Religion and Politics in
Post-Communist Romania

RELIGION AND GLOBAL POLITICS SERIES

Series Editor

John L. Esposito
University Professor and Director
Prince Alwaleed Bin Talal Center
for Muslim-Christian Understanding
Georgetown University

Islamic Leviathan
Islam and the Making of State Power
Seyyed Vali Reza Nasr

Rachid Ghannouchi
A Democrat within Islamism
Azzam S. Tamimi

Balkan Idols
Religion and Nationalism in Yugoslav States
Vjekoslav Perica

Islamic Political Identity in Turkey
M. Hakan Yavuz

Religion and Politics in Post-Communist Romania

LAVINIA STAN
LUCIAN TURCESCU

UNIVERSITY PRESS

2007

OXFORD
UNIVERSITY PRESS

Oxford University Press, Inc., publishes works that further
Oxford University's objective of excellence
in research, scholarship, and education.

Oxford   New York
Auckland   Cape Town   Dar es Salaam   Hong Kong   Karachi
Kuala Lumpur   Madrid   Melbourne   Mexico City   Nairobi
New Delhi   Shanghai   Taipei   Toronto

With offices in
Argentina   Austria   Brazil   Chile   Czech Republic   France   Greece
Guatemala   Hungary   Italy   Japan   Poland   Portugal   Singapore
South Korea   Switzerland   Thailand   Turkey   Ukraine   Vietnam

Published by Oxford University Press, Inc.
198 Madison Avenue, New York, New York 10016

www.oup.com

Oxford is a registered trademark of Oxford University Press

Library of Congress Cataloging-in-Publication Data
Stan, Lavinia.
Religion and politics in post-communist Romania /
Lavinia Stan, Lucian Turcescu.
    p. cm.—(Religion and global politics series)
Includes bibliographical references and index.
ISBN 978-0-19-530853-2
1. Church and state—Biserica Ortodoxa Româna—History—20th century.
2. Church and state—Romania—History—20th century.   3. Biserica Ortodoxa
Româna—History—20th century.   4. Biserica Ortodoxa Româna—Doctrines.
5. Orthodox Eastern Church—Doctrines.   6. Romania—Politics and
government—1989–   I. Turcescu, Lucian.   II. Title.
BX698.S73 2007
322'.10949809049—dc22   2006037206

Printed in the United States of America
on acid-free paper

To our son Luc Edward

Acknowledgments

In the mid 1990s when we were searching for a topic of common interest, religion and politics came to mind naturally. A trained theologian, Turcescu has had a keen interest in politics, whereas Stan once toyed with the idea of enrolling in a theology program. During the last twenty-two years we have engaged in lengthy discussions, passionate debates, and heated arguments over a number of general topics, including the appropriate boundaries between religion and politics. This volume comes almost a decade after we started exploring religion and politics together, and after several articles and book chapters written in collaboration on the general topic of religion and politics in post-communist Romania. While readers are the final judges of the quality of our work, we believe that this volume would have been impossible to write by either author working in isolation. By working together, we complemented our sources of information, criticized our points of view, and expanded our mutual understanding of the general topic. It has certainly been a rocky and often adventurous journey, but we both learned a great deal from it.

Research for this volume was undertaken with the generous support of a Social Science and Humanities Research Council of Canada standard research grant that has covered multiple trips to Romania in order to conduct indispensable personal interviews with religious leaders, academics, writers and journalists, government officials and regular faithful. We thank everybody in Bucharest, Iasi, Timisoara, Pitesti, Constanta, and Cluj who agreed to talk to us about what remains a highly sensitive and often controversial topic in that country. Gabriel Andreescu, Liviu Andreescu, Gabriel Catalan, Ioan Sebastian Chesches, Dorin Dobrincu, Stephanie Mahieu, Irimie Marga, Justina Sora, Sabina Stan, Laurentiu Tanase, Cristian Vasile, Rodica Milena, and Razvan Zaharia made valuable material available to us. Norm Seymour commented on our discussion of sexuality, Christopher Snook proofread some chapters, and Adriana Bara did some copyediting and helped with the bibliography. A number of anonymous reviewers offered constructive criticism. We also thank two anonymous reviewers for their comments on the project, and especially Cynthia Read and Julia TerMaat of Oxford University Press for their patience and support in having this book published. This is the first volume on Romanian politics the press has published since Ghita Ionescu's *Communism in Romania, 1944–1962* (1964), and we hope it matches Ionescu's high standards of scholarship. Above all, Sabrina P. Ramet deserves warm thanks for helping us improve the quality of the arguments, for agreeing to write the foreword, and for extending a helpful hand and an encouraging word in times of need. The remaining weaknesses are all ours.

Parts of chapter 3 were published in Lavinia Stan and Lucian Turcescu, "Church-State Conflict in Moldova: The Bessarabian Metropolitanate," *Communist and Post-Communist Studies* 36, no. 4 (2003): 443–465. The copyright of that version vests in the Regents of the University of California, and it is used here with permission. Other parts draw on Lavinia Stan and Lucian Turcescu, "Politics, National Symbols and the Romanian National Cathedral," *Europe-Asia Studies* 58, no. 3 (2006): 1119–1139. Used here with permission.

An earlier version of chapter 4 was published as Lavinia Stan and Lucian Turcescu, "The Devil's Confessors: Priests, Communists, Spies and Informers," *East European Politics and Societies* 19, no. 4 (Nov. 2005): 655–685, copyright 2005 by American Council of Learned Societies. Reprinted by permission of the American Council of Learned Societies and Sage Publications.

An earlier version of chapter 6 was published as Lavinia Stan and Lucian Turcescu, "Pulpits, Ballots, and Party Cards: Religion and Elections in Romania," *Religion, State and Society* 33, no. 4 (2005): 347–366. It is used here with permission from Taylor and Francis.

An earlier version of chapter 7 was published as Lavinia Stan and Lucian Turcescu, "Religious Education in Romania," *Communist and Post-Communist Studies* 38, no. 3 (2005): 381–401. The copyright of that version vests in the Regents of the University of California, and it is used here with permission.

An earlier version of chapter 8 was published as Lavinia Stan and Lucian Turcescu, "Religion, Politics and Sexuality in Romania," *Europe-Asia Studies* 57, no. 2 (2005): 291–310. It is used here with permission.

Contents

Foreword

Sabrina P. Ramet

It is a great honor for me to introduce this exciting new book written by Lavinia Stan and Lucian Turcescu about the Romanian Orthodox Church and its politics. They bring a fresh perspective to the subject, arguing that strict church-state separation is not an appropriate model for Romania and that, in any event, such separation "is not essential to democracy." Moreover, where others have dwelled at length on the vast changes which followed the collapse of communism throughout the Central and East European area in the course of 1989–90, they look at both continuity and discontinuity of the principles and institutions in religious policy and in the religious sphere over time. As they note, the post-communist transition offered an opportunity for Romania to redefine itself, and, within that context, to redefine its religio-political formula.

Stan and Turcescu allow us, as it were, to look behind closed doors. Indeed, they are uniquely qualified to write this book, bringing to the task training in theology (Turcescu) and in political science (Stan), as well as personal experience related to the subject of this book. Both of them spent about a quarter of a century living in Romania, both of them were under police surveillance, both of them had earned higher degrees by the time they left Romania, both of them changed fields of study. Stan began in economics, earning a bachelor's in commerce at the Academy of Economic Sciences in Bucharest before crossing over, after emigrating to Canada, to political science. Turcescu began as a student of computer sciences in Bucharest, but abandoned that course of study to switch to theology—at the risk of being labeled a "social parasite." Indeed, Turcescu's change of career path involved quite serious risk; every school of theology had a Securitate (secret police) officer assigned to it, and he was certain that the Securitate were keeping files on all students of theology. At the Faculty of Theology in Sibiu, where Turcescu began his theological studies before transferring to the faculty in Bucharest, the professors were urging their students not to go to restaurants or public places and talk to people about Christianity; Christian faith was to be treated, rather, as something very private, as something potentially dangerous.

Stan came under suspicion when her mother defected to Canada in 1988 and Stan herself was branded an "enemy of the state." Indeed, the secret police file kept on Stan eventually amounted to 100 pages of reports and notes, which, by Romanian standards, was by no means a thin file. Although she did not engage in any dissident activity such as political pamphleteering, local people would routinely spy on each other, and calling someone's political reliability into question was sometimes seen as a route to a promotion. This motivation may have lain behind the decision taken by a young agent in Alba Julia, where Stan landed in her first job, to build a case against the newly graduated economist. Reviewing Stan's private correspondence, which was replete with complaints about her workplace as well as about the communist party and the conducator, Nicolae Ceauşescu, the agent called Stan in for an interrogation. It was the first of three interrogation sessions. Co-workers and other people were pretending to be her friends in order to extract information to be turned over to the authorities. These interrogations, with their innuendoes and accusations, proved to be very difficult to endure. Soon after this, Stan left her job and moved to Sibiu to join Turcescu. Later, after the collapse of communism, she obtained confirmation that her parents' apartment had been bugged and learned of a plan to steal a key from her purse in order to implant a bugging device in the house. The entire episode also brought home the point that, in communist Romania, anyone might be placed under surveillance, even young people uninvolved in politics. By 1992, Turcescu and Stan had moved to Canada and enrolled at the University of Toronto for doctoral studies, completing their work respectively in theology and political science. They had shared some common difficulties in Ceauşescu's Romania and, in spite of training in different fields, found an overlap of interests in the intersection of religion and politics. The result of their collaboration is a tour de force, which, among other things, demonstrates the particular force with which the communist past haunts the post-communist present.

The relationship between communism and religion was always problematic. There are several reasons for this. First, each religion offers a set of values and, to the extent that a religious body is able to remain independent of penetration by the state, its value system presents itself as an alternative to the value system promoted by the state. Second, religious bodies have their own institutions and hierarchies which cannot so easily be placed under state control. Third, religious bodies offer programs of study (seminary, schools of theology) for those persons interested in working for or with or in the given church. Fourth, religious bodies have their own symbols, songs, and rituals—the cross rather than the hammer and sickle, Jesus Christ and the Virgin Mary rather than Marx and Engels, the "Ave Maria" rather than the "Internationale," the Holy Mass rather than the meeting of the party cell. To be a religious person, thus, was to be someone who might well be inclined to think in a way different from the way in which the regime wanted people to think; it was, in some sense, to be ranged *against* the communist state itself.

The communist states of Central and Eastern Europe dealt with these challenges in different ways. Only in Albania was religion banned outright, while, at the other extreme, only in the German Democratic Republic were faculties of theology funded by the state and allowed to continue their work as departments of the state universities. Between these extremes, there was a range of formulae available, but some commonalities stand out. To combat the challenge posed by the religious value systems, there were efforts to reinterpret Christianity in ways favorable to the communist state; thus, Jesus Christ was interpreted as an early communist and Martin Luther as a forerunner of socialism. The institutions of the churches, including their seminaries, their newspapers, and their parishes were penetrated by moles, who kept an eye on the local ecclesiastical functionaries and reported on their activities. In the case of Romania, as in the Bulgarian, Czechoslovak, and Soviet cases, church newspapers were heavily censored, with some articles even written by police agents assigned to work in "church journalism." In Hungary and Poland, prepublication censorship was the rule, but it was less severe than in the aforementioned cases, while in East Germany and Yugoslavia, church newspapers were subjected to post-publication censorship, which meant that as long as they did not violate some well-understood guidelines, they were able to distribute their issues.

Independent-minded clerics were considered undesirable throughout the communist world, and in several countries, including Romania, various devices were used in the early years to purge the ranks of the hierarchy and priesthood of such persons and to discourage courageous and independent-minded individuals from joining the priesthood. Indeed, being independent-minded was not considered a plus in any position or at any level in communist society. The churches were placed under the supervision of one or another state agency—under the Ministry of Foreign Affairs in Bulgaria, under the Ministry of Culture in Czechoslovakia—with small subsidies used to give the Churches an incentive to cooperate. And finally, alternative rituals were created, so that people wanting a public celebration of their marriages or of the birth of children, for example, could find that need satisfied through communist-approved rituals.[1]

Over the short run, the communists aspired to control religion and, where possible, to use religious bodies to advance the programs of the state. The Orthodox Churches of Russia, Bulgaria, and Romania proved to be especially amenable to such exploitation. Over the long run, however—at least until the Polish Summer of 1980 signaled the beginning of the end of communism[2]—most communists hoped that religion would steadily recede into the background, losing its place in the public sphere, and be increasingly seen as institutionalized superstition rather than as a competitive value system, eventually to die a quiet death. To push it out of the public sphere, the communists declared that religion was "the private affair" of each individual; although this formula, repeated in every communist country except Albania, seemed to signal a recognition of an individual right to believe, the stress here was rather on the fact that religion, being "private," had no place in the public sphere, no role to play in discussing the issues of the day, except to praise the insights and achievements of the communist party. In this regard, the Romanian Orthodox Church would eventually give the communist regime full satisfaction.

The collapse of communism left Patriarch Teoctist scampering to regain his footing, and shake off the residues of long collaboration with the communist authorities. Indeed, throughout the post-communist world, the opening of secret police files spelled trouble for local churches, since, whether one talked of the GDR or the Czech Republic or Romania, the files contained evidence of forms of collaboration on the part of even high-ranking church officials with the secret police.

The collapse of communism also presented the churches with new challenges, beginning with the new competition offered by both rival Christian

---

1. See Christel Lane, *Christian Religion in the Soviet Union: A Sociological Study* (Albany, N.Y.: State University of New York Press, 1978).

2. See Sabrina Petra Ramet, *Social Currents in Eastern Europe: The Sources and Consequences of the Great Transformation*, 2nd ed. (Durham, N.C.: Duke University Press, 1995), chapters 1–2, 4, 13, 15.

religions and various non-traditional religions, such as the Bahai, Hare Krishna, Scientology, and the Unification Church. Patterns of behavior to which clerics had become accustomed became irrelevant overnight, and new patterns of behavior had to be learned. Even the appeal to nationalism, which can reinforce a sense of community, put the nationalistic church on a national-communal foundation, and communicated the message that the nation is incomprehensible without reference to its religious loyalty, would now be situated in a new context, in which nationalism was neither a challenge to the regime nor a device whereby a fundamentally illegitimate regime could endeavor to find some alternative credentials placing it (and its church-partner) on the side of the nation.

The collapse of communism also opened up possibilities for Romania, like other countries of the region, to integrate into European institutions such as the Council of Europe, the European Union, and even NATO. For the Romanian Orthodox Church, the Council's condition that homosexuality be decriminalized was nothing less than a crisis for Christian civilization, as Turcescu and Stan show, while the European Union's draft constitution, the first 16 articles of which were promulgated in February 2002, sent shock waves throughout both the Orthodox and Catholic churches of Europe, especially in the post-communist world, where there were demands registered that the constitution of the secular EU contain references to God and to the continent's Christian heritage (with no Christian churches mentioning the Islamic and Jewish influences in Europe's heritage).[3]

The relegalization of the Greek Rite Catholic Church in post-communist Romania has presented a challenge of another kind, insofar as the communists had confiscated up to 2,500 churches and other facilities from that organization in 1948, turning many of them over to the Romanian Orthodox Church.[4] Now the Greek Catholics demanded a partial restoration of these properties, only to find their Orthodox brothers resisting any such transfer; even at this writing, 17 years after the fall of Ceauşescu, this dispute remains unresolved. Meanwhile, the Romanian Orthodox Church was itself seeking the return of 350 hectares of farm land, as well as other properties.

---

3. See my two chapters in Timothy A. Byrnes and Peter J. Katzenstein (eds.), *Religion in an Expanding Europe* (Cambridge: Cambridge University Press, 2006): "Thy Will Be Done: The Catholic Church and Politics in Poland Since 1989," especially pp. 137–143; and "The Way We Were—and Should Be Again? European Orthodox Churches and the 'Idyllic Past,' " especially pp. 163–166.

4. Sabrina P. Ramet, "Church and State in Romania before and after 1989," in Henry F. Carey (ed.), *Romania since 1989: Politics, Economics, and Society* (Lanham, Md.: Lexington Books, 2004), pp. 287–288.

Several of the core tasks with which post-communist regimes found themselves faced—privatization, political demonopolization and the deconstruction of political controls, an end to censorship of the press, coming to terms with the past, and lustration—have been reflected also in the religious sphere. With regard to the last of these, lustration (the prohibition of former communist officials and informers from holding public office in post-communist Romania) the church has manned the battlements, fearing that revelations about the past collaboration of hierarchy and clergy will not only result in banning some bishops from holding ecclesiastical office but also deeply embarrass the church. Indeed, there are suspicions that priests hearing confession in communist times may have routinely disclosed the content of these confessions to the authorities.[5]

It is no wonder, then, that the Romanian Orthodox Church sees itself as embattled. Faced with the demands of the Greek Catholics, the recently invigorated efforts by foreign neo-Protestant missionaries to evangelize in Romania, calls for the outing and lustration of former collaborators among the Orthodox hierarchy and clergy, and the liberal values being promoted by the European Union, the church has inevitably seen itself as on the defensive. Its stubborn opposition to Romanian membership in the European Union is one token of the church's fears, and unless that church can come to terms with the cultural and social change engulfing Central and Eastern Europe, including Romania, it may well drift into the role of cultural curator, preserving, almost as museum artifacts, values and behaviors which have nothing to do with the changing cultural context.

---

5. Catalin Bogdan, "Heavy Guilt," in *Nine o'clock*, issue #3758 (3 September 2006), at www.nineoclock.ro/index.php (accessed on 30 September 2006).

Religion and Politics in
Post-Communist Romania

I

Religion and Politics
in Post-Communism

The demise of the Eastern European communist regimes generated a flurry of studies proposing competing blueprints for the region's democratization. However, except for Sabrina P. Ramet, no other political scientist systematically examined the interplay between religion and politics or recognized that church-state relations represented an important dimension of the post-communist effort to move away from repressive dictatorship and closer to democracy.[1] Students of communist regimes who adopted institutional frameworks simply assumed that, as a result of the decades-long concerted campaign of the self-avowed atheist regime, religious sentiment had completely vanished or churches had been irremediably discredited by being transformed into obedient tools of the state. Modernization theorists dismissed religion as an impediment to political and economic development, meriting an occasional footnote only when discussing communist advances in the backward Eastern Europe. Religiosity was equally unimportant for dependency theorists and authors according a high value to cultural explanations, for whom secularization was an unstoppable trend bound to affect all predominantly Christian countries.[2] Thus, religion was not on the radar screen of students of political science, whereas politics was a topic theologians only reluctantly addressed.

The social reality of post-communism proved the authors sounding the death knell for traditional religion wrong. Religious sentiment reached unprecedented levels throughout the region, both in countries like Poland, where the dominant Roman Catholic Church remained strong in the face of communist authorities, and in countries like Romania, where the dominant Orthodox Church endorsed the strictest Stalinist and sultanist-cum-totalitarian rule, to use a term coined by political scientists Juan Linz and Alfred Stepan.[3] To the surprise of many analysts, religion, alongside nationalism, stepped in to fill the ideological void left behind when Marxist-Leninism was discredited, and churches assumed new roles in shaping the eastern European democracy. As the tragic events of 11 September 2001 demonstrated, religion and religiously motivated ideologies turned into the fiercest enemies of globalization. Instead of withering away, they are here to stay, at least for the foreseeable future.

This volume examines the interaction between religion and politics in the Balkan country of Romania, highlighting both the influence of religious actors and symbols on the political process and the effects of politics on the life of the most important religious denominations. As individual chapters suggest, the points of interaction between religion and politics are manifold, touching on a number of public affairs areas—from general elections and restitution of church property to sexuality and public education. Far from being a footnote to post-communist politics, religion has become a driving force of public affairs and a powerful legitimizer of political action that no longer can be ignored. The trend is not unique to Romania. Religion divides the public in Russia, Poland, and Bulgaria, either helping political parties define their target electorate and consolidate their power base or leading to bloody conflict, as was the case in war-torn Yugoslavia.[4]

The number of political formations whose platform includes an explicit religious dimension remains significant throughout the region. Among these parties we should mention the center-right Christian Democrats in Poland, Romania, the Czech Republic, Slovakia, and Hungary, as well as the extremist nationalist parties like the Greater Romania Party and the Movement for Romania that advocate a return to strict Orthodoxy. A growing number of politicians, even convinced former communists, have couched their electoral promises in religious terms and relied on religious symbols to strengthen their popular appeal. Some Eastern European countries present themselves as "Catholic" (Poland and Croatia) or "Orthodox" (Russia, Romania, and Bulgaria), glossing over their religious diversity and privileging the dominant religious group to the detriment of smaller religious minorities. In almost all countries in the region, religion was brought back to public school as a more or less mandatory subject for young children, while religious denominations have led the fight against recognizing homosexuals and the transgendered as full members of the political community.

The Old Paradigm: The Piecemeal Approach

Most studies investigating religion and politics in post-communist Eastern Europe have followed a piecemeal approach, discussing the relationship between state authorities and one religious denomination at a time. These studies underscore the majority or minority position of the religious denomination under examination but ignore the interaction and competition among the multiple religious groups active in a country. Let us exemplify this theoretical approach by presenting the concept of *symphonia*, traditionally used to describe the ties between the state and the Orthodox Churches, and the Concordats, the documents framing the relationship between the Roman Catholic Church and Eastern European states. It is interesting that these two markers are rooted in two different time periods. While *symphonia* was inherited from Byzantine times and faithfully upheld by Eastern European Orthodox Churches after the collapse of the Byzantine Empire, it was only in 1630 that the first Concordat between the Vatican and a European royal house was drafted to settle outstanding religious issues in an eastern European land. Negotiated by Pope Urban VIII and Emperor Ferdinand II, the Concordat with Bohemia allowed for the reestablishment of the Roman Catholic Church in the region following Ferdinand's anti-heretical campaign. According to the document, the church renounced the goods that had been alienated during the progress of the heresy but received compensation in the form of revenues derived from a salt tax levied for its exclusive benefit.

The Byzantine model of theocracy, also known as Caesaropapism or *symphonia*, presupposed the existence of a Christian emperor who stood at the center of the Christian empire and at the helm of the church. For Eusebius of Caesarea (c. 260 to c. 340), the Christian emperor (Constantine at the time) was God's representative on earth, a position which many interpreted as a Christian adaptation of the ancient Roman institution of the god-emperor, who played the role of *pontifex maximus* (high priest) in the state cult.[5] In the sixth *Novella* of his legal code *Novellae Constitutiones Post Codicem*, Emperor Justinian I (527–565) offered the classic definition of the relationship between church and state, stating that "if the priesthood is in every way free from blame and possesses access to God, and if the emperors administer equitably and judiciously the state entrusted to their care, general harmony (*symphonia*) will result, and whatever is beneficial will be bestowed upon the human race."[6] Thus, on the one hand, "the church recognized the powers of the emperor as protector of the church and preserver of the unity of faith, and limited its own authority to the purely spiritual domain of preserving the Orthodox truth and order in the church." On the other hand, the emperor "was subject to the spiritual leadership of the church as far as he was a son of the church."[7]

In Byzantium, *symphonia* was an ideal to be reached, as in practice harmony was rarely established. Emperors ruling like despots constantly sought to subjugate the Orthodox Church even in the area of the dogmatic definitions of the faith, where they had neither the qualifications nor the right to do so. In his analysis of Byzantium, Deno Geanakoplos identified three realms belonging to the temporal and spiritual relations. First was the purely temporal realm for which the emperor alone made the laws. Second was the spiritual or ecclesiastical realm, which dealt essentially with church organizational issues such as "the establishment and redistricting of sees, disciplinary matters affecting the clergy... and, perhaps the most important, the appointment to or dismissal from patriarchal office." Third was the realm of the church's sacraments and dogmas of faith.[8]

Drawing on Byzantine documents, Geanakoplos convincingly showed that emperors routinely controlled the first two realms, and, during the Arian, Monophysite, Monothelite, Iconoclastic, and unionist controversies, attempted to assert control over the third realm, too. Though some emperors gained influence over the third realm for short periods of time, in the long run the church was able to establish its own faith and dogmas in spite of the emperors' decrees. In their recognition of the emperors' divine rights, the Byzantines went so far as to allow the emperors to appoint the Patriarch of Constantinople from a list of three worthy candidates suggested by the Holy Synod, to convoke ecumenical councils, to sign proceedings of an ecumenical council for the council to become valid, to enter the church sanctuary, to preach to the congregation, to receive communion in the same manner as the priests, to bless the congregation with the three-branched candelabra symbolizing the Holy Trinity, and to cense the icons and the congregation. One last privilege reserved for the emperor was his anointment by the patriarch at the time of coronation. After the Monophysitic dispute marked the end of the sixth century, the patriarch could refuse to crown an emperor whose profession of faith he rejected as questionable or unclear.[9]

After the collapse of the Byzantine Empire and the fall of Constantinople in 1453, the concept of *symphonia* was upheld, in one form or another, by both the dominant Orthodox churches and the political rulers as a mutually beneficial partnership. Its essence was despotic more than theocratic since the religious ruler did not formally assume political powers but the political ruler (the monarch) was invested with religious attributes. The Russian, Romanian, Serbian, Bulgarian, and Greek monarchs were leaders of their country's dominant church and had to convert to Orthodoxy when born into another faith (the example of Catherine the Great, the Catholic who joined the Russian Orthodox Church, is well known). Collaboration with the Orthodox Church allowed monarchs to strengthen their control over the uneducated peasant population, prevent social conflict, rally local boyars against outside military threats, gain acceptance for their conservative or reformist policies, and facilitate relations with regional neighbors. The Orthodox Churches saw collaboration with the secular power as a much-needed shield against the eastern expansion of Catholic influence, prompted by the loss of support in western Europe following the Reformation, as well as the Islamic threat posed by the advance of the Ottoman Empire into southeastern Europe.

Symphonia never entailed a partnership of equals, but the communist regime tipped the balance in its favor, leaving the Orthodox Church little maneuvering room. Following centuries of collaboration with the secular power, it is not surprising that Orthodox leaders were reluctant to openly oppose the state, their former ally. Rationalizing the need to obey the party-state by claiming that the communist regime advantageously compared to other oppressors, both foreign and domestic, the Orthodox Churches missed the occasion to place church-state relations on new conceptual foundations. Throughout communist Eastern Europe, the old concept of *symphonia* became a cover for the silent endorsement of state-led anti-religious campaigns. To accommodate a hostile atheistic state, the Romanian version of *symphonia* entailed some theoretical ingenuity and considerable compromises on the part of the Orthodox Church.[10]

Compared with other denominations, the Orthodox Church continued to have a privileged position in the new state, but it remained only a privileged servant of the state. Collaboration helped the church avoid obliteration but failed to prevent its persecution; more important, the partnership was a state-dominated marriage in which church leaders could seldom, if ever, negotiate where the boundaries of religious activities and freedom were to be drawn. Not surprisingly, church leaders and many of the clergy became morally compromised in the eyes of many Romanian Orthodox faithful and intellectuals, international church and ecumenical circles, and Western governments because they reaped the benefits of open collaboration with the communist dictatorship, while so many people were suffering. Since 1989, Romanian Orthodox Church leaders have seriously questioned whether *symphonia*, a concept developed in Byzantine times, can appropriately describe church-state relations in the new democracy.[11] We argue that this is another argument for proposing new models such as those discussed in this volume.

Bilateral pacts were concluded between the Roman Catholic Church and European monarchs as early as 1122 to settle the investiture controversy that profoundly troubled Christian Europe in the eleventh and twelfth centuries. But it was only in the nineteenth century that Concordats became a preferred tool of the Roman Catholic Church to regulate ecclesiastical affairs in different lands, usually by promising to forego some of its natural rights in order to secure from the state a promise to refrain from further encroachment upon ecclesiastical rights.[12] According to Archbishop Giovanni Lajolo, the Vatican's "concordat diplomacy" aims "at ensuring stability and certainty for the activities of the Church and safeguarding the exercises of religious freedom for the Catholic faithful." While responding to precise historical and political needs, all concordats seek "to ensure the freedom of cult, of jurisdiction and of association of the Catholic Church" and "to open areas of cooperation between the Catholic Church and the civil authorities, especially in two areas: education and charitable activity."[13] Since 1965, over 115 agreements were concluded with countries spanning different continents, cultures, and political arrangements. The proliferation of concordats, and the implicit recognition they bestowed on sometimes undemocratic political regimes, has come under fire recently. For example, while it provided the church with important benefits, the 1934 Concordat with Germany also granted international recognition to Hitler's regime.

As mentioned, the first concordat governing territories in eastern Europe was dated 1630. Sixty years later, the Concordat with Poland of 1736 was signed by Pope Clement XII and King Augustus III. The one with Russia, signed on 3 August 1847 and published by Pope Pius IX a year later, dealt with episcopal rights and the dioceses of Russia and Poland. The Concordat with Austria was concluded on 18 August 1855 by Cardinal Viale Prela and Prince-Bishop Joseph Othmar von Rauscher. Although ratified by the emperor and the pope, it was rejected by the Austrian-Hungarian government in 1870, at a time when the multinational province of Transylvania was part of the empire. The Concordat of 8 July 1881 concerned the establishment of church hierarchy in the province of Bosnia-Herzegovina.

In 1927, the Vatican signed the Concordat with Romania, ratified by the Bucharest authorities two years later, after extensive negotiations designed to appease the Orthodox Church. Born a Catholic in Germany and anointed King of Romania in 1914, Ferdinand long wanted to regulate relations with the Holy See. With great effort, he managed to conclude the Concordat on 10 May 1927, two months before his death. Because his exiled son Carol had relinquished rights to the throne after a morganatic marriage, and Carol's son was underaged, Ferdinand was succeeded by the regency formed of Prince Nicolas, Carol's younger brother, the Orthodox Patriarch Miron Cristea, and the head of the High Court of Justice. In that position, the powerful Cristea procrastinated as much as possible in the ratification of the Concordat. The document governed relations between the Roman and Greek Catholic Churches and the Romanian government, and it touched on a number of issues vital for the life of the Catholic congregations. There were issues related to church organization (Articles 1 and 2); appointment of clergy and hierarchs (3 to 6); protection of church property (9 and 13); the life of religious orders (17); bishop's prerogatives (8 and 12); confessional schools (14, 16, and 19); religious assistance in hospitals, orphanages, and prisons (18); and religious instruction in public schools (20). In exchange for recognition and a promise that the Catholic Church and its members "will enjoy from the state a treatment that cannot be inferior to the one enjoyed by other religious denominations" (Article 10), the Holy See agreed to notify the Romanian government of new nominations for bishopric sees "to make sure, jointly, that no political reasons exist against that individual [candidate]" (Article 5.2).[14]

Throughout eastern Europe, the communist authorities denounced the concordats as an unwelcome foreign infringement of their countries' national sovereignty. Among the first were the Polish communists, who unilaterally revoked the agreement in September 1945, followed by Romania in 1948. After 1989, a number of eastern European countries redrafted agreements with the Vatican. A new Concordat with Poland was signed on 28 July 1993 (but ratified by the Polish parliament only on 25 March 1998). By 2005, Hungary, the Czech Republic and Slovakia, Slovenia, Albania, Croatia, and the Baltic states of Estonia, Latvia, and Lithuania were also bound to the Holy See by agreements touching on religious education, conscientious objectors, or sexuality.[15] While framing relations between the Roman Catholic Church and Eastern European states in somewhat clearer terms, the concordats promote a legalistic view not reflective of the informal ties that bind religion and politics in countries where Roman Catholicism remains a religious minority. Because they were not yet concluded with predominantly Orthodox countries like Romania, Bulgaria, Yugoslavia, and Russia, concordats cannot tell us anything about the way the Vatican relates to those states.

A New Framework: Models of Church-State Relations

We find the piecemeal theoretical framework unsatisfactory, both because it rests on the implicit assumption that religious groups always oppose the state and belong to the civil society and because it downplays the dynamic character of the competition between religious denominations in their struggle to obtain much-needed state support and recognition. By constantly dissolving the boundaries between state and society, the communist authorities showed religious groups how to turn what was probably their most important disadvantage into a valuable asset. Faced with weak post-communist states unable to deliver the most basic common goods, discredited communist political elites and disorganized opposition groups looking for a renewed political message, and powerful competition from Western-based religious groups coming into the country, Eastern European denominations understood that major gains can be obtained not by opposing but by collaborating with and manipulating the state apparatus. As previously explained, since Byzantine times Orthodox Churches in Bulgaria, Romania, and Russia have allowed for cooperation with state authorities and the rulers of the day, while vehemently resisting attempts to relegate them to the realm of civil society, where they would be on par with other religious denominations. The Roman Catholic Church also forged privileged ties with the Polish and Croatian states, lending support to conservative political actors who were promoting the revival of Christian values and strict moral family codes. In countries like Estonia and Latvia, where they form a majority, Protestant (Lutheran) churches have also sought to align themselves with the state in order to redefine the good citizen and the appropriate church-state relationship.

To understand the case of post-communist Romania, we recognize that different religious denominations and different political actors have simultaneously promoted different models of church-state relations that, in turn, have informed the interaction between religion and politics in public affairs. Thus, our theoretical framework departs significantly from the traditional examination of the ties between the (Romanian) state and each religious denomination by first proposing four broad models of church-state relations and then highlighting the way these competing models inform the church-state interaction in six areas of public affairs. Our approach is thematic, as well as multidimensional. To capture the wide range of positions put forth by political and nonpolitical actors, to highlight the fact that in Romania churches have constantly shifted positions between state and society, and to reflect the diversity of civil society approaches to religiosity and secularization, we have reconstructed the models promoted not only by the majority and minority religious groups but also by the political elite and the humanistic (largely atheistic) civil society.

Our discussion owes much to Stephen Monsma and Christopher Soper's comparative study, *The Challenge of Pluralism: Church and State in Five Democracies*, which convincingly proposed patterns of church-state relations at the level of entire countries instead of examining a particular government's attitude toward each religious denomination active in the country.[16] They did so by looking at church-state relations in established democracies primarily from the viewpoint of the state, with the implicit assumption that, while a government might assume different positions toward individual religious groups, all these positions must converge in a rather coherent model of church-state relations. In the strict church-state separation model used in the United States, "religion and politics are seen as clearly distinct areas of human endeavor that should be kept separate from each other."[17] Religion is a private matter on which the state should remain neutral. No religious denomination is funded from the public purse, but all are allowed to fundraise privately, if they wish to do so.

The established or partially established church model used in the United Kingdom, Norway, Sweden, Denmark, and Greece represents the very opposite to the first model.[18] Under it, "the state and the church form a partnership in advancing the cause of religion and the state." The state grants recognition and, in Scandinavian countries, financial support to the church, which, in turn, grants the state "legitimacy and tradition, recognition and a sense of national unity and purpose."[19] The Netherlands and Australia use the pluralist or structural pluralist model, which sees society as made up of competing or complementary spheres like education, business, the arts, the family, and religion. Each sphere enjoys autonomy in its attempt to fulfill distinct activities or responsibilities, and the government recognizes each of them as separate areas of life worthy to be funded and supported.[20]

In chapter 2 we provide a brief historical overview to reconstruct the models of church-state relations proposed by the Romanian political elite, the Orthodox Church, the other religious groups, and the intellectual elite. These four models are strikingly different, working on divergent premises, building on various arguments, and exhibiting few points of intellectual convergence. While the political elite traditionally embraced a managed quasi-pluralist model of church-state relations, after 1989 some prominent political actors were tempted to codify into law the privileged position they were ready to grant to the powerful Orthodox Church. Those attempts were rapidly quashed under pressure from other religious groups, the local civil society, and the European Union, from which Romania has sought acceptance as a full member. In turn, the dominant Orthodox Church has advocated an established church model that recognized its role as defender of Romanian identity, qualified it for record levels of state financial support, and guaranteed its formal representation in the national legislative assembly.

Not surprisingly, this perspective came under attack from religious minorities that proposed a pluralist model firmly grounding all denominations outside the state and in the civil society and recognizing religious minority and majority groups as equal before the law. The intellectual groups, which represent the best-organized and most vocal segment of the local civil society, have countered the unprecedented levels of religiosity and the growing reliance of the political elite on religious symbols by way of articulating a model calling for the strict separation of church and state. According to them, such a model would align the country with the consolidated Western democracies that Romania wants to emulate, reduce the likelihood of state persecution of religious minorities, allow the state to make more rational decisions free of religious bias, provide for a clear break with the communist past of state encroachment on religious life, and permit nonreligious Romanians to have much-needed church-free space to manifest themselves as full citizens of the polity.

To reconstruct these distinct models, our investigation surveys church-state relations before, during, and after the communist period; emphasizes the principles and institutions retained over time; and follows the twists and turns of the local debate exposing the merits and demerits of each model. Not surprisingly, the taxonomy of relations that link religious groups to established democratic states developed by Monsma and Soper does not perfectly fit the case of Romania, a former communist country located in the conflict-ridden Balkans whose historical experience with democracy has remained rather limited thus far. As such, we had to construct new categories that more adequately reflect the experience of that particular country. Indeed, while the visions proposed by non-state actors resonate with the models developed by the American analysts, the Romanian political elite has seemingly embraced an understanding of church-state relations that is a modified variant of the pluralist model. As explained in chapter 2, both political actors and religious minorities uphold different versions of religious pluralism, but we contend that the pluralism to which religious minorities subscribe comes closer to democratic ideals than the managed quasipluralism to which politicians remain committed. The model is "managed" because of the numerous registration requirements imposed for the official recognition of new religious groups to take place. It is "quasipluralist" because of the informal precedence given to the Orthodox Church by government agencies at all levels.

To understand which of the four models proposed in Romania is compatible with democracy, the political system the country aspires to consolidate, we compare these models to Alfred Stepan's "twin toleration" requirement.[21] A number of theoretical perspectives were proposed to explain which religion is (more) compatible with a democratic system. For Max Weber and Axel Hadenius, Protestantism is more able than Roman Catholicism to sustain capitalism, which, in turn, is essential to democracy.[22] For Serif Mardin and Chris Hann, democratic values may be tied to broader Western cultural values, which the Islamic world does not accept.[23] Probably the best-known opinion is that of Samuel Huntington, who believes that Christianity has had a distinctive positive influence in the making of Western civilization and whose understanding of liberal democracy rests squarely on separation of church and state. For him, Protestantism and Roman Catholicism qualify as prerequisites for democracy, whereas "in Islam, God is Caesar; in [Confucianism] Caesar is God; in Orthodoxy, God is Caesar's junior partner."[24]

Stepan's recent work challenges these assumptions, arguing that "twin tolerations," not separation of church and state, are needed for democracy to flourish. To define the necessary boundaries of freedom for elected governments from religious groups, and for religious individuals and groups from government, Stepan contends that democratic institutions must be free, within the bounds of the constitution and human rights, to generate politics. This entails that religious institutions should not have "constitutionally privileged prerogatives" to mandate public policy to democratically elected governments. At the same time, individuals and religious communities "must have complete freedom to worship privately" and "must be able to advance their values publicly in civil society and to sponsor organizations and movements in political society, as long as their actions do not impinge negatively on the liberties of other citizens or violate democracy and the law."[25]

When contrasted to the "twin tolerations," Romanian models of church-state relations are not equally akin to the democratic spirit. In our opinion, the country's chances to consolidate its budding democracy rest on the ability of the Romanian public to impose rules of political competition that marginalize nondemocratic church-state models while promoting the more democratic models. These four models inform our discussion of the six most important public policy areas.

Religion and Public Affairs

In chapters 3, 4, and 5, which benefit from a strong historical component, we discuss the interplay between religion and politics with respect to nationalism, the reconsideration of the recent communist past, and the restitution of church property that had been improperly confiscated by the communist regime. All three chapters deal with issues specific to post-communist countries. Barely a decade and a half after the collapse of the dreaded dictatorial regime imposed by President Nicolae Ceauşescu, Romania continues to be heavily burdened by its recent past, whose legacy affects its political, social, economic, and spiritual life in a number of important ways. As in other countries in the region, post-communism has represented a process of dealing with the past as much as with the present and the future. As we contend in these chapters, Romania's reluctance to honestly assume its recent dictatorial experiences (both communist and fascist) has informed its political and religious life, exacerbating nationalist and chauvinist sentiment, discrediting democratic political formations, marginalizing religious actors open to ecumenical dialogue, denying legally recognized religious minorities the constitutional right to seek the return of their confiscated property in court, and periodically fueling public scandals with revelations about the religious hierarchs' collaboration with, and silent submission to, the communist authorities. As our investigation suggests, the public discourse surrounding these topical issues and the adoption (or rejection) of relevant legislation have involved extensive negotiations between state, religious actors, and the civil society.

In chapters 6, 7, and 8, we shift the theoretical lens to the three policy areas that have constantly been in the public eye since 1989: elections, education, and sexuality. We argue that Romania's rocky exit from communism and its initial stages of post-communist transition have invalidated most predictions for these areas. While analysts expected countries that experienced a strict Stalinist regime followed by a bloody revolution to be more inclined to elect representatives of the democratic opposition to government, in Romania the first post-communist elections of 1990 were overwhelmingly won by Ion Iliescu, a former communist apparatchik and one-time collaborator of Ceaușescu, and his National Salvation Front, a large umbrella organization gathering together second-echelon officials of the Communist Party. A convinced communist who seemed to share Marx's belief that religion was the opiate of the masses and who blamed Ceaușescu more than the communist ideology for the country's bankruptcy, Iliescu initially refused to employ religion as an electoral instrument, convinced of its lack of importance for the Romanian electorate in the post-communist context. But in 1996, religion unexpectedly became the cornerstone of the presidential campaign, allowing Emil Constantinescu to win the popular vote. Since then, religious symbols have been a constant feature of local and national electoral campaigns. Not even Traian Băsescu, whose religiosity has proven lukewarm at best, dared to ignore religion during his bid for the Romanian presidency in 2004. Elections remain an area where politicians of all ideological persuasions and religious leaders of Orthodox, Catholic, Greek Catholic, and Protestant denominations closely cooperate, continuously forging new ties and renegotiating old ones to fit their respective goals.

By contrast, education and sexuality constitute two domains where the influence of the Orthodox Church has manifested itself most clearly, both because that church, by its sheer numbers, historical ascendancy, and political influence, was able to bend the will of the politicians and because religious minorities were reluctant to fight the battle with their limited resources. When it came to religious instruction in public schools, the Orthodox Church took the lead in preparing teaching materials, hiring teachers, and arranging for curriculum changes that would allow religion to enter the school at all pre-university levels. It was only much later, as suggested in chapter 7, that state officials codified into law a state of affairs that the Orthodox Church created to its own advantage, often to the exclusion and marginalization of other denominations from the public school system.

When it came to defining the politics of the body and the appropriate standards of sexual behavior, the Romanian politicians and state officials took the lead, agreeing to decriminalize homosexual behavior at the request of the European Union. As explained in chapter 8, all religious denominations in the country opposed the move, but none was more vocal than the Orthodox Church, closely followed by the Greek Catholics. Church opposition to homosexuality placed the Romanian state representatives between the hammer and the anvil, as it forced them to opt between alienating the powerful local churches and losing popular support, on the one hand, and risk endangering the country's accession to the European Union, on the other hand. Only the renewed calls of the European political leaders convinced Romanian politicians to ignore church opposition and operate the required legislative changes.

Chapter 9 concludes the volume with a discussion of Romania's accomplishments in adopting an understanding of religion and politics that is tolerant, inclusive, and respectful of religious diversity, together with the steps needed to further consolidate its democratic system. Our examination of the Romanian case suggests that strict separation of church and state is neither the only way to attain democracy nor particularly fitting that country. In their investigation of religion and democratic politics, David Marquand and Ronald Nettler insisted that "even in the absence of a . . . bargain keeping church and state apart, religion and democracy can coexist. Communities of faith do not necessarily imperil the foundations of pluralist democracy by seeking to pursue essentially religious agendas through political action."[26] While celebrated in North America and western Europe as the linchpin of democracy, separation of church and state is not essential to democracy. In all those countries, religious organizations and beliefs continue to influence political behavior to various degrees. As one observer noted, the structure of the American government, "far from rendering religion largely irrelevant to politics . . . may actually encourage a high degree of interaction."[27]

The separation of church and state has been an ideal more than a reality in Western European democracies where either Protestants or Roman Catholics form a clear majority. Scandinavian states have long recognized their Lutheran churches as state churches, a relationship that was only recently challenged in Sweden and Norway and upheld in Denmark. In the United Kingdom, the Church of England and the Church of Scotland have retained their national church status; in Italy, Spain, and Ireland, the Roman Catholic Church has forged special relationships with the state and the leading political parties. More important than the Western experience with church-state relations is the fact that Romanian society, whose outlook and lifestyle remain traditional in spite of sweeping modernization trends engulfing the urban areas, is unlikely to accept a foreign model without roots in the country's history. As our conclusion suggests, Romania might not have to travel all the way toward a secular state, given the European Union's renewed commitment to Christian values. As European Parliament member Hans-Gert Poettering recently said, acceptance into the larger European family does not require new members to renounce their national, including religious, identity.[28]

Romania's religious makeup shows the prominence of the Orthodox Church vis-à-vis the other religious denominations present in the country. According to the latest official census conducted in 2002, around 86.8 percent of Romanian citizens claimed membership in the Orthodox Church, whose rites are closer to the Greek than to the Russian Orthodox Church, and another 5 percent were in the Roman Catholic Church. There were fewer than 200,000 Greek Catholics,[29] some 67,000 Muslims, 6,000 Jews, and around 701,000 Protestant Reformed believers, mostly in Transylvania.[30]

To be sure, levels of religiosity are low and comparable with those of other eastern European countries. For Orthodox believers, active engagement in church life is quite significant by Western European standards but remains modest by Orthodox Church standards. (An often cited joke says that Orthodox Romanians visit the church three times in their lives: for baptism, marriage, and feet first before being buried.) Of all religious denominations, the Orthodox Church has been by far the most vocal when it comes to public affairs. This is why a good part of our discussion examines the position of that religious denomination on issues of public interest. Although we have made every effort to include the positions of other churches—gauged from personal interviews with church leaders and the faithful, Romanian-language monographs, and press reports or official statements released by those groups—not all religious minorities have formulated official positions on all issues raised in this volume. Moreover, subjects that recently attracted a great deal of media interest in the western world (such as, for example, the sexual harassment of altar boys by Roman Catholic priests and the church leaders' attempt to cover up the scandal) have so far been completely absent from Romania.

2

Competing Models of Church-State Relations

The collapse of the communist regime allowed Romania not only to launch a double political and economic transformation but also to redefine the relationship between religion and politics. The redefinition was called for by political leaders, church representatives, and the civil society, each feeling that new church-state relations were needed after the authoritarian communist state gave way to a democratic state, and new, mostly Western-based, religious denominations have entered the country to compete with old, more established religious groups. As in other Balkan countries, the advent of democracy forced the Orthodox Church in particular to confront the new political reality. Under the centuries-long Ottoman occupation, the Orthodox Church was not challenged by disruptive social, political, cultural, and religious phenomena like the Reformation and the Enlightenment, but after 1989 the confrontation with Western-style liberal democracy was inevitable. The church was called to rethink its understanding of church-state relations by abandoning the cherished Byzantine concept of *symphonia* in favor of a pluralist perspective that denied any one faith the power to organize the whole of social life. As part of the post-communist transformation effort, the other religious and nonreligious groups were also called to embrace democracy. Thus, the interplay between religion and politics had to evolve because both terms of the religion and politics equation had transmogrified substantially, and old management mechanisms, communication channels, state commitments, and church objectives could no longer adequately reflect post-communist realities.

While all sides realized the need to place church-state relations on new foundations, agreement has not yet been reached as to what kind of model the country must embrace. As various actors pursued various goals, the shape and content of the proposed church-state models differed substantially, depending on the initiators, all of whom sought to gain maximum scope for unfettered activity. Certainly, Romanian actors have made constant references to the experience of Western Europe, but they were reluctant to prefer one single model over all others. For example, rather than adopting the German model in its entirety, the Romanian Orthodox Church has selectively endorsed some of its elements while silently discarding others. Its vision has blended German and British elements, although several factors recommend Greece as a more appropriate example. A Balkan country that has fulfilled all requirements for democracy for several decades already, and the European Union's only predominantly Orthodox country, Greece has also faced the divide between two main religious groups (the Orthodox majority and the Islamic minority) and could offer Romania inspiration for addressing its own outstanding tensions between the Orthodox majority and Greek Catholic minority. Interestingly enough, Romanians have stubbornly ignored Greece and preferred to set their eyes on more remote, but more prosperous and consolidated, democracies.

Church-State Relations before 1989

One of Romania's most important redefinitions of church-state relations was launched by Prince Alexandru Ioan Cuza (1859–1866), as part of a comprehensive reform program inspired by the 1848 revolutions and touching on all aspects of life. In 1859, Cuza became the ruler of the united principalities of Wallachia and Moldova, the new state that came to be known as Romania when recognized officially by the European powers three years later. At the time, the dominant religious denomination was the Orthodox Church, while smaller Roman Catholic, Jewish, and Muslim groups were present in central Moldova, the large towns, and Dobrogea, respectively. Cuza's choice of a religion and politics pattern that allowed the state to strictly control religious affairs was determined by his desire to champion the local Orthodox Church's independence from the Patriarchate of Constantinople in order to subordinate it to his own ambitious projects.

The political leader thus hoped to take advantage of the church's traditional policy of accommodation with the rulers of the day and silent submission to them, co-opt the dominant church into the larger project of nation and state-building, and end the massive loss of revenue to the Greek Mount Athos monasteries and the Patriarchate of Constantinople (located in the infamously corrupt Phanar district of Istanbul). Wallachian and Moldovan rulers had previously bequeathed vast lands to the church to the point that by the time Cuza assumed the reign one-fourth of Wallachian and Moldovan agricultural land, orchards, and vineyards were listed as property of the Orthodox monasteries dedicated to Mount Athos, Constantinople, and other Orthodox patriarchates. These monasteries routinely directed their wealth and revenues abroad, a process that seriously crippled the financial strength of the principalities and their ability to fund much-needed infrastructure, social, educational, and cultural programs.[1] In a remarkable series of reforms that shook Romania's still feudal core, Cuza nationalized the land controlled by foreign monasteries and stopped the transfer of funds abroad, improved the educational standards of the clergy, endorsed the use of Romanian as the liturgical language, replaced the Cyrillic alphabet with the Latin script, and pledged state financial support for church activities and clergy salaries.

Following a clearer delimitation of the roles and responsibilities of both church and state, and the creation of a national organizational structure, the church eventually emerged in 1925 as an autonomous, self-governing patriarchate in the Orthodox world. In 1865, one year before Cuza was ousted from power, the local Orthodox Church declared its independence. Yet the Patriarchate of Constantinople recognized it officially only twenty years later in 1885, seven years after the principalities, by then organized as the Romanian Kingdom, won their political independence from the Ottoman Empire. The 1866 constitution recognized the Orthodox Church as the dominant church in the country: "The Orthodox religion of the East is the dominant religion of the state. The Romanian Orthodox Church is and shall remain independent from all foreign leaderships but it will retain its doctrinal unity with the Eastern Ecumenical Church."[2] While proclaiming that freedom of consciousness is absolute and that the freedom of all religious groups is guaranteed in Romania, the same article 21 gave little recognition to religious minorities that in practice continued to be merely tolerated (Roman Catholics and Muslims), if not openly persecuted (Jews and Protestants). The Romanian Orthodox Church became the established religion invested with the power to legitimize the national political leaders, who had to be Orthodox in faith. Ironically, the Orthodox Church was freed from outside influences and control only to succumb to local politics; it still did not have autonomous decision-making power in areas ranging from control over monastic revenues to the nomination and removal of its head.[3] The church was brought under regular government control, a move in line with the Byzantine understanding of church-state relations.

Cuza himself ruled as a benevolent despot. The ensuing financial distress and reform failures, combined with an awkward scandal revolving around his mistress, led to his forced abdication and exile in Western Europe. Cuza was succeeded by Prince Karl of Hohenzollern-Sigmaringen, proclaimed King Carol I on 26 March 1866. Invited to assume the leadership of Romania by the anti-Cuza faction of liberal and conservative politicians, Carol I eventually converted to Orthodoxy, thus validating the Orthodox Church as a legitimizing factor for political leaders. Subsequently, all Romanian kings who ruled in pre-communist times were baptized in the Orthodox faith, considered protectors of that religious group, and given most of the privileges accorded to Byzantine emperors. As in other Eastern European Orthodox kingdoms that were liberated from Ottoman rule in the nineteenth century, the young country assumed a form of nation-state infused with the concept of *symphonia*, whereby "the head of the state was expected to be an Orthodox Christian, the church and the state were to coexist harmoniously for the good of the 'Orthodox Christian' society, and the state was expected to support the preservation of an 'Orthodox Christian' culture."[4]

After the creation of the modern Romanian state following the incorporation of the multireligious and multiethnic region of Transylvania into the Romanian Kingdom in 1918, church-state relations were again redefined, but the 1923 constitution, which Romanians still hail as one of the most modern in Europe at the time, did not provide for a democratic system that allowed all religious groups to worship freely and the state to treat them equally. Article 22 of the constitution states that "the Orthodox and the Greek Catholic Churches are Romanian Churches. The Romanian Orthodox Church, being the religion of a majority of Romanians, is the dominant Church in the Romanian state; the Greek Catholic Church has priority over other denominations."[5] While this privileged position fell short of full autonomy from the secular power, it granted important privileges to the dominant national church, including government subsidies for clergy salaries and pensions. After 1989, the Orthodox Church insistently called for a return to interwar arrangements that awarded it so many privileges.

Romania's option for the established church model was never seriously questioned, though it was neither the only choice nor a particularly fitting reality. Whereas the Romanian Kingdom was relatively homogeneous religiously and ethnically, Greater Romania included several provinces once part of different empires (the Ottoman, Russian, and Austro-Hungarian Empires) and a mixed religious and ethnic population (Orthodox and Greek Catholic Romanians, Roman Catholic and Protestant Magyars and Germans, Muslim Turks and Jews). Instead of embracing a pluralist model recognizing the country's religious diversity, the new constitution underscored the national character of the new state by elevating the two churches of the Romanian majority above all other religious denominations and underscoring the unique position of the Orthodox Church as the dominant religion. By requiring official registration of religious groups that sought to function legally in the country, the government limited the activity of the religious and ethnic groups through which the Ottoman and Austro-Hungarian Empires had previously asserted control over the Romanian provinces (especially the Roman Catholic Magyars in Transylvania and the Muslim Turks in Wallachia and Moldova). Through financial support schemes privileging the Orthodox Church, the government tried to strengthen the country's Romanian, and by extension Orthodox, character. The partnership between the state and the Orthodox Church was apparently inspired by the politicians' desire to co-opt the dominant church as an electoral ally, as well as the latter's autocephalous status, which deprived it of the support of a leadership residing abroad that might challenge the hegemony of the Romanian state.

State control over religious affairs was effected through the Ministry of Religious Denominations, a new governmental structure Cuza created in 1859 to grant official recognition to religious groups, disburse public funds, oversee relations between the government (the ministries and their subordinated departments) and the denominations as well as among religious groups, and enact government policy pertaining to religious affairs in general. In one form or another, this structure was retained by all subsequent Romanian governments, irrespective of their ideological or political orientation. From 1867 to 1921, it was reorganized as the Ministry of Religious Affairs and Public Education, which oversaw the important network of confessional schools through which the kingdom offered public education. From 1921 to 1930, the government of Greater Romania separated the Ministry of Religious Affairs and Culture from the Ministry of Public Education, but in 1930 it brought back together religious affairs and education under one roof, and a decade later reorganized religious affairs, education, and culture into a single ministry. Political instability and corruption meant that during the period of sixty-three years between 1881 and 1944, Romania had as many as sixty different ministers overseeing religious affairs, some of them for less than two whole weeks. Over the same period, only three individuals fulfilled their four-year mandates, and probably as many went down in history as able administrators. The overwhelming majority of the individuals appointed as ministers were self-declared Orthodox believers.[6]

After World War II, Romania became part of the communist bloc. Like its Eastern European counterparts, the Romanian Communist Party initially saw religion as a capitalist remnant that was expected to wither away as its social basis disappeared, but the party's religious policy was ultimately determined by practical more than ideological considerations. The Law on Religious Denominations of 4 August 1948 gave the Ministry of Religious Affairs full control over religious life. (In 1957, the ministry was downgraded to the level of a department, to signal the communist state's belief that the "problem of religious denominations" was solved.) At first, the communists appointed Orthodox priest Constantin Burducea as religious affairs minister, but after November 1946 only apparatchiks with unwavering commitment to the official ideology and policy line were given the post. Article 1 of the Law on Religious Denominations formally upheld freedom of religion and conscience, but ambiguous stipulations obliged practiced religion to conform to the constitution, national security, public order, and accepted morality (Articles 6 and 7). The state continued to support financially the salaries of the priests and ministers representing the officially recognized denominations, at their request. However, "priests who voiced anti-communist attitudes could temporarily or permanently be deprived of their state-sponsored salaries" (Article 32), a stipulation invoked to curtail the activities of Baptist ministers and to punish outspoken Orthodox priests in the 1980s. Groups had to be officially recognized, and the government could revoke the recognition for unspecified reasons at any time (Article 13). The state controlled the appointment of bishops and members of the Orthodox Church's collective leadership, the Holy Synod, which was compelled to welcome party members in its midst. The state further nationalized church property, severely restricted the training of priests, closed down confessional schools, ceased religious instruction in public schools, and banned public religious celebrations of Easter and Christmas.[7]

The communist religious strategy was multipronged, aimed to divide and conquer. Several waves of repression were launched to weed out church members who supported "retrograde" anti-communist positions that challenged official views and practices. A dedicated secret political police department was set up to thoroughly penetrate the rank and file of religious groups and to marginalize unreliable clergymen (as explained in chapter 4). Churches whose leadership resided abroad were the first to be targeted for persecution. After the Concordat with the Roman Catholic Church was revoked in 1948, the communist state was never again able and willing to reach a compromise with that church, which continued its activity in the country under serious restrictions. In 1948 the Greek Catholic Church was disbanded, its churches and adjacent land transferred to the Orthodox Church, and its leaders imprisoned if they refused to convert to Orthodoxy. Some fourteen denominations historically present in the country were granted official recognition, but no other group was registered until 1989. The state let the faithful know that religiosity was not akin to the communist spirit by annulling the autonomy of religious groups. In a symbolic gesture, in 1950 the communist authorities ordered the Baptists, the Seventh-day Adventists, and the Pentecostals to unite into the Federation of Protestant Cults.[8] Threatened with obliteration, the groups in question could do nothing but obey.

Communist authorities persecuted but did not dismantle the dominant Orthodox Church, recognizing instead that a church respected by the bulk of the population could be useful for furthering the party's socioeconomic and political goals.[9] Until 1965, the state made considerable efforts to weaken the church's role in society and to bring its hierarchy under control by legally depriving it of its national church status and the right to pursue educational and charitable activities. Once the last remnants of resistance were crushed, the state forged a special partnership with the Orthodox Church that enlisted that religious group as an unconditional supporter of communist policies in return for the government's tolerating a certain level of ecclesiastical activity (including training priests in the university-level institutes of Sibiu and Bucharest, and publishing selected theological titles).

The Communist Party controlled the Orthodox Church by appointing obedient patriarchs. The three "red" patriarchs—Justinian Marina (1948–1977), Iustin Moisescu (1977–1986), and Teoctist Arăpaşu (since 1986)—only rarely had the courage to place the interests of their church ahead of the interests of the party-state, and they never openly defied the authorities or informed foreign governments of the plight of their religious group. Instead of opposing religious persecution, they turned a blind eye to it and constantly denied any form of discrimination, thus condoning the communist regime's actions against their church.[10] Throughout his reign, Patriarch Justinian, a former parish priest with socialist views and a personal friend of Gheorghe Gheorghiu-Dej (Romania's leader from 1948 to 1965), remained a staunch supporter of the communist regime, but his cooperation did not spare the church several waves of persecution, including depositions and arrests of clergy, closure of monasteries and monastic seminaries, and strict control of its relations with foreign churches.[11] After the 1949 "social reorientation" programs, numerous priests considered retrograde were arrested. Another wave of arrests took place in the late 1950s, when additional monastic seminaries and monasteries were closed down, and thousands of monks and nuns were jailed or forced to go "back into the world."[12]

In response, Marina tried to reform the monastic system to prevent its being regarded as an anachronism unrelated to the life of socialist Romania. He introduced "useful trades" that every monk and nun could practice. In 1949, when communists deposed fifteen Orthodox priests, the Orthodox hierarchy responded by issuing a communiqué denying any form of religious persecution.[13] Shortly after his appointment, Patriarch Iustin rendered homage to President Nicolae Ceauşescu for "securing complete freedom for all religious cults in our country to carry out their activity among the faithful" and for his forty-five-year-long activity "devoted to the progress of the Romanian people and fatherland."[14] His successor, Teoctist Arăpaşu, a political activist long before assuming the position of patriarch, served as a Grand National Assembly deputy, a delegate to the Socialist Unity and Democracy Front congresses, and a key member of the Ceauşescu-sponsored National Peace Committee.

During 1965–1977, there was a relative thaw in church-state relations. The state no longer saw a need to close monasteries, agreed to rehabilitate formerly imprisoned clergy, and financially supported the restoration of churches of historical importance. In a series of shrewd calculations, Ceauşescu used the Orthodox Church to gain independence from Moscow in order to ingratiate himself with the West, whose financial support he badly needed for his megalomaniac industrialization projects. At the same time, he sought to strengthen his position domestically by appealing to nationalism, which the church considered its turf. In 1968, Ceauşescu acknowledged the role of the Orthodox Church in the development of modern Romania, and in April 1972, he allowed his father's funeral to be conducted according to Orthodox ritual and be broadcast live on national radio. (His mother, a simple peasant with no formal education, remained a committed Orthodox believer fearful of God throughout her life.) Ceauşescu also tacitly tolerated the use of baptism, marriage, and burial services by communist officials who privately considered themselves Orthodox Christians. In May 1974, Marina brought the Orthodox Church into the Socialist Unity and Democracy Front, a national advisory organization totally controlled by the Communist Party. His death in 1977 coincided with the revival of an Eastern European civil society and the onset of a new anti-church campaign in Romania.[15]

By 1979, religious persecution in Romania was on the rise again, and the Ceauşescu regime continued its anti-religious policies unabated until December 1989. In contrast to the pre-1965 crackdown on religious activity, this time several voices stood up against Ceauşescu's blatant infringements on religious freedom. The best-known dissenter was Orthodox priest Gheorghe Calciu-Dumitreasa, sentenced in 1979 to prison and later banished into exile for preaching sermons labeling atheism as a philosophy of despair and for criticizing the regime's violations of human rights and church demolitions. Moisescu allowed the synod to defrock Dumitreasa and other priests who were later arrested for anti-communist opposition. Between 1977 and 1989, twenty-two churches and monasteries were demolished and fourteen others were closed down or moved to disadvantageous sites behind tall apartment blocks. Teoctist also struggled with Ceauşescu's desire to demolish the Bucharest patriarchal complex and transfer the see to the northeastern town of Iaşi.[16] This did not prevent him from sending the dictator a telegram of support days after the first popular anti-communist uprising started in Timişoara in December 1989.

In sum, in the mid-nineteenth century, Romania recognized the Orthodox Church as the main denomination, a position that de facto meant that the church acted, and was treated, as a state church. That privileged status was ratified by the 1866 constitution and upheld by the 1923 and 1938 basic laws, even after the old Romanian Kingdom incorporated the multicultural province of Transylvania. While the Orthodox Church towered over other religious groups, it progressively lost ground to the modern Romanian state, which freed itself from church dominance to become an independent governmental machinery able to use the church in its nation-building and modernization projects. Communist authorities favored secularism and atheistic Marxism-Leninism, but in time they realized the advantages of tolerating rather than completely eradicating religious denominations. During its consolidation phase, the communist state persecuted all religions, but by the mid 1960s, the Orthodox Church reestablished a new foundation for collaboration with the authorities based on a distorted *symphonia* in which the "emperor" was no longer a Christian Orthodox, or even religious, but a state seeking to subjugate the church.

Models of Church-State Interaction in Post-Communism

Since 1989, four models of church-state interaction have been advocated as solutions compatible to democracy by the politicians, who set the policy agenda; the Orthodox Church, which claims the allegiance of a majority of the population; the minority religious groups, which enjoy the protection of Western democratic governments in the name of the freedom of religion; and the local civil society, which has struggled to be accepted as a serious partner of dialogue. For now, only the model proposed by the political elite has bridged the gap between theory and practice and inspired the legislative agenda and the overall mission of the State Secretariat for Religious Denominations without, however, being codified into law.

Romania was the last country in the region to adopt a new Law on Religion (in 2006) to replace the 1948 communist bill. Before the new law was enacted, the state upheld an outdated atheistic model and preached pluralism, while practicing a church-state relations model giving precedence to the dominant faith. In 1999, it looked like a sympathetic Christian Democrat government would allow the vision of the Orthodox Church to prevail and place church-state relations on a new basis, but opposition from minority religions, civil society, and foreign governments killed the proposal before parliament could debate it. In 2006, steps were taken to translate existing practices into law.

To date, no model presented as a unified document has been officially endorsed by the four social groups, and as such some readers might take issue with our effort to piece together four coherent bodies of principles and prescriptions. Post-communist Romania has been governed alternatively by center-left and center-right governments with different policy preferences toward political and economic reform. The Petre Roman (1990–1991), Theodor Stolojan (1991–1992), and Nicolae Văcăroiu (1992–1996) center-left governments leaned toward incremental change, whereas the Victor Ciorbea (1996–1998), Radu Vasile (1998–1999), and Mugur Isărescu (1999–2000) center-right cabinets opted for more sustained reforms. Similarly, from 2000 to 2004, the Social Democrat cabinet of Adrian Năstase emphasized social protection, while afterward the center-right team of Călin Popescu-Tăriceanu has endeavored to fulfill the European Union accession requirements. But the religious policy of all these governments (with the notable exception of Vasile's team) did not vary widely enough to suggest commitment to different church-state models.

Because Orthodox Church leaders expressed preference for different church-state models, we identify here only those proposals that are most popular with members of that religious group. Although there has been divergence among minority religious denominations with regard to the model the country should adopt, all groups that did voice a preference endorsed versions of the pluralistic model. Last, the civil society has been notoriously divided and unable to speak with one single voice, but two broad tendencies can be distinguished in its midst. Some groups have favored a clear separation of church and state in public affairs, while others have advocated the established church model. Since this latter group's arguments have generally coincided with those of the Orthodox Church, we present here only the strict separation model. Let us reconstruct each of these models in turn.

The Managed Quasi-Pluralist Model

When it comes to religion and politics, the Romanian post-communist political elite has tried to find the middle ground between winning and maintaining the electoral support of its mostly Orthodox constituencies, enjoying autonomy from all religious groups in the policy-making process, and complying with the requirements of religious toleration and even-handedness imposed by European Union accession. The process of negotiating between such competing goals has turned proposals coming from political quarters into variants of the managed quasi-pluralist model by which the centralized state retained control over religious affairs through registration and fund allocation, while relaxing communist-era restrictions on religious activity and endorsing a privileged partnership with the Orthodox Church. Individual parties and politicians have forged close ties to different religious groups, but the state has refused to formally elevate any denomination above all others. From the viewpoint of the authorities, religious groups formally belong to the state-free areas of family, education, and the arts.[17]

The product of a largely secular society and self-declared atheistic politicians, the 1991 constitution sounded a clearly pluralistic tone in its provisions relevant to religious life.[18] References to religion and religious life were made in Article 29 that guaranteed the freedom of thought, opinion, and religious beliefs when manifested in a spirit of tolerance and mutual respect, allowed religions to be "free and organized in accordance with their own statutes," and they prohibited "any forms, means, acts or actions of religious enmity." The article further upheld the autonomy of religious denominations from the state and pledged state support for religious assistance in the army, in hospitals, prisons, orphanages, and elderly care homes. To steer the churches away from pernicious political influences, the legislators stipulated that statutory rules of religious denominations were organic laws passed by the majority vote of each of the two chambers of parliament (Article 72). Religious groups could set up confessional schools, and religious instruction in the public school system was guaranteed (Article 32).

A number of other pieces of legislation expanded religious freedom. According to the Law on Preparing the Population for Defense no. 46 of 5 June 1996, priests and theology graduates were exempted from military training. Decree Law no. 9 of 31 December 1989 recognized the Greek Catholic Church, and the highly controversial Decree Law no. 126 of 24 April 1990 prescribed the conditions for the return of Greek Catholic assets that had been in the possession of the communist state and the Orthodox Church. In December 1991, the government annulled Decision no. 810 of 1949 that banned Roman Catholic orders and congregations on Romanian territory. In 1996, Easter and Christmas as celebrated by the Orthodox Church were listed among national holidays, but at the same time faithful of religious minorities were allowed to take alternative days off work.[19] In 2006, the new Law on Religion clearly guaranteed the fundamental rights of freedom of opinion, conscience, and religious beliefs (Article 1).

Despite the pluralistic tone sounded for the benefit of the international community, the mandate of the State Secretariat remained unchanged, an oversight that signaled a desire on the part of the post-communist state to retain its grip over religious activity. Through the secretariat, the government continued to require religious denominations to gain official recognition according to criteria that were never fully spelled out and could be changed unilaterally at will. The religious groups registered by the communist regime retained their status, and the reconstituted Greek Catholic Church was recognized in December 1989. But afterward, only the Jehovah's Witnesses gained recognition as a religious denomination because of intense pressure from the local civil society and the international community more than as a result of the government's commitment to fairness and evenhandedness. There are now eighteen groups recognized as religious denominations in the country (see the appendix to this volume). Romanian authorities also registered 385 faiths, organizations, and foundations, but these religious associations do not enjoy financial advantages; the right to build houses of worship or to perform rites of baptism, marriage, or burial; the guarantee of state (largely police) noninterference in their religious activity; or protection against public stereotypes and negative media campaigns.[20] This is important since not all nonrecognized groups can worship freely and openly in the country. For example, in 2004, the government vigorously pursued the Movement for Spiritual Integration into the Absolute, a New Age, Tantra-practicing yoga group led by Gregorian Bivolaru, on charges of human trafficking, sexual exploitation of minors, and tax evasion. A year later, Sweden granted Bivolaru political asylum, admitting that the spiritual leader was persecuted in his home country for his religious beliefs.

More important, the state continued to treat the Orthodox Church preferentially. Instead of reversing by law the communist-era transfer of Greek Catholic Church property to the Orthodox Church, the authorities accepted the Orthodox view that the matter was a purely religious dispute that had to be settled not by parliament but by the two denominations. This position allowed the Orthodox Church to control the process by opposing and delaying the restitution, even when ordered by the courts. Certainly, the Orthodox Church has dominated the State Secretariat. After 1989, all but one secretary were graduates of the Faculty of Orthodox Theology, and there is no evidence that governments ever contemplated the possibility of appointing a non-Orthodox to the post. Through the secretaries, the Orthodox Church was allowed to influence the distribution of government subsidies to religious groups. The Secretariat has insisted that fund allocation among recognized groups was proportional to group membership, but time and again the Orthodox Church received financial support above its rightful share from special government funds. The Social Democrat Văcăroiu government granted Orthodox priests bonuses and in 1994 decided to differentially cover the wages of the heads of recognized religious groups.[21] The Orthodox patriarch was offered 4.5 times the average salary, whereas other leaders received only 3.9 times the average.[22] Subsequent governments failed to bridge the salary gap.

Through the secretaries, the Orthodox Church was also able to delay the adoption of a new law on religion as long as the proposed drafts did not recognize it as a national church and did not impose restrictions on the activity of new religious groups. As parliament passed a new law on religion only in December 2006, for the first 17 years of post-communism, the Decree on the General Regime of Religious Denominations no. 177 of 1948 remained effective but hardly appropriate for the new times, since it defined the relationship with a repressive state.[23] Eager to improve its relationship with the Orthodox Church, the post-communist state did not avail itself of some legislative prerogatives allowing it to appoint the patriarch and control church property, pastoral letters, public statements, and relationship with churches abroad. While encouraging that church's emancipation from state appointments and reviews, state representatives continued to confirm nominations to senior positions in the Orthodox hierarchy and attend the synod sessions and the National Church Congress meetings.

The Established Church Model

Although it has de facto dominated the country's religious landscape and enjoyed the support of formations on all sides of the political spectrum, the Orthodox Church has downplayed its privileged position and asked instead for additional de jure benefits, as protection against the whims of future government teams that might be less disposed in its favor. Church leaders have shown preference for an established church model combining British, German, and Romanian historical elements, allowing it to receive government favoritism and to serve as part of both the state establishment and the civil society.

With an eye to the Church of England and its established church status, the Romanian Orthodox Church has claimed the position of national church on the basis of its large membership, its historical contribution to state and nation-building, the interwar precedent, and the model's compatibility with democracy suggested by the British example.[24] For Orthodox clergymen, recognizing the church as the national church would set the clock back to the interwar period and redress communist-era injustices by granting the church its historical right and reflecting de jure a position that the church has occupied de facto after 1989. In the words of Patriarch Teoctist, "the history of the

Romanian people is intertwined with the history of the Orthodox Church, the only institution which has lasted since the birth of the [Romanian] people. Whoever denies that the church is the national church should deny the unitary character of the Romanian state."[25] The church has dominated numerically, and its political clout has been unmatched by other religious or nonreligious groups. As such, the legal changes would merely recognize the state of affairs rather than grant the church unwarranted additional privileges. Church leaders were disappointed that the 1923 constitution was not used as a blueprint for the 1991 basic law. Aware that its calls fell on deaf ears, and encouraged by its increased hold over the population, in 1994 the National Orthodox Church Congress declared the church "national, autocephalous, and united in its organization," that is, a national church.[26] In September 1999, the church moved one step closer to being officially recognized as the national church when Premier Vasile amended the draft law on religion in its favor. After the cabinet turned down the proposal, Patriarch Teoctist declared his surprise and went on "strike." Relations between the ruling center-right coalition and the church cooled down significantly. The proposal was set aside and never revisited.

With an eye to the British Lords Spiritual, the twenty-six senior bishops of the established Anglican Church appointed to the upper House of Lords, the Romanian Orthodox Church has demanded that leaders of officially recognized religious groups be accepted as lifetime members of parliament. During the constitutional debates in the early 1990s, the church repeatedly called on state authorities to appoint all synod members (the patriarch, metropolitans, and senior bishops) to the upper Senate. Bold as it seemed, the idea was not completely new to Romania but part and parcel of pre-communist constitutions. The 1923 basic law granted the same right to Greek Catholic leaders as well. As local mass media revealed, in July 1990 the Orthodox patriarch and metropolitans met President Ion Iliescu to discuss what was laconically described at the time as "the Church's representation in parliament."[27] When Iliescu rejected the proposal, the patriarchate presented the synod with amendments claiming to improve the 1991 constitution. The changes related to Article 58.1, which the church wanted to read: "The Orthodox patriarch, metropolitans and archbishops or their representatives, together with the leaders of the other churches recognized in Romania, are senators de jure."[28] The drafters of the constitution disregarded the suggestions, but the church did not give up on the proposal.

In 1998, Archbishop Bartolomeu Anania of Cluj, Vad, and Feleac reissued the request. Orthodox clergy overwhelmingly endorsed the church's political involvement as natural since, as one clergyman put it, "the Church was actually never separated from the state. Where the ruler was, there the prelate was too."[29] Church leaders did not conceal their disappointment that politicians ignored the proposal, especially since Orthodox leaders believed that their tacit support had brought the center-right government to power. Bishop Ioachim of Huşi insisted that a church legislative presence was nothing short of a moral obligation for the state.[30] Critics pointed out that, if adopted, the proposal could damage the fragile Romanian democracy. These senators (whose number has constantly increased[31]) would be lifetime senators, since Orthodox leaders are not required to retire. They would also be a formidable parliamentary faction with unmatched political influence given by the church's moral standing, along with unparalleled village and town penetration and the growing loss of popularity suffered by political parties and politicians as a result of their perceived inability to solve the country's transition problems.

In 1999, a group of legislators prepared a draft law allowing Orthodox leaders to become senators, but with general elections around the corner, parliament did not discuss the draft. Recently, Father Irimie Marga, an Orthodox canon law professor at the Sibiu Faculty of Theology, justified the proposal in terms of the precedent set by the 1866 and 1923 basic laws and the communists' willingness to appoint the patriarch as a Grand Assembly deputy. For Marga, it is legitimate for Orthodox bishops to be senators, as this way they would participate in national politics as opposed to party politics, which the synod disagreed with because of its alleged divisiveness. The bishops' political involvement is acceptable and required, as all citizens (including the bishops) should be concerned with the country's well-being.[32]

The British model did pose a challenge to the Romanian Orthodox Church in assuming that the state granted no financial support to religious groups but expected them to raise funds for their activity through fees and donations. Thus, when it came to government subsidies, the church turned to the German model and asked for the introduction of a state-collected church tax.[33] Unless they elect to pay a 9 percent surcharge to their tax bill and thereby officially become members of a religious denomination, German taxpayers do not have the automatic right to be baptized, married, or buried in their denominational church; in some cases, they may find it difficult to gain access to the Roman Catholic or Protestant hospitals and care homes for the elderly. As a result, the vast majority of German citizens choose to pay the church tax. The Romanian Orthodox Church has praised the German model for allowing religious groups to receive state financial support, while making the process less political. The church tax would make the link between contributing taxpayers and their church more evident, and it would ensure that the total level of governmental subsidies reflected taxpayers' high levels of religious self-identification more than the whim of the ruling political party.[34] Its historical dependence on state funds has made the Orthodox priesthood a salaried bureaucracy whose welfare depends on the political decision-makers, but the church needs government subsidies. Despite aggressive private fundraising, state financial support remains crucial to church activity, covering the salaries and pensions of the priests and public-school religion instructors and the costs of running dioceses abroad, building new places of worship and maintaining the old ones.

The Orthodox Church has sought to maintain a strong formal presence in politics. Informally, the church has been a powerful political actor, so much so that the state often had to react to developments initiated by the church without consultation with, and often in contradiction to, the political elite.[35] For example, the Orthodox Church offered religious instruction in public schools before parliament passed legislation on the issue, and the church hampered attempts to decriminalize homosexual behavior at the risk of endangering Romania's European Union integration. Direct and indirect political involvement of the church at all levels has been endorsed by powerful synod members, both conservative and reformist. In 1998, Archbishop Anania proposed that the church select candidates for parliamentary mandates and priests urge believers during sermons to vote for people whom the church trusted. Even respected Metropolitan Nicolae Corneanu of Banat further explained that the church "can neither be apolitical, as some fear, nor involved in political partisanship, as some wish," since it "must have a word to say in what goes on in the world, society and daily life."[36] Many Romanian intellectuals suggested that the Orthodox Church should stick to religious affairs.

The Pluralist Model

Recognized and unrecognized religious minorities criticized the two drafts for the law on religion as falling short of democratic requirements and insisted that only the pluralist model was appropriate for the country. According to them, Romania, as other predominantly Orthodox countries, never enjoyed a stable democratic regime for more than brief periods of time and, as such, offered no historical precedents worth revisiting. The country, therefore, should emulate not Romanian interwar church-state models but Western European states by recognizing a wide variety of religious groups as public entities and giving them equal chances to qualify for official recognition, government subsidies, tax exemption status, and other privileges. In turn, religious groups must remain part of the civil society, not seek political representation. Baptist Union president Vasile Talos made clear his option for what he termed a "plural society [providing] us with a wider range of experience and a wider diversity of human responses to experience, and therefore richer opportunities for testing the sufficiency of our faith than are available in a monochrome society," while he rejected "the ideology of pluralism" encouraging "a society where everything is subjective and relative."[37]

In response to the 1999 draft law on religion, religious minorities submitted amendments to the Human Rights Committee of the Chamber of Deputies. Minorities voiced two major sets of concerns. First, fearing that the recognition of the Orthodox Church as the national church placed them on lesser footing by rendering them non-national and foreign, minorities rejected the proposal on grounds that "the power of the [Orthodox] Church is spiritual," not worldly, and the adoption of the draft would lead to Romania's isolation in Europe.[38] According to Jehovah's Witnesses, the proposal was "medieval," although it did not call for "lighting pyres for the Holy Inquisition"; for Christian Democrat deputy Petru Dugulescu (a declared Baptist), the proposal ran counter to the constitutional provisions recognizing religious denominations as equal before the law and Romania as a "secular, not religious, fundamentalist, state."[39] Without elaborating, leader Marko Bela of the Democratic Union of Magyars in Romania, representing the predominantly Catholic and Protestant Hungarians of Transylvania, believed that the privileged status envisioned for the Orthodox Church reflected "an extremely dangerous mentality."[40]

A second set of concerns related to the elaborate procedure by which the State Secretariat granted recognition to new religious groups and to several other restrictions placed on religious activity. A group wishing official recognition as a religious denomination needed to submit a statement detailing why it should be recognized, a list of supporting members (including only Romanian citizens living in the country and representing at least 0.5 percent of the total population), and a copy of the group's credo and organizational statutes (Article 23). Religious minorities argued that almost no new group and many of the already recognized denominations were able to fulfill the "0.5 percent" condition, amounting to a membership of about 115,000. Another restrictive provision stated that, to become legal persons, parishes had to demonstrate that their membership represented at least 5 percent of the locality's adult population (Article 15). The bill further stated that only Romanian citizens residing in the country could be religious leaders and church staff members. The Orthodox Church Serb vicariate of Timişoara asked for the word "only" to be erased, while the Unitarian, Evangelical, Reform, and Roman Catholic Churches backed an amendment allowing all religious denominations to invite ministers from abroad.[41]

Of major concern was a provision that rendered illegal and punished with fines of up to $9,000 organized religious activity by groups not registered with the State Secretariat. Among the former communist countries, only Uzbekistan and Turkmenistan have gone that far in punishing unregistered religious activity.[42] The Seventh-day Adventists deemed the proposal "unacceptable," whereas the Baptists argued that "as long as religious groups are treated differently according to how old they are and how many members they have we cannot talk about real and full respect for freedom of conscience, opinion, faith or religion."[43] Non-Orthodox groups also criticized the secrecy that surrounded the preparation of the final proposal that ignored the months of active negotiation among religious groups aimed at producing a mutually acceptable text.[44]

The Strict Separation Model

As previously stated, Romanian civil society is divided when it comes to the proper interaction between religion and politics. Former supporters of national communism and promoters of the so-called protochronist (from protos-chronos, meaning "first in time") theory have tended to subordinate church-state relations to a nationalist perspective that privileges the Orthodox Church as uniquely positioned to sustain the nation-building process.[45] According to this latter group, since its foundation, the modern Romanian state has continuously been under attack from both external and internal factors bent on destroying the unitary nation-state and diluting the Romanian character of the nation. Orthodoxy alone has glued together the Romanians living in different regions. As the arguments they propose and the church-state model they promote echo the Orthodox Church's defense of the established church model, we present here the alternative model of strict separation of church and state supported by the humanistic intellectuals of Bucharest.

During the confrontation between unarmed protesters and the communist authorities who summoned army troops in a desperate attempt to avert a regime change, Bucharest intellectuals organized as the Group of Social Dialogue. The title of the group's official mouthpiece, the 22 magazine, referred to the day when Ceaușescu cowardly left the Communist Party Central Committee headquarters by helicopter, only to be apprehended hours later and then shot commando-style three days later on Christmas Day 1989. Thus, "22" represented the day when the tide turned in favor of the anti-Ceaușescu forces.[46]

The group presented itself as the voice of civil society, an authority on the art of conducting politics, and the best training ground for anti-communist opposition politicians. Its elitist views prevented the group from forging ties to the broader society, whose choice of voting former communists into government in the May 1990 elections was belittled as a bad decision made on "the

Sunday of the Blind."[47] Its support for a political system wisely led by phi-losopher-kings, no doubt selected from its midst, was criticized as self-serving, outdated, and unreflective of Romanian post-communist reality. Its members were well versed in philosophy and literary criticism but had no hands-on ex-perience with public policy and the business of running a country other than that described in the works of Aristotle and Plato or the odd Western book that occasionally arrived in Bucharest. For its critics, the group was misrepresent-ing its mission when claiming to foster social dialogue, as the only dialogue it allowed was among people who supported its political views.

The inability of the Group for Social Dialogue to open communication channels with the broader society prompted some of its members to look for greener pastures elsewhere. The splinter faction led by Gabriel Andreescu, a writer the communist political police pursued in the 1980s, has articulated most clearly the separation of church and state model. True, voices both inside and outside the Group for Social Dialogue have made occasional reference to the need to keep religion and politics apart, especially in reference to the pow-erful Orthodox Church.[48] For example, in 1999 journalist Mihai Chiper took a stand against the fact that "in a secularized state, the Romanian Orthodox Church has occupied a symbolic position which legally is unwarranted" and warned that "as long as the state has no institutional strategy for strict sepa-ration [of church and state], its secular discourse will be insufficient to compel the Orthodox Church to reconsider its responsibilities and merits in a modern state. To date, no Orthodox Church leader has recognized the secular character of the Romanian society."[49] Except for Andreescu, none of these individual voices have organized for political action on a platform explicitly favoring strict separation of church and state. As part of the Romanian Human Rights De-fense Association, the Save the Carol Park (Salvați Parcul Carol), or the Soli-darity for Freedom of Conscience, Andreescu and his son Liviu have inked down several documents defending the model.

According to their position, strict separation of religion and politics is com-mendable because it allows both the state and the churches to be independent and autonomous from each other, and therefore it allows a radical break with the recent past, a period when the communist state used and abused the sub-servient Orthodox Church. The church was reminded of its unholy collabo-ration with the repressive communist regime and the secret political police, its failure to stand up for the rights of freedom and religion, and its inability to mount sustained resistance to the atheistic state. Further loss of moral ground occurred when the Orthodox Church allowed itself to be turned into a tool against the Greek Catholic Church, choosing to disregard court decisions that ordered the transfer of property to that religious denomination. As the intellectuals contended, strict separation protected the Orthodox Church from the state and, by cutting the church's financial umbilical cord to the government, compelled the church to return to its traditional vocation for social work and the protection of the weak and needy. Free from the burden of maneuvering among capricious political actors, the church would thus be in a better position to rediscover its spiritual mission.

These writers have been equally concerned with keeping the state structure autonomous from the influence of the major religious groups. Ignoring the fact that the model overstates the divide between religion and politics in Western democracies, Romanian civil society representatives have argued that separation of state from church, notably the Orthodox Church, is essential for the consolidation of the Romanian democracy. The model, they argue, is consonant with democracy, as illustrated by the tradition of Western Europe, especially France, Romania's wealthier Latin cousin where republicanism and modernization have gone hand in hand with secularism. According to this approach, religious groups should be entities separate from the state, exist largely as part of the civil society, and receive no direct funding from the government. Strict separation privileges a nonreligious, secular perspective that allows the state to treat all religious groups equally. With an eye to France, intellectuals have opposed the idea of religious education in public schools.[50] With an eye to the United States, they have called for restrictions on the building of new Orthodox places of worship, "agents of religious colonization" whose very existence "may generate pressures on citizens lacking religious sensibilities or who would rather cultivate these sensibilities privately."[51] The job of the state is "to protect the demarcation between the secular and the religious," as Liviu Andreescu maintained. The steady presence of the Orthodox Church in public schools, military, hospitals, and penitentiaries endangers state neutrality and the separation of church and state and "may turn the state into an agent active in the dissemination of religious doctrines and practices."[52]

In Search of Twin Tolerations?

Thus, four different church-state relations models have been publicly debated in post-communist Romania. When compared using Stepan's criteria, the models proposed by the civil society and the religious minorities pass the test of democracy, whereas the models promoted by the state and the religious group most closely associated with it need substantial amendments. That is, both the pluralist and the strict separation models allow for the "twin toleration" between religious and political authorities, but neither the managed quasi-pluralistic model advocated by the political elite nor the established church model proposed by the Orthodox Church is conducive to democracy. These latter models represent major improvements over the communist-era strict control over religious affairs, but they are in need of some revising in order to pass the democratic threshold.

The major criticism that can be levied on the state-sponsored, managed quasi-pluralistic model is its failure to protect unrecognized religious groups. Stepan is silent on registration requirements, but he does speak of a core institutional requirement to democracy that "necessarily implies that no group in civil society—including religious groups—can a priori be prohibited from forming a political party."[53] Inspired by the North American experience, Stepan seemingly argues against a registration process that would punish some religious groups by denying them recognition before they engaged in questionable acts. The Western European experience is different. Democratic states can ask religious groups to register but must allow unregistered groups to worship freely, as long as they do not advance violence and hatred and do not endanger public order.[54] In other words, registration can be accompanied by privileges, but nonrecognition should not lead to punishment and persecution, especially when authorities systematically refuse registration to all new groups across the board.

In Romania, unrecognized groups cannot build places of worship, and thus they have no complete freedom to worship privately. Even the recognized Greek Catholics have been denied access to their former churches in some localities. In addition, major world religions like Hinduism and Buddhism remain unrecognized. Stepan further posits that the judiciary, not the executive, should decide whether a religious group and its upshot political formation violate democracy and the rule of law. As the Bivolaru case suggests, the Romanian judiciary is not independent from the executive. Without giving specific names, Bivolaru repeatedly claimed that his arrest and the persecution of his group were launched at the command of a high-ranking Social Democrat government leader (the press alleged that Prime Minister Adrian Năstase was the official in question). When accepting to shelter Bivolaru, Swedish authorities admitted that the Romanian courts failed to give that religious group the benefit of the doubt and, instead, tried to demonstrate a guilt that the executive branch of the government had already established.

By themselves, none of the Orthodox Church's requests raise major problems for democracy, but taken together they might. As we contend in chapter 1, the Western European democratic experience is compatible with the established church model. The Greek example further suggests that a country can consolidate democracy with an established Orthodox Church. Thus, the democratic task requires not church disestablishment but the elimination of non-democratic domains of church power that restricted democratic politics. At the same time, the religious majority should have the opportunity to argue its case in the public arena—not because it is the strongest, but because it is given a right granted to all other groups. However, in the Romanian context an established church model combined with a more or less compulsory church tax would elevate the Orthodox Church to a level unparalleled in the European Union. A senate with thirty to fifty Orthodox senators chosen for life would be a problem for the legislative decision-making process. A large church with many bishops, priests, and ministers all paid from the state budget would raise issues about what say, if any, taxpayers have in the allocation of their contribution to the common purse. On a more mundane level, Orthodox theology graduates would teach publicly funded religious instruction in a sectarian, as opposed to an ecumenical, spirit.

Of the two Romanian models that do pass the test of democracy, the least likely to be accepted in that country is the strict separation model. The reasons are mainly historical. For many Romanians, the model is reminiscent of the communist-era "separation" that subordinated every aspect of religious life to the all-powerful party-state and obliged the faithful to perform rituals in secrecy. Communist practice redefined religious liberty to limit its application in society. As in the Soviet Union, in Romania citizens were guaranteed the right to conduct "religious worship," but they did not have an equal right with atheists to engage in "propaganda" (for example, education and proselytizing). Whereas they would still be allowed to worship privately, the Romanians have traditionally seen the public and private spheres as being much more intertwined than the Western understanding allowed for.[55] It is worth stressing that, for Stepan, the separation of church and state model does not fail the twin toleration test, but it is not essential to democracy. The example of the United States of America suggests that, while strictly separated financially, church and state show mutual respect and toleration. Religious instruction is not offered in public schools, and confessional schools receive absolutely no public funds. With the exception of France, Western European democracies depart from the strict separation model. Thus, contrary to a widespread opinion, strict separation is not the sine qua non condition of good church-state relations and functional democracy.

The Romanian democratic project requires amendments to the church-state relations models proposed by both the political elite and the dominant Orthodox Church. Contrary to civil society representatives who see, in the name of pluralism and secularism, only the need to impose limits on the activity of the Orthodox Church, we argue that the post-communist state must relinquish some of its control over religious affairs, and recognize the country's increasing religious diversity. Contrary to nationalists who denounce any criticism of the Orthodox Church in the name of the nation, its sovereignty and its perpetuation, we argue that it is high time for the dominant church to admit that a model of church establishment adopted when Romania was religiously homogeneous fails to reflect post-communist reality. The most serious threat to the Orthodox Church is represented not by other religious groups, new and old, grown locally or imported from abroad, but popular dissatisfaction with the church's failure to fulfill its social mission. The church's most serious enemy is itself.

3

Religion and Nationalism

No single definition can cover all manifestations of nationalism, which remains an elusive concept. For the *Encyclopedia Britannica*, nationalism is an "ideology based on the premise that the individual's loyalty and devotion to the nation-state surpass other individual or group interests."[1] Sabrina P. Ramet stated that "if by nationalism one means merely cultural awareness or civic-mindedness, then it is apparent that a society is enriched and protected by the presence of these phenomena in large amounts." But more often, nationalism manifested its "destructiveness and chauvinism."[2] Although Ernest Gellner considered nationalism as the idea that political and cultural units should be congruent, political scientists have identified nationalism not only as an ideology but also as a movement that makes political claims on behalf of a nation and on the basis of national identity.[3]

Reviewing the twentieth-century literature on nationalism, nation, and nation-state, Paul Latawski distinguished between the political, social, or territorial nationalism of the West and the ethnic nationalism of the East.[4] Martyn Rady accepted the distinction between Western and Eastern European nationalism, noting that in the West notions of nationhood were grafted onto older concepts of citizenship, natural rights, and popular sovereignty, all protected by strong states. In the East, by contrast, these concepts were less developed, Rady contended. When they started to appear in the late nineteenth century, states lacked civic and political institutions to protect individual rights and citizenship. As a result, the nation subsumed the individual, and civic rights took second place to the doctrine of national rights.[5] Ina Merdjanova saw Eastern European nationalism as a political religion, due to the sacralization of the nation and the glorification of dying for the fatherland as the noblest exploit.[6] Thus, in the region, nationalism has assumed mostly negative connotations.

Numerous authors examined the relationship between religion and Eastern European nationalism, pondering over its meaning, questioning its nature, and highlighting its importance.[7] Some noticed that, since religion existed before nations and nationalism, its longer cultural influence allowed it to subordinate nationalism to its goals. National churches frequently sustained and protected national identity. Because they were traditionally better educated than the majority of the population, Eastern European clergymen were among the first to speak of nation and nationalism, the new realities taking shape in the region. Clergymen noticed that playing the nationalist card guaranteed popularity with the masses and the political elite, especially in countries where members of the ethnic majority belonged to the same religion, whether Eastern Orthodoxy or Roman Catholicism. One of the most striking examples of the use of nationalism by religion occurred at the end of the twentieth century during the Yugoslav wars.[8] Yet not all encounters between religion and nationalism ended up in bloody confrontation and ethnic cleansing. In his examination of the Romanian Orthodox Church, Olivier Gillet noted that communist authorities used the church's historical contribution to the nation-building process to acquire additional legitimacy. The effort aimed to show the essential "Romanian" character of a regime installed by a foreign power, the Soviet Union:

> The advent of communism is seen today as the implantation of a radically foreign ideology in Romania. This is why the problem of the Orthodox nationalism under Ceaușescu remains a taboo topic. The Orthodox discourse, even cleaned of its "socialist" character, remained unchanged after 1989, becoming considerably more radicalized. The survival of the intellectual and political elite, and of the Orthodox hierarchy, partly explains this phenomenon.[9]

In this chapter, we examine the link between nationalism and religion, paying close attention to the way the Orthodox Church, the religion of the Romanian majority, has used nationalism to its advantage. Nationalism has been present in the religious discourse before, during, and after communism. To contextualize the contemporary uses of nationalism by church leaders, we travel back in time to the nineteenth century, when the Romanian national identity emerged. After a historical overview of pre-communist and communist periods, we consider such post-communist manifestations of nationalism as the enlargement of the Orthodox Church by welcoming under its jurisdiction the Bessarabian Metropolitanate from the neighboring Republic of Moldova, as well as that church's insistence on building a cathedral for "national salvation" in Bucharest.

Orthodoxy and Nationalism before 1989

In the Balkans, the nation-building process was accompanied and enhanced by desires for religious emancipation. Greeks, Romanians, and Bulgarians resented the oppressing Muslim Ottoman Turks and sought independence from the Ottoman Empire. They also grew apart from their mother church and sought independence from it. At the time, the ecumenical patriarch of Constantinople had jurisdiction over the entire peninsula, where national Orthodox Churches were set up as metropolitanates or archbishoprics. In the case of the three young nations, successful attempts at political independence (Greece in 1832, Romania in 1878, and Bulgaria in 1878 and 1908) were accompanied by attempts at religious independence. One by one, the churches of Greece, Romania, and Bulgaria declared their independence from Constantinople (in 1833, 1865, and 1870, respectively) but received recognition only much later (in 1850, 1885, and 1945). In 1872, in reaction to the Bulgarian church's declaration of independence, Patriarch Anthimus VI convened a council in Constantinople. Notwithstanding the lack of support it received in the Orthodox world, the council condemned *phyletism*—the national or ethnic principle in church organization—and excommunicated the Bulgarians. Despite the condemnation, Orthodox Churches in Eastern Europe have time and again fallen prey to the heresy.[10]

After national consciousness emerged in the region, the Romanian Orthodox Church joined the bandwagon by positioning itself as pivotal for the very definition of Romanianism, an imagined shared identity supposedly superseding Moldovan, Wallachian, and Transylvanian regional allegiances. In promoting Romanianism after Greater Romania incorporated Transylvania in 1918, the Orthodox Church borrowed, and eventually monopolized, the Transylvanian Greek Catholics' nationalist discourse centered on the Latin character of the Romanian language and descent. This appropriation gave the Orthodox Church growing moral and political legitimacy in the eyes of Romanians, as well as more recognition from the state. Initially, the Orthodox embrace of the Latinist argument was not credible because "for every effort by Transylvania's [Greek Catholic] priests to gain Habsburg support and assistance, Orthodox Romanians were likely to solicit support from the Czar, the Serbian Orthodox hierarchy, or the Orthodox in the Principalities [of Wallachia and Moldova]."[11] Such ambiguous attitude prompted secular intellectuals (Tudor Arghezi, Onisifor Ghibu, and Constantin Rădulescu-Motru, most notably) to attack claims that the Orthodox Church had preserved Romanian identity through centuries of foreign rule and, instead, stress the church's subordination to the Slavs and the Greeks.[12] The nationalism promoted by the Orthodox Church eventually bore fruit. The 1923 constitution recognized the Orthodox and the Greek Catholic Churches as Romanian national churches, yet the former was declared the dominant church, while the latter was only accorded "priority over other denominations" (Article 22).[13]

Most of the literature defending Orthodox nationalism dates from the interwar period, when Orthodoxy was linked to fascist politics and anti-Semitic pogroms. Many Orthodox priests joined the pro-fascist Iron Guard movement, which, with Hitler's support, during the period September 1940 to January 1941, briefly became a partner in the government of Marshall Ion Antonescu. Among the authors most popular at the time was philosopher, poet, and University of Bucharest theologian Nichifor Crainic (1889–1972), who, in his magazine *Gândirea* (*Thought*), advocated Romanianism as *Gândirism*, a mixture of Orthodoxy and nationalism, blended with idealization of peasant culture. As an Iron Guard mentor, Crainic made Orthodoxy a touchstone of the unique "Romanian soul."[14] Another leading figure of the same political organization, University of Bucharest philosophy professor and journalist Nae Ionescu (1890–1940), was reputed for a logical fallacy popular among Romanian nationalists:

> We are Orthodox because we are Romanians, and we are Romanians because we are Orthodox. Can we become Catholic? By becoming Catholic we would have to transform ourselves spiritually in order to be able to realize this Catholicism. This transformation would mean renouncing our history and our spiritual structure. In other words, it means renouncing Romanianness. There are not three solutions: either we remain Romanian and our Catholicism is not a reality; or we become Catholic and then we are no longer Romanians.[15]

Both Crainic and Ionescu placed great emphasis on the religion, language, customs, and traditions binding the Romanian people together, while distinguishing it from ethnic minorities and neighboring peoples.

Around the same time, Dumitru Stăniloae (1903–1993), the most prominent Romanian Orthodox theologian of the twentieth century, wrote on the
relationship between Orthodoxy and Romanianism, a theme he returned to in
his *Reflecții despre spiritualitatea poporului român* (Reflections on the Spirituality
of the Romanian People), published in 1992. For Stăniloae, a nation was built
along ethnic, not civic, lines, whereas nationalism and patriotism were inter-
changeable. In his words, "nationalism is the consciousness of belonging to
a certain ethnic group, the love for that group, and the enacting of that love
for the well-being of the group."[16] To this understanding of nation (*națiune* or
popor in Romanian), one should add the meaning of *neam*. Reserved exclusively
for the Romanian people, *neam* represented an ethnic group with stability and
long-established historical roots. In an early writing, Stăniloae brought together
neam and religion:

> The Romanian *neam* is a biological-spiritual synthesis of [mainly]
> Dacian, Latin and Christian Orthodox elements.... The synthesis is
> new; it has its own individuality and a unity that goes beyond its
> components. The highest law of our *neam*, the one that most appro-
> priately expresses what the nation is, is experienced by the whole, not
> the parts. The parts are stamped with Romanianness, a new, both
> unifying and individualizing stamp. The highest law of our *neam* is
> Romanianness.... What is the Romanian way of communion with
> the transcendental spiritual order? History tells us it is Orthodoxy.
> Orthodoxy is the eye through which Romanians gaze at the heavens.
> Then, enlightened by the heavenly light, they turn to the world
> while continuing to attune their behavior to it.... Certainly, in the-
> ory it is hard to understand how it is possible for Orthodoxy to in-
> terpenetrate with Romanianism without either of them suffering. Yet,
> the bimillennial life of our *neam* shows that in practice this is fully
> possible.... Orthodoxy is an essential and vital function of Roma-
> nianism. Our permanent national ideal can only be conceived in re-
> lation to Orthodoxy.[17]

Stăniloae ingeniously grounded his ethnic nationalism in the Augustinian
theory of *rationes aeternae*, according to which the eternal reasons are the divine
archetypes of all created species and individuals. They are placed in the mind of
God, much like Plato's ideas or forms.[18] For Stăniloae, God desired and even
planned the formation of nation-states. Since God's creation is good and nations
were created by God, nations are good, and so is nationalism. Together with other
prominent interwar authors, Stăniloae helped to make nationalism palatable
and encouraged Romanians to think of their nation as an ethnic nation.[19]

Religion and National Communism

Initially, the communist authorities played the internationalist card. Until 1952, the Romanian Communist Party was dominated by the pro-Moscow faction of Anna Pauker and Vasile Luca, who denounced nationalism and domesticism (national communism) as deviations and then used such charges to eliminate local communist leaders as they became popular (Lucrețiu Pătrăș-canu was just one example of a party leader executed on trumped charges).[20] Once the Muscovites themselves were eliminated, First Secretary Gheorghe Gheorghiu-Dej embraced national communism while still subscribing to strict Stalinism. His skillful maneuvering between a nationalism that catered to Romanian communists and submissiveness to Moscow allowed for the withdrawal of Soviet troops from the country in 1958, the release of political prisoners during 1962–1964, and the rejection of Soviet plans for economic integration and specialization within the Council for Mutual Economic Assistance (COMECON). The nationalist drive was supported by frequent references to the founding myths of the Romanian people: ancient Dacia's ties to Rome and the exploits of Roman Emperor Trajan; the Dacian chieftains Decebal and Burebista; and the Romanian medieval princes Mircea the Elder, Stephen the Great, and Michael the Brave. In a process paralleling the way modern Serbs perceive their defeat by the Ottoman Turks in the Battle of Kosovo of 1389,[21] Decebal's defeat at the hands of Trajan in 101–107 CE and the resulting population mix were reclaimed as the cornerstones of Romanian ethnic identity.

The Orthodox Church became an important player in this game. At first, the church was ordered to reestablish relations with and emulate its sister in the Soviet Union, the Russian Orthodox Church, by becoming involved in the renewal and transformation of society along Marxist-Leninist lines.[22] But after they embraced national communism, the authorities celebrated the church's independence from Moscow, encouraging it to participate in the ecumenical dialogue as mediator between the Western churches and the intransigent Russian church and its satellite Orthodox Churches. Whatever the official state position, the Romanian Orthodox Church had to obey the communist authorities. Because of the large number of Orthodox priests who supported the Iron Guard, the church was vulnerable to blackmail. It further had to repay the favor of not being dismantled and of being allowed to avoid the fate of the Greek Catholic Church, whose property it received in 1948. The combination of threats and rewards rendered the Orthodox Church the malleable partner the party-state needed. Other religious denominations adopted similar attitudes of support and nonconfrontation. The leaders of the Lutheran, Calvinist,

Adventist, and Baptist Churches, as well as the Jewish community, became subservient to the state and renounced political activity in order to survive.[23]

During the first decades of communist rule, Romanian Orthodox writers drew heavily on notions like nation and fatherland, under the inspiration of reputed Soviet and Romanian authors. Theologian Gheorghe Moisescu, the future Patriarch Iustin Moisescu, relied heavily on the wisdom of Stalin, Lenin, Soviet Prosecutor Andrey Vyshinsky, and Gheorghiu-Dej to demonstrate that the nation comprised all ethnic groups inhabiting Romania and thus included, as Marx contended, a community of men and women, formed historically, without distinction of race or ethnicity. The theological journals further embraced the official internationalism of the communist rulers.[24] Their internationalism was limited in scope, expressing tolerance toward and understanding of the peoples living inside the communist bloc, while virulently attacking those living in the West. The Vatican was denounced as the instrument of the capitalist West to penetrate the Eastern bloc by means of religion. This understanding of nationalism, informing the notion of fatherland, together with the evangelical commandment to obey state authorities allowed Moisescu and Marina to justify collaboration with the communists for the good of both church and state.

After Gheorghiu-Dej's death in 1965, Nicolae Ceauşescu embraced an even more overtly nationalist version of communism. His condemnation of the Soviet invasion of Czechoslovakia in connection with the Prague Spring of 1968 inspired admiration for him and his party both inside and outside Romania. Inside the country, intellectuals otherwise opposed to or lukewarm toward the communist ideology became party members. Art historian Andrei Pleşu is one such prominent example. Outside the country, Western governments pledged financial support for the maverick communist leader who dared to defy Moscow. The policy of relative openness allowed Ceauşescu to consolidate his support base and quell dissent inside the party leadership.

The thaw did not survive Ceauşescu's "mini-cultural revolution," launched after his 1971 visit to Mao's China and Kim Ir Sen's North Korea. His cult of personality, rotation of cadres, and peculiar ideological preferences came to be known as Ceauşescuism, a phenomenon informing all aspects of life. The Romanian national heritage was employed in the service of rampant nationalism. Events and personalities were noisily celebrated for Ceauşescu to claim that the entire Romanian history culminated with his personal rule.[25] Inspired by the extravagant celebration of 2,500 years of Persian monarchy organized by the Iranian Shah Mohammad Reza Pahlavi, in 1978 the Romanian dictator lavishly commemorated the 2,050th anniversary of the coronation of Burebista, the legendary king said to have unified the Thracian population from

Hercinica (today's Moravia) in the west to the Bug in the east, and from the northern Carpathians to Dionysopolis in the south. In celebrating Burebista, Ceaușescu wanted to show the world and his people that he was a worthy successor to royalty. He also wished to flatter the Romanians' national consciousness by pointing to their bimillenarian existence. Ceaușescu exaggerated nationalism in order to unite the people internally and claim the superior contributions of the Romanian culture to world civilization.

In the 1980s, the policy that looked for Romanian cultural developments seemingly anticipating Western European accomplishments was amplified and systematized as protochronism (from proto-chronos, meaning "first in time"), a theory insisting that Romanians had every right to be masters in their own country because they were the first to occupy that territory.[26] The insistence on ethnogenesis and national historical continuity was not unique to Romania. Most Balkan countries have flirted with it. Albanians have taken pride in their historical continuity with the Thraco-Illyrians, and Macedonians have insisted on their Thraco-Slavic ethno-genesis, a claim Greece vehemently denounced in the 1990s, since part of ancient Macedonia is in Greece today.[27]

The Romanian Orthodox Church brought its own contribution to the thesis of the Romanian ethnogenesis and historical continuity. The official church history textbooks of Mircea Păcurariu, used in the Orthodox seminaries and university-level theology institutes, endorsed a vision of history arguing that the ancient Daco-Romans were exposed to direct evangelization by St. Andrew, one of Jesus' apostles who allegedly preached the Gospel in the province of Dobrogea, and learned the Christian message from Christian Roman soldiers. There is little historical evidence to support such claims, but Păcurariu used references to nationalism and protochronism to endorse the Orthodox Church's contention that it had been with the Romanian people for 2,000 years from its very beginnings. In its nationalist rendering of history, the Orthodox Church portrayed itself as the constant defender and champion of the Romanians' autonomy and self-governance, a position from which it could demand the national church status.[28]

Commenting on the mutual support the Orthodox Church and the state traditionally provided each other, Metropolitan Nestor Vornicescu of Oltenia (who died in 2000) wrote to endorse Ceaușescu's exaggerated nationalism:

> Since the beginning [of the Romanian people], the unity of the national state, its independence and national sovereignty have been constant preoccupations. The ethnic and geographic area [bound by the Carpathian Mountains and the Danube River] has always enjoyed unity of language, faith, and tradition. It is for that reason that the

Romanian people fought for the unity of all three Romanian provinces of Trajan's Dacia. The Orthodox Church fought alongside the people, and all the fundamental events in Romanian history leading up to the 1918 unification have formed an integral part in the life of the Orthodox Church. The church defended the people's unity of faith and contributed to the defense of the people's essence and to the accomplishment of national unity. The two holy entities, church and fatherland, cannot be separated.[29]

Despite the support national communism continuously received from church historians, Ceaușescu's policy toward religion was ambiguous at best. Trond Gilberg thought that, on the one hand, Ceaușescu was the last Eastern European communist leader to believe in the feasibility of creating the "new socialist man and woman" through ideological indoctrination and anti-religious policies. On the other hand, Ceaușescu recognized the enduring importance of religion for the masses and the need to enlist church leaders in his quest for personal and regime legitimacy.[30] Ceaușescu's anti-religious drive led to the punishment of clergy criticizing his rule, including the Hungarian Roman Catholic Bishop Antal Jakab, several Baptist ministers, members of the Seventh-day Adventist Church, and the Orthodox priest Gheorghe Calciu-Dumitreasa. Paradoxically, lesser-known clergymen were punished more harshly because they were not known to or protected by Western media outlets, as Calciu and Jakab were.[31] Ceaușescu also demolished dozens of centuries-old churches in downtown Bucharest to make room for his enormous House of the People and the Victory of Socialism Boulevard. Yet, some of the most notorious church collaborators with the communist regime, such as Orthodox Metropolitan Antonie Plămădeală of Transylvania (who died in 2005), justified these demolitions as key to the modernization of the nation's capital.

Religion and Nationalism after 1989

After the collapse of the Ceaușescu regime, the Orthodox Church continued to advocate nationalism, out of routine as much as conviction. In their search for more sophisticated explanations, Orthodox theologians have justified nationalism in theological terms by referring to Apostolic Canon 34, which reads that "the bishops of every nation (*ethnos*) must acknowledge him who is first among them and account him as their head, and do nothing of consequence without his consent."[32] The Greek word *ethnos* is the key word here because Canon 34 was issued in the fourth century, and thus it is closer to New Testament time than to today. The biblical meaning of *ethnos* is reflected in the instruction Jesus gives his apostles to "go and make disciples of all the nations (*ta ethnē*)" (Matthew 28:19). The plural *ta ethnē* refers to pagans, non-Jews, and Gentiles (*goim* in Hebrew): that is, people of non-Jewish descent inhabiting the same territory regardless of their ethnic origins.[33] This understanding of *ethnos* meshes well with the modern western notion of a civic state, meaning an ethnically diverse group sharing the same territory and bound together by allegiance to a set of common institutions and practices.

Despite Orthodox aspirations to the contrary, the ancient meaning of *ethnos* does not support the idea of a nation-state,[34] a political unit consisting of an autonomous state that is inhabited predominantly by a people sharing a common culture, history, religion, and language. Modern Orthodox theologians understand *ethnos* as an ethnic group that occupies a distinct territory and is defined by a common language, history, race, and religion. Romanian canon lawyer Ioan Floca, for example, argued that in Canon 34 *ethnos* could only mean an ethnic group and did not refer to all inhabitants of a province or land.[35] Metropolitan Nestor Vornicescu also wrote that "autocephalous Orthodox Churches are each constituted within the borders of a certain territory, an important role in this being played by the specifically ethnic elements of each nation."[36]

No analysis of the relationship between religion and politics in Romania can ignore the Orthodox Church's skillful use of nationalism for restoring its credibility in post-communist times. After decades of collaboration, the church's discourse has underscored the link between Orthodoxy and Romanianism, along with the importance of preserving Romanian national identity in the face of growing modernization, globalization, secularization, European Union integration, and religious competition. Keen local political analysts like Gabriel Andreescu believe that after 1989 the Orthodox Church has relied on two principles to endorse its nationalist discourse: the "majority principle" (which points out that the church has the loyalty of over 86 percent of the country's total population) and the "essentialist principle" (which asserted that being Romanian presupposes Orthodoxy). Conversely, Romanians who belong to other faiths betray their national identity.[37] Later events proved Andreescu right.

The Orthodox Church voiced its nationalism through pastoral messages, public declarations by the clergy, theological publications, and statements released by organizations set up under its aegis. For Andreescu, organizations like the Association of Christian Orthodox Students in Romania (Asociația Studenților Creştin Ortodocşi din Romania, or ASCOR) were used to fight important battles that the synod could not directly wage. An example of using nationalism against other religious denominations was ASCOR's open letter addressed to the Romanian president in 1997, when parliament was about to amend Article 30 of the investment law to allow foreign investors to buy Romanian land. Under the guise of a concern for preserving Romanian lands for Romanian citizens only, the association opposed the influx of non-Orthodox religions that were affluent enough to purchase land. According to ASCOR, the permissive amendment ran against "all policies which had hitherto protected Romanian land by written and unwritten laws" and placed Romanian citizens and organizations "in the humiliating situation of being unable to oppose the foreign partner." The letter warned that the lack of "land protection legislation would generate grave disfunction," because the law would allow "the representatives of states with direct interests in the region or the centers of religious propaganda and proselytism to strategically take control of the land."[38] Subsequent developments proved that ASCOR's worries were unwarranted.

The instances when the church used nationalist arguments to further its agenda or undermine political and religious rivals are too numerous to be included here. Far from being isolated cases, when taken together they suggest that the Orthodox Church has elevated nationalism on a par with its most cherished dogmas. As part of a nationalist-inspired campaign, the synod decided to canonize 19 Romanian saints and declare the second Sunday after Pentecost the "Sunday of the Romanian Saints."[39] On 21 June 1992, in the presence of some 5,000 people, including Prime Minister Theodor Stolojan, Patriarch Teoctist canonized Stephen the Great (Prince of Moldova from 1457 to 1504), as well as more than a dozen other saints. The inclusion of historical political figures among Romanian saints fostered confusion between saints and national heroes, the more so since canonized rulers like Stephen the Great were better known for their intrigues, marital infidelity, and cruelty than for their Christian sanctity. A special celebration for Stephen the Great alone took place on the anniversary of his death on 2 July 1992 when Patriarch Teoctist presided over a much larger gathering at the Putna monastery, the place where the politically active saint was buried. Speaking on the occasion to attendees like President Ion Iliescu, Minister of Foreign Affairs Adrian Năstase, and Minister of Defense Nicolae Spiroiu, Teoctist declared that "God has brought us [church and state] together under the same sky today, just as Stephen rallied us under the same flag in the past."[40]

In its fight against homosexuality (presented here in detail in chapter 8), the church managed to win several political formations to its side. In parliament, its staunchest allies were the representatives of the extremist Party of Romanian National Unity and Greater Romania Party, for which Orthodoxy and moral cleanliness was quintessential to Romanianism. During debates, deputies and senators representing the two political formations proclaimed that Article 200 of the Criminal Code prohibiting homosexual behavior was too lenient toward a "sexual aberration" and that toleration of homosexuality was damaging to national pride.[41] The limited debate around the issue of abortion in Romania led to a nationalist argument being advanced by the official moral theologian of the Orthodox Church, Father Ilie Moldovan, whose 1997 pamphlet on abortion and contraception received wide distribution through official church channels. Relying on theological and ethnonational perspectives, Moldovan contended that abortion was a threat to the very survival of the Romanian nation, therefore amounting to genocide.[42]

Two other initiatives best illustrate the Orthodox Church's use of nationalism. The first was the reopening of a metropolitanate in the independent Republic of Moldova under the jurisdiction of the Romanian patriarchate. The second was the controversial project of an ambitious Orthodox national cathedral to be erected in downtown Bucharest. Let us now turn to each one.

The Bessarabian Metropolitanate and Romanian Religious Irredentism

The unilateral establishment of a new metropolitanate in the independent Republic of Moldova in 1992 triggered a ten-year conflict between the new church structure and successive Moldovan governments, between the Romanian and Russian Orthodox Churches, and between the governments in Bucharest and Chişinău. It fueled the nationalist expectations of some Romanians that independent Moldova (once known as Bessarabia) would again become part of a reconstituted Greater Romania. Romanian-speakers represent some 65 percent of the total population of Moldova, historically a Romanian land.[43] Fortunately, the irredentism of the Romanian Orthodox Church did not lead to armed conflict, most likely because the Romanian political elite was interested in securing and maintaining the country's current borders more than in acquiring new territories inhabited by significant numbers of non-Romanians. Support for the irredentist cause would have also weakened Romania's position vis-à-vis neighboring Hungary, which voiced claims to its former province of Transylvania immediately after the collapse of the communist regime. Romania further sought to strengthen its chances for acceptance into NATO and the European Union by presenting itself as an oasis of stability in a region rocked by conflict and war (affecting Yugoslavia and Transnistria during the early 1990s). True, not all Romanian politicians rejected irredentist calls. The nationalist Greater Romania Party and its populist leader Corneliu Vadim

Tudor have remained committed to the re-creation of Greater Romania within its 1918 borders.

In the last two centuries, the territory of the current Republic of Moldova has been traded back and forth between Bucharest and Moscow before becoming an independent country in 1991 with the dismantling of the Soviet Union. The last time it belonged to Romania was between the two world wars, from 1918 to 1939, when the country included provinces previously part of neighboring states. Greater Romania was a multiethnic state with manifold problems, and national sentiment alone did not bridge the great divide separating the Bessarabians from their fellow countrymen. Historians concur in suggesting that the Bessarabians themselves were the greatest obstacle to the region's integration into Greater Romania. As the most diverse region of the new state, and the one in which the Romanian presence in urban areas was least visible, Bessarabia was torn between its ethnic majority and ethnic minorities, each of which had specific grievances against Bucharest.[44]

Bessarabian Romanians complained about their treatment as second-class citizens in a state controlled by politicians ignorant of regional problems, Russians deplored the closure of their schools and their removal from local administration, while Jews took a stand against the anti-Semitism pervading Greater Romania.[45] The interwar Bessarabian Metropolitanate belonged to the Romanian Orthodox Church, but when the Soviet Union acquired Bessarabia in August 1939, following the Molotov-Ribbentrop pact, the Orthodox believers in the region reverted back to the jurisdiction of the Russian patriarch, who rushed to downgrade the metropolitanate to the status of a bishopric in order to strengthen his dominance.[46] However, the major bone of contention was the ethnic balance of power within the Moldovan eparchy, not its status. While most of the faithful were Romanian speakers, the bishopric was led by Russian speakers, whose unwavering loyalty to Moscow alienated the flock. All these factors taken together meant that the Moldovan Orthodox community was unable to find a common denominator.

The crumbling communist system and rekindled republican nationalist sentiment ultimately led to the dismantling of the Soviet Union. In 1989, the Popular Front was formed by Romanian speakers from the Soviet Moldova calling for the reversal of Russification policies and reunification with Romania. Moldova's unsolved internal conflicts, compounded by Romania's problems with its own ethnic minorities, took a toll on Moldovan pro-unionist sentiments such that, by 1995, the Popular Front had lost much of its popular support and most Moldovans opted for independence from both Moscow and Bucharest. The expectations of Romanian speakers that political independence from Moscow would lead to religious independence rekindled the centuries-old conflict between the world's largest Orthodox Churches. Neither the Moscow Patriarchate nor the Bucharest Patriarchate was willing to relinquish traditional dominance over Moldovan church affairs.

To appease the Romanian speakers, on 1 September 1990, Russian Patriarch Aleksy II visited Chişinău and ordained Romanian speakers Petru Păduraru and Vichente Moraru as the bishops of Bălţi and Cetatea Albă, respectively. A year later, Moscow reorganized the bishopric as the Metropolitanate of Chişinău and All Moldova, the 117th of the 124 eparchies of the Russian Orthodox Church. Its statutes remained nevertheless heavily inspired by those of its Russian protector. The metropolitanate quickly asserted its control over religious matters in independent Moldova, claiming Romanian speakers and Russian speakers, as well as the Gagauz faithful, as its flock. Even its name closely emulated that of the Russian patriarchate.[47] Soon afterward, the Popular Front seriously challenged Moscow's continued domination over religious matters in Moldova.

Within two years of his appointment, Bishop Petru was driven out of his see by pro-Russian faithful disgruntled with his increasingly pro-Romanian stance. In September 1992, Bishop Petru and his Romanian-speaking followers announced the establishment of the autonomous Bessarabian Metropolitanate and asked Patriarch Teoctist to recognize it as an eparchy of the Romanian Orthodox Church. Without consulting the Russian Orthodox Church, Teoctist accepted the metropolitanate as the continuator of the interwar "Autonomous Bessarabian Metropolitanate (old calendar)" with the see in Chişinău, and declared it part of the Romanian Orthodox Church. Petru Păduraru became metropolitan of Bessarabia in 1995, having been its vicar between 1992 and 1995. Teoctist purposely recognized the metropolitanate in December, a month connected with both the 1918 unification of Transylvania and Bessarabia with Romania, and with the 1989 anti-communist revolution. The careful selection of the date suggested that Bucharest viewed the move as conducive to Moldova's future integration into Romania, a first step toward religious and possibly political integration.

The Romanian Orthodox Church took this view seriously enough to restructure its own Metropolitanate of Moldova and Suceava, which oversaw religious life on the right bank of the Prut River, into the Metropolitanate of Moldova and Bukovina, which inherited from its predecessor the see in Iaşi but referred to the land of Bukovina, today part of Ukraine. Both the recognition of the Bessarabian Metropolitanate and the reference to Bukovina amounted to an irredentist move, since neither Bessarabia nor Bukovina was politically part of the Romanian state at the time. By 2001, the Bessarabian Metropolitanate had established 117 communities in Moldova, three in Ukraine, one in each

Baltic state, and two in Russia.[48] Congregation members were Romanian-speakers who live in Moldova or were descendants of Romanians deported to other Soviet republics by communist authorities.

Having received religious recognition from Bucharest, the Bessarabian Metropolitanate proceeded to request political recognition from Chișinău in order to comply with the Moldovan legislation. From 1992 to 2002, it submitted as many as eleven applications for official recognition. However, they were all rejected by three Moldovan presidents, five cabinets, and three parliaments dominated by both left-wing and right-wing parties, fearful that its registration would fuel ethnic tensions in the republic, alienate the powerful Russian Orthodox Church, and endanger relations with Russia, on which the republic heavily depended for energy imports. Moldovan authorities feared that registration might give additional ammunition to groups favoring reunification with Romania and bring Romanian church politics and religious concerns into the independent Moldovan state. Having exhausted all domestic venues at its disposal, in July 1998 the metropolitanate approached the European Court of Human Rights with a complaint against the Moldovan government. After considering the arguments of both sides, on 13 December 2001 the European Court ruled in favor of the Bessarabian Metropolitanate, a decision the Moldovan government appealed.[49] The European Court turned down the appeal and warned that refusal to comply with the decision by 31 July 2002 would bring the country's exclusion from the Council of Europe, which Moldova joined in 1995. Two weeks before the deadline, Chișinău passed draft legislation liberalizing procedures for the registration of religious organizations and stipulating that any denomination that had already filed a request would be automatically registered. Days later, the communist-dominated parliament adopted the amendments, paving the way for the metropolitanate's recognition hours before the deadline set by the European Court.

The staunchest opposition to the recognition came from the Metropolitanate of Chișinău and All Moldova, whose might was augmented by the unconditional support it received from the Russian Patriarchate. Unwilling to see its membership dwindle and its jurisdiction fragmented, the Metropolitanate of Chișinău denounced the Bessarabian Metropolitanate as a "schismatic" group whose very name ignored the constitutionally stipulated name of the republic, Moldova, by favoring Bessarabia, "an imperial name" referring to the interwar Greater Romania. The Metropolitanate of Chișinău also criticized the new legislation allowing for the official registration of the Bessarabian Metropolitanate on grounds that the automatic granting of all requests for recognition encouraged the spread of "cults" alien to Moldovan traditions.[50]

This position was echoed by Russian Orthodox Church leaders like Metropolitan Cyril of Smolensk, who saw the recognition as a "church schism" that ran counter to canon law. According to Cyril, an eparchy can appear on the territory of another eparchy only if "the churches which they belong to do not recognize each other according to canonical law," otherwise "the creation of [such] an eparchy is against church law." He further stated that "there are no ecclesiastical precedents for the creation of a parallel jurisdiction on the territory of a legitimate Orthodox Church," despite the fact that separate Orthodox Churches did emerge in the former Soviet republics of Ukraine and Estonia that pitted the Russian Orthodox Church against the ecumenical patriarchate of Constantinople. For him, "politics, not church expediency" was at issue in a case that "created a most dangerous precedent." The Russian Church leader blamed Romania for the conflict, glossing over the internal divisions within the Metropolitanate of Chişinău. Cyril further criticized Patriarch Teoctist for turning down Patriarch Aleksy II's repeated pleas for dialog and negotiation.[51] This war of words culminated in May 2002, when the Metropolitanate of Chişinău, echoed by the Russian Patriarchate, called for the dissolution of the Bessarabian Metropolitanate at a time when the European Court called for its recognition.[52]

The National Salvation Cathedral

The commingling of religion, politics, and nationalism has been especially evident in the prolonged negotiations preceding the construction of the Romanian Orthodox national cathedral. Periodically resurrected during the last century and a half, the project was born after the Romanian Kingdom won its independence from the Ottoman Empire after the 1877 Russian-Turkish war. At the time, King Carol I and the political elite insisted that the country needed a national cathedral to symbolize the victory through Orthodoxy over the Muslim Ottomans and to accommodate all faithful eager to take part in national festivities and religious celebrations. While the project enjoyed widespread support, Orthodox leaders, politicians, architects, journalists, and intellectuals found it impossible to agree on the cathedral's location and dimensions. Since the political elite was unwilling and the Orthodox Church was unable to finance the cathedral, the project gradually took a back seat to other national priorities. Not even the letter of 10 May 1920 by King Ferdinand to Patriarch Miron Cristea, strongly endorsing the Cathedral for National Salvation, could move the project ahead.

In 1925, the Romanian Orthodox Church was recognized by other Orthodox churches as an independent patriarchate, with Miron Cristea as its first head. Cristea continued to use the Bucharest metropolitan see, which included residential and office space together with a small church. Strategically positioned on top of the highest hill of the relatively flat Bucharest, the see proudly shared this location with the impressive National Assembly building. The proximity of the two buildings symbolized the collaboration between the political (temporal) and religious (extramundane) powers and was viewed by church leaders and politicians as having national significance, bringing together the state and the largest ("national") church for the service of the Romanian nation. It also meant that lack of space prevented the expansion of the metropolitan see into a residence befitting a patriarch. As a result, the patriarchate was compelled to look for another site that was close to downtown Bucharest and the metropolitanate see, and which had a firm-enough foundation to allow for large-scale construction.

After much thought, Cristea proposed Carol Park as the site. A church property for centuries, the park had been restored into a green space reserved for Bucharest residents. Nevertheless, sustained media criticism and opposition from park users provoked Cristea to accept Bibescu Voda Square as site of the cathedral. To seal the deal, on 11 May 1929, politicians and Orthodox leaders erected a small cross memorial (*troiţa*) to mark the future cathedral's location, but lack of funds postponed the construction. The project was abandoned once Romania succumbed to the dictatorship of King Carol II in 1937 and was revisited only after 1989.

In September 1995, the Orthodox Church celebrated the seventieth anniversary of its independence. Patriarch Teoctist seized the occasion to ask politicians and ordinary citizens to support the project of the national cathedral, stressing that Romania was the only predominantly Orthodox Eastern European country whose patriarch had to celebrate mass in a metropolitan church. To show his determination, Teoctist appointed a committee to select the design and nail down the architectural and technical details of the project, envisioned as a gigantic 10,000-seat cathedral of unmatched proportions that would occupy, together with its additional constructions, three hectares of land, two of which were reserved for the church itself. To surpass all existing Orthodox worship places and deserve the title of national cathedral, the monumental construction was to be seventy-two meters long, forty-four wide, and fifty high, about 236 by 144 by 164 feet. According to some, the Romanian Orthodox Church aimed to erect a worship place as high as Moscow's new cathedral, recognized for its grandeur, as though a church's standing in the Orthodox world rested primarily with the dimensions of the national cathedral. Romanian Church leaders assumed that cooperation from government officials would be secured at a later time.

From the beginning, the proposal raised eyebrows. Opponents argued that the very idea of a grandiose cathedral was alien to the Orthodox spirit and was inspired by the Roman Catholic tradition of the grand Gothic cathedrals dominating Western European cities. They pointed out that Roman Catholic cathedrals are tall because they aspire to link the faithful to God, but that Orthodox churches are small, providing a space designed to bring the religious community together. Following this argument, the Bucharest metropolitan see and its church would better suit Orthodox theology and the needs of the Romanian people. Its rich history, not extravagant dimensions, recommended the old church as an appropriate patriarchal see. Other analysts pointed out that the cathedral did not fulfill "an urgent spiritual need of the Romanian people"; that the country's Orthodox majority needed catechization, since many were unfamiliar with the basic principles of Orthodox faith; and the church could use the money to help the poor and those in need.[53]

Still others took issue with the nationalistic connotations of the title of the new construction, pointing out that salvation was individual not national, as the title "cathedral of national salvation" would imply, and criticizing the cathedral's dedication to the Heroes' Day. In the Orthodox tradition, worship places are usually dedicated to Jesus, Mary, a patron saint (for example, Saint Andrew or John the Baptist), or a religious celebration (like the Assumption of the Virgin Mary), not a national or a political event with little religious relevance like Heroes' Day. From 1920 to 1948, National Heroes' Day was celebrated on Ascension of the Lord Day (forty days after Easter) to commemorate all the soldiers lost in war who were buried in Romanian soil, regardless of their nationality. Communist authorities decided to make the 9th of May Heroes' Day, but after 1989, celebrations were again organized on the Feast of the Ascension of the Lord, "in keeping with the Romanian tradition."[54] In responding to criticisms deploring the cathedral's dedication to the nation rather than to a saint, Archbishop Bartolomeu Anania of Cluj, Vad, and Feleac contended that the nation is a sociohistorical, metaphysical, and theological reality and that salvation cannot be obtained individually, but only collectively—that is, nationally.[55] The assertion fits the bill for what the Orthodox churches themselves condemned in the nineteenth century as the heresy of phyletism, the view privileging race, tribe, or nation over the religious community in matters of salvation.

In February 1999, seventy years after Patriarch Cristea marked Union Square for the cathedral, Patriarch Teoctist blessed the same site in the presence of President Emil Constantinescu, Christian Democrat Prime Minister Radu Vasile, and the speakers of the Senate and the Chamber of Deputies. Rising to the occasion, Vasile pointed out that the construction would create much-needed jobs, and Constantinescu insisted that the monumental building was needed because "too many Romanians asked themselves whether the blind fight for wealth, power, and privilege that plagued our history would continue to waste our energy in the next millennium."[56] With general elections scheduled for late 2000, both politicians were desperate to rally the support of the Orthodox Church. The ceremony allowed the ruling Democratic Convention, which included the Christian Democrats, to claim that it solved the problem by convincing the Orthodox Church to renounce claims to the park. Union Square offered plenty of space for the large cathedral and was situated close to the metropolitan see, allowing religious processions between the two, but was located on top of one of the largest and busiest junctions of the country's only subway, where two key subway lines intersected with an underground system that allowed the Dimbovita River to flow through. Architects believed that the underground maze prevented the square from supporting heavy construction at ground level and that the costs of mitigating these problems and strengthening the cathedral's foundation were prohibitive.

Faced with all these objections, exasperated Orthodox leaders became adamant that Carol Park was the best location for the cathedral. They reminded the government that the park was close to the metropolitan see and thus allowed the patriarch to fulfill his administrative and religious duties, and it allowed construction of the cathedral to be on an elevated surface, as required by the Orthodox tradition. Carol Park presented its own challenge, in addition to the fact that it was one of Bucharest's few remaining green spaces. In 1923, the park became home to the Tomb of the Unknown Soldier dedicated to the memory of the soldiers who lost their lives in combat. During communist times, the park's most elevated section, where the Orthodox Church envisioned the cathedral, became the site of the Mausoleum of Communist Heroes, a unique dark burgundy granite structure housing the tombs of the first Romanian communist leaders, Petru Groza and Gheorghe Gheorghiu-Dej, who ruled the country from 1945 to 1965.

Civil society criticized the plan to locate the cathedral in Carol Park. The Group for Social Dialogue, uniting intellectual luminaries and anti-communist dissidents, became the project's most vehement critic and raised concerns regarding its every aspect. Respected writer Alexandru Paleologu called for the project "to be stopped at all costs" because "nation and nationalism are transitory, whereas a cathedral testifies to something eternal, defies time." He added that such a construction was unwarranted when the infrastructure was inadequate, historical monuments were ignored by indifferent and incompetent local authorities, ordinary citizens were unable to make ends meet, and the country was in misery. Not even Stephen the Great, who erected a church after each victorious battle, was able to build a cathedral because the Romanian "understanding of space has no room for cathedrals." Paleologu claimed that

the result would be "a catastrophic, fatal kitsch," "an ecclesiastical Ceauşescuism," "parasitical, immoral and impertinent," and "a monument for our
esthetical and ethical doom" on a par with communist symbols like the Soviet-
style Casa Scânteii and Ceauşescu's eclectic House of the People.[57] This position was echoed during a roundtable where architects claimed that a tall
central cathedral was unsuited for a city "formed of small parishes lined up
concentrically around the center."[58]

Despite criticism, the government transferred a 52,700 square meter lot
to the Orthodox Church; but erecting the cathedral in the park sparked old
flames. Bucharest residents organized as the Group of Solidarity with Carol
Park started peaceful protests and marches against the project. Bucharest
mayor Traian Băsescu, leader of the opposition Democratic Party, denied approval for the construction site. Even the ruling Social Democrats were divided
on the issue. Minister of Culture and Religious Affairs Răzvan Theodorescu
announced that the mausoleum in the park, illustrative of contemporary art,
should be preserved as a historical and artistic piece, not demolished as a symbol of a defunct ideology.[59] Premier Adrian Năstase insisted that only public
debate could find a compromise acceptable to the residents, the church, and
the politicians. Since construction would extend over several electoral cycles,
Năstase argued, the church needed the support of as many political parties and
civil society groups as possible.[60]

In May 2004, however, the Social Democrat majority in the Bucharest
municipal council approved the church's request to build the cathedral in the
park. Some 200 representatives of the Save Carol Park ad hoc group organized
a peaceful demonstration, asked President Iliescu to spare the park and the
mausoleum (which were protected by the law on historical monuments), and
voiced its preference for transforming the communist symbol into a monument for the victims of communism. In a letter to Iliescu, the group noted that
"there is no need for a megalomaniac national cathedral, a replica of communist buildings like the House of the People," at a time when the church
should rebuild historical monuments like the Văcăreşti monastery, and criticized the gigantic cathedral that "needed the widest support."[61] Counterdem-
onstrations were organized by the Romanian Orthodox Foundation, the Society of Romanian Orthodox Women, the Bucharest Theology Students'
Foundation, and other University of Bucharest student associations, which distributed flyers in all Bucharest parishes criticizing Băsescu for refusing to
allow the cathedral in the park, "concocting the most perfidious plot to divide
Bucharest residents and the most humiliating ways to bury the symbol of our
Christianity—the Cathedral of National Salvation," and asking politicians to

understand that "the [Orthodox] Mother Church should remain above political interests and interpretations."[62] ASCOR declared that the communist mausoleum "no longer corresponded to the aspirations of the Romanian society, which sees itself as Christian, democratic and European."[63] The League of Mayors took a stand against "those delaying the building of the cathedral. When everything was set, the Bucharest general mayor's office asked again to clarify an already clear issue, forgetting that it must wholeheartedly support morally and financially an idea celebrating our people." The association chided that "this is the third location being challenged. It is revolting to say that a project seeking to unite all Romanians, including those living abroad, would bring only misfortune and environmental damage."[64]

Two lengthy articles published in the *Adevărul* daily provided insight into the nature of the controversy surrounding the cathedral. In the first article, journalist Lelia Munteanu criticized supporters of the cathedral for insisting on a gigantic construction. She rhetorically asked them: "Why do we need a huge cathedral? Why can't the nation attain salvation in a small, less costly village church?" She then turned against the opponents of the cathedral, who poked fun at the cathedral project, saying that "the initiative [to build the cathedral] was good and opportune if the sacred place is built with its foundation in heaven, where there is plenty of real estate for free, and where people strolling in the park would not smell incense and myrrh." Munteanu wondered about the real motives animating the members of the Save Carol Park initiative group:

> Where were they when in Bucharest entire hectares of parks were cleared to make way for the Cathedrals of Embezzlement, the Mausoleums of Bank Bankruptcies? . . . . If a site near the National Library is proposed, they will shout "Save the National Library"; if a lot near Glina landfill is found, they will shout "Save Glina landfill!" When deputies found their chamber too small, civic groups said nothing; when senators found their building too cramped, there was no reaction; when the government found the Victoria Palace insufficiently large, everybody kept silent. But when it comes to a church, pompously named the Cathedral of National Salvation, a nonprofit organization creates a circus atmosphere.

The politicians' refusal to find a site for the church, their strategy of "moving its site from here to there in the hope that construction never starts," reminded Munteanu of pregnant Mary's efforts to find a place to give birth on Christmas Eve. The journalist warned that "it would be humiliating for all of us if, rejected everywhere, Mary were to give birth in the garbage bin."[65]

In the second article, Cristian Tudor Popescu wrote that those asking for the Cathedral of National Salvation did so not because they needed forgiveness but because they believed that the nation needed it because of its sins:

> One by one, Romanians should pass through the cathedral as through a gigantic communal bath where they could wash their sins of poverty, despair, confusion, and alienation . . . In the West, as the churches distanced themselves from the political power, the building of cathedrals slowed down. In Orthodox countries, religion has always been close to the state. In Romania, even today, the Orthodox Church is close to the worldly power. The political elite and the church need this cathedral of party and state. If one cannot eradicate corruption and its sister poverty, one erects a cathedral. . . . What would this cathedral mean for ordinary people? Could they relax and be closer to God in this church-palace of protocol? . . . Do Romanians need a God-Mall? Or do they need churches in every community, in villages, in town districts? I believe we do not lack churches, small or big. We need true church leaders, servants of God and humans.

Commenting on the lavish donations politicians offered for the cathedral, Popescu wrote, "there are lots of people wishing to obtain this great indulgence, but not even a cathedral as big as the House of the People would wash away our leaders' sins in an impoverished, politically weak, miserable country whose symbol is not Salvation, but Superficiality."[66]

In late October 2004, deputies unanimously approved construction of the cathedral behind the mausoleum. Democratic Party deputies supported the proposal for fear of losing popular support, although their leader Băsescu still opposed the project mostly on technical grounds.[67] The public opinion remained divided on the issue. For one writer, "the cathedral is but an implicit discourse for the unity between the nation and Orthodoxy, which inherits all the features of collectivism and nationalism that the Romanian Orthodox Church always associated its strategies with." Moreover, the cathedral belongs to an outdated scenario, to "the old nationalist sentiment that says nothing to our youth."[68] In an article suggestively titled "The Shadow of Theocracy over Carol Park," Gabriel Andreescu reported that Solidarity Association leader Remus Cernea claimed that, before the vote, deputies allegedly told association representatives that "we need youth like you; we have our dignity, we cannot vote in favor of the draft, after former Securitate members, that is, the priests, were the greatest evil to this country." But after the vote, the same deputies told them, "the Romanian Orthodox Church is powerful and we cannot do anything."[69] While vociferous before the vote, politicians of all ideological persuasions joined forces to pass the law on the cathedral as an organic law, taking precedence over the simple laws.

With a new government in power after the November 2004 general elections and Băsescu as the country's president, in February 2005, the media announced that the cathedral site was again moved to Dealul Arsenalului (Arsenal Hill), behind the House of the People. The site is firmer, more resistant to earthquakes, visible from all corners of Bucharest, and higher than the rest of the capital, allowing the Orthodox Church to erect an even higher building with even more additions than initially contemplated. Architect Anca Petrescu, who designed the House of the People and oversaw its construction alongside Ceauşescu, commended the idea of placing the cathedral and the national legislature side by side. Another architect, Adrian Bold, also said that the site will see a "nice closeness of the most important institutions in the state: parliament, church, and army," alluding to the nearby Ministry of Defense headquarters.[70] The proposal for the national cathedral made full circle, as the new location had been proposed by King Ferdinand in his 1920 letter to Patriarch Cristea. Ironically, Ceauşescu himself had unknowingly cleared the area to make room for the future cathedral. After the 1977 earthquake, he envisioned the possibility of erecting a monumental House of the People on the hill. As a result, five churches and an entire residential district were demolished. Another church was moved 245 meters behind some new buildings.

Conclusion

The interpenetration of religion and nationalism remains a salient feature of Romanian post-communist political life. Because nationalism had its roots in the nineteenth century, our examination considers the Orthodox Church's use of nationalism historically and shows that, far from diminishing in importance, religious nationalism acquired new forms of expression following the collapse of the communist regime. After initial resistance to adopt a position that distanced itself from its sister Orthodox Churches in the Slavic world, the Romanian Orthodox Church managed to appropriate the Romanian nationalistic discourse. It shared this nationalist spirit with the communist government, but it reasserted its nationalism after 1989. In so doing, the Orthodox Church not only appropriated this discourse from the Transylvanian Greek Catholics, who developed a national consciousness as early as the late eighteenth century, but eventually employed that same discourse against the Greek Catholics and its other critics. It also used nationalist rhetoric to promote two projects whose magnitude reveals the pervasive effects of nationalism in

Romania: controlling the Bessarabian Metropolitanate, an eparchy on the territory of the independent Republic of Moldova, and promoting the project of a large cathedral dedicated to "national salvation" in the very center of Bucharest, next to the national legislature.

More than eighty years after the formation of the modern Romanian state, nationalism is there to stay as a sentiment strongly shared by large segments of the population. The trend is perhaps unsurprising, given the fact that the young country had suffered significant loss of territory in the 1940s and had to face irredentist calls from neighboring Hungary as recently as the early 1990s. Romanians will likely fall on nationalism as long as they feel insecure within the borders of their nation-state. Strangely, the often-unquestioned commitment to nationalism goes hand in hand with tolerance and inclusiveness. A recent effort of the Romanian national television station to identify the "great Romanians"—the individuals who had the greatest (presumably positive) effect on the Romanian people—allowed the general public to submit candidates for that coveted honorary position. The results, released in mid-July 2006, produced a list of ten names, including historical figures like Stephen the Great and Michael the Brave alongside fascist dictator Marshall Ion Antonescu. The great surprise was the fact that not all nominated "great Romanians" were of Romanian origins. The list also included King Carol I among national luminaries.[71]

4

Confronting the Communist Past

Father Ionică, if the devil writes on a piece of paper "God exists" and signs, don't sign beside him.
> —Rohia Monk Nicolae Steinhard, *Jurnalul fericirii*
> (Cluj Napoca, Romania: Dacia, 1991, 268)

In the early 1990s, as other former communist countries had done, Romania initiated a transitional justice process that was fueled by repeated calls for the condemnation of the communist past, for the banning of communist officials and collaborators from post-communist political life, and for the disclosure of the names of informers who provided the political police with information on their neighbors, friends, and relatives. The Romanian Orthodox Church hierarchy was included in the criticisms brought against the old regime. After 1989, it came under fire for its longstanding collaboration with the communist authorities and their dreaded political police, the Securitate. The Romanian transitional justice process eventually lost momentum and never achieved the success of similar initiatives undertaken in Central European countries. Romania has lagged behind other nations in disclosing the identity of former political agents, in the adoption of a legislative framework granting citizens access to the files compiled by the Securitate, and in honestly reevaluating the communist regime and its human rights abuses. For example, the Czech Republic opted for lustrating thousands of former communist officials, and Germany quickly offered citizens and researchers access to the Stasi archive. In Romania, by contrast, a former collaborator of Ceauşescu became the first post-communist president (Ion Iliescu ruled post-communist Romania for eleven of its first fifteen years), and communist officials and political agents control both politics and the economy. It was only in 2000 that the country offered access to a limited number of Securitate files, the result of the personal crusade of Christian Democrat senator Constantin Ticu Dumitrescu, who had to overcome public apathy and considerable opposition from the political elite.

Like other Eastern European secret political police, the KGB-styled Securitate aimed to quash dissidence and opposition to the Communist Party and its leaders, and to ensure the party's unchallenged monopoly over all spheres of life. Accountable only to the top communist leadership, the political police used full-time agents—with covered, uncovered, or partly covered identities—and an extensive network of part-time informers drawn from inside and outside party ranks. Estimates of the number of agents and informers have varied widely, ranging from as few as 400,000 to as many as 1 million in a total population of about 23 million. The informers represented the bulk of the Securitate personnel. Allegedly, each agent had to maintain a network of some fifty active informers. There were many reasons that citizens became Securitate spies. Informers could be blackmailed, inspired by misled patriotic sentiment, or attracted by the compensations informants received: passports, better jobs, transfers from rural to urban areas, or money. Victims included pre-communist dignitaries and party leaders, individuals critical of Communist Party policies and President Ceauşescu's megalomaniac projects, and people who unsuccessfully attempted the illegal border crossing. Over the course of a lifetime, a person's relationship to the Securitate could easily change from torturer to tortured, then back again. An individual might even be a victim and a victimizer at the same time. The Securitate compiled individual files on both spies and their victims.[1]

Dismantled after the December 1989 uprising, the Securitate was reorganized shortly thereafter through an unpublished presidential decree as the Romanian Information Service (Serviciul Român de Informaţii, or SRI, as Romanians know it). Although supposedly this service is under parliamentary supervision, it seems as if the reverse is true: the service has been supervising parliament for the last seventeen years. Scores of press reports maintain that former Securitate members control key post-communist institutions, becoming the country's top entrepreneurs, politicians, judges, and ambassadors. The "old boys network" of informers and the secret officers to whom they reported have masterminded scandalous financial schemes in which thousands of ordinary citizens have lost their life savings, while spies acquired ownership of profitable, state-owned enterprises and vast stretches of land. From the beginning, the service insisted that it was a new security and intelligence agency with little connection to the Securitate. It professed a completely different philosophy, different policies, and different aims. It made a firm commitment to accountability and employed new, younger personnel. Despite these claims, however, the service consistently refused to make public the internal workings of the communist political police, the Securitate file archive, and the identity of its spies. This decision has raised serious doubts about its credibility. Observers agree that since 1989 the Securitate archive has been modified, some say beyond recognition, by the destruction, addition, and alteration of key documents.[2]

In Romania, the transitional justice process has revolved around access to the Securitate archives, estimated to some twenty-five linear kilometers of documents (less than one-sixth of the Stasi archives). According to the Law on File Access no. 187 of December 1999, the National Council for the Study of Securitate Archive is the government agency that grants Romanians access to their own files and investigates citizens' past involvement with the Securitate, including public officials, electoral candidates, bureaucrats and administrators, diplomats, religious leaders, journalists, and university professors.[3] The council is led by a parliament-appointed eleven-member college, which judges whether an individual was an "angel" or a "villain." The college bases its decisions on information collected from the Securitate archive and other archives, interviews with the individual, and additional relevant sources. Decisions are adopted with a simple majority of present college members, if at least eight members attend the meeting, and can be contested in court within a month. The names of individuals found to have collaborated with the communist secret political police are published in *Monitorul Oficial*.

Observers agree that the legislative framework for file access is deficient. Rather than being chosen from among independent civil society representatives, college members were nominated by political parties represented in the Senate. They therefore tended to support the unmasking of former spies in all political parties but the one that supported their candidature. The council must determine past collaboration based on the Securitate files, but because until 2005 the archive was housed with the Information Service, the council had no direct access to the shelves. As a recent case showed, the service was not always candid when asked to release the files of prominent politicians, hiding valuable documents on their collaboration with the political police. Nobody knows how many files are extant, except for the service, which has been extremely reluctant to share information with the public, legislators, and the council. Due to its virtual monopoly over the archive from 1990 to 2005, the service was in a position to destroy and alter the archive as and when it pleased, protecting some public figures and discrediting others. Legally, the service is not required to release all Securitate files to the council, but only those that are not endangering the "national interest," which are to be selected jointly by the council and the service. The Supreme Council for the Defense of the Country, which includes representatives of the Information Service but not the council, settles disputed cases. While the law compels the council to answer petitions within a specified timeframe, it does not compel the service to respond promptly and with dispatch to the council's requests for information.[4]

The Romanian Orthodox Church is the denomination most severely implicated in the transitional justice process. This is not surprising. That church collaborated closely with the communist regime in exchange for protection of its assets from nationalization and for a privileged position among denominations in Romania. Four major themes illustrate how transitional justice affected the Orthodox Church. They include (1) Patriarch Teoctist's undignified resignation in 1990 and his controversial return, (2) allegations that Orthodox priests broke the secret of the confessional by reporting information to the Securitate, (3) the reevaluation of the pros and cons of the church's collaboration with the communist regime, and (4) the church's insistence that the names of political police agents and informers drawn from the Orthodox clergy should be kept secret. We will now consider each one of these themes that illustrate the difficulties of separating church and state during communist and post-communist times.

Patriarch Teoctist: The Unrepentant Penitent?

Born in 1915, Teoctist Arăpaşu became a monk in 1935 and the head of the Orthodox Church in 1986, after the death of the fourth Romanian Patriarch Iustin Moisescu. Teoctist attended the University of Bucharest's Faculty of Orthodox Theology from 1940 to 1945, starting his university education when Romania plunged into fascist dictatorship and graduating after Soviet troops imposed a communist regime. By the time Teoctist became its head, the Orthodox Church was firmly under the control of the communist state, which appointed its leaders and drastically reduced its role in politics, education, and social work. Both coercion (in the form of imprisonment of clerics with anti-communist views and the close monitoring of all priests and church leaders) and the granting of privileges (including Greek Catholic Church property transfer) were used to win the Orthodox Church's submission. Teoctist became patriarch not so much due to extraordinary intellectual and spiritual accomplishments but, rather, because of the support of the third patriarch, Justinian

Marina. After the death of Marina in 1977 and the appointment of Moisescu as patriarch, Marina's supporters managed to appoint Teoctist to the position of Metropolitan of Moldova, the second most important post in the Romanian Orthodox Church because, traditionally, the occupant of this office became the patriarch. Teoctist's propensity for compromise and obedience ensured that the communist authorities approved of his nomination.

Both before and after 1986, Teoctist was seen as a supporter of Ceauşescu's anti-religious policies. These included the suppression of religious denominations, church demolition, and the defrocking of priests who stood up to the communist dictator. Though he occupied the patriarchal seat for only the final three years of communist rule, Teoctist found it difficult to defend his church against the totalitarian state. The written record of his communist-era public interventions included countless congratulatory and adulatory telegrams and speeches praising Ceauşescu, but making no mention of the regime's suppression of religious life. Without protest, Teoctist allowed scores of churches recognized as historical monuments to be demolished or moved to less conspicuous locations. Some twenty-two churches in Bucharest alone were destroyed before 1987, after which the communist regime gave in to Western pressure to stop the demolitions. Instead, they opted to move churches behind high-rise apartment buildings. Western democracies interpreted the patriarch's lack of official reaction to church demolition as a sure sign of collaboration.

Teoctist failed to criticize the nation's dictator even after the anti-Ceauşescu revolt started in the western town of Timişoara, Banat region. On 19 December 1989, three days after the massacre in front of the Timişoara Orthodox cathedral, Teoctist sent a telegram to Ceauşescu, marking the end of the National Church Assembly annual meeting and congratulating the dictator for his predictable reelection as Communist Party leader at the fourteenth party congress held a month earlier. Immersed in the adulatory lingo of the time, the telegram claimed that Romanians were living "in a Golden Age, properly and rightly bearing the name of [Ceauşescu]." The dictator was praised for his "brilliant activity," "wise guidance," and "daring thinking," at the very time when he inflicted irreparable damage to the country's religious fabric.[5]

The public outcry following the telegram's disclosure after Ceauşescu's overthrow was considerable. It placed the Orthodox Church in an unflattering and difficult position, showing it to be an institution that sided with an oppressive tyrant against the people in revolt. The daily *România liberă* described the telegram as nothing short of irresponsible and spoke of "the great disgrace that has fallen upon the Orthodox Church, tarnishing its traditions and martyrdom."[6] For the intellectuals, the telegram proved once again the church's unconditional submission to communist authorities, its abandonment of

Christian morality, and the insincerity of Teoctist's and the synod's commitment to the December revolution. In the first hours of the uprising, the patriarch called on Romanians to support the National Salvation Front, a revolutionary formation with deep roots in the second-echelon communist
nomenklatura. Later, Teoctist denounced Ceauşescu as "a Herod of our
times," while the synod came out in favor of the front.[7]

Facing criticism from all corners, Patriarch Teoctist resigned his position
for what he diplomatically called "reasons of health and age" during the Holy
Synod's extraordinary session of 18 January 1990. At the end of the meeting,
Teoctist asked God and believers for forgiveness for lying under duress and for
failing to oppose the dictatorship.[8] Accepting the resignation, the synod appointed an interim committee to lead the Orthodox Church until the election
of a successor. Reporting the news, Le Monde talked about a crisis in the
Romanian Orthodox Church and suggested that Archimandrite Bartolomeu
Anania had the best chance of becoming the next patriarch, though Anania
was not the Metropolitan of Moldova at the time. In reply, Anania declared that
he did not seek the position, while Sibiu Faculty of Orthodox Theology canon
law professor Ioan Floca rejected "suspicions of a power vacuum" as unfounded and appealed for "the maintenance and consolidation of the unity of
the Romanian Orthodox Church."[9] Teoctist's resignation opened a vivid debate
on accepted norms of patriarchal vacancy and succession. According to Orthodox canon law, a person cannot resign as patriarch unless physically or
mentally incapacitated; otherwise, succession is settled after the incumbent's
death. Some Romanian Orthodox theologians believed that Teoctist's unprecedented resignation could set an undesirable precedent by opening the
way for the removal of other Holy Synod members and by allowing public
pressure to sideline hierarchs for reasons more political than spiritual.

Teoctist's penitent mood did not last. Practical considerations related to
canon law prevailed over the need to deal with the painful communist past with
sincerity and compassion. Reclaiming the patriarchal seat barely three months
after his resignation, Teoctist suggested that he had no choice in sending the
adulatory telegram, which the Securitate agents overseeing religious affairs in
communist Romania had automatically filed, as was customary at the time.
Dismissing the telegram as "a party-imposed ritual" unreflective of his or the
Orthodox Church's position vis-à-vis Ceauşescu and his policies, Teoctist insisted on the pressures to which the communist authorities exposed him, and
claimed that he was a prisoner of his patriarchal residence during his first three
years in office. The information was contradicted by earlier statements in which
the patriarch described his 1988 trip to Rome, where he secretly met Pope John
Paul II, and admitted that he was allowed to travel, though with restricted

movement and under constant Securitate surveillance. The complete secrecy surrounding his brief meeting with the pope spared Teoctist the wrath of communist authorities and political police.[10]

The halfhearted apology Teoctist delivered in late 1989 was considered sufficient to heal the old wounds and restore public confidence in the Orthodox Church. As such, Teoctist and synod members made no further mention of their collaboration with communist authorities until a BBC interview early in 2000. During that interview, Teoctist asked for forgiveness for concessions the church made during the communist era, and he expressed his regrets that believers suffered because he lacked the courage to defend the church. The timing of the declaration, the first in which Teoctist spoke on communist-era church demolitions, coincided with calls for opening the Securitate files of Orthodox Church leaders. Rather than taking the opportunity to elaborate on the issue and present the reasons for collaboration, Teoctist adopted a one-step-forward, two-steps-back strategy and tried to recast himself and the Orthodox Church as the main anti-communist opposition force in the country. He declared that in 1987 he adamantly opposed the proposal of communist dignitary Ion Dincă to move the patriarchal see from downtown Bucharest to a remote location unbefitting the patriarchal church. Many wondered, however, why he did not seek Western help and why he kept silent on the regime's intentions on grounds that disclosure "would have affected the faithful" in unspecified, but presumably negative, ways. In the same interview, Teoctist reiterated that the communist Department of Religious Affairs, not he, had filed the ill-fated December 1989 telegram, "written and sent in an act of routine" bearing "no relationship to the Timişoara massacre." The interview was received with skepticism in Romania.[11]

In 2001, *Ziarul de Iaşi* reported that local historian Dorin Dobrincu, while working in the Information Service archive, discovered a secret document portraying Teoctist as an Iron Guard member and a participant in the January 1941 fascist rebellion, which resulted in the death of 416 people, of which 120 were Jewish. The rebellion was a failed coup d'état launched after leader Marshal Ion Antonescu ended an alliance with the guard that had begun at a time of deep political crisis in September 1940. Because Orthodox clergy supported the rebellion, Antonescu adopted Decree Law no. 314 of 15 February 1941 banning priests from politics. At a December 1941 meeting of the Council of Ministers, Antonescu was told that 422 priests had been sent before military tribunals for their part in the rebellion. The communist regime forced many Iron Guard members to collaborate under threat of disclosing their past fascist sympathies. The document, which the Securitate agents drafted based on information supplied by unnamed informers, suggested that the twenty-six-year-old Teoctist ransacked a Bucharest synagogue, together with other priests and Iron Guard members. It read that Teoctist was "once an active legionary, participant in the rebellion and the devastation of the synagogue on the Antim street" in Bucharest, and was "close to and a great influence on the Patriarch [Justinian Marina], who supported Arăpaşu's nomination as Metropolitan of Moldova."[12]

Teoctist remained silent about this damning public revelation, and the patriarchate spokesman dismissed the document as "pure fabrication," but the public scandal could not be averted. In the following days, the *Ziarul de Iaşi* report was supported by other independent sources. The Bucharest-based daily *Evenimentul Zilei* corroborated Teoctist's involvement in the Iron Guard and claimed that it had been known within Orthodox circles for some time before reaching the public. High school history teacher Gabriel Catalan reported that in fond D, file 7755, volume 3, page 239 of the Securitate archive he found Note no. 131 of 4 October 1949 linking Teoctist to the Iron Guard and the synagogue destruction. Catalan also ventured to say that the note's source appeared to be the then Metropolitan Nicolae Bălan of Transylvania. Historian Cristian Troncotă, who had access to Teoctist's Securitate file, confirmed Teoctist's adherence to the guard but not his participation in the synagogue destruction. Troncotă described the file as "impressive," containing eight thick volumes, and revealed that Teoctist "was followed until he became the patriarch. Some bishops reported on him, and many synod members opposed him."[13]

Asked to comment on the patriarch's tainted past, maverick poet and anti-communist dissident Mircea Dinescu said that "[Teoctist] could have no career if Securitate had nothing on him."[14] The implication was that Teoctist's reluctance to denounce communist abuses stemmed from his fear of being publicly unmasked as a fascist collaborator, a revelation that would have destroyed his reputation with the Romanians, Western governments, and sister Orthodox Churches. *Evenimentul Zilei* journalist Cornel Nistorescu urged the Council for the Study of Securitate Archives to examine Teoctist's file and the patriarch to confess and ask for forgiveness for his fascist past. Nistorescu dismissed suggestions that the confession would make the Church unpopular with the Romanians. In his words, "for a long time the Romanian Orthodox Church assumed no responsibility for [its actions during] the communist period. When Patriarch Teoctist asked to be forgiven for lacking the courage to raise [his voice] against church demolition no tragedy ensued, and the Romanians' trust in the Orthodox Church did not diminish."[15]

The scandal escalated when the council fired investigator Catalan, who publicly declared that before working for the council he was a doctoral candidate, and in that capacity he found archival evidence that Teoctist belonged to the Iron Guard, collaborated with the Securitate, and was a homosexual.[16] President Iliescu disapproved of the "ungrounded and indecent" attack against the patriarch, declaring that "the council was set up for studying the communist past, not for its employees to carry out personal vendettas against public figures," and that "the compilation of blacklists, the unauthorized and partial use of information increased the confusion and suspicion of the Romanian society, discrediting traditional institutions like church and army."[17] It is unclear which "blacklists" Iliescu was referring to.

On 23 March 2001, the Information Service announced that, after carefully analyzing Teoctist's secret file no. 62046, it concluded that the Securitate pursued the patriarch, who was its victim, not its informer. The next day, the Council for the Study of Securitate Archives, the only Romanian institution entitled to distinguish villains from angels, asked the Information Service for the release of Teoctist's file in order to give its own verdict on the case. When it became evident that council president Gheorghe Onişoru seemed inclined to exonerate the patriarch, the opposition Democrat Party criticized him for rushing to clear Teoctist of collaboration charges before studying the file and despite the fact that immediately after the revolution rumors had it that Teoctist had been a Securitate agent. For the Democrats, the rumors seemed clear proof that the council was unable to find the incriminating evidence whose existence they failed to question.[18] The case speaks for the tremendous difficulties facing transitional justice in a divided country like Romania. It is unlikely that Teoctist was a Securitate informer consciously and zealously providing damning information about others. Rather, the patriarch seems guilty not for what he did but for what he failed to do. This is not necessarily reflected in the Securitate archival documents and is not punishable by the Romanian legislation in force today.

The Securitate's Confessors: Between Sacrament and Sacrilege

Patriarch Teoctist was not the only contested Orthodox leader. Since the collapse of the communist regime and the opening of previously inaccessible archives, compelling evidence has mounted to support the thesis that numerous Orthodox clergy and hierarchs actively collaborated with the Securitate. Much public debate has surrounded revelations that some Orthodox priests broke the seal of the confession by reporting information obtained therein to the communist political police. In its characteristic style, the Orthodox Church leadership dismissed such reports as completely unfounded, but this attitude only fueled public mistrust, with scores of journalists, intellectuals, politicians, historians, and theologians joining the debate and analyzing the political and theological consequences of such spiritual trespassing.

Orthodoxy harshly condemns breaking the secret of the confession. Together with the Roman Catholic Church, the Orthodox Church recognizes confession as one of the seven sacraments, which are seven means of communicating divine grace. Sacraments occupy center stage in the doctrine of salvation, which itself is key to Christian theology. According to theologian Dumitru Stăniloae, "the person confessing knows that the priest will not divulge the secret," and "trusts the priest because he feels that the priest is responsible for his salvation before Christ, listens in the name of Christ with a strength which comes from Christ."[19] Patriarchate spokesperson Vincentiu Ploieşteanu further explained the sacrament of confession as "a secret between the confessor and the penitent that needs to be strictly guarded. If by mistake or carelessness we divulge a word, we automatically are defrocked before Christ, not before men."[20] Trust and secrecy go hand in hand for the confession to be complete and for the priest to act as an effective link between believers and God. Orthodox canon law confirms the confessor's obligation to keep the secret. Canon 28 of Nicephorus of Constantinople reads that "a Father Confessor must forbid divine communion to those confessing secret sins to him, while letting them enter the church; he must not reveal their sins but should advise them gently to remain repentant and keep praying; and he must adjust the amercements to befit each one of them according to his best judgment."[21]

The news that information obtained during confession may have been leaked to government authorities broke in mid 1998. It provoked a public uproar to which the mass media contributed substantially, despite the fact that no hard evidence was produced to prove the accusation. Christian Democrat and Greek Catholic Senator Ioan Moisin voiced the indignation of many ordinary Romanians when he demanded to know "in whose service were the [Orthodox] priests who told Securitate what they heard at confession, Christ's or the Securitate's? The patriarch and the bishops should tell us what punishment the church law prescribes for breaking the secret of the confession, and whether the punishment was enforced!" At the same time, Ziarul de Iaşi noted, "it is well known that many priests were Securitate informers, offering information to which repression organs normally had no access. Through confession, priests found [out] almost everything about the personal life of the faithful." Ticu Dumitrescu also revealed that he found out from his own Securitate file that two different priests informed on his father.[22]

While ties between Orthodox clergy and the Securitate remain shrouded in secrecy, we can distinguish four kinds of association. The first two include priests who did not break the secret of the confession. There were priests who avoided collaboration but refused to take a stand against the regime. Some observers argue that most priests belonged to this category, but others say that such a politically neutral position was untenable. Archbishop Andrei Andreicuţ of Alba Iulia claims to have been one such. In his book *S-au risipit făcătorii de basme* (Mythmakers Have Vanished) he recounts his life based on his Securitate file. The volume includes copies of twenty-five memos filed by agents and reports signed by informers obtained from the Council for the Study of Securitate Archives. Pupils attending his catechism classes, occasional acquaintances, fellow priests, and theology professors were among the spies who reported on him. Andreicuţ became a Securitate target when he abandoned a career as an engineer to pursue theological studies. A note in his file explained that he continued in his pursuit of theology, "even after being warned." The note continues: "His intense religious activity meant to counteract the official atheistic education. He is a good Romanian, a true patriot, but dislikes the communist or socialist system and is determined to free the people from our socialist ideology, even with the price of self-sacrifice."[23]

Not an active dissident, Andreicuţ was pursued for his religious commitment and friendship with individuals critical of communism. He applied four times before the Securitate and the State Department of Religious Affairs allowed him to enter the doctoral program in theology. His nomination to become a missionary priest stationed abroad was rejected, and his transfer to Cluj city was blocked. Devices planted in his home allowed a Securitate agent nicknamed Nicu to listen to all of Andreicuţ's conversations, and even his confession.[24]

Second, a number of priests openly resisted the regime. Orthodox leaders insist that close to a hundred thousand priests were imprisoned in the 1950s, but the claim seems exaggerated.[25] Most of the arrests occurred in 1945–1948, when the fragile Communist Party took control over the country by eradicating the opposition and replacing the old elite and bureaucracy. The methods were brutal, often leading to death or long-term disability, or giving the victims a choice only between arrest and collaboration. Persecution was random, designed to inspire fear and destroy support networks. Communist leader Vasile Luca justified the terror by arguing that "it is better to arrest ten innocent than to let one bandit go free."[26] Authorities knew that "the clergy are worried of the recent arrests. It is rumored that some eighty priests are kept in the Ministry of Interior dungeons, facing harsh conditions, with little food and hygiene."[27] While jailed in the Caracal prison camp in 1945, Professor Onisifor Ghibu identified "some eighty priests, most of them Orthodox, and seven Greek Catholic." Early in his detention, Ghibu sadly remarked that of the fifty-seven jailed Orthodox priests, whom he suspected of having converted to communist "democracy," "not even one felt the need to say mass."[28] That year, Orthodox priest Ioan Bardaş counted "one hundred Orthodox priests, three Catholics and three Lutheran pastors" in the Aiud jail.[29]

By contrast, the Sighet prison housed twenty-seven Greek and Roman Catholic priests and bishops, but no Orthodox prelate.[30] For supporting the anti-communist resistance movement in Constanţa county and refusing to break the secret of the confession, Father Stelică Popovici spent thirteen years in the worst communist prisons. Father Alecsandru Capotă, a political prisoner from 1958 to 1962, provided another example of moral rectitude that needs to be commended. Recounting his painful memories of communist prisons, Capotă revealed that "in jail [the authorities] promised to set me free in exchange for information on the bishopric. When I asked why they did not ask their informers inside the bishopric for such information, they said that they wanted information on the informers."[31] Without divulging names, Andreicuţ's testimony revealed that the State Department of Religious Affairs was closely cooperating with the Securitate to elicit information reports from members of the Alba Iulia archbishopric.

The number of active clergy dissidents dwindled to a handful by the 1980s. A well-known dissenter was Father Gheorghe Calciu-Dumitreasa, whose *Şapte cuvinte pentru tineri* (Seven Words for Youth), delivered at the Bucharest seminary, broadcast by Radio Free Europe, and circulated in samizdat form, described atheism as a philosophy of despair.[32] In retaliation, the Securitate imprisoned Calciu in 1979, and the synod defrocked him in 1981, apparently according to Apostolic Canon 84, which reads that "whosoever shall insult the king, or a ruler, contrary to what is right, let him suffer punishment. If he be a clergyman, let him be deposed; if a layman, excommunicated."[33]

Two entries from Andreicuţ's Securitate file speak of Calciu's beliefs and prison conditions. The Securitate reported that on 24 December 1980, teacher Tudor Petre told Andreicuţ that

> Calciu pitied the people destroying churches to build taverns. He referred to the Enei church [in downtown Bucharest], replaced by a restaurant. [Petre] urged [Andreicuţ] to become a good servant of the church, saying that many clergy were immoral, even those teaching in the theology departments, and that the situation is hard to remedy because the current [communist] regime encourages future priests to be immoral so that the church is destroyed from inside out.[34]

Later, retired priest Aurel Olteanu told Andreicuţ that he knew from Calciu's wife that

Calciu's food ration was reduced because the regime wanted him dead. He was told that if in need of more food he should work for it. [Calciu] refused for fear of being killed under the false charge of trying to escape. This happened to Professor Liviu Munteanu...imprisoned in Aiud, a chain smoker. When taken out for a walk, he leaned to pick up a cigarette butt and was shot, allegedly because he tried to flee.[35]

At the insistence of Western governments, Calciu was allowed to emigrate. After 1989, the synod reinstated him.

The next two categories included priests who acted at the command of the Securitate to denounce parishioners, priests, and prelates. Both groups include informers, some of whom never recanted (although they made every effort to hide their collaboration), and others who bravely confessed and asked for forgiveness. Metropolitan Nicolae Corneanu of Banat and priest Eugen Jurcă belong to this latter group. A bishop since 1961, Corneanu made compromises with the communist government, but in a 1997 interview he candidly admitted to defrocking five dissident priests in 1981 under pressure from the Securitate. One of the five priests was Calciu-Dumitreasa. After 1989, the church rescinded all politically inspired punishments. In a festive roundtable organized in late 1998, the Group of Social Dialogue praised Corneanu for being "one of the few Orthodox Church leaders who managed with word, deed, and public presence to show us how the church must be present in society in order to bring us together." Corneanu modestly insisted that "besides small things, I made only concessions," and said that his need to publicly reveal his collaboration stemmed from "a feeling of culpability and the urge to recover the past."[36]

In a March 2001 open letter to Orthodox leaders and the civil society, Jurcă confessed he had been a Securitate collaborator for ten years and in 1980 signed a pledge to spy out of fear, cowardice, ignorance, and despair. After 1989, Jurcă stopped meeting his Securitate liaison officer, and four years later he had to turn down a call from the officer asking him to provide information on old religion books brought into the country. In his public confession, Jurcă urged the Orthodox clergy not to give in to intimidation and blackmail over their personal sins and declared that Romanians needed "to find out the truth such that the youth avoid the shadows of the past and the horrors we once lived. Real national reconciliation is impossible without cleansing us of the moral ambiguity we live in. The truth must be known, however painful and shameful." Civil society representatives praised Jurcă's confession as an important act of conscience and an opportunity for Romanians with similar experiences to reflect. They urged informer priests to confess their sins and set an example of morality for the entire society. Jurcă was the first priest to confess publicly, after the press published excerpts of Teoctist's Securitate file.[37]

Lack of reliable data on the number and socioeconomic background of Securitate agents and informers does not allow us to estimate the percentage of informer priests. Press reports suggest that a high percentage of Orthodox priests collaborated in one form or another, charges the Orthodox Church vehemently denies. Following Father Capotă, only one or two priests in the eastern county of Galați refused to collaborate. In his words: "Until 1991, for seventeen years I worked as an accountant with the bishopric, and I could see that the communist authorities infiltrated there a person representing the State Department of Religious Affairs and controlling all personnel hires, fires, and transfers. The Securitate also had a colonel overseeing church problems." Bishop Casian Crăciun of Dunărea de Jos refused to comment, on grounds that the past was no longer important for Romanian society, but his cultural advisor said that he knew of no informer priests and that those who collaborated "did so in their personal name, not in the name of the institution [the Orthodox Church]."[38]

In 1999, *Evenimentul Zilei* reported that former informer priests were trying to become operative in the Information Service, to avoid exposure (according to law no. 187). Anonymous sources said that Orthodox informer priests volunteered to work for the service by resuming contacts with Securitate officers whom they reported to during communism. The newspaper quoted a former Securitate officer in Timişoara, who claimed that over 80 percent of the Orthodox priests had collaborated.[39]

Days later, the identity of the officer was disclosed when the paper carried a lengthy article on the ties of Orthodox priests to the Securitate. Former Securitate officer Roland Vasilievici (directly responsible for recruiting priests for the Timişoara branch from 1976 to 1986) explained how the political police used priests to gather information. He noted that priest recruitment targeted all denominations and started in the 1960s at the order of an unnamed Securitate leader, who reportedly declared that he wanted to see "no Orthodox priest un-coopted as an informer. We spent so much money educating them, they even know dialectic materialism and history, but contribute nothing. They should at least collaborate with us for [building] socialism to serve their country and cease wasting time, chasing women, and getting drunk. Comrade officers, make these lazy priests work, they have enough spare time to collect information. They should be our survey polling organ." After 1989, the Securitate officer allegedly became the head of an extremist party and a wealthy capitalist. "Based on written [collaboration] pledges, almost all Orthodox clergy became informers," Vasilievici declared, "recruited for their nationalist sentiment."

Vasilievici estimated that informers accounted for 80 to 90 percent of the Orthodox clergy, and added:

> This information network [of priests] was gradually educated in a nationalist, chauvinist, and xenophobic spirit. Church leaders were supervised by the intelligence and counterintelligence departments, were subjected to complex training programs, and sent abroad to serve their socialist country by collecting information, participating in nationalist-communist propaganda activities and disinformation campaigns, providing false information to emigration leaders, infiltrating Radio Free Europe, and mending the broken image of Romania and its communist leadership.[40]

The article is important for detailing the relationship between the Securitate officers and informers, the criteria for maintaining a good profile with the secret police, the methods the Securitate used to verify the reliability of its informer network, and the steps of the recruitment process. As such, the article presents a rare glimpse into the inner workings of the secret organization that kept Romanians under the thumb of the Communist Party for forty-five years. Vasilievici reveals that "the communist-era Department of Religious Affairs was the Securitate's KGB-styled annex. Whoever says that he was sent as a priest to a Western parish without collaborating with the Securitate lies with un-Christian nonchalance." Doctors, professors, engineers, journalists, and priests were allowed to travel abroad as part of the highly secret Atlas program. According to the Securitate officer:

> All of them wrote reports after their return, and all were subject to draconian verifications with respect to their political beliefs, future intentions, and loyalty to the communist regime. Their phone calls were monitored, their mail intercepted, their every move followed, and their homes and workplaces bugged. There was a general and a specialized training; this way individuals indoctrinated by communism, nationalism, and chauvinism were formed during an era when reason slept. The origin of the current paranoid and outdated nationalism lies in the Securitate reeducation and training programs. This also explains the excessive nationalism of the clergy, who ceased to think critically and search for rational arguments, adopting instead paralogical thinking patterns praising Marx and Ceauşescu, a self-imposed schizophrenia. This training resulted in the [Orthodox clergy's] intolerance toward other religious denominations and the Greek Catholic Church.

Vasilievici further explained that after contact was established and collaboration was agreed upon, the Securitate compiled two files for each priest. While
both files had the same reference number, the first referred strictly to the informer himself, while the second contained reports on other individuals filed
by the priest. Securitate agents met with the clergy at least monthly to gauge
popular mood.[41]

During the past seventeen years, a number of Orthodox leaders and priests
have been embarrassed by revelations of their tainted past. Despite claims by
some Romanians that collaboration was the rule for the church, revelations
have generally dealt with isolated individual cases. They do not represent the
entire Orthodox Church as a corrupt organization with a majority of priest-
informers. Vasilievici's estimate that close to four in five priests collaborated is
important, but remains unsubstantiated and vague. He does not offer specific
names, places, dates, or actions. As a larger part of the Securitate archive is
transferred from the Information Service to the Council for the Study of Securitate Archives, a process scheduled to end in the near future, it is possible
that more clergy will come under intense public scrutiny. This will result in
many clergy coming forward to confess, though it is likely that many more will
dismiss the gravity of their actions and defend their past activities.

Communist Servant or Shrewd Negotiator?

The Romanian Orthodox Church's multifaceted collaboration with the communist authorities is relatively well documented.[42] The church flattered Ceauşescu and glorified him as a "secular 'god,' 'demigod,' and 'savior'"; it contributed to the manipulation of religious symbols; it tacitly agreed to a church
demolition policy sacrificing its interests to the whim of communist leaders; it
served as the communists' faithful instrument in the destruction of the Greek
Catholic Church; and it quashed anti-communist sentiment and dissidence
among its clergy. In analyzing the contribution of the Orthodox Church to
Ceauşescu's personality cult, Dan Ionescu revealed that one of the oldest Orthodox publications, the *Telegraful Român*, published in the Transylvanian city
of Sibiu, enthusiastically quoted a French biographer of Ceauşescu, who had
compared him to Moses "leading his flock toward the promised land of welfare and independence."[43] Every year, prelates praised the communist leader,
party, and regime for their commitment to defend human rights and build a
"multilaterally developed" Romania. However, as soon as it became clear that
Ceauşescu would not return to the country's helm after his overthrow, Or-

thodox leaders changed sides, blessed the anti-communist revolution, and turned against their communist allies. In their January 1990 declaration *Ora adevărului* (Hour of Truth), synod members admitted their guilt and their compromises with the communist regime, and they apologized for those "who did not always have the courage of the martyrs."[44] Unfortunately, the belated condemnation of Ceaușescu and his anti-religious policies from the pulpit did not quell public opposition to the Orthodox Church. The controversial past of its leaders continues to be a stumbling block for the church and is the subject of periodic campaigns aimed to discredit it. At issue are its unconditional submission to communist rulers and its ties to the Securitate.

After 1989, two major views on the position of the Orthodox Church toward the communist regime emerged. On the one hand, hierarchs insisted that their actions were intended to secure the church's survival as a religious organization. No sacrifice was too large and no price was too high as the Orthodox Church tried to avoid obliteration at the hands of the atheistic political regime. Individual priests were defrocked, denied moral and financial support, or thrown in jail, but the church as an institution survived a period of unprecedented persecution. Defenders of the church's collaboration argued that the Romanian Orthodox Church's strength relative to other religious denominations in the country and elsewhere in the communist bloc proved that their relationship to the state was justified. According to such authors as George Enache, Cristina Păiușan, and Radu Ciuceanu, the Orthodox leadership understood early on that open opposition to the regime was pointless, as demonstrated by the wave of arrests and forced retirements that followed the nomination of a communist government in 1946. This is why Patriarch Justinian Marina supported the regime openly, while he opposed it tacitly. Marina's inner opposition was evidenced by his occasional puns directed against the communist leaders, his willingness to promote and protect priests with anti-communist views, and his notes informing the communist leadership of the priests' arrest. Marina, the "Red Patriarch" who reigned unchallenged over the most controversial period in the church's history, was thus recast as a prelate who resisted the regime.[45]

In contrast, critics maintained that as God's institution on earth, the church had the resources to remain unblemished in even the direst circumstances. No mundane individual or institution could undo the work of God and destroy his church. Critics responded by pointing to the example of the Russian Orthodox Church, which demonstrated that even when communist authorities banned a religious denomination, confiscated its property, and harassed its clergy and followers, the church could survive clandestinely. The plight of the Greek Catholic Church in Romania (examined here in chapter 5) further suggested that defiance represented an alternative to active collaboration.[46] Independent voices wondered whether leaders had the interests of the Orthodox Church at heart more than their own, as they retained their lavish residences and opulent lifestyle even during the late 1980s, when ordinary Romanians scrambled for mere necessities. When evaluating Marina's position, they saw his collaboration as genuine and his dissidence as apparent. A committed socialist, Marina was anointed patriarch by the communist regime, whose leaders he had long courted. His actions did not reflect dissidence or opposition to a regime whose basic ideological tenets he fully embraced, but a desire to build a personal power base that would guarantee his complete dominance over the Romanian Orthodox congregation.

Opposition to Orthodox leaders first came from within the church. The most notable initiative took place on 9 January 1990, when Anania, Andreicuţ, and Stăniloae set up a seven-member Group for Reflection on Church Renewal to regenerate the church by replacing tainted leaders. The group targeted the Holy Synod, the collective Orthodox Church leadership, which at the time included contested hierarchs like Patriarch Teoctist, Metropolitan Antonie Plămădeală of Transylvania, and Metropolitan Nestor Vornicescu of Oltenia. When asked to resign and make way for younger, reform-minded leaders, synod members turned down the proposal, though public confidence in the church stood at an all-time low. A week later, the patriarchate denounced the "insulting campaign" directed against the church, reminiscent of the Stalinist drive of the first years of communist rule in Romania. After this setback, the group never again challenged the leadership and ultimately lost importance. Its failure to attract support from the clergy and theology students followed the death of its most prominent member, Stăniloae, in 1993. The group's small successes contributed to its very demise, since every time the Orthodox hierarchy co-opted a group member, the group lost another voice, gradually turning into a defender of the status quo. Anania became Archbishop of Cluj, Vad, and Feleac and, with Metropolitan Antonie Plămădeală's deteriorating health in the 1990s, the de facto, if not de jure, Orthodox leader of Transylvania. In 2006, Anania became the first Metropolitan of Cluj, Alba, Crişana and Maramureş, leading a majority of Plămădeală's flock. Ironically, he remains one of the most conservative Romanian Orthodox leaders. Young theologian Daniel Ciobotea was appointed Metropolitan of Moldova, occupying the second most important position in the church hierarchy, which had remained vacant after Teoctist's 1986 nomination as patriarch. Andreicuţ replaced the controversial Emilian Birdaş as archbishop of Alba Iulia, and Theodor Baconsky was appointed Romania's ambassador to the Vatican from 1997 to 2001.[47]

Representatives of minority churches also mounted criticism. On 29 September 1997, on the eve of a synod meeting, Christian Democrat and Greek Catholic senator Ioan Moisin attacked the Orthodox Church. Citing pre-1989 newspaper reports and books, Moisin denounced the church for collaborating with the communists and interfering with the democratization process, arguing that the church "cannot solve its crisis without telling the truth," and he named senior clerics who allegedly abetted communists. They included the late Metropolitan Nicolae Bălan of Transylvania; Bishops Vasile Leu, Roman, and Antonie; priest Dumitru Cumpănașu; and Patriarch Iustin. "Before Soviet troops even reached [the Metropolitan see of] Sibiu," Moisin said, Bălan "sent a telegram to Metropolitan Aleksy of Leningrad praising 'the freedom brought by the Soviet Army' and blaming Romania's 'political mistake of fighting against the Soviets' on the 'weakening of the Romanian people... and the existence of [the Greek Catholic] Church in communion with the Papal Church in Rome.'" During the Bucharest congress of religious denominations held on 16–17 October 1945, Bălan publicly thanked the Soviet Union.[48] In 1993, Roman Catholic Bishop Ioan Ploscaru identified Leu as the inmate who denounced Roman Catholic prisoners to the communist guards. Each time a Roman Catholic priest prayed, Leu alerted the guards with a big sign of the cross.[49] Moisin further revealed that Cumpănașu was a communist official and a Securitate agent, Roman and Antonie denounced Calciu to state and party organs, and Moisescu "reached the lowest possible levels of cowardice," while Plămădeală "did the work of the Department of Religious Affairs."[50]

In his statement before the Senate, Moisin cited Orthodox theology professor Nicolae Dura, who boldly wrote that "some church leaders appointed during the Ceaușescu era (1965–1989) pledged allegiance first to the 'Secu monastery,' and then to the Holy Altar. Those appointed after 1989 got their education [abroad] with support from the 'Secu monastery' and later became leaders with the help of their National Salvation Front protectors."[51] Playing on the identity between the name of a Romanian monastery (Secu) and the first four letters from the name of the infamous institution (Securitate), Dura referred to the latter as the "Secu monastery" in order to emphasize the collaboration between the Orthodox Church and the communist secret police. Elsewhere, Dura spoke of the communist-era Orthodox theology students as "Securitate creatures" and "communist tools of collaboration," an assessment Moisin confirmed with reference to a 1978 letter to Radio Free Europe in which Bucharest Seminary students condemned its jail-like atmosphere, the beatings, and the informer networks controlling their institution.[52] After accusing Patriarch Teoctist of assisting the communists' forced conversions of Greek Catholic priests to Orthodoxy and of not opposing Ceaușescu's church destruction, the senator asked for the secret files of Orthodox leaders to be opened to the public.

Along the same lines, in 2001 journalist Cornel Nistorescu wrote:

> Not us, the believers, turned God into a Communist Party member or wrote in 1952 Patriarch Justinian's speech [praising communist leader] Gheorghe Gheorghiu-Dej and in 1948 an Ode to Stalin the Great in *Telegraful român*. . . . In March 1989, the synod, not the believers, sent Ceauşescu a telegram pledging "our full support for your ongoing activity as a great and brilliant hero of peace, a fighter of international détente, disarmament, understanding and peaceful cooperation between nations."[53]

The Orthodox Church's ties with the Securitate became the subject of another article written by analyst Neculai Constantin Munteanu, a former Radio Free Europe correspondent. Trying to provide a balanced view on the subject, Munteanu claimed that until 1951 laypeople, not clergy, filed most reports, and only afterward did the Securitate proceed to compile files on the clergy:

> When repression failed, [communists] obliged church leaders to participate in quasi-political activities—peace marches, the National Assembly—to compromise them in the eyes of the faithful. The church hierarchy had to give Caesar what was Caesar's. Some gave more and, with their consciousness, their soul. . . . The church leaders' collaboration with the Securitate remains an open wound, though the proof is thin and there are debatable testimonies of police agents, who avoid specifying names, dates, and places. . . . Periodic interest in the [issue] stems from the fears, distrust, and suspicions poisoning our existence. Unfortunately, Orthodox leaders consider it part of a campaign to discredit the church. This is a regrettable exaggeration. The church is not reducible to its leaders or to those who signed the pact with the devil. Refusal to clarify the situation can only fuel suspicion.

According to the same writer, the Securitate was "far more blamable than the priests." The Secu monastery gathered "the servants of evil, who forgave nothing and left nothing and nobody untainted." Munteanu lamented the authorities' determination "to keep this monastery closed with seven locks" and concluded that "the truth, however painful, must come to light because . . . the moral resurrection of the Romanians involves the church, too."[54] The debate will no doubt continue.

Revealing the Names of Informer Priests

The Council for the Study of Securitate Archives began verifying the histories of candidates running in local and general elections in 2000. At the same time, the institution accepted citizen requests for the investigation of journalists and university presidents. Frustrated with the Orthodox leaders' conservative position and continued opposition to democratic principles of accepting sexual, ethnic, and religious diversity, civil society activist Gabriel Andreescu asked the council to reveal the Securitate informers within the synod, a request Teoctist denounced as "an inadmissible act of blackmail and intimidation." Andreescu told journalists he could explain Orthodox opposition to democratization only as the "perpetuation of church collaboration with communist authorities." This collaboration was demonstrated by the prelates' support for communist policies, by Corneanu's allegations that Orthodox leaders worked with the Securitate, and by the revelation that collaboration affected other Orthodox Churches in the communist bloc. Indeed, Moscow newspapers alleged that Russian Patriarch Aleksy and four of the six Russian synod members had been undercover KGB agents.[55]

Initially, the council pledged to answer Andreescu's request promptly, but then it announced that investigating only Orthodox leaders amounted to discrimination. Under considerable pressure from the Orthodox Church to either investigate the heads of all officially registered religious denominations or no religious leaders at all, and insistence from other churches that Andreescu's request did not refer to them, the council took a full year to launch verifications into the past of all religious leaders in Romania.[56] In August 2001, without specifying names, the council announced that it had studied the files of sixty religious leaders and found out that some had been both tortured and torturers.[57] The council's final results never reached the public, either because archival data analysis was never finalized or because the council chose to keep it secret. In either case, the failure to report to the public violated the legislation. Andreescu's request and the council's hesitant response was the subject of a great deal of journalistic investigation. Some writers denounced Andreescu for daring to discredit the most credible institution in the land and a pillar of the Romanian ethnic identity; others criticized the church for not coming clean and admitting its past mistakes. Still others pointed out that the church must not be equated with individual priests and hierarchs tainted by their collaboration with the communists.[58]

The Orthodox Church's proposal for the exemption of clergy from background checks (despite law no. 187) received support from the ruling Social

Democrats and from the main opposition party, the chauvinistic Greater Romania Party, which saw Orthodoxy as the cornerstone of Romanian identity. Pro-democratic opposition parties were far less enthusiastic. Leaders of the center-leftist Democratic Party rejected limiting the scope of the law and allowing priests to hide their past, on grounds that informer priests could not claim any Christian moral standing.[59] However, the parliamentary committee overseeing the Information Service, where the Social Democrats and the Greater Romania Party formed a clear majority, viewed the proposal favorably. While not formally overseeing the council, the committee is able to affect council activity indirectly by restricting the number of files the council can access.

The Orthodox Church presented its proposal in a 2001 letter, which argued that, as an independent institution, it was not obliged to obey secular laws. If it were, then the separation of church and state, which Romania's commitment to democracy presupposed, might be called into question. In response, council member Mircea Dinescu threatened to resign if the institution "looked for devils [Securitate informers] only outside the church," and his colleague Andrei Pleşu said that "church representatives cannot have a special status, they are part of the society." Dinescu believed that "it is beneficial for the church if names of tainted priests are disclosed. The people will trust the church more knowing there are no informers among those hearing confession." Ticu Dumitrescu said, "there were informers in all social categories. What would the notary public say if the priest is exempted?"[60]

Liberal leader Radu Stroe commented, "Church representatives must obey the law, which must be the same for everyone. As the most trusted institution, the [Orthodox] Church should hide nothing. The priests who sinned are individually responsible, not the church."[61] *Ziarul de Iaşi* contended, "the moral foundation for disclosing the names of tainted priests is the monopoly on sincerity priests enjoy in a society harassed by the state." Unless names were disclosed, "Romania's moral rebirth would take place only after several generations die," and the church would be placed in the privileged position of "judging itself its tainted clergy." The newspaper rejected the Orthodox claim that exemption was needed to protect the sacrament of confession by saying that the informer priest was the first to break the secret of the confession and by doing so "entered the land of the mundane," governed by secular laws.[62]

Some clergy members agreed with this position. Known for his moral rectitude and anti-communist position, Father Sandi Mehendinţi declared that "the priests are part of the Romanian society and should not be exempted from our past and present mistakes. We should not refuse to take responsibility before our flock."[63] For Father Costică Popa:

> We, the priests should know our hierarchs, who evaluate us and de-
> cide for us. Relations among clergy are tense and administrative is-
> sues are affected because former Securitate collaborators were pro-
> moted to church leadership positions.... To forgive is to know,
> repent, and give up evil. Even if the civil society does not care, we, the
> priests, should try to clarify things. Files of Securitate collaborators
> should be open at least to the clergy, for us to understand how many
> priests had a double discourse.[64]

In mid-2001, Capotă and Popa publicly asked for the opening of the files of all
Orthodox priests.[65]

Most church leaders opposed verifications. Archbishop Pimen of Suceava
said priests were obliged to inform, and admitted that after a visit abroad he
"of course signed reports, but gave information that could harm no one."[66]
Without offering details, Vincenţiu Ploieşteanu admitted to having a Securitate
informer file. Insisting that the church was innocent until proven guilty, he
reminded the public that thousands of priests refused to collaborate and that
no hard evidence proved that information from confession reached the Securitate. Ploieşteanu made several points of note. First, he said Dinescu was
wrong to "equate informer priests with breaking the secret of the confession."
It was not likely, he argued, that the Securitate was interested in the information obtained this way, either because it could get it by some other means or
because it was too personal to be of real use. The political police did use the
most trivial data to blackmail informers and their victims, however, and no
other means of data gathering could penetrate so deeply into a person's intimate life as confession.

Second, Ploieşteanu complained that the press "grossly manipulated" the
position of the church, which did not oppose clergy verification but merely
voiced "dissatisfaction" with the process and the "anti-Christian and anti-
Orthodox" stance of some college members. However, the Orthodox Church
did not simply state its "dissatisfaction" with the process of verification; it
vigorously lobbied the government to amend the legislation in such a way that
priests were not verified.

Third, Ploieşteanu announced that the church wished to be part of verifications. However, the council must remain independent from the political
elite and the accused groups, and current legislation allows no institution or
social group to interfere in investigations. Fourth, Ploieşteanu noted that the
clergy was the only social category verified in toto (from the priest in the remote
village to the patriarch).[67] The law lists other social groups subject to investigation, but none is so strictly hierarchical or so well-represented in both urban

and rural areas as are religious denominations, and especially the Orthodox Church.

The church's request for the amendment of the law won the support of President Ion Iliescu, who in July 2001 publicly stated that, in his opinion, law no. 187 violated the constitutional principle concerning the separation of church and state. "No state institution," he commented, "should decide on church matters."[68] Dinescu replied that the council "deals not with churches and priests but with those engaged in political police activities, [and] if we do not disclose all files and all informer names, then the council is useless."[69] Without consulting their colleagues, the council president Onişoru and Ion Stan (leader of the parliamentary committee supervising the Information Service) agreed that clergy files be verified only at the request of religious leaders. This private agreement, which was not binding unless the council and the committee adopted it, was denounced as capitulation to pressure from the Orthodox Church.[70] In April 2004, the committee proposed changes to law no. 187. The changes read: "Verifications of clergy members are started only at the request of religious leaders."[71] By denying ordinary citizens the right to demand investigations of priests, the changes effectively exempt the clergy from verifications, a privilege other social groups are likely to ask for in the near future.

Conclusion

Despite some positive developments in the process of coming to terms with the communist past, the Romanian public is yet to have access to key documents revealing the activity of the Securitate, its vast network of spies and informers, and its relationship with the Orthodox Church. Based on previously unavailable secret archives, we now know that the Orthodox Church was a victim as much as a beneficiary of communist policies. It is high time to honor the many priests thrown in jail or killed in the 1940s and 1950s and to denounce the hierarchs' and priests' compliance with the atheistic regime. However, in a country where conspiracy theories abound, delayed transitional justice has bred a web of convoluted scenarios and a myriad of contradictory "revelations" that have gradually blurred the line between victims and their victimizers and turned the shame of individual guilt into collective indifference.

Many Romanian intellectuals believed that, as the country's major religious denomination, the Orthodox Church must lead the way toward moral rebirth and an honest reassessment of the past. They were disappointed when church leaders defended their collaboration with communist authorities and explained it away as mere human weakness or a carefully orchestrated strategy to keep the church alive. Its unholy past cooperation with a political regime reputed for human rights trespasses will likely haunt the Orthodox Church as long as its leaders refuse to assume their own mistakes.

To the surprise of many Romanians, the opening of the secret files could lead to the discovery of active collaboration with the repressive communist organs of members of religious minorities. The recent opening of formerly secret archives revealed the hidden face of collaboration by members of other religious denominations active in the country. On 17 January 2007, Baptist pastor Iosif Ţon admitted to having been a long-time secret informer and claimed that collaboration with the Securitate was widespread among members of the Baptist community in Romania. Ţon later became one of the most outspoken critics of Nicolae Ceauşescu's regime and was eventually forced into exile.[72] In another recent article, Baptist pastor Marius Cruceru reflected on his father's spying activities for the Securitate in the 1970s and alleged that his father might have been murdered by the state security service in a staged accident when he decided to end his collaboration.[73] Ministers, pastors, rabbis, and priests representing other faiths were also identified or identified themselves as former Securitate informers. As in Poland, file access may taint members of the anti-communist opposition more than former communist officials, because the secret political police sought to penetrate social groups that opposed the system, not those that supported it. Similarly, in Romania, a higher percentage of religious minority members will likely turn out to have collaborated with the Securitate. These groups, so far shielded from the public scandal that affected the Orthodox Church, must also honestly face their past.

5

The Politics of Orthodox-Greek Catholic Relations

The Greek Catholic Church in Transylvania was constituted around the year 1700 when the Hapsburg regime, through the skillful mediation of the Jesuits, persuaded the local Romanian Orthodox clergy that their acceptance of Catholic dogma and the authority of the pope would earn them equal status with the Catholic and Protestant clergy.[1] The reasons for the conversion remain disputed, with the Orthodox viewing Greek Catholicism as the result of political pressure, and the Greek Catholics arguing that the Orthodox Romanians of Transylvania accepted Catholic dogma more or less freely in their desire to join the Western European nations. Truth is that, within a century of the Greek Catholic Church's inception, Transylvanian Romanians "were transformed from a mute society of serfs and shepherds subservient to the will of Western European regional masters into a vocal class expressing 'national' aspirations."[2] Church members gathered around the Şcoala Ardeleană (the Transylvanian School) were instrumental in highlighting the Latin origins of the Romanian language and promoting the theory of Romanians as direct descendants from the Roman legions that once conquered Dacia and were then stationed there under Emperor Trajan and subsequent Roman emperors until 272 CE. Not only did the Greek Catholics play a major part in securing for the Transylvanian Romanians equal status with their Hungarian and German neighbors, but, as prominent politicians, they also continued to dominate the political scene in interwar Greater Romania from 1918 until 1940.

A great number of the leaders of the National Peasant Party, which ruled Romania alternatively with the Liberal Party during the interwar period, were Greek Catholic and proud of their heritage.

On order from Moscow, the Romanian communists disbanded the Greek Catholic Church in late 1948, after Patriarch Justinian denounced the Vatican as "the center of the oldest imperialist tradition,"[3] and the communists unilaterally revoked the Concordat that interwar Romania signed with the Vatican. The scenario was similar to the disbanding of the Greek Catholics in Ukraine in 1946 and was to be repeated in Czechoslovakia in 1950. Metropolitan Nicolae Bălan of Transylvania stirred things up as early as 1944 by writing a letter to Russian Patriarch Aleksy I in which he blamed the Greek Catholics for Romania's alliance with Nazi Germany during World War II: "If Romania made mistakes in its past, if it participated on the side of the Germans in the war against Russia, all of these were done out of a weakness of the Romanian nation due to its split into two by a church in its midst that is in communion with the church of the popes in Rome."[4] The Greek Catholic Church was forced to merge with the Orthodox Church, and its priests were promised state-sponsored salaries if they declared themselves Orthodox. In November 1948 some 600 Greek Catholic priests and all their six bishops went to prison because they refused to convert, and many of them died in terrible conditions. Faced with the alternative of arrest, other clergy and faithful joined the Orthodox Church.[5]

As with the 1700 union, the 1948 incorporation of the Greek Catholic Church into the Orthodox Church resulted in bitter controversy. On the one hand, the Orthodox Church supported the merger and saw the Greek Catholics' return to the church from which their ancestors were separated in 1700 as long-overdue reparation of a grave historical injustice. Until 1989, many Orthodox clergy and theologians naively believed that the 1948 suppression of the Greek Catholic Church had put an end to Greek Catholicism in Romania, but the unrecognized denomination survived clandestinely until 1989, when it resurfaced and received official recognition. On the other hand, the Greek Catholics denounced the 1948 merger as an unlawful act perpetrated by a communist state willing to disregard basic human rights, and they harshly condemned the Orthodox Church for its role in suppressing another Christian denomination. The Greek Catholics refused to acknowledge that the Orthodox Romanians of Transylvania, too, were entitled to an apology for their forceful conversion of 1700 or to any form of compensation for the property they lost to the Greek Catholics at the time.

Several pieces of legislation sealed the fate of Greek Catholicism in communist Romania. Article 27 of the 1948 constitution paid lip service to reli-

gious freedom, allowing only those religious groups whose "rite and practices do not run counter to the Constitution, the public morals, or the national
security." Article 27 also banned religious education in public schools, dismantled confessional schools, and singled out the Orthodox Church as an autocephalous and unitary church.[6] Two laws adopted in July and August 1948
redefined the role of religion under the new regime by subordinating religious
denominations to the atheistic state. While this legislation applied to all religious groups in the country, Decree Law no. 358 of 1 December 1948 and
Council of Ministers Decision no. 1719 of 27 December 1948 referred specifically to the Greek Catholic Church. The first article of the decree law disbanded
the church and all its juridical units "as a result of the return of local Greek
Catholic communities to the Orthodox Church." The second article transferred
all Greek Catholic property except places of worship to the Romanian state and
set up a committee of representatives of the Ministries of Culture, Finance,
Interior, Agriculture, and Education to decide on "the destination of these assets, which in part could be given to the Romanian Orthodox Church."[7]

Decision no. 1719 enlarged the committee that oversaw the transfer of
Greek Catholic property by including representatives of the Orthodox and
Greek Catholic Churches, but it remained silent on the balance of power
within the committee, although presumably the Orthodox were called to
nominate more representatives than the Greek Catholics (Article 2). Ironically,
the decision allowed the Greek Catholics to have a say in the way their property
was taken away from them, at a time when their leaders were thrown in jail
and could not effectively represent the church on the committee. The same
article provided for the Orthodox Church to receive all Greek Catholic Church
property not yet transferred to the state—that is, cathedrals, churches, chapels,
monasteries, and sketes, together with their adjacent land (Article 3). For unknown reasons, the committee never functioned and never met. In 1998, Ştefan
Ioniţă of the State Secretariat of Religious Denominations told legislators that
"we believe that after the arrest of the Greek Catholic clergy, the [Greek Cath-
olic] assets were simply taken over by local administrative bodies with the help
of the political police, and then transferred to various institutions according to
their use, the churches going to the Orthodox Church."[8]

The transfer did not always entail a transfer of property rights, although in
all cases the Orthodox priests received the keys to the local Greek Catholic
church building, a fact many understood as further endorsement for the Orthodox Church's privileged ties with the repressive communist authorities.
Following unconfirmed reports, some Transylvanian Orthodox priests and
communities organized weekly mass in Greek Catholic churches that formally
continued to be registered as Greek Catholic property. The reasons for this

blatant disregard for the law are not easily evident. It is possible that former Greek Catholic local administrators conveniently "forgot" to record the property change in the official registry. It is equally possible that local officials believed that formal registration was unnecessary, since the Greek Catholic Church was dismantled and hence could no longer claim any property. It is difficult to indicate precisely the number of such cases, but it seems that they were the exception rather than the rule. Whatever the motive for them remaining Greek Catholic property, these churches should have been the first to be returned by the Orthodox Church. As we will see, this was not the case, because the Orthodox Church refused to surrender these worship places to their rightful owner.

Post-Communist Issues and Actors

The ousting of communist dictator Nicolae Ceauşescu brought new hope to the Greek Catholics. The church quickly reorganized itself, and its clergy and faithful launched a sustained campaign for having their rights recognized. But forty-five years of communist rule and underground activity took a great toll on Greek Catholic membership. While as late as 1995 insisting that the vast majority of its pre-1948 1.5 to 2 million believers had remained loyal, the Greek Catholic Church found out that only a fraction still considered themselves Greek Catholics, and the rest had converted, willingly or not, to Orthodoxy, Roman Catholicism, or other faiths. As late as 2000, the Vatican's *Annuario Pontificio* was reporting an official Greek Catholic membership of around 1.4 million, but many local observers considered the figure unrealistically high. To the surprise of both the Greek Catholic leaders and the Vatican, the 2002 Romanian national census counted only some 200,000 Greek Catholics—that is, about 1 percent of the country's total population. Independent reports claim that the number of Greek Catholics is slightly higher and that some census workers registered Greek Catholic families as Orthodox.

This claim is hard to verify. Mahieu argued that the discrepancy between the membership figure claimed by the Greek Catholics and the figure reported by the National Institute for Statistics may be due to the fact that the Oaş and Maramureş areas, where the return to the Greek Catholic Church was the most significant, were for ten years regions of massive legal and illegal migration to the West.[9] In our view, the migration factor does not satisfactorily explain the discrepancy. According to the Institute for Statistics, the combined population decrease for 1992–2002 was around 60,000 in Maramureş and Satu Mare counties (including Oaş).[10] Thus, the decrease affecting Greek Catholic membership can also be attributed to negative population growth rates. The figure of some 600,000 additional Greek Catholics in the two counties alone is highly unrealistic, as it implies migration rates ten times higher than the officially registered population loss. Mahieu further explained the difficulties in accurately counting the Greek Catholics by "multiple attendance," the practice of visiting churches belonging to more than one denomination. In Mahieu's study, a respondent indicated attendance of three different churches belonging to the Orthodox, Roman, and Greek Catholic denominations. According to the respondent, each church offered services that attracted her. An Orthodox by baptism, the respondent liked the Orthodox church for the Saturday evening Vespers because of the beauty of the songs, the Roman Catholic church for the service of the Adoration of the Virgin Mary (which she first witnessed on a visit to Medjugorje), and the Greek Catholic church because of the impressive oratorical qualities of the priest serving there.[11] Regardless of the actual number of followers currently, Greek Catholics are vocal defenders of their church's rights.

The first legislation adopted by the revolutionary National Salvation Front government included Decree Law no. 9 of 31 December 1989 that annulled as many as twenty pieces of communist legislation, the very last one being the 1948 decree that dismantled the Greek Catholic Church. Four months later, Decree Law no. 126 of 24 April 1990 officially recognized that religious group (Article 1) and set the general framework for Greek Catholic property restitution. Article 2 provided for the return of Greek Catholic Church assets in state hands at the time, identified by a committee of state and church representatives. According to Article 3, another committee of Greek Catholic and Orthodox representatives was formed to discuss the possible return of former Greek Catholic churches, worship places, and parish houses used or owned by the Orthodox Church, not without taking into account "the wishes of the faithful in communities with such churches." Article 4 further stipulated that "for the localities with an insufficient number of worship places, the state will support the building of new churches and give the denominations the needed land."[12]

Setting the tone for property restitution, the decree's omissions and commissions had a major impact on subsequent efforts to find a solution acceptable to both churches. The decree divided the process of Greek Catholic property restitution into two distinct components by separating the return of worship places from the return of all other assets, a fact echoing the 1948 decision to transfer Greek Catholic property to other organizations according to its use. Post-communist authorities believed that the two distinct restitution processes had two distinct solutions and that the settlement agreed to by the state in its relationship to the Greek Catholic Church was not binding for the Orthodox Church. At the same time, the state refused to legislate the restitution of Greek Catholic churches and worship places used by the Orthodox Church, thus signaling that the state viewed restitution as a strictly religious problem it could not or would not interfere with, neither as a mediator nor as an active participant.

Instead of admitting that an injustice perpetrated by the state had to be settled by none other than the state, the post-communist authorities refused to involve themselves in a divisive issue. In doing so, they allowed the tensions to escalate into a full-blown conflict. While the two contending denominations were supposed to settle their differences through dialogue and negotiation, state noninterference gave the Orthodox Church the upper hand—since they had access to, and in many cases the property right over, the churches—and left Greek Catholics unprotected and without any means of appeal. When Greek Catholics insisted on the urgency of being allowed to organize mass inside their former churches rather than on the street, in public parks, or in ad hoc worship places, state representatives prescribed more dialogue, although procrastination benefited only the Orthodox. Surprisingly, Article 4 of the decree implicitly suggested a possible solution to the conflict: the construction of new churches. It represented another concession to the Orthodox, who were no longer required to return the old Greek Catholic churches in the localities where new state-sponsored churches would be built.

While reluctant to search for a solution to church restitution, post-communist authorities started returning some Greek Catholic property kept in their hands. By contrast, the Orthodox Church mounted formidable resistance and used every conceivable method and argument in order to delay the loss of property on its part. By 1997, parliament representatives had met four times with the Transylvanian Orthodox and Greek Catholic leaders, Antonie Plămădeală and Lucian Mureşan, and identified and returned eighty state-owned buildings. During the same period, some 100 church buildings went back to the Greek Catholic Church, and the two denominations made arrangements for organizing alternate masses in thirty other buildings.[13] Most of these churches were located in the southwestern region of Banat, where an agreement between the Orthodox Metropolitan Nicolae Corneanu of Banat and the Greek Catholic Bishop Ioan Ploscaru of Lugoj allowed the Greek Catholics to get back their churches as early as 1990.[14] Differing statistics on the exact number of churches and assets to be returned to the Greek Catholic Church further complicated a division of property that has been highly contested from the beginning. According to some Greek Catholic sources, a total of 1,800 churches, cemeteries, and chapels must be transferred from Orthodox to Greek Catholic hands. Others indicate a figure of 2,400.[15] As of 2006, a number of churches had been built by both Greek Catholics and Orthodox. Although in many cases they were not sponsored by the state, as initially suggested, the new church buildings have taken a major role in somewhat calming down the conflict. Tensions continue between the two churches, as explained below.

Parliamentary Debates on Greek Catholic Property Restitution

After 1989, the conflict over the ownership and use of Greek Catholic churches became the subject of hot debates and intense political bargaining in the Romanian bicameral parliament. While paying lip service to the cherished democratic principles of equality before the law of all religious groups and the protection of private property, post-communist authorities decided early on to treat Greek Catholic church restitution as a purely religious problem in which the state should not involve itself. The state's policy of noninterference, informing Decree Law no. 126 of 1990, resulted from the claim of breaking up with the communist regime and its practices, the prominence of political actors praising communist-era accomplishments, and the Orthodox Church's privileged position in the post-1989 ideological void.

   The Orthodox Church's adamant opposition to the rebirth of the Greek Catholic Church persuaded an intimidated parliament and State Secretariat for Religious Denominations to decline to actively participate in property claims settlement. Politically, the position benefited the rulers of the day, who could blame lack of progress on church leaders. Morally, the state's refusal to intervene in a conflict heavily skewed in favor of one denomination was questionable. The 1948 confiscation of Greek Catholic property was undertaken by the state, a fact transforming the old Orthodox-Greek Catholic dispute over possessions into a conflict involving three actors (the injured Greek Catholic Church, the Orthodox Church beneficiary, and the state as mediator). Moreover, the aspiring democratic post-communist state could hardly single out church property as an area where property rights should not be fully protected. As discussed later in this chapter, the central authorities' refusal to mediate interconfessional negotiations, along with the active involvement of the local authorities and the police on the side of the Orthodox Church, led to escalating tension and violence that could have easily been prevented by upholding the rule of law.

While drawn predominantly from the second echelon of the Communist Party, President Ion Iliescu and the Social Democrat governments of 1990–1996 argued that the new Romanian state was not the successor of its communist predecessor and, as a result, was not compelled to redress the latter's injustices but, if it wished to show benevolence, could do so selectively. Legally, the position was untenable. On 29 November 1984 Romania had ratified the Vienna Convention on Succession of States in respect of State Property, Archives and Debts of 8 April 1983, which asked states to adopt legislation prohibiting abuse of power and granting reparations to victims of such abuse, and further read that "in cases where the government that perpetrated such acts no longer exists, the successor state or government must compensate the victims."[16] The Greek Catholics certainly were not the only group to ask for reparations and justice at the time, but they were the most vocal, and they benefited from unflinching support from international actors.

Greek Catholics were joined by the former political prisoners who wanted a formal apology and financial compensation for their many years of jail; ordinary Romanians seeking to regain the dwellings the communists took away from them; individuals demanding access to the files the secret political police compiled on them; the sons and daughters of anti-communist dissidents asking that the prison guards who killed their parents be put on trial; the peasants attempting to regain the land they lost in the collectivization drive; and the civil society groups looking for ways to ban communist officials and political police agents from post-communist politics. The Social Democrats rejected all such claims. Had the country implemented resolute transitional justice, the Greek Catholic demands might have been satisfied more quickly and comprehensively. In the aftermath of the 1989 revolution, however, Iliescu and his collaborators insisted the consensus was to bury the past because Romanians were preoccupied exclusively with their falling living standards.

Not all political actors turned a blind eye to the recent past. The nationalist Greater Romania Party, a junior governmental partner, and its leader Corneliu Vadim Tudor, known for his anti-Semitic outbursts, underscored the accomplishments of communism. Unfortunately, these politicians were the least inclined to side with the Greek Catholics, as their interventions during parliamentary debates reveal. It is no less true that whenever legislators launched debates on the topic, the Orthodox Church denounced parliament's interference in religious affairs and decried Romania's inability to separate church from state as guaranteed by the 1991 constitution.[17]

A legislative proposal seeking the restitution of Greek Catholic property was introduced in parliament as early as 1992, but the house was unable to settle the issue. The reasons for this inability went beyond the politicians' unwillingness to legislate a religious conflict. Lack of political will on the part of both the Social Democrats and the Democratic Convention was perhaps the most important factor hampering the search for a political solution to the interconfessional dispute. Politicians representing other regions saw the issue as a Transylvanian problem in need of a Transylvanian solution. The great disparity in numbers between the two churches intimidated even the atheistic politicians, who proved unwilling to risk losing political capital and alienate the predominantly Orthodox electorate. The exacerbation of claims on both sides made serious and sober dialogue impossible. Several times the Greek Catholics insisted on nothing short of *restitutio in integrum*—that is, an immediate and unconditional restitution of all their buildings confiscated in 1948, regardless of whether there were any believers left to use them. The Orthodox subsequently rejected even the most reasonable Greek Catholic proposals.

Over the years, pragmatic dialogue for finding an imperfect solution acceptable to all sides made room to exhortations on each denomination's historical precedence and the cruelty of communist injustices, incorrectly suggesting that the legitimacy of Greek Catholic claims hinged on their contribution to the state-building and nation-building processes more than on their legal right to get back what was once theirs. Greek Catholic demands for church restitution allowed the Orthodox Church to advance its own claims for the restitution of property it lost in 1700 to the then nascent Greek Catholic Church. As is usually the case, instead of uniting the two churches, remembering history became one more factor dividing them.

The Christian Democrat senator and Greek Catholic priest Matei Boilă introduced the first legislative proposal on the use of Greek Catholic church buildings in November 1992. The two-article proposal, registered at the Senate as PL 189, received the support of Greek Catholic Archbishop Lucian Muresan and Orthodox Metropolitan Nicolae Corneanu, though other Orthodox Church leaders denounced it. According to parliamentary rules, proposals are first discussed by the chamber where they are introduced, and then sent to the other chamber for approval. Before the final vote, each chamber asks the parliamentary committees to review the proposal and make a recommendation that is, nevertheless, not binding on the full house. Four months later, the Senate sent it to three, instead of the usual two, parliamentary committees for discussion. The committees endorsed the proposal, but on 3 November 1994 the Senate leadership met with church leaders without reaching common ground. A week later, the chamber set the proposal aside, as requested by Senate secretary Tudor.[18]

During the 1992–1996 legislature, the house made no further attempts to discuss the Greek Catholic restitution issue. Its reluctance to involve itself in the conflict transpired in an open letter Senate Speaker Oliviu Gherman sent in 1994 to the leaders of the two churches. The letter noted that "five years after the December 1989 revolution in some Transylvanian localities the Greek Catholic cannot worship because of lack of churches" and that the December 1989 and April 1990 decrees remained a dead letter in most rural and urban Transylvanian localities because of dissensions, tensions, or open conflict between local church representatives. Although recognizing that "there were many failed attempts to solve the problem through dialogue," Gherman called on the Orthodox and Greek Catholic leaders to "solve their divisions in an ecumenical spirit so that there was no need for the Senate to adopt a law regulating a problem whose solution must be exclusively the result of Christian love."[19]

The Greek Catholic Church saluted with renewed hope the change in government and the transfer of power to the Democratic Convention after the 1996 general elections. As the Convention's driving force, the National Christian Democrat Peasant Party appointed several high-ranking cabinet members, including the State Secretary for Religious Denominations, but its accession to power did not lead to significantly more Greek Catholics entering parliament. (Until 1996, only the Christian Democrats nominated legislators from among the Greek Catholics.) Instead of appointing as secretary a person independent from all major religions recognized in the country, the Democratic Convention first chose Gheorghe Anghelescu, a graduate of the Sibiu Faculty of Orthodox Theology, and then Nicolae Brânzei, the Orthodox priest of the tiny village of Boteni, Argeş county, where Christian Democrat leader Ion Diaconescu resided. Unsurprisingly, neither was willing to champion the Greek Catholic cause, allowing the State Secretariat to continue to defend the Orthodox position. After Iliescu won the presidency in late 2000, and his Social Democrats formed the government, Orthodox theologian Laurenţiu Tănase became the State Secretary but was unable to settle the property restitution conflict during his four-year term. Despite the change in government brought about by the 2004 general elections, the politicians were unable to contribute significantly to the Orthodox–Greek Catholic property settlement.

In 1997, convinced that the government, through its legislative branch, had to settle a conflict it generated, Greek Catholic legislators registered with each chamber similar proposals allowing their church to use some of its former worship places. PL 158/1997 proposed to the Chamber of Deputies was rejected in September 2000 at the recommendation of the parliamentary committees. PL 312/1997 presented to the senators gained the approval of the committee on human rights. Believing that the bill placed it at a disadvantage, the Orthodox Church mounted pressure against both the proposal and the

Greek Catholic calls for legislating property restitution. In March 1997, the Holy Synod asked the Greek Catholic Church for reconciliation and unity but fell short in explaining how the Orthodox Church was to meet those standards. In response, Christian Democrat deputy Vasile Vetişanu blamed the previous Social Democrat government for refusing to address the issue and asked the Orthodox Church to relinquish the property soon because in the northern Transylvanian town of Satu Mare the Greek Catholic faithful had to celebrate Easter mass in the rain. Senator Peter Kovacs Eckstein pointed out that Orthodox priests "afraid of church leaders and community members refuse to return the churches [to the Greek Catholics]. The bill speaks to such priests and allows for an amiable solution to concrete problems." The Senate eventually adopted with a slim majority a modified version of the bill reading that "in villages where the Orthodox Church uses several churches that belonged to the Greek Catholic Church before 1948, at least one is to be returned to that Church at the request of the local Greek Catholic eparchy."[20]

Expecting opposition from the Chamber of Deputies during debates of the modified bill, Greek Catholics made an important concession and enlisted Pope John Paul II to their cause. In 1997, the pope called on Romania to hand back Greek Catholic property. While the country was predominantly Orthodox, he noted, Catholics constituted a "vital community," and "any tendency to see communities that came from abroad and sought to integrate themselves as dangerous can only weaken the country and its institutions."[21] Two years later, Greek Catholic negotiators declared their readiness to give up the request for *restitutio in integrum* if some 160 church buildings were handed over promptly. Their willingness to reach a compromise did not help the process. Two Chamber of Deputies committees examined the bill. Because the judicial committee rejected it, while the committee on human rights proposed amendments, the committees had to settle their differences in a common report, adopted in a session without quorum.[22] The chamber subsequently turned down the bill, though some deputies were sympathetic to the Greek Catholic cause. Vetişanu deplored the fact that "the [Orthodox] Church promotes hatred and discord. . . . We proclaim that the Orthodox Church is national but forget that it is first of all Christian, belongs to God first and only then to men."[23] Curiously, the bill was reintroduced in the Senate in late 2001, only to be rejected two months later with ninety-three votes against and only twenty-three in favor, after the committees on human rights and culture turned it down on technical grounds.

Blocked from all sides, in November 2001, the Greek Catholics and other minority religious groups appealed to the European Union for the elimination of discrimination against them and for the return of confiscated property as a precondition for Romania's acceptance in the union. Patriarch Teoctist's response summarized the Orthodox position. In his 12 February 2002 letter to Social Democrat Minister of Justice Rodica Stănoiu, the patriarch argued that, according to Decree Law no. 126, the legislature agreed to allow the mixed church commission to decide all issues pertaining to the worship places confiscated by the communists, and accepted church dialogue as a binding extrajudicial procedure to settle church restitution with the accord of local communities. The Supreme Court of Justice Decision no. 901 of 1996 and the Constitutional Court Decision no. 23 of 27 April 1993 upheld the procedure. In his plea, the patriarch referred to the 1993 Balamand document, which laid down the procedure for conflict settlement between the Orthodox and Greek Catholic Churches. Article 31 of the Balamand document recommended that "Christians resolve their differences through fraternal dialogue, thus avoiding recourse to the intervention of the civil authorities for a practical solution to the problems which arise between Churches or local communities. This applies particularly to the possession or return of ecclesiastical property."[24]

"The courts erroneously apply the secular law to church property ownership," the patriarch lamented, denouncing the "abusive interference" of the Ministry of Justice in the Orthodox-Greek Catholic litigations, together with the court decisions ordering the Orthodox Church to give up churches, chapels, and cathedrals. Stănoiu, in turn, sent the letter to all courts of appeal to be taken into account in the future, a gesture Greek Catholic lawyers vigorously criticized.[25] They pointed out that Decree Law no. 126 allowed for church dialogue without making it a requirement, the Constitutional Court and Supreme Court decisions recommended church dialogue without banning churches to petition the courts, and the constitution guaranteed for every citizen the right to petition the courts. In fact, they said, the Supreme Court ruled many times in cases of disputed churches, thus admitting that the secular law was applicable to such situations.[26]

As Romania was reviewed for European Union membership, the Social Democrat government stepped up pressure on both sides to find an acceptable compromise. On 5 April 2002, State Secretary Tănase mediated a meeting of Orthodox and Greek Catholic leaders, but the feisty negotiating partners were unable to bridge their differences. During discussions, Greek Catholic representatives deplored the fact that a mixed Orthodox-Greek Catholic committee met six times since 1998 without making real progress. Weeks later, 100 Greek Catholics participated in a mass organized in front of the Alba Iulia Orthodox cathedral. Priests from twenty-nine parishes appealed to Social Democrat Premier Adrian Năstase to end the discrimination against the Greek Catholic Church.[27]

In reply, Năstase suggested the government could initiate legislation to solve the conflict, because such restitution "is a promise we made to ourselves and the European Committee," but the State Secretariat retorted that most of the problem was already solved, since most Greek Catholics had remained Orthodox and 160 churches had been returned. "The restitution of the remaining Greek Catholic churches would block many [Orthodox] faithful from exercising their freedom of religion," the Secretary declared. When Greek Catholic Archbishop Lucian asked President Iliescu to convince the government not to limit restitution of Greek Catholic property confiscated by the communists, Iliescu replied that justice must be done to the extent that it does not lead to other injustices and reiterated the view that the state could not and should not interfere in the religious conflict.[28]

In October 2002, Orthodox and Greek Catholic leaders met again in Arad in a search for middle ground. The Greek Catholics requested the right to organize alternate mass in the church in localities with a single church that formerly was Greek Catholic (a practice known as *simultaneum*, using a Latin word). They also claimed back the Baia Mare and Oradea cathedrals and the Bucharest St. Basil church, together with all unused churches kept under lock by the Orthodox (far fewer than the roughly 1,800 worship places confiscated in the 1940s). The Orthodox side rejected even these reasonable demands, pointing out that 160 churches, including the Blaj, Cluj, and Lugoj cathedrals, had already been returned. The Orthodox negotiators were unwilling to make further concessions. For them it was evident that "you cannot take a church from 500 people and give it to twenty, because it would stay closed all the time," but Greek Catholics argued that people did not return to the Greek Catholic Church precisely because the churches were not given back.[29] Around 350 Greek Catholic parishes were still forced to celebrate mass in the open air, while seeking resources to build new worship places. For small, rural, Greek Catholic congregations, fundraising was a daunting task. For this reason, the government, through the State Secretariat, allotted the Greek Catholic Church funds three times larger than those warranted by its percentage in the population. From 1990 to 2001, the Secretariat had financially supported the construction of 220 new Greek Catholic churches, without being able to guarantee all Greek Catholic congregations the right to worship in consecrated churches.[30]

Arguments for and against Restitution

Different arguments have been proposed for and against the restitution of Greek Catholic churches still in the hands of the Orthodox Church. Supporters

saw them as persuasive, but these rationalizations have rested less on systematic and dispassionate reflection and more on circumstantial considerations and untested assumptions. Both sides have claimed that their position
was grounded rationally and historically, although their reading of the complex
history of Transylvania was often self-serving and selective. These justifications
have never before been systematized, but we believe that their identification
helps readers to grasp the markers of the debate on church restitution and to
understand that, ultimately, there is no real winner of the conflict.

The Church Involvement Argument

A justification frequently used to postpone parliamentary debates on alternative solutions to the Orthodox–Greek Catholic property conflict was the absence from debates of church representatives from either side. Several par-
liamentarians invoked this argument, although the parliament statutes
prohibit such a presence, especially when a bill is debated. In 1992 before the
Senate discussed Boilă's proposal, senators ignored the seriousness of claims
that many Greek Catholic congregations were forced to celebrate mass outdoors and argued, instead, that debates could not proceed in the absence of
church representatives. The call stemmed less from preoccupation with procedure and fairness, since bills affecting the life of other societal groups had
been debated in the absence of representatives of those groups, and more from
the desire of pro-Orthodox legislators to delay discussion of the legislative
proposal supported by their Greek Catholic colleagues.

On 24 April 1997, the Senate started debating a similar bill. In an unprecedented move, meeting chairman Cristian Dumitrescu read a letter from
Patriarch Teoctist, requesting that Orthodox Church representatives participate in the debates. Ironically, Dumitrescu represented the Democratic Party, a
junior partner in the government dominated by the Christian Democrats, who
were represented by the initiators of the Greek Catholic bill. The call opened
the gate for a heated debate pitting the government partners against each other
more than against the opposition. Rallying to the Orthodox viewpoint, Social
Democrat senator Vasile Văcaru asked for the chamber to send the proposal
back to the committees rather than discuss it in the absence of Orthodox
leaders, but independent senator Laurențiu Ulici reprimanded Dumitrescu for
reading a private letter addressed to the Senate Speaker, not the senators.
Taking the floor, Boilă doubted the Orthodox Church's intention to participate
constructively in debates, while Ioan Moisin lamented that "church dialogue
will not bring justice to the Greek Catholics! We have no other choice but to
adopt a law on the restitution of Greek Catholic churches and assets." Social

Democrat Sergiu Nicolaescu (arguably Romania's most popular movie director) noted that he did not remember ever, for a party other than the initiator,
that the cabinet ministers and the legislators had to give parliament permission to discuss bills. "According to our Statutes," Nicolaescu said, "we have to
discuss the proposal today, since the representatives of the government, the
initiator, the parliamentary committee, and the Senate are present." Presented
with such arguments, the senators agreed to discuss a bill stipulating that in
localities with two churches at least one of which previously belonged to the
Greek Catholic Church, reconstituted Greek Catholic parishes must be allowed
to use one of the churches.[31]

The Governmental Solution Argument

Also in 1997, another argument was used to delay the debate on the same bill.
It proposed leaving it to the government to solve the church restitution issue.
Democrat Senator Corneliu Gavaliugov deplored the fact that the agreement
reached in the early 1990s in trilateral discussions involving parliament and
the two churches remained unimplemented, but he offered no details on the
nature of the agreement. "This easily-solved problem remains prone to dem-
agogic discourse," he said, urging his colleagues to "allow the executive,
through the State Secretariat for Religious Denominations, to continue the
dialogue before adopting laws like the one proposed today." Christian Democrat Şerban Săndulescu reminded Gavaliugov that the State Secretariat
"had seven years to solve the problem" and rhetorically wondered "why our
[Orthodox] clergy do not address the rise of neo-protestant groups, but fight the
officially registered Greek Catholic Church, whose historical activity was so
beneficial to our Romanian people?" Nicolaescu best captured the essence of
the Orthodox accusation against Greek Catholics, when declaring:

> After the December 1989 regime change and the recognition of the
> Greek Catholic Church, fundamentalists on both sides hampered the
> property restitution process and sought to pit faithful against faithful
> in Transylvania. The Orthodox against their Greek Catholic brothers!
> They used calumnies and lies, skillfully manipulating the flock. . . . By
> accepting that "Romanian" equals "Orthodox," and "Catholic" equals
> "Hungarian," we negate the beginning of Christianity on our territory
> and the contribution of the Greek Catholic faith to the liberation of
> Transylvanian Romanians during the first half of the 18th centu-
> ry. . . . Are these Greek Catholics not Romanians because they have
> different Christian beliefs?![32]

The Membership Argument

The Orthodox have often pointed out the discrepancy between the small number of members of Greek Catholics in Romania and their enormous restitution claims. In 1997, Christian Democrat deputy Ioan Vida Simiti deplored the fact that, for some Romanians, the Greek Catholic property restitution represented the problem of "an insignificant religious minority, whose exaggerated claims run counter to the national interests." Instead, he contended that the small Greek Catholic congregations were the result of nothing short of a "religious genocide" that needed to be promptly stopped in its tracks. To support his position, Simiti read in parliament a letter from the General Association of Greek Catholic Romanians applauding the Senate's endorsement of legislative proposal PL 312/1997 and reminded senators that the bill allowed the church to get back "only the church buildings it needed for its eparchies." The letter reaffirmed that conversion to Greek Catholicism "opened for the Romanian people the road to Europe and launched the national building process." The dismantling of the Greek Catholic Church in 1948 represented "an arbitrary act against human rights." During communist times, the Greek Catholic Church "offered sustained resistance, losing over 1.5 million faithful, including its bishops." According to the letter, the church's losses constituted a "veritable spiritual and physical genocide, the largest and gravest among communist injustices. To cite statistics showing that today the Greek Catholics constitute less than 1 percent of the country's population (compared to 10 percent in 1948) should give no satisfaction but call for reflection over a tremendous historical error."[33]

The New Constructions Argument

As a corollary to the membership argument, one could add the Orthodox pleas that Greek Catholics abandon their restitution claims in order to rely instead on the state or the local communities to build new churches for them. On 27 May 1997, legislators received a programmatic document from Archbishop Bartolomeu Anania and seven archpriests of the Orthodox Archbishopric of Cluj, Vad, and Feleac titled "Concrete Proposal for Confessional Reconciliation." The document noted that the interference of secular forces marked the two most painful historical moments in the life of the Transylvanian Greek Catholic and Orthodox Churches:

> In 1700, the Catholic Church took advantage of the historical context and, with the support of thirty-eight Orthodox priests, implanted

Greek Catholicism in Transylvania. Secular forces quashed the Orthodox resistance. The persecution was long and painful. In 1948, the Romanian Orthodox Church took advantage of the historical context and, with the support of thirty-seven Greek Catholic priests, considered its right to recover the faithful it lost in 1700, thus proclaiming religious unity. Secular forces quashed the Greek Catholic resistance. The persecution was long and painful.

The document contended that "for reconciliation to become a reality both parties should make practical, realistic proposals in good faith." Surprisingly, the plea for rationality was immediately followed by the rather unreasonable demand that the Greek Catholic leaders "give up proposals such as church restitution, equal church division, and alternate church use. To continue to press forth these proposals is to fuel long-term confessional hatred." Thus, the petitioners dismissed all proposals allowing Greek Catholics to enter their former churches on a full-time or part-time basis. Regretting that in their eparchy "the Orthodox have good ecumenical relations with all traditional Christian churches of the Hungarian ethnic minority but not with our Romanian brothers," the Transylvanian Orthodox leaders proposed "that churchless Orthodox and Greek Catholics build their own worship places with the generous support of peace-loving Transylvanians, even if the state ignores the obligation it assumed through Decree Law no. 126 of 1990 and contributes nothing."

The proposal conveniently allowed the Orthodox to keep and use formerly Greek Catholic churches even when they did not strictly need them, and it transferred the financial burden of settling the conflict from the Orthodox Church to the Transylvanian local communities and the Romanian state. Christian Democrat deputy Pavel Tănase Tavală criticized the document for presenting exclusively the Orthodox Church viewpoint on the Transylvanian confessional conflict and the history of Orthodox-Greek Catholic relationships. Noting that "differences in interpretation of the post-1948 events and clergy vanity hampered church dialogue," the deputy suggested that the conflict stemmed from "lack of understanding and tolerance between the two Churches." For Tavală, "the Greek Catholic Church has always considered itself a Romanian Church and has actively promoted the cause of Romanianism," a reason that strengthened its claim to church restitution.[34]

The Unconstitutionality Argument

Before the vote on PL 312/1997, the Senate invited State Secretary for Religious Denominations Gheorghe Anghelescu to voice the executive's position vis-à-vis the bill. In his address, Anghelescu declared that the adoption of a restitution law amounted to unconstitutional state interference in church affairs: "We [the State Secretariat] believe that the adoption of a law on the use of churches can be construed as state interference in church affairs," in virtue of Article 29.5 of the 1991 constitution, which provided for the separation of church and state. Anghelescu recommended further church negotiations and insisted that the conflict was purely religious in nature. His position was embraced by the opposition Social Democrats. Dumitru Pâslaru and Stefan Cazimir believed that church dialogue had already led to significant progress, many restitution claims being "bridged amiably" without state interference. For Petre Turlea, the bill was unacceptable on a number of levels. First, it was undemocratic "because it disregarded the community's right to democratically decide the use of the churches it built." Second, it ran counter to the Balamand document signed in 1993 by the Orthodox and Roman Catholic international ecumenical dialogue partners, which encouraged the two churches to recognize that "church dialogue must start from current realities, recent censuses must be trusted, the religious majority must choose the owner of the worship places, and disputes over Greek Catholic churches must be solved through dialogue with the Orthodox." Third, the bill "created the premise for serious religious conflict among Transylvanian Romanians with potentially grave consequences for our unitary nation-state. The initiators play into the hands of those who would wish for Romania to cease to be a unitary state."

By contrast, Liberal senators condemned the State Secretary for his partiality and wondered whether "somebody who took so violently and blatantly the side of one religious denomination deserved to remain a member of the executive." The bill had its enthusiastic supporters from among the government and opposition representatives. Damian Brudașca, representing the opposition Greater Romania Party, saw the legislative proposal as "the only way to make justice to the Greek Catholic Church." "The fact that an ecclesiatical commission was set up does not guarantee the successful solution to Greek Catholic problems," Brudașca said, voicing a comment other politicians endorsed but were reluctant to say aloud. The deputy considered "the executive and legislative branches of government directly responsible for the way this problem is solved. We need a law because the state created the problem in the first place." After the vote, Brudașcă declared that he was 'shocked' by the bill's rejection, but his Social Democrat colleague Viorica Afrasinei insisted that the rejection "reflected the bill's shortcomings, not parliament's rejection of the Greek Catholic Church."[35]

The Dissolution Argument

Both the Orthodox and the Greek Catholics have occasionally favored either the merger of the two religious groups (through more or less voluntary conversion) or the return to the communist state of affairs. However unrealistic, these arguments demonstrate the wide range of proposals considered in an effort to end the dispute. In 1997, Turlea denounced the Greek Catholics' "Jesuit reading of Romanian history" and provided his own interpretation of Transylvanian history:

> In 1700, the churches of Transylvanian Romanians came under papal jurisdiction.... In 1948, the Orthodox Church received all Romanian churches in Transylvania. What kind of injustice are we called to address? The 1948 one? Why not the 1700 one? Recently, the Roman Catholic Church launched an offensive against Orthodoxy and the states that support it.... The destruction of Orthodoxism means Romania's destruction, since the Romanian people were born Orthodox, as was the Romanian state.... It is absolutely necessary to unite around the Orthodox Church. Such unity is an act of patriotism.

Greater Romania Party deputy Dumitru Bălăeţ embraced the view, insisting that "the Romanian people were born Orthodox. Orthodoxy protected and helped us through good and bad times. The creation of the Romanian principalities and their unification was the result of many factors, the most important one being the Orthodox Church." Independent senator Costică Ciurtin rhetorically asked, "Why the fight for church supremacy, for conquering the souls of the believers, when the normal course is the [Greek Catholics'] return to our mother [Orthodox] Church? Did anybody ever ask ordinary people what they believe in and what faith they opt for? Or do church leaders decide their faith as they did 300 years ago?" Deploring the Greek Catholic attacks against the Orthodox Church, Ciurtin voiced satisfaction that the 1948 "political act" leading to the dismantling of the Greek Catholic Church did not result in closure of churches. For him, "churches belong to the eparchies turned Orthodox, and many Greek Catholic priests celebrate mass in their old church. Part of the Greek Catholic clergy converted, and many of those who have attacked our national church receive their pensions from the Orthodox Church."[36]

In 1999, a Greek Catholic senator put forth a rather surprising suggestion for Orthodox–Greek Catholic reconciliation. In a passionate speech, Moisin told legislators that opinion polls suggested that over half of the Romanian citizens

want political and military alliance with the West, although the latter
is predominantly Catholic, while Romania is Orthodox. Whereas the
West had Rome as a spiritual reference point, Romania looked at
Constantinople and Moscow [for guidance]. The time has come to
choose. It is impossible to lead a boat whose political motor steers
toward the West, while the spiritual motor leads in the direction of the
Slavic and Byzantine East. You cannot look politically to the West and
spiritually to the East because sooner or later you will enter a vicious
circle.[37]

Moisin offered the Greek Catholic Church, "the Romanians' only spiritual
bridge between the West and the East," as a solution to post-communist Romania's conundrum. Not only did the Church "obey Rome, but it maintained
the Orthodox rite and tradition." Greek Catholics recognized the primacy of
Rome, "as did the Romanian people in the first millennium when it was
entirely Catholic." Thus, the Orthodox conversion to Greek Catholicism has a
historical precedent and would help the people revert to their initial state of
religious awareness. Moisin continued:

> Church unity is possible in Romania if we keep the rite, tradition,
> organization, books, and churches but during mass remember
> first the Holy Father. There is no difference between the Orthodox
> and Greek Catholic churches besides papal primacy. If this [unity]
> happens before the year 2000, then: (1) the West would accept
> us without reserve, (2) we would become an example for all the other
> Orthodox churches today, when Orthodox and Catholic Christians
> must unite against the rise of Islam, (3) God would bestow on us
> his help because he wishes more than anything that divisions among
> Christians end.[38]

While extremely original, the proposal was seen as utterly simplistic
and historically inaccurate, and therefore it was never seriously considered by
the leadership of the two churches or their faithful. For the Orthodox, conversion to Greek Catholicism at the prompting of political or religious luminaries would resemble the 1700 top-down introduction of Greek Catholicism
in the country. For the Greek Catholics, conversion to Orthodoxy would re-
mind them of 1948 and betray the memory of all the hierarchs, clergy, and
faithful who spent years or died in communist prisons for refusing to abandon
their church. Contrary to Moisin, the doctrinal differences between Orthodoxy
and Greek Catholicism extend beyond papal primacy to touch on fine dogmatic
points.

The Memorandum

In September 2002, after a decade of disappointment with the way the Romanian authorities managed the church restitution process, an "action committee" of Greek Catholic laypersons addressed a memorandum to President Iliescu, Prime Minister Năstase and his cabinet, the parliament speakers, and the Supreme Court of Justice president. The document asked for an end to the discrimination against their religious denomination in a number of areas. The most important demands referred to the restitution of Greek Catholic property the communist authorities confiscated in 1948. The Greek Catholic Church asked for the right to approach the courts, as negotiations with the Orthodox Church had proved inefficient. They demanded an end to the illegal demolishing and dismantling of their former churches by Orthodox congregations, legal protection for Greek Catholic churches listed as historical monuments, and the unconditional restitution of all Greek Catholic goods nationalized by the state (including land and forests). For the signatories, Decree Law no. 126 of 1990 was unconstitutional and the implied transfer of juridical powers from the state to a mixed ecclesiastic commission was illegal and abusive, because they limited the Greek Catholics' right to justice and allowed the state to give up its constitutional obligations. The memorandum appendixes reported on the situation of the Greek Catholic Church property in early 1948; the communist attempts to suppress the Greek Catholic Church through restrictive legislation; the unconstitutionality of Decree Law no. 126 of 1990; the fruitless dialogue with the Orthodox in the mixed commission; the discrepancy between the number of churches claimed and those returned as a result of the Orthodox–Greek Catholic dialogue; and the Greek Catholic churches demolished, dismantled, burned, or left derelict after 1989.[39]

The memorandum represented an important marker in the relations between the Greek Catholic Church, on the one hand, and the Orthodox Church and the state, on the other hand, because it shifted the responsibility for property restitution from the church to the state. While Decree Law no. 126 of 1990 encouraged the two churches to form a mixed commission in order to return Greek Catholic property found in Orthodox possession to its rightful owners, and implicitly exonerated the state of the responsibility for overseeing the process, the memorandum highlighted the shortcomings of the existing legislative process and the serious delays in settling the church restitution issue. While previous Greek Catholic positions condemned the Orthodox Church, the memorandum referred to it as "our sister church" that was the beneficiary of confiscated property, but not the actor who confiscated and nationalized the Greek Catholic worship places.

To persuade state representatives to make justice to the Greek Catholic Church, the authors of the memorandum proposed three types of arguments: juridical, historico-religious, and social. Each argument adopts a different angle to examine the church restitution issue. Taken together, these arguments form the clearest and most coherent Greek Catholic position on the topic to date.

The Juridical Argument

The juridical argument highlighted the promise that the rights to private property and religious freedom were constitutionally protected in Romania. In trying to respect them, the state was encouraged to act on a strictly juridical basis and ignore the small number of faithful in each Greek Catholic community. Following the memorandum, if other states were to guide themselves by the number of faithful, then the historically important but numerically small Orthodox Churches of Istanbul, Jerusalem, and Alexandria should have their property confiscated as well. Churches must return to the Greek Catholic Church because they were once the property of that denomination, belonging to the eparchy (as religious juridical person), not the parish community. The Greek Catholic Church in Romania is a juridical person and, according to Catholic canon law, only its bishops and metropolitan can represent it. In 1948, only the church leaders had the legal ability to transfer property, but most of them were already jailed at the time and could not do so. The memorandum went further to refute the Orthodox argument that a parish church belonged to the parish community, which could thus decide whether the building should be returned. Citing Metropolitan Corneanu, the memorandum argued that, following Orthodox canon lawyer Iorgu Ivan, a consecrated church ceased to be the property of the parish community, becoming instead the property of the Orthodox Church as an institution.[40] Thus, following the memorandum, even by Orthodox canon law a parish community had no input in the destination of its places of worship. Contrary to Decree Law no. 126 of 1990, Orthodox parish communities using formerly Greek Catholic churches should not decide on their return.

Orthodox theologians contradicted Corneanu's interpretation of canon law. In an e-mail to Turcescu, Rev. Dr. Alexandru Stan, a former canon law professor at the University of Bucharest Faculty of Orthodox Theology, wrote that Article 186 of the Statute on the Organization and Functioning of the Romanian Orthodox Church recognized "parishes, protopopiates, monasteries, eparchies, metropolitanates, and the patriarchate as juridical persons of public right."[41] Together with other Orthodox Church administrative structures, parishes were juridical persons able to represent their interests, including those related to property restitution. For Stan, the article showed that Orthodoxy emphasized the role of the local church, whereas Roman Catholicism emphasized the universal church and the role of the bishop and the pope. Patriarchate legal councilor Ion Neagu further argued that

> the restitution of [Greek Catholic] worship places and parish houses cannot be realized within the limited framework of property rights consecrated by civil right. Acknowledging a property right on the basis of an existing property title is not always fully acceptable, given the special character of the property under consideration. By their nature, places of worship are sacred goods, and the property of the community of faithful. [They] are inalienable and imprescriptible goods available for the use of that community.[42]

Orthodox theologian Nicolae Dura referred to several canons of the early church in order to suggest that no bishop was allowed to transfer or sell property belonging to local communities under his jurisdiction.[43] Following Dura, Metropolitan Corneanu wrongfully ignored the canons when returning property to the Greek Catholics against the wishes of the local Orthodox parishes using those churches. In 2004, the metropolitan indicated that he returned all Greek Catholic churches in his diocese because he was shocked by the abuses the Greek Catholic Church endured when it was forceably disbanded in 1948. He further suggested that, in the interwar period (1918–1944), intercommunion between the Orthodox and Greek Catholic Churches was widely practiced and accepted in Transylvania and Banat, where it was customary for the Greek Catholic priest to replace the Orthodox priest in the church when the latter went on vacation. Because Orthodox Church leaders in Bucharest have remained oblivious to that attitude of collaboration, Corneanu argued that many Orthodox regard the Greek Catholics as their competitors.[44]

The memorandum raised two additional issues concerning the respect and defense of property rights in Romania. First, it asked the state to end discrimination against minority groups by returning property confiscated from the Greek Catholic Church, the Roman Catholics, the Reform Church, the Jews, the Germans, and the Hungarians. Whereas non-Romanian groups have enjoyed the protection of foreign governments, the predominantly Romanian Greek Catholics have not. True, the Vatican intervened on behalf of the Greek Catholics, but not as strongly as for the Roman Catholic Church, and not so much with the Romanian state, but with the Orthodox Church. The Holy See perhaps was reluctant to push too hard at a time when the late Pope John Paul II wished to heal the rifts between the Roman Catholic Church and the Eastern European Orthodox Churches. Second, the memorandum noted that Decree Law no. 126 of 1990 was unconstitutional, because it was never amended to accord with the 1991 Romanian constitution. It did not provide for the return of landed domains that represent a large part of Greek Catholic property. It allowed the state to control the restitution process, although the state confiscated the property in 1948. It permitted the executive branch of government to delegate authority to a mixed ecclesiastical commission. It allowed the state to ignore its responsibility of discharging justice through its law courts and leave this task to the commission dominated by the beneficiaries of the confiscated Greek Catholic churches and parish houses, the Orthodox.

The Historical-Religious and Social Arguments

While less developed and generally less persuasive than the juridical argument, the historical-religious arguments made reference to Romania's desire to join NATO and the European Union to argue that the Greek Catholic Church provided one of the best links to Western Europe. The section started by watering down the differences between the Romanian Orthodox and the Greek Catholics. "One doctrine, different rites" was the message the memorandum promoted. Both religious groups affirm one faith but do so in different ways and with the help of different rites. The document then engaged in a lengthy presentation of oft-cited historical arguments crediting the Greek Catholic Church with Romanian national awakening. Most of these arguments have already been presented in this chapter, and therefore are not mentioned below.

According to the memorandum, the union with Rome in 1700 allowed Transylvanian Romanians to have access to better Western education and culture and thus to discover the Latin roots of the Romanian people. Greek Catholic priests were educated in the Latin language in Rome, not in Slavonic in St. Petersburg as some Orthodox clergy were. It was the Greek Catholics who first pointed to the Latin origins of the Romanian language and people, while downplaying their ties to the Eastern, Slavonic world. The memorandum engaged in an ampler historical discussion before mentioning the eighteenth-century Greek Catholic Bishop Inochentie Micu, "a remarkable personality" who gave his life promoting the rights of all Transylvanian Romanians, regardless of their religious affiliation. For the authors of the memorandum, the recognition of Transylvanian Romanians as a nation, not just a tolerated population, as a result of Micu's efforts represented the historical equivalent of

Romania's current efforts to be accepted as a full member of the European Union. This historical parallel was viewed as another argument in favor of church restitution in Transylvania.

The social argument emphasized the social role the Greek Catholic Church traditionally played in Transylvania. The social role, materialized in aid programs and charitable work benefiting the children, the elderly, persons with special needs, and the poor, could be reinstated if the Greek Catholic Church would regain its proper place and status in Romanian society. The memorandum further quoted the opinions of important Romanian cultural and historical luminaries who held the Greek Catholic Church in high regard. The document concluded by summarizing its major demands: respect for human rights, including freedom of religion, self-determination and collective autonomy, peaceful coexistence with the Orthodox Church, and *restitutio in integrum* of property seized by the communists. Thus, the document signaled the Greek Catholic Church's willingness to return to its initial position, the one least palatable to the Orthodox Church.

Conclusion

Today, the restitution of the Greek Catholic churches abusively confiscated by the communist regime remains as divisive and as far from an amiable settlement as it was in 1990, when it first emerged. Small concessions were made by both sides over the years. Some Orthodox leaders have surrendered Greek Catholic places of worship in their diocese, as reparation for the communist injustices inflicted on the Greek Catholic Church. The Greek Catholics have progressively scaled down their requests, abandoning *restitutio in integrum* in favor of receiving only the churches that would allow congregations to organize mass inside rather than outdoors. In the end, neither side was fully committed to solving the conflict. The Orthodox turned down the reasonable demand for alternate use of churches, while Greek Catholics recently returned to the *restitutio in integrum* request.

In this conflict, the two denominations have spoken from strikingly different positions. As the aggrieved party and a small religious minority, the Greek Catholic Church has had little leverage in making its voice heard during the conflict mediation process other than by adopting a more intransigent or more conciliatory position, or by asking for help from international actors. Initially, the church asked for *restitutio in integrum* in the hope of getting at least some of its property back. The strategy backfired, prompting the Orthodox Church to demand compensation for the churches it lost in 1700. Some would dismiss such claims as unjustified, but in divided Transylvania, historical arguments never fully support only one view. Retribution for past injustices opens the door for competing claims that are never more legitimate just because they are more recent. The Greek Catholic Church received major recognition in December 2005, when Pope Benedict XVI raised it to the status of a Major Archbishopric and promoted its head, Lucian Mureşan, to the rank of major archbishop with authority similar to that of the Eastern Catholic patriarchs. In churches at the rank of Major Archbishopric, the key decisions, including the election of bishops in the home territories, are made by their synods of bishops rather than imposed from above by the Vatican. The papal decision made the Romanian Greek Catholic Church the fourth major archbishopric in the Catholic Church, after the Ukrainian Catholic Church and the Indian Syro-Malabar and Syro-Malankara Catholic Churches.[45]

As the main beneficiary of the status quo and the country's dominant religious group, the Orthodox Church has had the ability to set the terms of a dialogue in which procrastination has worked solely in its favor. In dozens of Transylvanian villages, the Orthodox priest and faithful denied Greek Catholics access to their former church, even when the Orthodox had no plans to use the Greek Catholic church building, either because they already had their own or because the Greek Catholic place of worship was old and crumbling. Except for Banat, where Metropolitan Corneanu ordered the return of the churches, in no other Transylvanian region did the Orthodox priests voluntarily relinquish the Greek Catholic churches. Officially, the Orthodox Church leaders called for continuous dialogue and fraternal understanding. Unofficially, they allowed and encouraged the Transylvanian priests to adopt extreme positions that went far beyond mere protection of their interests and escalated into full-blown conflict, led to the destruction of historical monuments, and resulted in the illegal selling of Greek Catholic land. It seems as though the conflict is not limited to church restitution but hides a larger Orthodox campaign of intimidating and harassing Greek Catholics who are unwilling to convert to Orthodoxy.

The major culprit for this state of affairs remains the Romanian state, whose unwillingness to treat all religious groups evenhandedly has allowed the Orthodox Church to impose its view on church restitution. While paying lip service to democratic principles, successive Romanian governments of all ideological persuasions have denied Greek Catholics and other groups wronged by the communist regime the right to approach the courts. Not surprisingly, these groups have sought justice outside the country by petitioning the European Court of Human Rights for recognition of their rights. In 2003, the European Court admitted the petition of the Greek Catholics in Suciu de Jos, a small Maramureş village, for the return of their former church. A number of other Transylvanian Greek Catholic congregations announced their plans to approach the European Court in Strasbourg in the near future. Regardless of the final decision reached by the European justices, the Suciu de Jos case could set an important precedent for the Orthodox-Greek Catholic property restitution.[46]

The United States government's annual reports on human rights around the world continue to single out Romania for discriminating against the Greek Catholic Church. In its 2004 and 2005 reports, issues such as property restitution, church registration, harassment by Orthodox clergy, and access to cemeteries figured prominently.[47] Recent cases demonstrate that the Romanian local authorities continue to disregard the law and side with the Orthodox against the Greek Catholics. In January 2005, the local council of the Pesceana village, Vâlcea county, illegally forbade registration of the Greek Catholic parish in the locality. The police disregarded Greek Catholic complaints of verbal and physical abuse by Orthodox villagers and their priest. The police chief was fired, but only because the case became known to the national mass media. In an unprecedented move, the local council was reprimanded for its discriminatory decision by the National Council for Combating Discrimination, a government structure that never before intervened in the Orthodox–Greek Catholic property conflict.

6

Religion and Elections

The literature on elections in Romania has grown exponentially since citizens won the right to elect and be elected to public office after the collapse of the communist regime, but to date no study has dealt systematically with the influence of religious actors and symbols on electoral campaigns. Nevertheless, elections and party politics have best illustrated the politicians' readiness to take advantage of church-state ties, and the religious denominations' eagerness to reassert their role and shape democracy according to their vision.[1] In the aftermath of the December 1989 regime change, Romania moved quickly to adopt permissive legislation encouraging political parties to compete in elections for the right to form the government. Parties needed only 251 members to register, and as a result some 200 formations spanning the entire political spectrum were set up in a matter of months. Polls were organized in 1990, 1992, 1996, 2000, and 2004 (local elections in June; parliamentary and presidential elections concomitantly in November). In local elections, citizens chose mayors directly and local and county council members indirectly. A mixed proportional representation system with party lists and deputy seats set aside for designated minority groups was adopted for electing the 140 members of the upper Senate and the 345 members of the lower Chamber of Deputies. The president is elected directly from among candidates who gather at least 100,000 support signatures. A runoff between the two candidates who won the highest share of the national vote was organized in every electoral year but 1990, because no candidate won a majority of the vote in the first round.

In 1990, Ion Iliescu, former collaborator of communist dictator Nicolae Ceauşescu, became Romanian president. He renewed his mandate in 1992 but lost four years later to geology professor Emil Constantinescu, whose candidacy was supported by the Democratic Convention, a coalition including the Christian Democrats and Liberals as main partners. After serving as Social Democrat senator for four years, in 2000 Iliescu made a spectacular comeback, winning the presidency in the second round and defeating the country's staunchest nationalist, the Greater Romania Party leader Corneliu Vadim Tudor. Four years later, Iliescu's successor at the helm of the Social Democrat Party, Adrian Năstase, lost the presidential race in favor of Democrat Party leader Traian Băsescu. In 1990, the Salvation Front, representing the revolutionary anti-Ceauşescu forces, won parliamentary representation and appointed Petre Roman as premier, but a year later, under pressure from disgruntled Jiu Valley miners, technocrat Teodor Stolojan replaced Roman. The following year the Front—by then renamed the Social Democracy Party—won a plurality of seats in parliament and nominated Nicolae Văcăroiu as premier, but in 1996 political power reverted to the Democratic Convention. Plagued by internal dissension, the Convention appointed three cabinets in four years, was unable to fulfill its electoral promises, and became entangled in scandals of corruption and nepotism.

With little support from within and without the Convention, Constantinescu abandoned politics, leaving the Convention without a presidential candidate just months before the poll. Caught off guard, the Convention imploded and failed to secure parliamentary representation in the general elections of 2000. The Social Democrats formed the government under Năstase's leadership. Although registering success in some limited areas, the cabinet came to be known for rampant corruption, economic mismanagement, and intimidation of its critics. Despite its shattered reputation, in 2004 the Social Democrat Party won a plurality of seats in the house, but President Băsescu refused to accept a government that did not include his Truth and Justice Alliance. Behind-the-scene negotiations allowed the Alliance to appoint Călin Popescu Tăriceanu as head of an unstable cabinet reuniting Democrats, Liberals, Conservatives, and representatives of the Democratic Union of Magyars in Romania.

Religion and Party Politics

The interplay between religion, on the one hand, and elections and party politics, on the other, is best illustrated by several interrelated areas reflecting the continuous negotiation between religious and political actors in search of a balance acceptable to both sides. These areas are the following: (1) direct involvement of priests and prelates in politics as members of parties and as electoral candidates running for either local or central (or both) governmental office; (2) support given by religious leaders and clergy to electoral candidates in exchange for promises to adopt legislation favorable to their religious group; and (3) electoral candidates' use of religious symbols to win additional votes.[2]

In Romania there are substantive differences between religious denominations in terms of what they can offer to and can demand from the political elite. The dominant Orthodox Church has proved to be a force to be reckoned with and an indispensable ally for any presidential candidate and political party seeing the support of a large electoral segment. By contrast, evangelical Protestant groups and new religious movements lack the numbers that would make them attractive to politicians and parties, and they seldom play a role in electoral campaigns. Most Roman Catholic and Reformed faithful are drawn from among the Transylvanian German and Hungarian minorities, each represented politically by a democratic federation of political parties. While ethnic political formations enjoy the support of their specific churches, a host of political parties compete for the support of the Orthodox Church and its predominantly Romanian faithful. This makes for a different dynamic in the relationship between religious and political leaders and explains the vocal and prominent role the Orthodox Church has tended to assume in electoral campaigns, compared with other religious denominations.

The political involvement of religious leaders is not a novelty to Romania. In pre-communist times, the clergy were actively involved in elections, advising parishioners to vote for candidates, blessing electoral banners, and praising their favorite parties from the pulpit. For a brief period, Patriarch Miron Cristea was a member of the regency that ruled the country on behalf of child King Michael, after King Carol II nonchalantly gave up the throne to marry divorcee Elena Lupescu. The 1923 constitution recognized Orthodox and Greek Catholic Church leaders (including the Orthodox patriarch, metropolitans, and bishops and the Greek Catholic cardinal, archbishops, and bishops) as senators. In the interwar period, many Orthodox priests joined the fascist Iron Guard and Legion of Archangel Michael, paramilitary organizations opposing Soviet communism and extolling Orthodoxy as central to Romanian identity. In the 1946 elections, priests actively campaigned against the communist forces.[3]

Communist authorities sought to build a society where religion had virtually no place and launched a sustained campaign against religious organizations. Monasteries were dismantled; thousands of religious leaders were imprisoned, beaten, and murdered in communist detention centers; the Greek Catholic Church was banned and its property transferred to the Orthodox Church. Elections had predetermined outcomes, so there was no need to enlist clergy support to ensure a good voter turnout or a result favorable to communist candidates. However, the authorities did forge a tacit understanding with the Orthodox Church, which became ever more subservient to the regime to the point that Patriarch Teoctist joined the leadership of the Socialist Democratic Front, an organization controlled by the Communist Party.

Clergy Political Involvement

After 1989, the Orthodox Church leaders advised clergymen to refrain from participating in politics, joining parties, running for public office, and influencing their parishioners' political options. At a January 1990 meeting, the Holy Synod banned priests from engaging "in any form of political partisanship," including party membership; allowed bishops to sanction politically active priests and monks; and obliged priests holding public office to cease their priestly activity for the duration of the political mandate. This latter provision forbade priests to collect a salary from the church while receiving wages for performing public office duties. But at a time when the Orthodox leadership was vehemently opposed for its collaboration with the communist regime and the synod was divided between reformers and conservatives, most priests and monks disregarded the recommendation.

Synod Decision no. 1066 of 1996 reiterated that "according to the canon law, bishops, priests, deacons, and the spiritual fathers of all faithful will abstain from running in elections to become deputies or senators. Priests and monks are called to fulfill their spiritual mission, incompatible with a systematic party engagement." The decision banned clergy from becoming active party members, but left the door open to political involvement by permitting priests to run in elections as independent candidates.[4] In February 2000, at the beginning of another electoral year, the synod reminded priests that they could run in local but not general elections and only as independent candidates, if they secured the approval of their superiors. The Orthodox leadership further specified that, in light of canonical laws on political neutrality, clergy should abstain from openly supporting parties and candidates. Because of its vague formulation and lack of sanctions, the decision was treated as a mere recommendation. Bishops failed to sanction politically active priests and allowed priests holding public office to say mass, perform religious services like marriage and baptism, speak from the pulpit, and hear confession. By design or accident, the decision offered priests the possibility of contributing to politics in the hope of obtaining tangible advantages for the Orthodox Church or their parish, while showing general society, the political elite, and other religious denominations that the Orthodox Church as an institution opted for political neutrality.

Political neutrality was the Orthodox Church's official policy during subsequent elections, but clergymen did not live up to that commitment. Scores of Orthodox clergy joined or supported political parties. In the early 1990s, Metropolitan Nestor Vornicescu of Oltenia, Bishop Calinic Argatu of Argeş, and Archimandrite Simeon Tatu of the Plumbuita monastery were among sympathizers of the Salvation Front and its subsequent incarnations. Known for his steadfast support for Ceauşescu, Vornicescu even agreed to be included on the Front's electoral lists, only to withdraw his candidacy at the last minute because of public protests over his decision. Less intimidated by public resentment, Tatu represented the same party as a senator from May 1990 until his death in 1998. Metropolitan Nicolae Corneanu of Banat joined the pro-democratic Civic Alliance in December 1990 but never ran for political office. Father Ioan Roman represented the Christian Democrats in Parliament in the 1996–2000 period. An active participant in the June 1990 anti-government demonstration in Bucharest University Square, Father Simion Mehedinţu joined the Christian Democrat Alliance, a radical splinter group of the Christian Democrat Peasant Party, ten years later. Though not all Orthodox Church leaders became party members, most were rather open about their political loyalties. Archbishop Pimen Zainea of Suceava more than once admitted to his monarchist preferences, and Vornicescu and Metropolitan Antonie Plămădeală of Transylvania voiced their support for the nationalist Greater Romania Party.[5]

After 2000, an ever-growing number of Orthodox priests entered politics. Ilie Sârbu became minister of agriculture, and Ioan Aurel Rus renewed his mandate and continued to represent the Greater Romania Party in the Senate. The 2000 local elections allowed an unprecedented number of priests to become mayors and deputy mayors, as well as local and county council members, with party support. Gheorghe Radu and Gheorghe Supeală represented the Social Democrats in the Bucharest district councils, Ion Văran became a Democrat Party councillor in Caraş Severin county, and Viorel Mitru was a Greater Romania Party town councillor for Roman. In Cluj county, Titus Popovici joined the Greater Romania Party and Ioan Roman the Liberal Party, while Costin Morar became a county councillor for the Party for Romanian National Unity before switching sides to the Social Democrats. Teofil Bradea was elected mayor in Bihor county, while Dumitru Nistor, Gheorghe Bărănescu, and Petre Popa became mayors of villages in Argeş county. Accurate statistics are unavailable, but observers believe dozens of priests have held public office at all levels and have been committed to party ideology more than to Christian dogma. In late 2002, a Social Democrat priest refused to bless the new headquarters of the Suceava Christian Democrat Peasant Party organization. The refusal was seemingly determined not by the proposal's novelty, since Romanian priests customarily bless buildings, cars, and even animals, but by the fact that in 1997 a Timişoara Christian Democrat priest allowed former President Iliescu to be painted as Satan on one wall in his church.[6]

Orthodox priests were not the only ones to receive party cards, serve as electoral candidates, and be elected or nominated to public office. Greek Catholic priests Ioan Botiza and Matei Boilă became Christian Democrat Party members, and Boilă represented that party in the Senate from 1992 to early 2000, when he defected to the Christian Democrat Alliance. Social Democrat deputy Vasile Suciu was a leader in Oastea Domnului (an Orthodox revivalist movement) and admitted that his parliamentary adviser, Ion Pop, was a Baptist minister. A prominent Greater Romania Party leader was evangelical minister Ioan Miclea; former honorary president of the Democratic Union of Magyars Laszlo Tokes was the Reformed bishop of Piatra Craiului; and Reformed minister Sogor Csaba represented the Democratic Party in the Senate.

In the early 1990s, the synod turned a blind eye to priests becoming party members and running in elections, but by the end of the decade it became clear that the cases of politically involved clergy threatened to become the rule. The first attempt to reformulate the church's position on clergy political involvement occurred in April 1998, when Archbishop Bartolomeu Anania of Cluj announced plans to ask the synod to reverse its position and allow Orthodox clergy to get involved in politics and be elected to state office on party lists. Anania maintained that political neutrality exposed the Orthodox Church to vicious and unfair attacks from mass media and other denominations that did not observe this principle, and that in any case the synod's recommendation of political neutrality had been disregarded by Transylvanian priests, who took sides during electoral campaigns and ran for parliament without the blessing of their superiors. Thus, Anania maintained, the policy revision would merely keep up with reality.

The proposal was supported by Metropolitan Daniel Ciobotea of Moldova and popular University of Bucharest theology professor Constantin Galeriu, who declared that the Orthodox Church should openly promote luminaries known as "the nation's conscience" as candidates for parliament. Deputy Archbishop Gherasim Pruteanu of Suceava also said the church must enter politics for the country to preserve its Orthodox tradition and mentioned that political involvement did not necessarily mean that priests would join political parties but, rather, would warn parties that some of their legislative proposals "ran counter to our Christian Orthodox traditions." Pruteanu pledged to "support Anania's proposal because church and state were never truly separated. Wherever the ruler was, there the patriarch was, too!"[7]

While warmly embraced in Orthodox circles, the proposal was criticized by politicians and the mass media, which saw it as a serious impediment to the separation of church and state and the democratization process. The press campaign against the proposal was so sustained that the synod even refused to consider it seriously on grounds that it was not the right moment to discuss the Orthodox Church's political involvement. Quite unexpectedly, Anania's proposal forced the Roman Catholic Church to take a stand on clergy political involvement, although there were no reported cases of politically involved Roman Catholic priests. A declaration presenting the position of the Roman and the Greek Catholic Churches stressed the commitment of those two religious groups to political neutrality, added that they "will respect the citizen's right of opinion" (indirectly suggesting that their clergy will refrain from endorsing specific parties or candidates), and reiterated that the Second Vatican Council forbade Roman Catholic clergy and leaders to engage in politics.[8]

While the Orthodox synod rejected the proposal, some of its members quietly embraced its spirit. Bishop Calinic Argatul of Argeş decided to allow, even encourage, priests to secure eligible positions on party lists in the 2000 local elections. In an unprecedented move, the bishop personally sent letters to political parties asking for eligible positions on party lists for local priests. When his letters became known to the public, Calinic told the press that

> it is absolutely necessary for the priest to be first among citizens in his preoccupation for the spiritual and material problems of ordinary people. That is why we need priests as village and town councillors, mayors and deputy mayors. We also need priests in culture, social work, parliament, and even government, as ministers.... Since the Romanian Orthodox Church accounts for 86 percent of the country's population, [Orthodox] clergy should represent it in all state leadership structures.

Wary of the bishop's extraordinary sway on local affairs, and his tremendous popular appeal, the Social Democrats nominated Fathers Iulian Chiriţă, Cristian Ichim, and Nicolae Mărgăritescu to local councils.[9]

After the 2000 local poll, Anania came out strongly in favor of political neutrality and announced that the synod planned to discuss the increasingly numerous cases of politically active priests and propose sanctions for those who endorsed parties and candidates in their sermons. Anania warned that this time the synod was ready to hand out sanctions that could take the form of wage reductions or delays in promotion. It is unclear why Anania had a change of heart. Apparently, his support for sanctions against politically active clergy was a response to the fact that two priests of the Mănăştur parish in Cluj openly endorsed Gheorghe Funar's bid to renew his mayoral mandate against Anania's warning not to do so. The mayor of Cluj-Napoca from 1992 to 2004, Funar was known for his chauvinistic and anti-Hungarian stance and for painting the city garbage bins, benches, and signposts with the Romanian tricolor flag.

Anania found unexpected support from Calinic. When the Socialist Party announced that in Argeş seven priests were among its members and it planned to make Calinic a "serious offer" to convince him to join the party, Calinic retorted that "a clergy member should not climb down from the silence of the Holy Altar into the noisiness of politics." The bishop warned priests that if they wished to join parties, they would have to do so without his blessing, and if they already were party members, they should "rush to give up politics; otherwise they will be suspended." Jokingly, Calinic advised parties to take up "a confessor to whom party leaders and members tell their sins from time to time."[10]

Opposition to clergy political involvement mounted in early 2003, after Greater Romania Party leader Damian Brudaşcu boasted that three Cluj priests had joined the party. Hours later, Fathers Adrian Mitrea, Cristian Berinţan, and Constantin Neguţ resigned from the party under pressure from Anania, while the press revealed that the priests were not new party members. Mitrea had joined the party in 1998 because it had helped him build his village church. In 2000, Berinţan became a village councillor with Christian Democrat help, and a deputy mayor soon afterward. Unhappy at having to give up his party card under pressure, Berinţan bluntly told the press that "only mad people can believe that priests are not politically engaged. All of them are. We live in a democratic state, and nobody can limit my political options." In response, Anania reiterated that priests cannot be included on party lists or become party members but can run in elections as independent candidates.[11]

Opinions were divided with respect to enrollment of clergymen in political parties. Greater Romania Party senator Ioan Aurel Rus, the parish priest of Nepos village (Bistriţa-Năsăud county), described his situation as follows: "During my legislative mandate, I am suspended; that is, I am not remunerated as a priest. But each weekend I say mass, hear confession, and take care of all other parish problems." He saw his two positions as compatible and stressed that "as a Romanian citizen, I have the right to occupy public office, and as a priest I have never engaged in politics in my church, never urged people to vote for my party." But patriarchate spokesman Constantin Stoica said that priests like Rus

> ignore not only the synod's decision, but also church canons. . . . Of course, all of us have personal political opinions, but priests should not display them because this would divide the flock. The priest's only politics should be the Bible. A priest can make politics, as any other citizen, but then he must give up his activity within the church, stop saying mass and hearing confession, and refer to himself not as "Father X" but as "Mr. X."[12]

Romanian journalists believed that by becoming party members, priests "gave up the independence stipulated by [church] canons. They continue their religious activity and, even if not preaching from the pulpit the ideology of their respective parties, their party membership can influence parishioners." *Evenimentul Zilei* further noted that

> every four years, just before elections, the synod must review the priests' political engagement, a delicate problem since priests are "opinion leaders" and the church is among the most trusted institutions. If divulging their political preferences or dedicating themselves wholeheartedly to politics, priests can lead the flock "astray" towards one party or another. . . . Without declaring it openly, each party has a secret strategy for attracting the clergy [because] each one would like the church to become its turf. . . . Political engagement endangers [the religious principle of] "penitence." A Greater Romania Party bishop with two Social Democrat and two Liberal deputies, who oversees the activity of ten Democrat, two Christian Democrat, three Humanist [Conservative], and four Union for Romania's Rebirth priests does not have the same authority, cannot give the signal for unity.[13]

As new elections were slated for 2004, the Orthodox Church divided among those favoring political neutrality and those supporting political involvement of the clergy. In January 2003, Anania announced that the synod would hear the cases of the three Cluj priests who joined the Greater Romania Party and of Archbishop Teodosie of Tomis, known for his close ties to the ruling Social Democrats. Anania also announced that all Cluj priests who were party members or held public office were under investigation. According to the press, in the Cluj-Napoca council eight priests represented the Social Democrats, one the Liberals, and four the Democratic Party. Parties unanimously pleaded for priests to be allowed to take part in political and party life. Funar hoped that priests could continue to act as politicians and represent their communities in governmental structures, and Brudaşcu pleaded with the synod to permit the three priests to return to the Greater Romania Party. Brudaşcu criticized the priests for being unaware of the interdiction to engage in politics and recommended that the bishops clearly state the prohibition and identify the canons banning priests from politics.

Politicians joined forces with politically active priests to argue that party membership should be the personal choice of each Orthodox priest and to note that other denominations did not embrace political neutrality. The Cluj campaign manager of the Democratic Union of Magyars announced that party lists were open to priests who agreed to participate in internal elections. Since its founding in the early 1990s, the Union allocated 15 percent of its leadership positions to youth representatives, and another 15 percent to civil society and clergy. The Reform Church did not embrace political neutrality.[14] The Romanian constitution allows churches to decide whether priests can enter politics.

Reflecting the mood of the Orthodox leaders, the Archpriest of Moldovan county of Botoşani asked local priests not to engage in politics or run in local elections because, as he explained, the message of a party member targets a limited segment of the community, whereas the priest must talk to the entire flock. In response, Social Democrat Octav Cosmânca, leader of the strongest political formation in Moldova, argued that priests should be allowed to engage in politics since only the constitution and parliament could limit an individual's political right to be elected to public office. Cosmânca's position was echoed by premier Năstase, who said that as local and county councillors, priests bring a measure of morality to the political process and the way community problems are addressed. These political declarations were denounced by the opposition Liberals, who criticized the Social Democrats for their attempt to transform the Orthodox Church into their electoral tool.[15]

In February 2004, the synod upheld its decisions of January 1990, September 1992, February 1996, and February 2000 forbidding Orthodox clergy from engaging in politics, joining political parties, participating in electoral campaigns, running in elections, becoming members of parliament and local and county councils, becoming mayors or deputy mayors, and being nominated to positions in the local and central state administrative structures. Synod Decision no. 410 of 12 February 2004 asked priests to abstain from becoming politically active, even as independent candidates, and pleaded with political parties not to accept clergy as members and not to use clergy and places of worship for political purposes. On behalf of the patriarchate, Stoica announced that "the church is politically neutral, but not indifferent to the life of the polis. Its position remains the same: the only politics that priests should make is the Bible," and he warned that Orthodox priests had ten days to choose between politics and priesthood. He insisted that giving up the priesthood for short-term political gain was an irreversible act, with the priest being defrocked in perpetuity. That position was supported by Anania, who warned that "up to now the Synod made recommendations, but it can also give orders, if recommendations are disregarded," noted that priests could no longer suspend their religious activity for a four-year period to assume public office, and said that cases of politically active priests will be heard and settled by ecclesiastical courts.[16] No exceptions were to be made. Even mayor-priests had to make a choice, though they had been democratically elected and their mandate was about to expire in a matter of months when new elections were scheduled. According to Anania, the Orthodox Church leadership did not know the number of priests who became politicians because they entered politics without informing their bishops. Journalists announced that of Romania's 14,000 Orthodox priests, fewer than 200 held administrative positions and only a handful were active politically.[17]

Months after the synod meeting, unnamed sources revealed that the synod was presented with an alternative proposal allowing priests to enter politics as independent candidates. Supported by Teodosie and two unnamed "older hierarchs, extremely obedient to political rulers both during and after communism," this initiative was rejected in favor of Anania's proposal because Teodosie's close ties to the Social Democrats were seen as detrimental to the Orthodox Church. Though it reportedly "scandalized" politician-priests, the synod's ban was hailed by civil society and journalists as a step forward in the effort to end Social Democrat attempts to enroll the clergy politically. The press saw the decision to defrock politician-priests as unprecedented and reflective of the fact that the dominant religious group had consolidated its position: not only did it remain the country's most trusted institution, but also it found the courage to adopt a critical stance toward the state and the parties that vied to control it.[18]

It took considerable determination to enforce the ban and to convince politician priests that it was definitive and irrevocable. Two weeks after the synod adopted the proposal and four days after the deadline, the archbishopric of Cluj announced that only one priest—Greater Romania Party Senator Rus—had renounced the priesthood, while eighty-seven priests from Cluj and Bistriţa counties had given up politics. Of the sixty Cluj priests who renounced politics, thirty-two represented the Social Democrats, one the Liberals, and three the Democratic Party. In Argeş, one of the three Social Democrat mayor-priests announced that he would choose politics over priesthood because "I served the church for thirty-five years, now it is time to serve the community." The Băiculeşti mayor, nicknamed Părintele Furtună (Father Storm), pledged to ignore the synod's call, run in the 2004 local elections, and, if needed, "start a new revolution because I cannot choose between being a mayor and a priest, since the two go well together. If I have to give up the mayor's office, I will start another revolution [within the Orthodox Church]!" Priests Aristarh Cojocaru and Aurel Goraş, representing the Social Democrats and the Liberals on the Suceava town council, gave up politics. Teodosie announced that nine Constanţa priests were ready to renounce their local councillor mandates, but he said nothing about his own ambiguous situation. The ban led to significant changes on electoral party lists, as most politician-priests chose religion over politics. In Tulcea county, the Social Democrats had to find new candidates to replace several priests who had secured eligible positions on party lists. The press alleged that the priests had been included on lists following an informal agreement between Archbishop Teodosie and local party leaders.[19]

During the 2004 local elections, efforts to separate religion from politics were not entirely fruitful. The ban took politician-priests by surprise, and many made contradictory declarations within a matter of days. In Braşov and Galaţi, no priest engaged in politics, but this was not the case in other counties. The Social Democrat mayor of Ştefăneşti (Argeş county), Dumitru Nistor, sought to renew his mandate, but lost to the Liberal candidate. Petrică Florea of Costeşti (Iaşi county) competed for the mayoral position with Liberal support, declaring that "a priest cannot be indifferent to what happens in his parish. For eighteen years I struggled to help people here as much as possible. As a local councillor, I could have done much more."[20]

While Calinic ignored the ban and gave Nistor his blessing, the Metropolitanate of Moldova ecclesiastical tribunal announced it would punish Florea if he did not give up politics, since that was not the first time he disobeyed his superiors. After losing the race to the Social Democrat contender, Florea defended himself by saying that he had the constitutional right to elect and be elected to office, and he hoped the metropolitan would be lenient: that instead of defrocking him, he would temporarily suspend him from his priestly duties. Even when renouncing party membership and public positions, priests found new methods to support their political preferences. On 16 May, Social Democrat leaders traveled to Satu-Mare to participate in the Sunday mass. Taking advantage of the occasion, their candidate for the mayor's office, "with the priest's blessing, addressed the faithful, presenting the main objectives of his electoral platform and promising to solve rapidly the problems related to the [legal ownership] of the land surrounding the church [building]." The candidate was allowed to speak from the pulpit, a move the media saw as a case of religious manipulation for political reasons.[21]

The synod's support for the political neutrality of the clergy was criticized by the ruling Social Democrats, their partner in government, the Humanist (later Conservative) Party, and the main opposition political formation, the Greater Romania Party. Cosmânca labeled the ban a "mistake," his party colleague Nicolae Mischie called it "abnormal," and Greater Romania Party leader Petru Calian deemed it "discriminatory." For Cosmânca, the ban was a mistake "because the Orthodox Church has two obligations. First, the presence of priests in local councils guarantees that church problems are solved directly by local communities. Second, as shepherd of his flock, the priest must see how citizens' administrative problems are addressed inside and outside the church." Cosmânca qualified his earlier statements, arguing that "I did not say that priests should make politics, only that they should be part of local government. This means that they should be included on party lists as independent candidates." As other churches allow priests to enter politics, Cosmânca could not understand "why the Orthodox Church would act differently." Talking to the Chamber of Deputies, Orthodox priest and Humanist Party deputy Pavel Cherescu deemed the ban unconstitutional, since "only parliament can restrict the citizens' fundamental rights and liberties by adopting an organic law. Because of the synod's decision, Romania runs the risk of becoming Europe's Afghanistan and transforming its clergy into a minority deprived of constitutional rights." For Cherescu and priests wishing to give up neither politics nor priesthood, the ban revealed the Orthodox Church's propensity "toward a religious fundamentalism that could divide church leaders."[22]

By contrast, the democratic opposition supported the ban. The outside-parliament Civic Alliance saluted the synod's "extremely clear" decision and hoped it would lead to "an increase in the church's trust capital, and contribute to the needed moral rebirth of the Romanian people." Radically changing their position, the Liberals also supported the "correct" decision confirming "the political neutrality and the moral and spiritual standing of the Orthodox Church and its clergy," called on other religious denominations to adopt similar bans, and criticized the Cluj Social Democrats for asking the synod to reverse its decision. To preempt expectations that once again the Orthodox Church leadership would tacitly allow clergy to engage actively in politics, Anania insisted that the ban was irrevocable, definitive and unanimously adopted, and that therefore "not even the patriarch can reverse it." Social Democrat leaders announced that the initiative of the Cluj party branch was a unique gesture they did not support.[23]

Opposition against the ban on clergy's political involvement came not only from outside, but also from inside the Orthodox Church, as more and more prelates began to either challenge it openly or (mis)interpret it in ways that suited them. While initially few dared to question Anania or the synod, later on some leaders announced that priests with public offices could fulfill their mandates but would have to give up politics definitively after the 2004 elections. Others noted that the ban specified no deadline for priests to opt between religion and politics. Stoica suggested that "the ten-day deadline was Anania's personal interpretation," argued that "it is pointless to deprive localities of their mayor or local councillor for the next two months" until new elections were organized, and insisted that the ban referred to priests seeking to renew their political mandate: "There are several hundreds priests attracted to politics. They cannot run again, but if their bishops approve, they can fulfill their current mandates. In that case, they cannot participate in the electoral campaign, and cannot run again in the upcoming elections." Calinic embraced this position when he asked priests in his eparchy to give up party membership to avoid being defrocked but allowed mayor-priests to fulfill their mandates.[24]

By far the most vocal and adamant opposition to the ban was mounted by Rus, the Greater Romania Party senator and the only priest in the archbishopric of Cluj to choose politics over priesthood. On 2 March, the archbishopric ecclesiastical tribunal controlled by Anania defrocked Rus. The senator asked the senatorial judicial committee if parliamentary immunity protected him from sanctions imposed by the Orthodox Church, since the synod's ban applied to future political mandates, not to his own case. Rus claimed that he informed Anania of his plans to run for political office but did not specify whether Anania had given his approval. In its response, the committee noted that, according to the constitution, there was no incompatibility between priesthood and political office, and they promised to ask Patriarch Teoctist for details on the case. Rus appealed the ecclesiastical tribunal decision, but on 20 April the tribunal upheld the decision. A bitter Rus claimed that his defrocking was the result of Anania's personal vendetta, and that for electoral reasons he chose not to sue the synod or Anania for the damage they had inflicted to his public image in an electoral year. According to Rus, "former servants of the communist regime like Plămădeală and Teoctist now have the courage to hold accountable a true patriot [like myself]. The constitution, not the synod, stipulates my rights." The senator criticized the Orthodox prelates for driving around in "luxurious cars, when Jesus rode a donkey," and he encouraged his Greater Romania Party to open its electoral lists with his name.[25]

Writer Liviu Ioan Stoiciu pondered why the Orthodox Church had adopted such a firm position in favor of political neutrality only months before new local elections were scheduled. According to Stoiciu, "the [Orthodox] Church's moral credibility was challenged by its own leaders. All of a sudden, priests who became senators or deputies on the electoral lists of various parties refused to obey the church, and even dared to give orders to their superiors (the bishops and the metropolitans). The authority of the clerical hierarchy was challenged." To explain why Anania asked priests to give up public offices obtained through free and fair elections, Stoiciu argued that Teodosie, whom Anania named among clergy in a problematic situation, was the key to the speedy ban of priests from politics: "Teodosie likes power and with the help of the [ruling] Social Democratic Party dreams of becoming first Metropolitan of Tomis and Dobrogea [a position that does not yet exist] and then the patriarch. He wants the church to discontinue following the tradition of nominating the metropolitan of Moldova as the patriarch, and he is fighting a life and death struggle to become a metropolitan" since the patriarch is chosen from among metropolitans. For Stoiciu, the commitment to political neutrality stemmed from the power struggle within the synod between the supporters of the young, ambitious Teodosie, who relied on Social Democrat support to advance his ecclesiastical career, and his opponents led by Anania, who wanted the established tradition to be observed and to have Metropolitan Ciobotea of Moldova enthroned patriarch after Teoctist's death. Stoiciu believed that "the decision to ban priests from politics is not enough to stop Teodosie's ascendance."[26]

The Roman Catholic Church was the second religious denomination in Romania to adopt a formal policy of political neutrality, banning clergy from politics. In doing so, the Catholic leaders invoked the Roman Catholic canon 285.3, which reads that "clergy are forbidden from assuming public office that implies participation in state decision making"; canon 383.1 of the Greek Catholic Church Code; and paragraph 33 of the *Directory on Ministry and Priestly Life* of the Vatican Congregation for the Clergy (1994), which states:

> The priest, as servant of the universal church, cannot tie himself to any historical contingency, and therefore must be above any political party. He cannot take an active role in political parties or labor unions, unless, according to the judgment of the ecclesiastical authority, the rights of the church and the defense of common good require it. In fact, even if these are good in themselves, they are nevertheless foreign to the clerical state since they can constitute a grave danger of division in the ecclesial communion. . . . The reduction of [the priest's] mission to temporal tasks, of a purely social or political nature, is foreign to his ministry, and does not constitute a triumph but rather a grave loss to the church's evangelical fruitfulness.[27]

Roman and Greek Catholic priests were asked to give up political involvement as soon as possible, and a number of politician-priests throughout the country made the choice. In Sălaj county, all Orthodox and Roman Catholic priests gave up politics, including priests representing the Social Democrats and the Liberals. In Cluj, Social Democrats had to remove the names of thirty-two priests who were all party members included on electoral lists, and in Bistrița-Năsăud twelve priests gave up party cards and council positions. In Constanța county, seven councillor-priests renounced their party membership, while Father Gheorghe Stoica chose politics over priesthood. The five or six Reform clergymen who were members of the Democratic Union of Magyars refused to turn in their party cards or give up their public office.[28]

Use of Religious Symbols by Politicians

After 1989, the dependence of Romanian political parties on religious actors and symbols became stronger and increasingly accepted. Whereas in the first post-communist elections only a handful of political parties made systematic efforts to woo the country's main religious denominations (primarily because only a few parties understood that religion successfully filled the ideological void left behind by the collapse of the dictatorial communist regime), by 2004 all parties without exception claimed a special relationship with the churches, tailored their political platforms to the needs of targeted religious communities, and encouraged their candidates to use religious symbols and perform religious deeds that would make them popular with the electorate. The Romanian Orthodox Church was uniquely positioned both to receive requests from political parties and electoral candidates and to promise much-desired support. The church as an institution avoided taking the side of specific parties, a move that would commit it to lend support even when party policy was disadvantageous and return it to the position of servant to politicians reminiscent of communist times. Rather, it preferred to allow bishops and priests to choose between competing politicians and forge ties to those from whom the clergy hoped to gain the most. As a result, at any given time there were some Orthodox bishops working closely with the government and others with the opposition, with bishops often advocating different political positions in the synod.

In electoral campaigns, candidates of various political persuasions wooed the Orthodox Church in an attempt to gain the votes of the country's largest religious community. Although it played a role in the 1990 and 1992 campaigns, it was only in 1996 that religion moved to the forefront of electoral debates, compelling all contenders to define their position vis-à-vis the Orthodox Church and Christianity. The 1996 presidential candidates were careful to include visits to Orthodox churches in their electoral itineraries; to show up for religious services on major Orthodox feast days; and to be photographed surrounded by Orthodox icons, calendars, and symbols. Some made substantial donations for church enlargement and reconstruction, others godfathered orphans and witnessed marriages in widely publicized ceremonies, and one candidate chose "He Who Votes for Me, Votes for God!" as his electoral slogan. The highlight of the presidential race was the televised debate in which the Christian Democrat Constantinescu surprised the incumbent Iliescu, a self-declared atheist, by asking him whether he believed in God. In the end, Constantinescu won and, in a token of gratitude, became the first post-communist Romanian president to take his solemn oath, hand on the Bible, in the presence of the Orthodox patriarch. Since then, the patriarch has opened each legislative session by encouraging senators and deputies to fulfill the mandate entrusted to them by the electorate.

Candidates for the 1996 general elections also sought the support of the Orthodox Church. A written request by Transylvanian Social Democrat leaders pleading with the synod to urge believers to vote for Social Democrat candidates caused much discussion. The letter reminded the Orthodox Church that "the Social Democrat government was the first in Romania's history to grant priests' bonuses" and claimed that Roman Catholic and Greek Catholic priests actively encouraged believers to vote for the major opposition coalition, the Democratic Convention, although this contention was not supported by the evidence at hand. Religion maintained its saliency in 1998, when contenders for the Bucharest mayor's office went on record as attending Orthodox religious services, giving alms, and receiving the unusual honor of being invited inside the altar sanctuary. By 2000, the Romanians had accepted the electoral cooperation between parties and the Orthodox Church, earlier decried as one of the inevitable evils of a distorted political life. Just before the second round of the presidential elections organized that year, prominent Orthodox leaders—including Patriarch Teoctist—urged the electorate to vote for a candidate "who has proven to be balanced, and not for an extremist" for "Romania to place itself among European nations." Bishop Vincentiu Ploieşteanu called for an end to political extremism and expressed dissatisfaction that in the first round young people supported a "crazy" candidate. Though no names were specified, the "balanced" candidate was Iliescu, while the "crazy extremist" was Tudor. In the first round, Tudor mustered greater support from an electorate dissatisfied with both Iliescu's center-left regime of 1990–1996 and Constantinescu's center-right regime of 1996–2000.[29]

Months before the local poll of 2000, laypeople and clergy from Bucharest, Maramureş, Cluj, Alba Iulia, Harghita, and Covasna approached the synod with an unusual request. Addressed to "all clergy from Romania and abroad and all Romania's well-wishers," and authored by Emil Hossu, the parish priest of Boiul Mare village (Maramureş county), the open Letter for the Soul (*Scrisoare de suflet*) read as follows:

> We witness the most serious political crisis Romania has faced in the last decade, when all sorts of politicians asked the clergy to sup-
> port this or that party's bid to form the government. We are neither upset nor pleased, but we resent the yoke that burdens our con-
> fused country. . . . We responsibly ask the Holy Synod to reflect on the election of a church leader able to pull the country out of chaos. We know that [running for the presidency] will be a great sacrifice for the selected bishop, a crucifixion, but we need a doctor. . . . During these crucial times, the future Romanian president must be a Ro-
> manian Orthodox Church leader. Following his crucifixion [on the political altar], he will be hurt, attacked, smeared, accused, but we firmly believe that the clergy realizes that sending a bishop into "the lion's den" is essential for a church that has always stood by its people.[30]

After revealing that this was not the first plea of its kind to reach the Orthodox leadership, the synod rejected the proposal and reiterated the church's com-mitment to political neutrality, reassuring the public that it continued "to be sensitive to the problems of our society." Indeed, in the 2000 general elec-tions, no Orthodox Church leader entered the presidential race.

The symbiotic relationship between politicians and the Orthodox Church was manifest during but also between elections, each time the government sought to consolidate its popular support and gain approval for policy pro-posals. An example of politicians transforming a religious celebration into a propaganda tool was the mass of the Dormition of the Virgin Mary feast on 15 August 2002 at the Nicula monastery, when the Social Democrats distributed free small paper icons of Virgin Mary specifying the party as the donor. The move prompted *Adevărul* to write a critical article titled "Virgin Mary, the Social Democrats' Electoral Agent." Upset that nobody sought his approval, the head of the monastery criticized the icon distribution, adding that "desecrating icons by turning them into party tools shows us that political propaganda was pu-shed too far." Instead of apologizing, the Social Democrats argued that the believers had to know that the icons were paid for by the party. The following year, the party again distributed the controversial icons and obliged the faithful gathered at the monastery to listen to a political message of Premier Năstase read aloud by Minister of Interior Ioan Rus. Anania criticized the politicization of the religious celebration and the Social Democrat initiative as "a gesture of impiety and political amateurism," but Năstase denied that his party sought to gain electoral support through the Orthodox Church, noted that his message "reflected the state's support to the church," and assured Anania that the government was committed to support financially the completion of all (church) constructions in his diocese.[31]

At around the same time, the Orthodox Church blessed a new church in Talpa village (Botoşani county), "an edifice of [Minister of Public Administration] Octav Cosmâncă and the government," in a celebration attended by Social Democrat luminaries, including the Chamber of Deputies speaker; four ministers; and dozens of senators, deputies, prefects, and county council presidents. The blessing was conducted jointly by Metropolitan Daniel and Metropolitan Petru of Bessarabia. The next day, Cosmâncâ lost his ministerial portfolio, prompting journalists to write ironically that God finally heard his prayers and to suggest that the minister had used a combination of public funds and funds derived through corrupt methods to finance the construction of the enormous church. Liberal leader Dan Morega built a church in Padeş village (Gorj county) and ordered a painting on the church wall representing him according to the Byzantine iconography, though his saintly posture contrasted with his public image as a corrupt businessman and politician. Morega was not the first Romanian politician to build a church, but others preferred to immortalize their financial contribution in a small inscription mentioning their name, not a full-scale portrait. The Social Democrat Party also got into the business of building churches. In 2003, it announced plans to construct a new church in Dumbrăveşti village (Prahova county), and a year later it helped build a monastery in Crucea village (Constanţa county).[32]

Today, most politicians dream of building churches that will mark their contribution to the welfare of the Romanian people and the prosperity of their natal villages. While politicians in other countries are busy setting up student scholarship funds, building public libraries, and founding nonprofit organizations that promote community interests, politicians in Romania prefer to erect churches in the belief that their stone and brick structures will stand the passage of time better. They also seem to have a fascination with Byzantine paintings covering the church interior walls, which present them as worthy preservers of Romanian values, on a par with revered historical figures like Stephen the Great, Michael the Brave, and Mircea the Elder. Not surprisingly, Romania is the Eastern European country with the highest number of Orthodox churches relative to its total population.

God and the Ballot in 2004

Until 2004, the balance between religious denominations and the political elite seemed inclined in favor of the latter. Generally, politicians decided when exactly to enter negotiations with religious groups, which groups to approach, which promises to make, and to what degree and when to meet their promises. Time and again, religious leaders felt betrayed and deceived by politicians who, once in office, conveniently forgot to honor their pledges or insisted that more urgent problems had to be addressed before any matters of importance for the religious denominations. It was only in 2004 that the Orthodox Church tried to redress the balance of power and to make its relationship with the political elite more equitable, by insisting that its key demands be honored before general elections were organized that year.

As the local poll approached, reports about politicians seeking support from priests and bishops and clergy taking sides in the electoral campaign became more numerous. With Teodosie's approval, priests distributed pamphlets detailing the accomplishments of Social Democrat Tulcea mayor Constantin Mocanu. In Stefăneşti village (Argeş county), Liberal candidate Mihai Bărbuceanu complained that Social Democrat mayor Nistor joined party street demonstrations and meetings dressed in priestly robes and thus "uses religion and church for electoral purposes." In Petroşani, Father Octavian Pătraşcu encouraged voters to support the Social Democrats, "the only party in Romania to believe in God," endorsed—in priestly robes—the party's mayoral candidate, and was quoted as saying, "Pray and work! This is the golden rule of our Christian faith and tradition, which [Social Democrat candidate] Dr. Benor Voicescu observes in his daily life and activity. This is why we support him and wish him success in the race and in his work for the community." People visiting the social canteen organized by Pătraşcu's parish were told that the Social Democrats had paid for the food, which had in fact been covered by foreign donations. The Liberal Party complained to the synod that "through his explicit political activity, Father Pătraşcu disregarded the synod's ban on clergy political involvement," but the priest argued that he was helping the Social Democrat campaign as an ordinary citizen, not a church representative.[33]

The press reported many similar examples. In Runcu Salvei village (Bistriţa county), Ilie Furcea interrupted mass to invite Social Democrat leaders to present the candidate for the mayor's office. Parishioners sent a protest letter to Anania, but the priest was never punished. In Gătaia village (Timiş county), the Social Democrat mayoral candidate Iosif Sargan was allowed to speak from the pulpit of a Reform church, and he gave hefty donations to the local Reform and Orthodox parishes for the clergy to support his candidacy publicly. Again, parishioners protested and petitioned the police and the courts, but nothing was done. The Social Democrat Party targeted evangelical churches in Cluj-Napoca, tailoring its electoral message to suit each church (Adventist, Baptist, Pentecostal). Electoral fliers distributed in the Adventist church included the Social Democrat slogan "Together for Cluj-Napoca," a verse from Jeremiah ("seek the good of the community because its happiness is yours"), and photos of Social Democrat mayoral candidate Ioan Rus, candidate for county council and Baptist minister Victor Faragan, and candidate for municipal council and Baptist believer Ioan Pop. Bishop Epifanie Norocel of Buzău was photographed next to controversial Social Democrat leader Marian Oprişan; he told the faithful that Satan is "right-wing," that "the center-right Romanian Liberals were sent by the devil to do his bidding," but that "they will be punished, either in this life or in the afterlife." The opposition also wooed the Orthodox Church, but instances of collusion were fewer. Zimnicea councillor Father Filip Bubureanu, a long-time sympathizer of the Democratic Convention, turned his yearly pilgrimages to Moldovan monasteries into electoral propaganda for the opposition Liberal Party.[34]

In the local elections of that year, the Orthodox Church contributed in no small part to the Social Democrats' coming second in terms of number of county councillor mandates, and to their losing to the opposition Justice and Truth Alliance by just a narrow margin (32.6 to 33.8 percent). The church expected to be rewarded for all its efforts soon after the local poll, with the government meeting a number of important demands like returning property (land and assets) that had once belonged to the archbishopric of Suceava and launching the construction of the Cathedral for National Salvation in Bucharest, two controversial projects that civil society and local government had opposed on mostly practical grounds. Facing the government's refusal to meet the demands, the church changed its tone and started to criticize President Iliescu and Prime Minister Năstase, as though to show the two that the Social Democrats could not afford to lose its valuable support in the months preceding the general elections.

While Social Democrat leaders were busy distributing gifts, food, and money at Easter time, Anania warned that the high levels of political corruption could endanger Romania's integration process into the European Union.[35] Some weeks later, during the lavish 500-year celebrations of the death of Moldovan king Stephen the Great, recognized as Saint Stephen the Great by the Romanian Orthodox Church, Archbishop Pimen of Suceava criticized the Social Democrat leaders gathered at Putna monastery. Iliescu and Năstase attended the celebrations under the protection of 500 police officers brought in

from neighboring counties. Pimen scolded the Social Democrat youth organization for politicizing the effort to bring Stephen's icon to the monastery, in
the process marginalizing the initiator, the Association of Orthodox Students
from Romania (Asociaţia Studenţilor Creştini Ortodocşi din România, or
ASCOR). The archbishop also admonished them for committing "a condemnable act at a time when our Christian roots are threatened throughout
Europe, when morality is forgotten, when men live beneath the level of animals, when few statesmen believe in God. We see these double-faced politicians entering the church only during electoral campaign or at major events.
While we cannot judge them, we should pray to God to enlighten them!"[36]

Pimen further criticized the "excessive" security measures adopted at
Putna, which allowed only press representatives and politicians to enter the
monastery and obliged the faithful to wait outside the monastery walls:

> Stephen the Great was saddened to see that the faithful were brutally
> stopped from entering the church and were treated as terrorists and
> thieves at the order of the country's leaders, [who only] sought elec-
> toral capital, as religious and patriotic sentiment is foreign to them.
> They are remnants of the Communist Party. . . . Only God knows how
> they were elected to rule our country! God sought to make us wiser, to
> show us where the dishonesty and unfaithfulness with which they
> surround themselves can lead. They are elected, but this does not
> justify their undignified behavior.

He characterized the country's leaders harshly, declaring that "President
Iliescu is a true believer in the communist doctrine and does not support the
idea of private property, while Năstase is a very proud man." Pimen added that
"Ceauşescu said clearly 'I am an atheist' and did not interfere, but [Iliescu and
Năstase] say 'We are with the church' when in fact they are against the church
and the people."[37] Metropolitan Daniel of Moldova distanced himself, arguing
that "organizational deficiencies cannot be attributed to President Iliescu and
Premier Năstase," and State Secretary for Religious Denominations Laurenţiu
Tănase said that Pimen's statement "risked unnecessarily poisoning church-
state relations."[38]

The press believed that Pimen's stand signaled a change in the church's
position toward state and government. Writer Dan Ciachir argued that "we are
witnessing a change of attitude on the part of the Orthodox Church from
servility to independence. Anania and Pimen are the first to discuss with the
state as equals, they are the root of renewed church-state relations" since
Pimen's position reflected the position of many other church leaders whom
the state treated arrogantly. For Ciachir, "Pimen told our rulers some hard

truths that nobody else dared to in the history of modern Romania," and in this "we witness signs of the church's emancipation," though the church continued to be subordinated to the state through the share of the national budget it received. Theologian Vincenţiu Cernea believed that in 1990 the Orthodox Church missed the chance to redefine its relationship to the state, and as such in 2004 it "faced an identity crisis, it was hesitant and did not know how to act in a free society," but he was pessimistic with regard to the church's chance to become independent from the state and the ruling party.[39]

As the general elections drew closer and the Orthodox leaders grew more critical, Social Democrats made extra efforts to bridge the divide. In September, the government sponsored an international congress on Romanian spirituality organized under the aegis of the Archbishopric of Alba Iulia and reminded the patriarchate that 1,554 churches were renovated and the construction of 1,050 others was launched during the 2000–2004 period.[40] Some weeks later, the government proposed (and parliament endorsed) the building of the monumental Cathedral for National Salvation in Carol Park, close to the Bucharest commercial district and the patriarchal see. The project met the opposition of civil society groups and Bucharest general mayor Traian Băsescu, representing the opposition Democratic Party. The government also returned vast stretches of Moldovan forest that had once belonged to the Archbishopric of Suceava, a gesture of good will toward its most adamant critic, Pimen. After receiving the news, Pimen declared that by agreeing to the restitution, Năstase "entered the select circle of founders and protectors of historical churches and monasteries," apparently forgetting his earlier references to Năstase's arrogance and corruption.[41] Once its two main demands were met, the Orthodox Church again lent support to the Social Democrats.

For their part, parliamentary candidates turned celebrations of Saint Paraskeva's Day (14 October) into a public relations success. Local public servants and the wives of Social Democrat leaders prepared 60,000 cabbage rolls to distribute to the poor, together with 200,000 liters of wine and beer. The Orthodox Church arranged for a fragment of the Holy Cross to be brought from Greece, while the mayor's office entertained pilgrims with choral songs, parachute stunts, and fireworks and offered them hot tea during the unusually cold night. Arriving in Iaşi at the last moment, Premier Năstase took the opportunity to renew his electoral promises of better social protection for the elderly.[42] Both the Orthodox Church and the Social Democrats draw most of their support from the economically backward province of Moldova, whose capital is Iaşi.

In the presidential elections, Năstase competed against Băsescu, representing the Justice and Truth Alliance; Corneliu Vadim Tudor, representing the Greater Romania Party; and nine other minor candidates. At first, Băsescu burned bridges with the Orthodox Church when he voiced support for homosexual marriages and the legalization of prostitution. On 28 October, the patriarchate condemned Băsescu's position, while the press, the opposition, and Anania criticized the church for taking a position against a presidential candidate during the electoral campaign. Social Democrat Cosmâncă took the occasion to argue that "Băsescu is Satan, not a genuine Christian. His position toward homosexual marriages is the position of the Antichrist, not of a normal Christian fearful of God. He is Christian only in his troubled mind. Adrian Năstase is a good Christian, a man who really helped the [Orthodox] Church as lots of churches were built in the last four years."[43] In the end, Băsescu claimed that he neither supported nor opposed the legalization of prostitution and homosexuality, and he attended mass, offered donations, and pledged to return additional property to the Archbishopric of Suceava.[44] Hours before the poll, Băsescu visited a Bucharest church, attended mass, made the sign of the cross, mumbled the Our Father, and was blessed and sprinkled with holy water by the priest.[45] The visit was the divine sign he looked for, helping him to win the presidency in the runoff.

Among presidential candidates, Tudor was the keenest on employing religious symbols.He centered his entire electoral campaign on Christianity; wore white clothes similar to the patriarch's symbolizing purity, honesty, and correctness; and insisted during each visit, debate, demonstration, and declaration that he would be "the first Christian president in Romania's history." A photograph of him with Patriarch Teoctist and Pope John Paul II was published in newspapers with wide circulation several times during the campaign. In a letter to the Central Electoral Bureau, the patriarchate complained of Tudor's use of Christian and religious symbols and his failure to seek the patriarch's consent before using the photograph as an electoral tool. The Greater Romania Party remarked that the photo had been taken during Pope John Paul II's visit to Romania, had been published before, and had therefore already been in the public domain at the beginning of the electoral campaign.[46] It is difficult to estimate how many more votes Tudor gained by employing religious symbols. He gathered only 13 percent of the national vote and was unable to enter the presidential runoff.

Conclusion

During the past two decades, many more priests have become politically involved and many more politicians have employed religious symbols to gain

electoral support. Whereas in the early 1990s politicians were generally controlling the process of marrying religion and politics for electoral gain, recently
religious actors have become more assertive, threatening to withdraw support
if political parties fail to meet key demands. The strategy has apparently
worked and has allowed the Orthodox Church to obtain restitution of some of
its property and launch construction of the gigantic Cathedral for National
Salvation, two projects that civil society bitterly opposed. The involvement of
religion in electoral politics clearly benefits the Orthodox Church more than
other religious denominations, further solidifying that denomination's ascendancy over religious affairs in the country. While beneficial for the resurrection of religious activity after forty-five years of communist rule, the interplay between religion and electoral politics could eventually prove detrimental
to democratization if the umbilical cord that ties the Romanian political elite to
the powerful Orthodox Church is not cut.

7

Religious Education
in Public Schools

After the collapse of the Nicolae Ceauşescu regime, religious denominations vigorously exercised their public voice for the first time
since 1946, the year when the Communist Party formed the government and set about to transform the country into an atheistic state
along Marxist-Leninist lines. Education was an area where the legally recognized denominations, especially the dominant Orthodox
Church, registered success in the early stages of post-communist
transition. They pressured authorities to introduce religious education in public schools and to offer substantial financial support for
theological institutions.[1] In this chapter, we provide an overview of
post-communist legislation on religious education in public schools,
examined against the background of the 1991 constitution and international provisions protecting freedom of conscience. We also
critically assess the pre-university textbooks used in Orthodox and
Roman Catholic religion courses offered in the public school system and discuss religious groups' attempts to ban evolutionary
theory from school curricula and the Orthodox Church's efforts to
introduce religious symbols in public universities. Throughout the
chapter, we use concrete examples to illustrate how religion is
being taught in Romanian schools today.

The Pre-Communist Public School System

The origins of the Romanian public education system date to the beginning of
the nineteenth century, when European states began to assume the responsibility of setting up networks of schools that offered basic instruction at the
primary level and revamped curricula at higher levels.[2] As the principalities of
Wallachia and Moldova, while still under the control of the Ottoman Empire,
opened their Western borders, the sons of local boyars traveled to Austria,
Germany, France, and Italy. They brought home new ideas and a genuine
commitment to change that would align the country with the developed nations of Western Europe. On their return, for example, Gheorghe Lazar, Ion
Heliade-Rădulescu, and Dinicu Golescu opened schools to train instructors,
while Eufrosin Poteca and Simion Marcovici proposed blueprints for educational reform. At the time, schools were largely the product of private initiative.
The state did not favor the general education of rural peasant masses but,
instead, wanted instruction that produced public officers or individuals whose
skills successfully met market constraints.[3] It was in this context that the
Orthodox Church stepped in.

   The 1834 law on theological seminaries provided an interim solution to the
lack of teachers and teaching materials in rural areas, by calling on the village
priests to teach basic reading, writing, and mathematics during the winter
months, when the children of peasants were not working in agriculture or
performing chores in the household. Instruction, which often did not extend
beyond the second grade, included basic calculus. It was centered on Orthodox
religious dogma and liturgical songs because, as one historian stressed, "rural
schools should give peasant children not so much instruction to get into
boarding schools and colleges, but basic knowledge they could use in the
household, coupled with familiarity with religion and the methods of toiling
the land."[4] These principles were reflected in *Regulamentul Organic*, Moldova's
first proto-constitution of 1832. Teachers were called to inspire in their students "the chastity of thinking, love in God and men, duty toward the country,
respect for and belief in the ruler and his laws."[5] The village priest taught
catechism and, together with the teacher, monitored the students' fulfillment
of religious duties. The intent was to blend religious, moral, and applied instruction to mold peasants into obedient and useful citizens. Despite the
enormous progress it registered in the first half of the nineteenth century, the
Romanian school system was unable to bridge the significant qualitative differences between urban and rural schools, and between boys' and girls' instruction.[6]

In 1833, for the first time, the Wallachian school board called for proposals for a textbook. They were looking for a catechism textbook discussing "the citizen's duties as Christian, member of the society, and thinking person capable of moral deeds." The winner of the competition, a bestseller throughout the century, was the textbook of Bucharest high school teacher Aaron Florian, who called pupils to observe their individual duty toward God, themselves, and others, as well as their duties toward rulers and parents, siblings, teachers, friends, the poor, and their country.[7] Christian ethics was the basis of the Romanian civic spirit, and throughout the nineteenth century civic education was closely related to catechism. Through civic spirit, a citizen manifested love for the country (patriotism) and obedience to its rulers, both of which the catechism promoted on the grounds that "besides God, here on earth, the rulers take care of the people's well-being and happiness . . . order and peace . . . and protect our life, our assets, and everything against the enemies and those who bring evil."[8] Pupils were encouraged to "show respect for the nation" because "whoever attacks the king attacks the head of the nation, and whoever attacks the head wants to kill the body, and [thus] is a slave, a tyrant, or a thief. Those who seek to become greater than the government are tyrants, adulterous, ignoramuses, pagans." At the same time, the textbook admitted that "the government that encroaches on the people's legitimate rights is despotic."[9]

Important for our discussion is the continuous presence of the Orthodox Church in the public education system, though it is true that its influence gradually eroded, first in towns and much later in the rural areas. At the beginning of the century, the church was the single most important organizer of public instruction in the villages, where most of the population resided. Yet by the middle of the century, more and more trained teachers had assumed the priests' teaching duties in a concerted campaign, supported by the political elite, to make the public education system more civic. But the priest remained the moral example for communities, using weekly sermons to educate the people for whom he was the most likely adviser in times of doubt, confusion, and trouble.[10] Thus, while priests were replaced by teachers, and the Bible by new educational materials, religion remained important. In 1859, the government advised teachers that "moral education is closely linked to religious instruction. The former forms the man, the latter forms the Christian. Since early Christianity, nobody is a man in the true meaning of the word unless he is a Christian."[11]

Teachers were further advised that "the study of religion is the first and most important [subject presented] in primary school. Instruction must foster the children's intelligence and good heart to make them useful to themselves and the society, but such a goal cannot be attained without the study of religion . . . which strengthens virtue and morality."[12] Beyond classes of religion, instruction as a whole was delivered in an active religious frame-work: "school days should always start and end with a prayer" for which the school should use "a blessed icon, strategically placed, for students to get used to pray daily, because man can never rise above his humble condition without first praising God. Nothing without God!"[13] To prevent dogmatic heresy, teachers were advised to consult with clergymen, but at the same time "to never allow Romanian Christianity to lose its characteristic toleration" or "make the mistake of transforming the school into a place of exclusivism or proselytism, never turn down pupils of other religion or impose on them requirements and practices running counter to their parents' religion."[14]

Toward the end of the nineteenth century, Romanian national political rulers were intent on using the educational system to foster national identity. Religion was blended with nationalist beliefs claiming that "to be Romanian means to be Christian, and to be Christian means to grow within the Orthodox Church."[15] Educators also started to advocate the separation of church and school, as well as the complete replacement of priests with teachers as public educators at the primary level. One such voice contended:

> The priest can no longer be teacher for the same reason he cannot teach mathematics in church, because Jesus Christ himself drove out of the temple the [money-chargers] who were using computing op-erations. So far, the Romanians were never religious enough to defend themselves only with the icon, as did the Byzantines. In the future, they will understand that they can live neither without church nor without the school because, as man has two natures, body and spirit, he needs two directions.[16]

Transylvania was the first to open public schools, but they largely catered to the ruling Magyar and German ethnic groups to the exclusion of the poor Romanian ethnic majority, whose language was not even included in the curriculum. When the province belonged to the Hapsburg Empire, the Roman Catholic Church dominated the local school system, a supremacy similar to the Orthodox Church's in the Romanian Kingdom. Once Transylvania was in-corporated into Romania, Bucharest made every effort to unify the educational system under its control, reducing the number of schools catering to Hun-garian and German minorities and promoting the creation of schools for the Transylvanian Romanians. According to the Treaty on Minorities Romania signed in Paris on 9 December 1919, the state subsidized minority schools, but neither the 1923 nor the 1938 constitutions safeguarded unrestricted and equal access to education for minorities. Romanian became the compulsory language in all Transylvanian schools, and geography and history were to be taught in Romanian. Unable to offer Romanian-language training and attract students, many Roman Catholic private schools ceased to exist altogether. Hungarian elementary schools sponsored by the Roman Catholic, Unitarian, and Evangelical Churches decreased from a total of 421 in 1913 to 339 in 1932, while all schools sponsored by the Greek Catholic Church closed their doors.[17] In parallel with this trend, the Romanian Orthodox Church increased its influence throughout the country.

Institutionally, church involvement in public education remained unchanged until the advent of the communist regime. In consultation with state authorities, recognized religious denominations were allowed to offer religious instruction at pre-university levels, mostly at their own expense. Neither new groups (primarily Protestant) nor old groups (most notably Jewish) were granted such privileges. If they wished to offer religious instruction, it had to occur in their places of worship, not in the public school system.

Religious Education under Communism

Shortly after 1945, religious education came under the scrutiny of communist authorities and the secret political police, the Securitate. The State Secretariat for Religious Denominations, a government body dealing with religious matters since pre-communist times, continued to exist but was transformed into an agency enforcing more strict state control over religious affairs in the country. The Securitate included a special department supervising religious life that tried to solve the so-called problem of the denominations, especially the problem of religious groups and individuals hostile to the new regime.[18] The "problem of the denominations" was code language for a systematic attempt to discourage religious participation and to transform the country into an atheistic state. Theology schools were regarded as especially dangerous places where anti-communist ideas were spread among students.[19] All but four theology schools were disbanded by the communist authorities, and numerous theological seminaries met the same fate. Some theologians teaching in these schools ended up collaborating with the communist regime by informing on their students and colleagues, while those who opposed the communists were arrested.[20] Numerous Greek and Roman Catholic professors, priests, and bishops were also arrested.

As late as the 1970s and 1980s, the Securitate closely monitored the composition of the student body in seminaries and theology schools. From recently released Securitate secret documents, we see that in 1980 a total of 1,142 students were enrolled in Romania's four theology schools, of which 1,097 attended the Orthodox schools of Bucharest and Sibiu. Of the 1,007 seminary students, 872 studied in six Orthodox seminaries, while the rest were enrolled in two Catholic seminaries, one Baptist, and one Pentecostal. A Securitate report dated 12 December 1980 noted the high number of candidates competing for seats in theology schools and seminaries (around five candidates per seat, a number comparable to technical programs), and the fact that almost half of the students (1,500 of a total of 2,973) were members of the Communist Youth Union. Three students even belonged to the Communist Party. After summarizing information unavailable to the larger public, the report mentioned that serious efforts were made to recruit faculty members teaching in those schools as spies.[21]

The communist authorities retained the structure of the state education system (including eight primary and secondary grades, followed by four years of high school training, and finally four to six years of university education at the bachelor level), but revamped the curriculum to suit their needs. Research and teaching were disjoined, with the latter conducted in universities and the former reserved to the Romanian Academy institutes. Social sciences and humanities university-level programs were drastically curtailed in favor of economic and technical programs preparing specialists for a sustained industrialization program. Vocational training was expanded to accept an ever-increasing number of students wishing to become welders, carpenters, cooks, or bus drivers. Most high schools preparing students for entrance into universities were turned into institutions training clerks, accountants, or nurses. Applied training was introduced as early as the fifth grade, alongside a month-long practicum, which obliged students to engage in the "voluntary work" of harvesting fruits and vegetables without just remuneration. The Ministry of Education designed all curricula and eliminated electives at all levels. As a result, all students enrolled in a given program had to take the same courses in a preapproved order.

In this process of unprecedented change, religious education was greatly affected. The teaching of religion in public schools was discontinued in 1947, denominations were banned from organizing catechesis, and confessional schools were closed a year later, as part of a larger program designed to allow political authorities to shape Romanians into new atheistic communist persons. At the same time, the history curriculum in the public school system was amended so that the role of religious groups in shaping Romanian ethnic identity and their involvement in nation-building and state-building processes were denied and Darwinist evolutionary theory was presented uncritically.

Post-Communist Developments

Not surprisingly, after decades of officially supported atheistic propaganda, the resumption of pre-university religious education in public schools represented one of the first demands religious groups in Romania put forward after December 1989. In January 1990, less than a month after Ceauşescu was killed by a firing squad and well before post-communist authorities had time to revamp the education system, the new Secretary of State for Religious Denominations Nicolae Stoicescu, together with the Orthodox Church's collective leadership structure, the Holy Synod, pledged their support for the introduction of religious education in public schools at all pre-university levels. An optional religion class, for which students were not to be graded, was to be included in the pre-university curriculum, with students declaring their religious affiliation in consultation with their parents. For students taking Orthodox religion, the basic curriculum was to be selected by a synod-appointed mixed commission of clergymen and lay people. Defending the proposal, Stoicescu argued that religious education would contribute to the moral recovery of the nation, while the future Metropolitan Daniel Ciobotea of Moldova explained that religious education was needed because "atheistic humanism cannot be replaced by a nihilist, indifferent, and confused humanism."[22]

Working on the premise that Romanians would welcome the proposal in the months to come, the Orthodox Church labored to solve the most important issues related to the introduction of religious education in public schools, including the allocation of time slots and classrooms, the preparation of teaching materials, and the training of teachers familiar with church doctrine and ritual. The church was right to presume that if it did not solve these practical problems, the introduction of religion could be deferred indefinitely. Two different reasons seem to have prompted the Orthodox Church to take the lead. First, it was the religious group that benefited the most, as a majority of Romanian students were expected to opt for Orthodox religious classes, a choice reflecting their parents' declared religious affiliation. Second, during the first years of the post-communist transformation, the Ministry of Education was too disorganized and overwhelmed by public demands for reform to be able to redesign the already existing programs efficiently, let alone manage new projects like the introduction of religious education.

Because the quest for initiating religious education was met with mixed feelings outside Orthodox circles—with some prominent intellectuals opposing the idea of mandatory religious education altogether, and others criticizing the potentially poor quality of religious instruction and of the related literature—not many of the patriarchate's efforts to address such practical issues were documented in the press. The most reliable information we have to date comes from a case study of the Bishopric of Buzău undertaken in 2002 by high school philosophy teacher Emil Moise. While the study is limited to only one of the twenty Orthodox bishoprics in Romania, it is likely that many events unfolded similarly in the rest of the country.

On 14 June 1990, the Bishopric of Buzău learned that the synod discussed the pedagogical training of priests wishing to teach religion in public schools during the September 1990 to September 1991 academic year, and decided that each eparchy should send a priest to attend the intensive pedagogical course offered by the Bucharest Theology Institute from 16 to 27 July 1990, and then instruct the other priests in the eparchy on the course content. In reply, the bishopric suggested that schools mark the start of the school year with the Orthodox *Te Deum* ceremony, that both parents and priests become involved in the organization of religious education, and that the patriarchate launch a "national radio station to present the teachings of our Church, to inform correctly and promptly on all religious events."[23]

Eight priests representing the Bishopric of Buzău traveled to Bucharest to take part in the summer training and then presented the program and the requirements for teaching religion in public schools to the other Buzău priests. After hearing the presentation, the priests admitted that "this subject [of religious education] makes us think hard, and we wonder whether we can offer so many classes of religion, if we can be both priests and teachers at the same time."[24] The priests felt that their resources were stretched to the limit if they were required to take on additional responsibilities on top of those demanded by the priesthood. Even in small villages with a single primary school, the local priest was asked to give eight different one-hour-long religion classes, one for each grade in which the school enrolled students. In larger localities, the teaching load was far greater since there was either more than a single school in every parish or a school had multiple student groups in each grade taking classes at different times.

During 1990–1991, religion classes were offered, but not from the beginning of the school year and not in all schools. Classes depended on the resources available locally, including the availability of teachers, and the willingness of school principals to introduce into the curriculum what many saw as a controversial subject. Most teachers offering religion classes in the public school system were Orthodox priests or graduates of university programs of Orthodox theology, and as a result more students enrolled in Orthodox religion classes than in classes presenting other faiths. This was partly because there were more Orthodox than non-Orthodox priests to begin with, and other religious denominations were unable to muster enough teachers for the classes in which their believers numbered significantly. Moreover, most school principals, themselves Orthodox, encouraged the introduction of Orthodoxy to the neglect of other denominations. This early success occurred outside an adequate legal framework for religious education in public schools and later came to haunt the Orthodox Church. The denomination was accused of trying to turn religion education into a tool of Orthodox indoctrination, of undermining the right of other denominations to offer religious instruction in schools, and of taking advantage of a disoriented and disorganized Ministry of Education to introduce religion in the public school system through the back door. Some of these charges were unfounded.

While religion was a tolerated subject during the 1990–1991 school year, it was agreed that its presence in the curriculum had to be stipulated officially in a protocol signed by the Ministry of Education, which oversaw all matters related to education in Romania, and the State Secretary of Religious Denominations, which covered the salaries of religion teachers and represented the interests of the churches. On 11 September 1991, only four days before the start of the new school year, the protocol was signed, providing for the introduction of "moral-religious training" in public schools to "highlight elements of ethics and cultural history." In accord with their parents, students could choose the denomination and theological doctrine covered in their religion class. Theological school graduates could teach religion in public schools, thus allowing priests to dedicate their time and efforts to helping the community, engaging in social work, and performing religious services. Religion was to be taught in an ecumenical spirit, without disparaging other faith traditions, and textbooks were to be formally approved by the Ministry of Education. The protocol made religion an optional and a facultative subject but failed to define the terms precisely—an oversight church, state, and civil society representatives have struggled ever since to take advantage of or to correct. Apparently, "facultative" meant that students had the option to take or not to take a particular subject included in the school curriculum, whereas "optional" meant that students had to choose between two subjects, one of which was religion; the other was selected by the Ministry of Education.

The protocol framed subsequent debates on religious education in Romania. It revealed the denominations' powerful influence and imposed an understanding that gave them the upper hand. Offering religion classes taught by graduates of religious studies programs might have been another option. The graduates could teach religion from an ecumenical and comparative viewpoint, thereby eliminating the need both for students to be divided in smaller groups according to their faith and for teachers to instruct their students from the viewpoint of different denominations. This option reduces the number of classrooms and teachers required, as well as reducing the costs of teaching materials. In addition, the arrangement prevents teachers from extolling the virtues of one faith while denigrating others. The proposal was not without its problems. Romanian universities include theological, but not religious studies, departments. They train students in Orthodox, Roman Catholic, Greek Catholic, Reform, or Baptist dogma and social work, and, despite sustained efforts to promote ecumenism, local churches still have a long way to go before they embrace its spirit. Still, the long-term benefits would have greatly exceeded these short-term difficulties. At no point was such a proposal put forth—not even by human rights activists or civil society representatives—not because it was unfeasible, but because the involved parties were unable to envisage it.

The protocol allowed religion to officially enter the curriculum and set legal limits to religious education in public schools, but what it both said and failed to say raised some unrealistic expectations. Some argued that the protocol deliberately kept the status of religion in relation to other subjects unclear to allow denominations, and especially the powerful Orthodox Church, to reach as many children as possible. Following the protocol, religious groups expected most of the resistance against religion teachers to fade away, and the ministry expected religion to be taught in an ecumenical spirit though teachers presented exclusively the viewpoint of their own denomination. The schools expected the ministry to give them clear guidelines on how to offer religious education. The teachers expected the schools to make classrooms and time slots available. And students expected to have the chance to enroll in classes presenting the fundamentals of the religious denomination of their choice. But there were important unresolved issues. Students not choosing an officially recognized denomination were in effect denied religious education because the State Secretariat was unwilling to cover the cost of training teachers in their traditions, and the ministry forbade the organization of religious classes for denominations not officially acknowledged. Since students could choose the denomination of their religion class, more than one classroom had to be available to accommodate students of different denominations, a fact that placed a considerable burden on the Romanian schools, whose lack of space remains proverbial. It took time for some of these problems to be sorted out.

Even after religious education was made official, the Orthodox patriarchate received letters from priests reporting problems. The Bishopric of Buzău complained that its clergy faced problems in delivering religion classes and mentioned that it insistently asked the Ministry of Education to advise local school principals to "enter [religion] in the timetable, include it in the grade sheet and keep a record of all religion classes held," presumably because schools still refused to do so. In their petition to the synod, the priest and parishioners of Cănești village presented the "acute difficulties we faced [in our attempts] at reintroducing religion in school mounted by the school leadership, represented by Principal Florica Iordan, who belongs to the old communist nomenklatura, formerly served as the deputy secretary of our mayor's office, and was improperly installed as school principal after the December 1989 revolution." The petitioners hoped that Patriarch Teoctist personally "will intervene with the government for our village school to reintroduce religion [as a subject] as it was before 1948, since this is our right. This measure will contribute to the healthy education of the new generation in the spirit of Christian morality and honesty, truth, justice, and all the virtues inherited from our ancestors for the good of our Fatherland, the glory of our Holy Mother Church and the welfare of our nation." In a separate letter, the local priest offered additional reasons for resolute intervention, including the fact that the principal did not allow the *Te Deum* to be performed and an icon to be introduced in the school. Without the principal's approval, the *Te Deum* was sung on 1 October 1990 and an icon was hung on a classroom wall, but it soon disappeared. The letter mentioned that the Ministry of Education representatives sided with the principal against the priest, but "under the pressure of the faithful" the principal agreed to introduce religion in the curriculum more than a month after the start of the school year.[25]

In May 1991, priests in Buzău complained to the Ministry of Education that a number of school principals did not allocate time slots and classrooms to religion classes, and alleged that the principals interpreted erroneously the terms "facultative" and "optional" in the collaboration protocol to mean that students could choose not to take religion at all. In the town of Râmnicu Sărat, priests reported that religion classes were scheduled either too early in the morning, when students and teachers had trouble getting to school, or too late in the afternoon, when students were eager to leave school to go home or attend to other activities. This encouraged students to skip class or to opt out of religion altogether. Another reason for concern was the fact that some schools had no classrooms where religious instruction could take place, and attendance was low because teachers made students aware that religion was not mandatory. A report on religious education in the public schools located on the territory of the Bishopric of Buzău mentioned that "in some schools priests were received with a cold shoulder and even hostility, while in other schools only after two to three weeks of insistence [on their part] were religion classes allowed to start," and that principals of schools in urban areas mounted resistance, whereas schools in rural areas created no problems. The report blamed the ministry for not ordering town schools to introduce religion into the curriculum as a subject as important as the traditional disciplines of mathematics and history.[26]

It was only in mid-1995 that parliament adopted a new law on education providing for religious instruction. The delay was due not so much to the controversy around religious education as to the endless debates surrounding education in minority languages that the law also covered. According to the parliamentary statutes, the draft bill was sent for discussion to two standing commissions, including the Commission on Education, before being debated in the Chamber of Deputies and the Senate in separate sessions. The Senate discussed the bill on 13 June 1995 in the presence of the Social Democrat Minister of Education Liviu Maior. Much of the debate centered on Article 9, which recognized religion as a school subject. First, Senator Gheorghe Dumitraşcu, who sat on the parliamentary Commission on Education, proposed that Article 9 read: "Mandatory school curricula include religion as a school subject. The study of religion is mandatory in primary school and optional in secondary school, the optional subject being ethics. The study of religion is also optional, depending on the religion and denomination of each student." Maior agreed with the proposal with one exception: he wanted the elimination of any alternative to religion, since, in his view, the presence of an alternative created confusion among students and teachers, and religious denominations did not like alternatives. Maior added that religion dealt with ethical issues, and as such it was pointless to propose ethics as an alternative to religion; he explained that in mandatory school curricula for the first eight grades there were no optional subjects, and the ministry was unwilling to grant religion a different status. Maior's new proposal stated: "Mandatory school curricula include religion as a school subject. The study of religion is mandatory in primary school and optional in secondary school. The study of religion is also optional, depending on the religion and denomination of each student." To this proposal, Emil Tocaci asked the minister to consider the word "facultative" instead of "optional," because "optional" implied an option or alternative that needed to be specified. After the minister embraced the suggestion, several senators argued in favor of the mandatory character of religious education.[27]

The Legislative Framework

The Law on Education no. 84 of 31 July 1995,[28] dealing with all forms of education in Romania, was the first post-communist law to legalize the teaching of religion in public schools. Only Articles 9, 11, and 12 pertained to religious education. The law made religion classes mandatory in primary schools (grades 1–4), optional in secondary schools (grades 5–8), and facultative in high schools (grades 9–12) and vocational schools (Article 9.1). With the consent of their parents or legal guardians, students could choose to study religion in a particular denomination (Article 9.2). The law banned religious proselytism in public schools to avoid subordinating education to the purposes and doctrines promoted by political parties and other societal groups (Article 11.3). The organization and content of instruction could not be structured according to exclusive and discriminatory criteria with respect to ideology, politics, religion, or ethnicity, but Article 12 provided exceptions to the rule. Educational institutions created because of religious or linguistic needs were not considered exclusive and discriminatory. Instruction in such institutions corresponded to the choice of the students' parents or legal guardians.

The day parliament adopted the law, a record number of fifty-seven deputies asked the Constitutional Court to examine the constitutionality of Article 9.1. In their petition, deputies claimed that, by making the study of religion mandatory in primary schools, the law ran counter to the 1991 constitution, which guaranteed "the free development of human personality" (Article 1.3) and freedom of conscience (Article 29), provided that "any person has the right to freely dispose of herself" (Article 26.2), and obliged public authorities to "ensure the conditions necessary for the youth's free participation in the country's political, social, economic, cultural and sportive life" (Article 45.5).[29] Before ruling on the petition, the court asked for clarifications from the Ministry of Education and parliament, which replied that, in their view, the controversial Article 9.1 was constitutional.

Based on provisions of the Romanian constitution and international law, the court nuanced its position and deemed constitutional one specific reading of Article 9, itself not readily apparent. Constitutional Court Decision no. 72 of 18 July 1995 stated that the Romanian constitution provided that "in state schools religious education is organized and guaranteed by law" (Article 32.7), that "nobody can be constrained to adopt an opinion or adhere to a religious belief that are contrary to the person's beliefs" (Article 29.1), and that "parents and [legal] guardians have the right and responsibility to ensure, according to their own convictions, the education of their minor children" (Article 29.6). The court cited Article 18 of the Universal Declaration of Human Rights, stating that "everyone has the right to freedom of thought, conscience and religion; this right includes freedom to change his religion or belief, and freedom, either alone or in community with others and in public or private, to manifest his religion or belief in teaching, practice, worship and observance"; Article 18.2 of the International Covenant on Civil and Political Rights, which provides that "no one shall be subject to coercion which would impair his freedom to have or to adopt a religion or belief of his choice"; and Article 13.3 of the International Covenant on Economic, Social and Cultural Rights, according to which "the States Parties to the present Covenant undertake to have respect for the liberty of parents and, when applicable, legal guardians to choose for their children schools, other than those established by the public authorities, which conform to such minimum educational standards as may be laid down or approved by the state and to ensure the religious and moral education of their children in conformity with their own convictions." Article 9 of the European Convention for the Protection of Human Rights supported a similar view.[30] The court insisted that Article 9.1 of the Law on Education should be interpreted in strict conformity with Article 29 of the constitution, in the sense that "nobody can be constrained to adopt an opinion or to adhere to a religious belief that is contrary to the person's beliefs" and that "parents and [legal] guardians have the right and responsibility to ensure, according to their own convictions, the education of their minor children." For the court, any other interpretation was unconstitutional.

Thus, for the Constitutional Court, the provision of Article 9.1 allowing "students, with the consent of their parents or legal guardians, to choose to study religion in the denomination of their choice" was constitutional, since the right to choose allowed the possibility of either having or not having a religious option. The choice made with the consent of the parents or legal guardians was an expression of parental authority and ensured the right of the child's legal representatives to make decisions, according to their own convictions, on the education of their minor children. For the court, the introduction of religion as a "mandatory subject" of study in primary schools was unconstitutional, unless it allowed the student not to study religion at all. The court interpreted the word "mandatory" to mean that religion must be present as a subject of study in primary schools, but the choice to study it or not was optional. In other words, primary schools should be prepared to offer religion as a subject of study, but students, with the consent of their parents or legal guardians, may choose not to study it.

The ruling baffled human rights organizations like the Association for the Defense of Human Rights in Romania–the Helsinki Committee (APADOR-CH), which expected the Constitutional Court to explicitly strike down all interpretations of Article 9.1 as unconstitutional rather than propose a compromise between the law on education and the constitutional guarantees for freedom of conscience. According to human rights activist Renate Weber, the ruling equated "mandatory" with the right to have religion in the curriculum, an interpretation that was unjustified judicially and betrayed a compromise

between constitutional guarantees and the pressure exerted on the court justices by the Orthodox Church.[31] Indeed, in December 1996, the synod sent to
the Senate an initiative supported by 1,049,853 citizens asking for the modi-
fication of Article 9 to state that "the primary, secondary, high school, and
vocational school curricula include religion as a basic subject of study. Participation in religion classes is done in accordance with [each student's] religious
affiliation." The revised article denied students the right not to enroll in religion classes, but the Minister of Education remained silent on that issue and
only noted that no subject was recognized as "basic."

APADOR-CH insisted that, in practice, few Romanians were aware of the
Constitutional Court ruling and few knew that their children had the option of
not having religion in school. Pressure from the religious denominations,
teachers, and fellow students, along with the schools' reluctance to explain to
the children their rights and list religion as an optional and facultative subject,
ensured that students not keen on religion remained enrolled in religion
classes. The situation was complicated by the fact that, as explained earlier,
children declaring their religious affiliation had to choose an officially recognized denomination. This meant that students embracing unrecognized faiths
were denied the right to pursue religious education.

Human rights groups criticizing Article 9.1 continued to lobby the government to amend the law in order to make it clear that students could take no
religion at all, if they and their parents so desired. With new elections around
the corner, the Social Democrat government was unwilling to bring changes to
the law on education that would make it unpopular with the powerful religious
denominations, commanding support from large segments of the electorate. It
was only after the Democratic Convention won the November 1996 parliamentary elections, and Christian Democrat Emil Constantinescu replaced Ion
Iliescu as the Romanian president, that the new government issued Emergency Ordinance no. 36 of 10 July 1997, which amended Article 9 of the law on
education to read:

> (1) Religion is part of the school curriculum in primary, secondary,
> high, and professional schools. (2) The student, with the consent of
> the parents or legal guardian, chooses to study religion in a particular
> denomination. The student may choose not to enroll in religion
> classes if parents or the student's legal guardian request this in
> writing. In the latter case, the grade point average is computed with-
> out religion grades. The computation method is similar for students
> who, because of objective reasons, do not have the possibility to attend
> religion classes.[32]

In its new version, the article recognized the students' right to take no religion classes, but placed the burden on the students to let the school know their wishes by submitting written requests for exemption. Critics noted that the new version better met the churches' demands for a more comprehensive coverage of religious instruction in schools. While formally giving students the option not to study religion, the new article observed the letter but not the spirit of the Romanian constitution and international legislation protecting freedom of conscience because it made the study of religion the default option and the process of choosing not to study it more cumbersome by requesting a written notice from parents. Out of convenience, some parents might not submit such exemption requests, and parents in rural areas might be deterred to behave differently from other parents and let their children study religion out of peer pressure or because they were intimidated by the priest, the teachers, or the larger community.[33]

Defenders argued that the new article rightly predicted that there would be few exemption requests. If students wishing to take religion classes had to submit written requests, the school system would be unnecessarily burdened with paperwork. Other observers noted that the ordinance was a way for the major coalition partner, the Christian Democratic Peasant Party, to repay the Orthodox Church for its support in mobilizing the electorate against the Social Democrats. As a commentator noted, "except for electoral rhetoric, only the enforcement of religious instruction in public school curricula showed the party's dedication to Christian Democracy."[34] When asked how this fit in with Romania's application to the European Union and its commitment to the separation of church and state, the new Liberal Minister of Education Andrei Marga answered vaguely that Romania's overwhelmingly Orthodox population had to be considered.

Emergency ordinances are adopted without parliament debating them individually. Usually, most of the discussion surrounding ordinances is carried out in the legislative standing commissions, with the full chambers allotting little time for discussion. In the case of Emergency Ordinance no. 36/1997, the Chamber of Deputies struggled with the constitutionality of revised Article 9. In its session of 5 November 1998, Democrat Party deputy Alexandru Brezniceanu saw Article 9 as contradictory.[35] While paragraph 1 made religion part of the school curriculum at pre-university levels, implicitly giving it a mandatory character, paragraph 2 spoke of the students' choice not to enroll in religion classes, thus giving them the option not to attend such classes. Brezniceanu unsuccessfully tried to amend the article to state that "in pre-university schools, the study of religion is guaranteed at all levels by the school curriculum." Christian Democrat Gheorghe Andrei asked for high schools and vocational schools not to be required to offer religion. In his view, "thousands of high school students declared themselves outside of any religious denomination" to avoid taking religion classes usually scheduled at the beginning or the end of the school day. There was also a shortage of trained teachers able to answer intelligently the more sophisticated questions of high school students, and the students' workload was already heavy enough.

The proposal was defeated. Before the vote, Social Democrat Dan Marţian criticized the ordinance for making religion mandatory at the pre-university level and thus ignoring the Constitutional Court ruling upholding the constitutionality of only a very precise interpretation of Article 9. In reply, Christian Democrat deputy Virgil Petrescu claimed that the ordinance followed the procedure laid down by the constitution: after mentioning a rule, it specified the exceptions to the rule. In Petrescu's view, paragraph 1 of the revised Article 9 introduced the rule, while paragraph 2 introduced the exceptions to the rule.

The 1999 law on education was unable to eliminate confusion. It recognized religion as part of the "common curriculum," a formulation that could make religion mandatory, since only mandatory courses are common to all pre-university levels, but also an optional and facultative subject the student could opt out of. While formally all pre-university students had the choice of not pursuing religious education in public schools, in practice that choice could not be taken advantage of. In its internet documents, the Orthodox patriarchate presents religious education as mandatory, in spite of the constitutional guarantees for freedom of conscience, the Constitutional Court Decision no. 72 of 1995, and the human rights conventions Romania adhered to. The site states that "the subject Religion is mandatory at the pre-university level and organically integrated into the education legislation and all current Ministry of Education orders and decisions."[36] Sorin Otelariu, an Orthodox priest and a high school religion teacher maintaining a website on religious education in Romanian public schools, believes that Emergency Ordinance no. 36 of 1997 allowed religion to gain a "somewhat mandatory status" but failed to help students choose the denomination in which to study religion. According to him, students should not be allowed to choose denominations "subjectively, but the choice should be determined "objectively" by baptismal certificates.[37]

Journalists have reported instances where the practice of teaching religion in schools ran counter to the constitutionally guaranteed freedom of conscience. Under pressure from local churches, schools in the Transylvanian city of Cluj-Napoca scheduled religion classes among other mandatory classes during the school day and gave up the practice of offering religion at either the beginning or end of the day. Whereas the old schedule encouraged students with an interest in religion to skip class for the convenience of having more spare time, the new timetable kept students taking no religion classes prisoners of the school for that hour.[38] Survey polls conducted in the 2002–2003 school year among high schools in Buzău revealed that, on average, fewer than 20 percent of students enrolled in religion classes and as many as 90 percent of students did not know that religion was facultative and could be dropped, without the student being asked to opt for another subject instead. When told that religion was not compulsory, only 14 percent of students still opted for religion as a subject of study.[39] These low percentages do not reflect high levels of interest in religion classes, as churches have consistently suggested.

Other press reports reveal that some Orthodox religion teachers adopt a position toward other denominations that is far from ecumenical. In some schools, students were asked to cross themselves in front of Orthodox icons placed permanently (not just during the religion class) in the classrooms. In Buzău, an Orthodox religion teacher told students in grades 1–4 that if they did not wear crucifixes the devil would inflict evil on them; another teacher drew the devil on the blackboard to scare the students; students of rural schools were compelled not only to attend religion classes but also to go to the local Orthodox church and buy candles; and one report even claimed that a girl was so scared by the teacher-priest's story about burning in hell that she ended up having nightmares and being psychologically traumatized.[40] A religion teacher at School no. 1 of Buzău town denigrated other legally recognized religious groups and told students that if they ever entered a Seventh-day Adventist church they would then be run over by a tractor. At another school, the religion teacher asked students to refer to non-Orthodox denominations as sects and claimed that "Jehovah's Witnesses is one of the most dangerous sects, promoting religious fanaticism."[41] In 2003, a school in a small Argeş village unveiled a classroom dedicated to religion classes that resembled a chapel with wall paintings of biblical scenes, martyrs, and saints alongside portraits of the local bishop, the school principal, and the mayor, who was also the village Orthodox priest. The priest was draped in the Romanian national flag. When questioned by journalists, he defended the traditional Orthodox character of the paintings and the inclusion of the three portraits.[42]

Another religion teacher told students in grade 5 that God loved only the Orthodox. After objecting to such teaching and arguing that God loved all children, the two non-Orthodox students in the class were ostracized during the break, with Orthodox students refusing to play with them on grounds that they were "dirty." The Orthodox priest teaching religion at the primary school in Joseni village (Buzău county) punished a child in grade 4 by ordering him to stand up for the entire hour-long class because he confessed to having watched a movie brought to the village by a Protestant group. According to Gabriel Andreescu, the attitude toward education of some religion teachers went against "modern education principles that envision the student as a responsible person endowed with reason and democratic values." He blamed the state for "failing to meet its obligation to guarantee conditions for children's education and their completely free affirmation of freedom of conscience." Because of the concessions they made to the churches, "state institutions supported the infringement of principles without which we cannot discuss European integration."[43] Indeed, the Ministry of Education seems unwilling to stand up to the Orthodox religion teachers. When Moise complained of the abuses committed by these teachers, the ministry representative laughed and dismissed the reports as mere "exaggerations."[44]

Before Romania adopted a new law on religion in 2006, two proposals were drafted by the executive and discussed by the legislative branch before being abandoned for electoral reasons. The first draft—introduced in parliament in September 1998, discussed in 1999, and withdrawn in February 2000 by the Mugur Isărescu cabinet—was pieced together by Christian Democrat Premier Radu Vasile. When it came to religious instruction in public schools, it stated that "parents or legal guardians have the right to educate their children in their religion or in the religion of their choice" (Article 3). The second proposal was prepared by Social Democrat State Secretary for Religious Denominations Laurenţiu Tănase and presented to religious groups for discussion in 2004. Its stipulation that "parents or legal guardians have exclusive right to opt for the religious instruction of their minor children according to their own faith" (Article 3) came under attack for not allowing children any input in the decision.[45]

But the draft went a step further to regulate church involvement in public schools. According to Article 33, "religious instruction may be undertaken in public schools exclusively by registered religious denominations. Public school religious instructors are appointed with the consent of the religious denomination they represent." The article also allowed for the possibility of dismissal on doctrinal grounds: "If an instructor gravely departs from the doctrine and ethics, the religious denomination can withdraw the permission [to that individual] to teach religion, a move which leads to dismissal." It is unclear who exactly is to determine what "gravely" means.[46] In early 2006, the Senate adopted the proposal in virtue of Article 75.2 of the constitution, which states that if a chamber fails to pronounce within sixty days of the introduction of an "extremely complex law," "it shall be deemed that the bill or legislative proposal has been adopted." The draft was finally adopted as Law on Religious

Freedom and the General Regime of Religious Denominations no. 489 of 28 December 2006. Article 32 of the law deals with religious instruction in schools and reads:

> 1. In public and private schools, religious instruction is provided to recognized denominations. 2. Religion teachers in public schools are appointed with the consent of the denomination they represent. 3. If a teacher seriously trespasses the doctrine and moral values of the denomination, the denomination may withdraw the support it gives that individual to teach religion, a move leading to the teacher's dismissal. 4. If a school cannot provide teachers of religion for students belonging to a particular denomination, students can request to demonstrate that they study religion by providing proof from the denomination to which they belong.[47]

Religious Education Textbooks

We had the opportunity to study Orthodox and Roman Catholic religion textbooks used in Romanian pre-university public schools. While under communism all public schools used unique textbooks for each subject, since 1989 the Ministry of Education has allowed teachers to choose between alternative textbooks written by different authors and published by different presses. Textbooks are distributed free of charge to all students at pre-university levels, and this is probably why they can hardly be found in bookstores. The following discussion is based on seven Orthodox and two Roman Catholic textbooks, as well as the officially approved curricula for religious education. We had access to the Roman Catholic textbooks for grades 1 and 2 and to all pre-university Orthodox textbooks except those for grades 3, 6, 7, 8, and 12.

All Orthodox religion textbooks we consulted have the approval of the Ministry of Education, a mandatory condition for textbooks for all subjects. With one exception, all textbooks were "printed with the blessing of His Beatitude Teoctist, Patriarch of the Romanian Orthodox Church," a formula equivalent to the Catholic imprimatur representing an endorsement of the textbook. For grades 1–4, the curriculum for the Orthodox religion classes includes elements of the Old and New Testament, Christian ethics, and liturgy, ministry, and mission. Each grade presents these general areas in gradually more complex terms, building on the knowledge students acquire in previous grades. Students in secondary schools become familiar with the history of the early church and the history of the Romanian Orthodox Church up to the present day. Catechesis is introduced in grade 2 and continued up to grade 10. High school students in grade 9 review issues related to Christian ethics, liturgy, spirituality, and mission, but they also learn about other religions (Islam, Hinduism, Buddhism, Judaism). Students in grades 10 to 12 study elements of Orthodox dogma and Christian art and reflect on "Christianity and the Problems of the Youth," including music, drugs, mass media, sexuality, superstitions, reincarnation, Asian religious practices, unidentified flying objects, and sectarian aggressiveness. In addition, grades 10 and 11 are exposed to "Orthodoxy and National Culture," a broad theme including lessons on Romanian religious folk art, early Romanian manuscripts, Orthodox metropolitans and their contribution to nation building, and the unification of the provinces of Wallachia, Moldova, and Transylvania. Some textbooks respect the approved curriculum more strictly than others. For example, out of two grade 2 textbooks consulted, the one approved only by the ministry followed the curriculum strictly, while the one approved by both the patriarchate and the ministry followed the Orthodox liturgical cycle, with Christmas and Easter as highlights.[48]

Approved by both the ministry and the patriarchate, the curriculum includes elements that are potentially problematic from the viewpoint of the twin tolerations democratic requirement and the state's need to be impartial with respect to denominations. It could be argued that the inclusion of catechesis in religion classes directs public resources (teacher's salaries and classrooms) toward activities that should be carried out by the Orthodox Church on Sundays, an exercise the church has yet to consider seriously. It could also be argued that catechesis seems to have been introduced not so much to provide students with additional information regarding the Orthodox faith but in the hope of turning them into committed Orthodox believers.[49] The "Orthodoxy and National Culture" section could be problematic if it does not begin to acknowledge the role of other religious groups, most notably the Greek Catholic Church, in the emancipation of Transylvanian Romanians and the formation of the Romanian Kingdom in 1918. We consider concrete examples of this, but first we turn to evaluating the general characteristics of the Orthodox textbooks.

The Orthodox religion textbooks provide a level of detail that seems unnecessary for the average student who does not plan to enroll in higher theological education. The textbooks, especially the most advanced ones destined for high schools, cover almost the same material that is covered in seminaries and theological institutes. In addition, higher-level textbooks repeat in greater detail topics studied in earlier grades.[50] This is characteristic of pre-university textbooks for all subjects, not only Orthodox religion, and a constant concern for parents, who believe that the school curriculum in general is heavy, too much being covered in almost every subject and too many subjects being studied.[51] Senator Angela Bălan voiced these concerns on 21 May 2001 when she demanded the Social Democrat Minister of Education Ecaterina Andro-nescu to revise the school curriculum and rhetorically asked whether every student must have an advanced knowledge of religion. The senator received no convincing reply, and the religion curriculum remained unchanged.[52]

Unlike other subjects, Orthodox religion makes little effort to update the language of its textbooks to make it more accessible to children. Their language has been used in theological schools since the seventeenth century and is burdened by archaic words and formulas used neither in the literary language nor in colloquial Romanian. Textbooks for grades 2–8 include excessively long lessons, accompanied by primary text readings starting in grade 5. Most readings are from the Bible, but some are commentaries on a biblical episode discussed in class.[53] For Andreescu, the Orthodox religion textbooks contain sexist and authoritarian elements, both because they quote passages from the Old Testament where women are listed among men's possessions alongside animals and land and because a grade 1 lesson speaks of God harshly pun-ishing children who abuse animals. "Moral-religious training" should be the first to embrace modern educational models stressing reward instead of punishment, but the Romanian educational system in general has not entirely eradicated child abuse and physical punishment.[54]

Many textbooks blend Orthodoxy and nationalism, and they alternate lessons about Jesus with lessons about the lives of Romanian saints and po-litical rulers. The Orthodox Church is presented as the most important religion of the Romanians, key to their ethnic identity, nation and state. The country's major literary figure, nineteenth-century poet and political commentator Mihai Eminescu, is quoted as saying that the Orthodox Church is "the spiritual mother of the Romanian people"; Kings Constantin Brâncoveanu and Stephen the Great are presented as Orthodox saints; and the grade 9 lesson on "Love of Nation and Country" mentions that the "Romanian law [is] belief in God and love of the country."[55] In grade 12, students are familiarized with Romanian Christian thinkers, some of whom were interwar figures such as Nae Ionescu, Mircea Eliade, Nichifor Crainic, Vasile Băncilă, and Petre Țuțea, but no men-tion is made of their anti-Semitism and collaboration with or sympathy for the fascist Iron Guard. Moreover, nothing is said about the compromises the Orthodox Church made during communist times.[56]

The textbooks adopt a critical position toward the new religions that en-tered the country after 1989. Echoing the official position of the Orthodox Church, which believes that new religious movements have lured Orthodox faithful with false promises of short-term financial assistance, the textbook for grade 9 presents proselytism as "a form of manifesting intolerance toward the religious beliefs of one's fellow humans." It mentions that the Orthodox Church condemns it but does not mention that proselytism is not illegal in Romania (p. 29). Its definition of proselytism, "the attempt to change one's religious beliefs through various means: material objects, moral pressure," differs markedly from the definition provided by the *Romanian Dictionary of Neologisms*, which views proselytism as "zeal to make proselytes; ardent devotion for a newly adopted belief."[57] The textbook sees only the free preaching of the word as acceptable because it does not involve material gifts or moral pressure.

While Roman Catholic textbooks are written in a more accessible language and use everyday examples and stories instead of biblical stories, they seem more expressly directed toward teachers than students. The textbook for grade 1 contains several three-page lessons that are inaccessible to children who have barely begun learning the alphabet. It focuses on God the Father, Jesus, and the Holy Spirit. The textbook for grade 2 is more appropriate to the age group it targets. It discusses Jesus and Mary and God as the creator of the world. The textbook for grade 1 has the imprimatur of Archbishop Ioan Robu, the head of the Roman Catholic Church in Romania, but the textbook for grade 2 does not (although it was sold in the bookstore of the Roman Catholic Archdiocese of Bucharest).[58] More important, neither textbook bears the official approval of the Ministry of Education.

Darwinist Theory and Christian Values

The Orthodox Church's involvement in education did not stop with the introduction of religion classes. At times, calls have been heard for the revision of textbooks in consonance with Christian values. In 1990, the Group of Reflection on Church Renewal asked for a "de-Marxization" of pre-university textbooks so as to adequately reflect the contribution of Orthodoxy to Romanian culture.[59] While the group failed to offer details, it presumably referred to textbooks for traditional subjects like history, philosophy, biology, and Romanian literature. Three years later, Metropolitan Antonie Plămădeală of Transylvania called on parliament to adopt educational programs and literature based on fundamental Christian values and ideals. His position was echoed in 1998 by Greek Catholic priest and Christian Democratic senator Ioan Moisin, who asked the Ministry of Education to set up a commission of "knowledgeable" Orthodox and Catholics to revise philosophy and biology textbooks to avoid contradictions with religious creationism. The senator complained that students were told by their religion teacher that humans are God's creation and by the philosophy and biology teachers of Darwinist persuasion that humans descend from apes. The proposal also envisioned the formation of a Council of Public Morality, directly subordinated to the Romanian president and formed by church and teachers' representatives, which would supervise public education.[60] Neither the parliament nor the ministry seriously considered these proposals.

Orthodox Symbols in Universities

Until 1945, the Faculty of Orthodox Theology was part of the University of Bucharest, the country's most prestigious higher education establishment, but the communist anti-religious campaign turned it into an independent institute offering four-year bachelor in theology degrees. Admission was strictly monitored, and graduates had a single career choice: priesthood. After 1990, the institute was reincorporated into the University of Bucharest, though many university administrators and faculty felt it did not meet university standards of excellence. The institute, directly controlled by Orthodox Church leaders, responded to these criticisms by diversifying its programs, hiring younger faculty (some with doctoral degrees from Western universities), and making admission and grading criteria more transparent. The number of corruption cases implicating theology professors has constantly diminished in the last seventeen years.

Since 1990, some Orthodox students have launched a massive campaign to make the University of Bucharest Orthodox. Classrooms were used to host student debates on religious issues; student residences, offices, and classrooms were blessed by Orthodox priests; and candles and Orthodox icons became a permanent fixture of classrooms. A spring 1998 incident highlighted the deep divide between Orthodox believers and more secularized societal groups and raised questions about the limits of religious activity in Romanian universities. The dispute ensued after four philosophy and law students asked the university senate to ban religious activity from the campus and reject a proposal of the Association of Christian Orthodox Students to build a new church on the grounds of the Faculty of Law.[61] Other students denounced the "excessive politicization of the academia and the imposition of an ideological monopoly" by the Orthodox Church, "the proliferation of extreme right groups," and the "toleration of and the support given to fundamentalism" by university administrators, calling students to resist these tendencies.[62]

The senate initially passed the required resolution but then rescinded its decision in response to a threat that the names of those voting against building the new church would be revealed. For a week, the university was covered with posters supporting both sides of the issue. Patriarch Teoctist and the Orthodox protesters proclaimed that communist-era religious persecution had returned, but the students opposed to the project saw the construction of a worship place on campus as a threat to a pluralist and tolerant academic ethos. The latter group also opposed a 1997 decision of the Law Students' League to introduce Orthodox icons into classrooms as infringing on the rights of non-Orthodox students. On 9 April 1998, the senate banned religious symbols (including icons) from campus and set up a committee to enforce the decision. The committee proved unable to make good on its promises. Even in 2004, there were icons on campus. The academic year continues to start with an Orthodox mass in which all faculty and students are invited to participate.

During a roundtable organized by the respected Group of Social Dialogue, gathering the country's prominent intellectuals, Professor Mircea Flonta revealed that a December 1995 proposal envisaged the inclusion in the academic charter of a provision saying that the University of Bucharest was based on the principles of Christian ethics. When the proposal met with a cold response because it might hamper the activity of non-Christian professors, the Association of Christian Orthodox Students asked for the recognition of an Orthodox patron saint for the university. This move, according to Flonta, revealed that the association viewed the leading Romanian university as a semiconfessional institution. Andreescu argued that "by introducing Orthodox and Catholic symbols in a university or school, one forces the students to study in a religiously defined atmosphere, a thing which runs counter to their religious freedom."[63] Though construction of the church was halted, it was due to the lack of necessary funding more than the university senate's realization that Romanian higher education should remain secular.

In 2004, another university faced pressure from Orthodox Church leaders seeking to build an Orthodox chapel on campus. The University of Suceava categorically refused to allow construction to start and petitioned the courts against decisions of the Social Democrat government and municipal council that ceded to the Archbishopric of Suceava 150 square meters next to the university convocation hall in one of the town's parks. University vice president Mihai Iacobescu challenged claims that the construction marked the 500-year anniversary of the death of Moldovan King Stephen the Great. He argued, instead, that it was the result of political pressure and the Social Democrats' desire to woo the Orthodox Church in search of electoral support. Indeed, the Orthodox Church draws much of its support from the province of Moldova, where Suceava is located.[64] Not all universities steered clear of religious influence. The University of Oradea in northwestern Transylvania boasts a centuries-old wooden church placed right in the middle of its campus, as well as a new chapel inside the main building that houses most of the classrooms. Both worship places are Orthodox, as have been all its university presidents since 1989.

Conclusion

The religious groups' most celebrated post-communist achievement was the introduction of religious instruction into public schools. In this chapter we analyzed the new law on education against the background of the 1991 constitution and international provisions protecting freedom of conscience. With an eye to historical precedents, we went beyond the legislation to present actual case studies, analyze religion manuals, and discuss attempts to ban the teaching of evolution in public schools. Romanian denominations have successfully pushed for legislation making religious education in public schools the default option, with parents who do not want their children to take religion having to opt out in writing. The way churches undertake the teaching of morality in an effort to heal the Romanian moral fiber after decades of communist atheism often goes against modern principles of education and guarantees for freedom of conscience. Due to this excessive zeal, students may end up rejecting religious values. Romania's high levels of political corruption suggest that religious morality has yet to make a difference in that country.

8

Religion, Politics, and Sexuality

Religious groups have worked both with and against the state to change public mentality and lifestyle. Sexual behavior and practices have been a contested territory for church and state throughout the last century. In a traditional society like Romania, popular mores are informed by the practices and contradictions of conservative villages, which have traditionally rejected homosexuality and scorned prostitution while at the same time tacitly accepting adulterous husbands. Villages have traditionally denounced abortion, even as they have developed an impressive knowledge of medicinal plants and potions able to induce it. Communist authorities were no kinder toward homosexuality. Under their rule, jail sentences for homosexual behavior increased. Homosexuality was used as an accusation against outspoken dissenters and was seen as a barrier undermining the creation of the "new socialist man."[1] The communists also imposed a comprehensive pro-life program that ultimately failed to protect the country against population loss.

After 1989, homosexuality, abortion, and prostitution became deeply divisive issues in Romanian society. They sparked heated public debates involving politicians, religious leaders, local academic communities, the mass media, and the public at large. Discussions generally revolved around the adoption of new laws that would align Romanian legislation with European Union standards. A combination of internal factors (such as shifts in accepted mores) and external factors (including pressure from the European

community) determined the formulation of new, liberal legislation with respect to these three areas of sexuality. The ban on homosexuality was lifted at
the insistence of the Council of Europe, which threatened to recommence
monitoring Romania's human rights record if the ban were not removed.
While the international community took a decisive role in ending discrimination against gays and lesbians, it remained silent on Romania's position vis-
à-vis abortion and prostitution, mostly because European Union member
states do not themselves embrace a common position on these two sensitive
issues.

In this chapter, we examine homosexuality, abortion, contraception,
family planning, and prostitution, several issues upon which religious groups
made pronouncements. We also discuss the churches' condemnation of artificial insemination, a topic that briefly gained media attention in early 2005.
We conclude by discussing the Orthodox Church's struggle to regulate additional aspects of the sexual life of its married clergy and their families, as well
as those of unmarried monks.

Lifting the Ban on Homosexuality

When Romania formally applied for membership in the European community
in the early 1990s, Article 200 of its Criminal Code, punishing sexual relationships among same-sex persons with prison terms of up to five years, came
under heavy criticism. It did not meet European standards of tolerance and
went against European legislation regarding the recognition of minority
groups and nondiscrimination. Three years after becoming the country's supreme leader, in 1965 Nicolae Ceauşescu introduced Article 200 which, together with an earlier sweeping pro-life program, was part of a larger campaign
to increase the available workforce, regulate sexual behavior, and rid the
country of what he considered unacceptable behavior. All of this served the
creation of the new socialist man and woman.

For decades, gays and lesbians kept their sexual orientation secret for fear
of prosecution, and many endured long prison terms for the slightest infringement of the communist moral code. After 1989, gay and lesbian groups
began lobbying against the ban on homosexual behavior, but their demands
met with fierce resistance from the general public, political elites, and religious
groups. A 1993 opinion poll showed that four out of five Romanians believed
homosexual acts were never justified and the complete eradication of homosexuality served a legitimate national interest. Eight years later, another poll
found that 86 percent of respondents would not want a gay or lesbian person

as their neighbor.[2] A 2004 poll reported that 61 percent of respondents avoided homosexuals, 36 percent of them would not want a homosexual neighbor, and 43 percent believed that homosexuality is a disease that can be treated. In the same poll, an unnamed gay man expressed his distrust of the National Council for Fighting Discrimination. In his view, as well as that of his friends, the council did not help homosexuals. Rather, it was a façade assisting Romania's bid to join the European Union.[3]

The denominations first voiced their position on homosexuality in 1995, when the Constitutional Court asked them to comment on Article 200. That year, the court of the Transylvanian town of Sibiu asked the Constitutional Court to rule on the article's constitutionality and to state whether behavior condemned by the Christian churches should be prosecuted for endangering the "normal evolution of social relationships." To develop a response, the Constitutional Court asked legislators, recognized religious groups, the academic community, local administrative bodies, and civil society representatives to discuss the ban on homosexuality. Summarizing these responses in its final ruling, Decision no. 81 of 15 July 1995,[4] the Constitutional Court listed the denominations that answered its request, naming the Orthodox, Greek Catholic, and Old Calendar Churches, alongside representatives of the Jewish, Muslim, Seventh-day Adventist, and Pentecostal communities. The court remarked that all denominations without exception condemned homosexuality and upheld the ban.

The Senate rejected charges that Article 200 ran counter to the 1991 Romanian constitution and the European Human Rights Convention, while the academic community asked for more time to study the issue. Only the civil society groups asked for the ban to be scrapped. In its ruling, the Constitutional Court noted that Article 200, which banned any kind of homosexual behavior, ran counter to important pieces of international legislation the country adopted after 1989. To reconcile the Romanian Criminal Code with European legislation, the court ruled that Article 200 was unconstitutional "to the extent that it refers to consensual sexual relations between adults of the same sex, not taking place in public and not producing public scandal." The court's bold move paved the way for decriminalizing homosexuality.[5]

Under international pressure, the Social Democrat government of Prime Minister Nicolae Văcăroiu initiated procedures to modify the code in accordance with European standards, but only after years of bitter arguments did changes partially liberalizing homosexual activities come into effect by Law no. 140 of 5 November 1996.[6] Under the new version of Article 200, homosexual activities were punishable with prison terms if they were carried out in public or if they caused public scandal. The article punished those "inciting or encouraging a person to the practice of sexual relations between persons of the same sex," as well as "propaganda or association or any other act of proselytism committed with the same purpose." While seemingly more lenient than its predecessor, the new formulation did not specify what exactly constituted a public scandal and where the fine line between private and public behavior should fall. Some politicians believed that any homosexual act was potentially public because "what is damaging and immoral on the streets cannot be permissible and moral in intimacy," while others justified their hesitation to fully decriminalize homosexuality by pointing to opinion polls showing that Romanians regarded homosexual relations as abnormal.[7]

It took four more years to erase Article 200 from the Criminal Code. In May 1998, the Christian Democrat government of Prime Minister Radu Vasile adopted amendments to decriminalize homosexual behavior, while punishing coerced sexual relations and relations with children younger than fourteen years of age with jail sentences of up to seven years. Addressing the press, Minister of Justice and Liberal leader Valeriu Stoica stressed that the changes were meant not to change the de facto situation, since apparently "homosexuality ceased to be prosecuted in 1996," but the de jure position of homosexuality and to eliminate the Council of Europe's "suspicions" toward Romania. To shift the blame away from itself and preempt criticism coming from conservative segments of Romanian society, the government pointed out that Article 200 had been scrapped as part of a larger drive to harmonize Romanian and European Union legislation that included lifting jail sanctions for calumny and decriminalizing the insult of public authorities.[8]

While the senators supported the changes the government proposed, the deputies were much less willing to jeopardize their popular support and risk losing the impending general election of late 2000 by voting for an unpopular bill. At the end of a fierce debate in which only Democratic Party representative George Stancov dared to praise the amendments, the ruling Christian Democrat and the opposition Social Democrat and Greater Romania Party deputies unexpectedly joined hands to reject the changes. One deputy who voted against the proposal defended his position stating, "we want to enter Europe, not Sodom and Gomorrah."[9]

Prime Minister Vasile's proposed changes again took center stage after Romania started accession talks with the European Union in March 2000, at a time when addressing the problem of discrimination against minority groups became a formal commitment for Romania to enter Europe. On 28 June of that year, deputies voted to decriminalize homosexuality, in accordance with Council of Europe Resolution no. 1123,[10] which deemed the Romanian Article 200 discriminatory. Once the lower legislative chamber approved them, the changes were sent to the upper chamber for examination. To quash the amendments, the Orthodox Holy Synod met ahead of the debate in the Senate, with spokesman Archbishop Nifon of Târgovişte announcing that the synod had decided to ask President Emil Constantinescu not to sign the changes into law, should the Senate also vote for decriminalizing homosexuality. Local gay rights activists set up a lobby in parliament and petitioned Patriarch Teoctist in a bid to temper the Orthodox clerics' wrath.[11] Ultimately, the international factor decided the fate of Article 200. When it became clear that the Romanian political elite was ready to postpone eliminating Article 200 in the electoral year 2000, the Council of Europe threatened on 9 September 2000 to renew the monitoring of Romania's human rights record. Hours before the deadline, the Romanian bicameral legislative assembly passed the amendments.

Though the law marks a groundbreaking step for the rights of homosexuals in Romania, it does not necessarily respond to the problem of discrimination. The changes still regard as illegal "abnormal sexual practices, including oral and anal sex, if performed in public." In the minds of legislators, these practices seem to be associated exclusively with homosexuals. Article 152 of the Criminal Code defines the phrase "in public" as applying to situations when the act is committed in public: in a place that by its nature or destination is always accessible to the public (even though no other person is there when the act occurs); in any other place accessible to the public, if two or more persons are present; in any place not accessible to the public, if there is the intention for the act to be heard or seen; in a multiperson reunion, except for family reunions; and in any situation wherein the act might be brought to public knowledge. This last provision is the most controversial. Potentially, it renders the changes to Article 200 meaningless since any homosexual act might be made public. Since 2000, the interpretation of the law has been in the hands of the Romanian courts, which are reluctant to impose jail sentences for homosexual behavior. As a result, no cases of gays and lesbians being jailed for their sexual activity have been reported.[12]

A joint Human Rights Watch and International Gay and Lesbian Human Rights Commission report published in late 1998 singled out the Orthodox Church as one of the most formidable opponents to decriminalizing homosexuality. True, the overwhelming majority of Romanian religious denominations came out in favor of the ban, but the Orthodox Church was far more vocal than others. Orthodox canon law condemns homosexuality in the harshest terms, a view that is consonant with the position of the overwhelming majority of Romanian Orthodox theologians and married clergy.[13] In his influential *Jurnalul fericirii*, respected monk Nicolae Steinhardt articulated his position against homosexuality by calling it a disease in need of urgent treatment. Commenting on the U.S. practice of building separate churches for homosexuals, Steinhardt provided two arguments against such segregation and indirectly against homosexuality:

> First, Christ accepts all those coming to Him, even the homosexuals, not for them to justify and confirm their sin but to give it up. Christ neither rejected whores and thieves nor blessed their position. It is wrong to believe that homosexuals are entitled to the special treatment of being accepted before cleansing themselves of sin. The Lord, merciful and good, listens to each prayer not calling for strengthening the sin. . . . Second, Christianity has a universal vocation and is hostile to segregation. Christ is not calling us to build a church for whites and another for blacks, a church for women and another for men, a church for the rich and another for the poor, a church for homosexuals and another for heterosexuals, a church for the intellectuals and another for the illiterate.

For Steinhardt, it would be "un-Christian and ridiculous" to build churches for victims of diseases like "heart stroke, hepatitis, kidney stones. . . . It is enough that we pray to God in different languages and we divide ourselves into nationalities and religions."[14]

Various Orthodox leaders took a stand against homosexuality and used their political clout to block amendments to Article 200. Patriarch Teoctist repeatedly came out against "the acceptance of the degradingly abnormal and unnatural lifestyle as normal and legal," and tried to influence the outcome of the parliamentary vote on lifting the ban. Days before deputies were to vote on decriminalizing homosexuality, the patriarch wrote to members of parliament voicing opposition to striking down Article 200, which he praised for banning "unnatural behavior." Claiming to represent Christian moral and spiritual consciousness, Teoctist argued that Romanians always respected the traditional family and were able to distinguish "sin from virtue, natural from unnatural, normal from abnormal, right from wrong." While further stating that "the church condemns sinful love in order to protect sacred love, rejects the tyranny of egotistic passions unable to bear fruit to protect the freedom to live in virtue, rejects the unnatural to protect the dignity of the human being," the patriarch reminded legislators that "the Orthodox Church works for the salvation of all, even the spiritually and physically sick," and "appeals to its believers in parliament to defend human dignity, the moral health of the people, the stability of the family, and the spiritual rebirth of the Romanian society." Torn between the desire to enjoy the benefits of European Union membership and the harsh criticism coming from the powerful and insistent

Orthodox Church, the deputies chose to support the changes to Article 200, with 180 votes for, 14 against, and 40 abstentions.[15]

A number of Christian organizations helped sustain the momentum for an anti-homosexuality crusade within the Orthodox Church's higher echelons. After denouncing homosexuality as "propaganda for human degenerates," the outspoken Association of Christian Orthodox Students (Asociaţia Studenţilor Creştin Ortodocşi din România, or ASCOR) persuaded Teoctist to ask legislators to maintain the ban on homosexuality, and they mounted a tireless intimidation campaign against those members of parliament who were willing to decriminalize such behavior, accusing them of atheism and immorality.[16]

In its fight, the church used state television to vehemently criticize the proposed changes to Article 200. In a number of religious programs, Orthodox theologians, priests, and monks extolled the virtue of the traditional position vis-à-vis sexual relations and rejected any "Westernization" of Romanian mores. The patriarch's chief of staff at the time, Deputy-Patriarchal Bishop Teofan Sinaitul, attacked liberalization as fostering confusion between "normal and abnormal, good and evil," and he deplored the fact that "homosexual practices received the status of normal behavior." He further declared that Christian churches condemned the sin, not the sinner; contended that the state should not allow homosexuals to voice their position publicly in journals and newspapers, clubs, mass media, or street demonstrations; and argued that renunciation of Article 200 was the first step toward "recognizing same-sex marriages and the right of homosexual couples to adopt children and to enjoy the privileges of the normal family."[17]

Deputy-Patriarchal Bishop and Holy Synod Secretary Vincenţiu Ploieşteanu added that "we need healthy young people in mind and body, like any civilized country, and we must try to protect them from contamination by such serious sinners."[18] Father Sandu Medinţi deplored liberalization as "the devil's work," signaling the country's renunciation of its century-old Christian ethics, and Archbishop Andrei Andreicuţ of Alba Iulia accused politicians of "encouraging societal aberrations."[19] The most outspoken Orthodox leader was Archbishop Bartolomeu Anania of Vad, Feleac, and Cluj, who remarked that "Europe asks us to accept sex, homosexuality, vices, drugs, abortions, and genetic engineering, including cloning" and attacked the "impoverished Europe . . . built exclusively on politics and economics, lacking any trace of spirituality, culture, or religion."[20]

Even after parliament had eliminated Article 200, the Orthodox Church tried to pressure it to reverse its decision. In September 2000, in a last attempt to intimidate the government and parliament, church leaders threatened to call for a national referendum, since by decriminalizing homosexuality "the political elite placed itself in opposition to the overwhelming majority of the electorate, a fact ultimately amounting to a coup against our democracy." The push for the referendum came from Archbishop Anania, who led the Metropolitanate of Transylvania after Metropolitan Antonie Plămădeală fell sick in the mid 1990s. The call for a referendum drew support from neither the government nor the opposition. Before the Senate again discussed the amendments decriminalizing homosexuality, the Liberal Party, to which Minister of Justice Stoica belonged, declared its opposition to the referendum, and Social Democrat representatives said that "even if the Orthodox Church is against [the changes], what one does under one's blanket is one's business."[21]

More important, the referendum call received no response from the presidency. Under Article 90 of the 1991 constitution, only the Romanian president can call a referendum on matters of national importance, but decriminalizing homosexuality was dismissed as a matter of little importance for the country. The timing was not the best, either. Romanians were preoccupied with the general elections of late 2000, mounting political corruption, and falling living standards, and they could hardly turn their attention to other issues.

In response to the referendum call, human rights activist Gabriel Andreescu accused the Orthodox Church of endangering the country's national interest by not allowing legislators to comply with the Council of Europe requirements:

> By pressuring the Senate, the church interferes with the activity of the state. In fact, we are not talking about legalizing homosexuality but about eliminating discrimination. It refers to a person's right to private life, nothing else. At stake is the very future of Romanian society, which by [eliminating the ban] adheres to modern, democratic values needed for entry into the European Union. By its position, the Orthodox Church opposes Romania's global interests.

Not a homosexual himself, but a nonpracticing Orthodox, Andreescu asked for the ties of Holy Synod members to the communist secret political police, the Securitate, to be disclosed publicly. The activist, who insisted that he had concrete proof of certain synod members' involvement with the Securitate, was thus trying to demonstrate that the moral principles the Orthodox Church invoked in its fight against homosexuals were nothing but a façade concealing long-term collaboration with the atheistic communist authorities. In response, the patriarchate condemned Andreescu's position as "an inadmissible act of blackmail and intimidation of church leadership for its firm position against repealing Article 200."[22]

Days later, the synod met to discuss homosexuality and again urged politicians not to amend Article 200. "Everybody should know that homosexuality is a sin against religious, family and social values, which are at the core of our church," Archbishop Casian Craciun of Dunărea de Jos said after the meeting, adding, "I do not believe that European Union integration hinges on the [homosexuality] issue." Only Metropolitan Nicolae Corneanu of Banat had a different attitude. In 1998 he declared: "I cannot understand the condemnation of homosexuals . . . with the help of the Criminal Code. I see the need to explain to the faithful why homosexuality cannot be accepted or why it is in fact a disease. But this physical and spiritual disease cannot be treated with imprisonment."[23]

In its fight against homosexuality, the Orthodox Church managed to win the support of some political parties. The extremist Party of Romanian National Unity and the nationalist Greater Romania Party, which uphold Orthodoxy and moral cleanliness, argued that Article 200 was too lenient and that toleration of homosexuality affected national pride. The Greater Romania Party was among the very few to oppose decriminalization of homosexuality until the very end, with its representative Dumitru Bălăeț claiming that the annulment of Article 200 would mean that "homosexuals will wander on the streets, not only in the woods."[24] The Christian Democrat Peasant Party felt compelled to justify its Christian Democratic commitment by adopting a strictly traditional view on the subject. Its leader, respected politician and Greek Catholic believer Corneliu Coposu, categorically opposed "sexual aberrations," arguing that the party's Christian moral foundation led it "to combat every deviation from the law of nature and from the moral principles of a future balanced society." He further claimed it to be imperative for "liberty of some to be blocked by the liberty of others when the collective sentiment of a group or a tradition is injured by some initiative pretending to be 'progressive' and modern."[25] Christian Democrat deputy Emil Popescu took this view to an extreme when he suggested that "incest is preferable to homosexuality since at least the former preserves the chance of procreation."[26]

The Orthodox Church has continued to voice opposition against granting homosexuals some of the same rights heterosexuals enjoy. Speaking in 2001 at a congress on the family organized by the Orthodox and Roman Catholic Churches, Patriarch Teoctist protested against child adoption by homosexual couples, on the grounds that "without the love and affection only the [traditional] family can provide, the child would become a being lacking goodness, mercy, faith, and love and would be incapable of distinguishing right from wrong."[27] To be sure, the Orthodox Church was not the only denomination to oppose legalization of homosexual behavior. In 2000, Metropolitan Vlasie Mogîrzan of the Old Calendar Orthodox Church, which follows the Russian-style Julian calendar and claims the allegiance of some 40,000 Romanians, declared that "as an Orthodox people, we cannot agree with decriminalizing homosexuality."[28]

Many members of the Christian Democrat Peasant Party, which mounted the fiercest parliamentary opposition to legalizing homosexual behavior, were devout Greek Catholics. Because of this campaign, Romania was among the last Eastern European countries to decriminalize homosexuality. While recognizing that the new legislative framework was an important step forward because "finally the state is out of [the people's] bed," Adrian Coman, director of the only gay rights group recognized in the country, admitted that repealing Article 200 "does not necessarily show that people in this country became more tolerant toward gays and lesbians."[29] Attitudes against homosexual behavior remain intransigent, and homosexuals continue to be derided and discriminated against.

In May 2005, the first weeklong gay festival in Romania culminated with a colorful Gay Pride parade through downtown Bucharest. The event was organized by Accept, a nonprofit organization promoting the rights of lesbians, gays, bisexuals, and transsexuals. Though initially Bucharest Mayor Adriean Videanu opposed the parade, President Traian Băsescu and Minister of Justice Monica Macovei endorsed it.[30] The event attracted some sympathetic participants, as well as small protesting groups like the New Right (Noua Dreaptă), a neo-Nazi, white-supremacist group opposed to gays and ethnic minorities in the name of Christianity. The group, which claims to be the heir of the interwar right-wing Legionary Movement, has ties to similar European organizations. A group member was arrested for throwing a lit torch in the midst of the parade, while group leader Tudor Ionescu was fined for "initiating an unauthorized demonstration" during the authorized gay march.[31] That day, another meeting organized by the Conservative Party attracted several dozen participants who listened to an Orthodox priest denounce homosexuality.[32]

Abortion, Contraception, and Family Planning

According to Romanian observers, the reason for the religious groups' opposition to decriminalizing homosexuality was the fact that public sentiment favoring the liberalization of abortion after more than two decades of communist pro-life policies had rendered abortion a highly sensitive issue, which the religious denominations were unwilling to tackle right away. Under the Ceauşescu regime, abortion was prohibited by the unpopular Decree no. 770 of October 1966.[33] The decree was supposed to help realize demographic targets set by the government. In turn, these targets were meant to fulfill Ceauşescu's megalomaniac ambition of ruling over a populous nation. In 1969, the prohibition of abortion resulted in a birthrate almost double the national average (the largest generation ever recorded in Romania), but such increases were not sustainable and were lost by the late 1980s. Lack of birth control devices and alternative family planning programs, sharply deteriorating living conditions, and the state's unwillingness to recognize the existence of family problems (abandonment, abuse, physical disability, and mental afflictions) compelled Romanian women to undergo illegal abortions, even at the risk of losing their lives, giving birth to malformed children, or going to jail if the interrupted pregnancy was discovered.[34]

The post-communist leaders abrogated the anti-abortion decree only days after the December 1989 uprising, and the sudden liberalization gave Romania one of the highest abortion rates in Europe. Estimates vary widely, from over 1.2 million abortions conducted yearly in a population of around 23 million to half that rate.[35] According to official figures, there were 1,009 abortions for 1,000 live births in 2003, compared to 3,100 abortions for 1,000 live births in 1990–1991.[36] Pro-life Romanian doctors contended that 70 percent of all conjugal and extramarital conceptions were terminated before term, often in the third trimester, while a further 20 percent of women became sterile due to complications. By comparison, in Britain outside London, only 19 percent of conceptions were ended before term. On average, Romanian women have five abortions during their sexually active years. Legalization of abortion did not curb illegal abortion, which continues to be the method of choice for teenagers and women from disadvantaged, large families, who cannot afford birth control. In Romania, the female mortality rate due to botched terminations is up to six times higher than in Central Europe, though it is likely below communist-era levels.[37]

As a result of these abortion rates, those worried about the "endangered Romanian nation" and its dramatic loss in population launched a massive pro-life campaign. Religious groups joined forces for this initiative, but the Orthodox and Greek Catholic Churches were its most vocal supporters. Because abortion in Romania was legalized through a decree of the provisional revolutionary government, feminist groups desired a law that would recognize a woman's right to terminate unwanted pregnancies. A pro-abortion legislative proposal introduced in the 1992–1996 legislature garnered the support of the Senate, but the Chamber of Deputies quashed it. In January 1994, when the proposal moved from the upper to the lower chamber, on behalf of the Orthodox Church, Christian Democrat Senator Ioan Alexandru condemned the law on abortion as "a disaster for our people, which ranks first in Europe in the killing of babies," and complained that legislators had legalized abortion too soon, since Romania's population was rapidly decreasing in number. But he voiced his hope "to stop the bill in the Chamber of Deputies and discuss the issue again." A well-known poet who defied communist authorities by teaching the Bible in an attic at the University of Bucharest in the 1980s, Alexandru was known for his close ties to the Orthodox patriarchate, whose views he championed in parliament.[38] Days later, the Orthodox Church leader drafted an open letter urging the state to take legal action to curb the explosive increase in abortions.[39]

The only legislative initiative banning abortion was introduced by the Christian Democrat senator and Greek Catholic priest Ioan Moisin in December 1997 (PL 646). According to parliamentary procedure, the Senate asked two permanent committees to discuss the proposal before the full chamber voted on it. In March 1998, the Committee on Human Rights rejected the proposal, while the Committee on Health Care decided to support it. The two opposing resolutions reflected the two primary positions regarding abortion. On one hand, Romanians recognized the inadequacy of the existing legal framework, under which, unless complemented by programs in social work and sexual education, abortion risked raising more medical and social problems than it solved, especially in a country facing deep economic recession. On the other hand, the emotive vocabulary of pro-life activists, who spoke of mass murders of fetuses and "the maiming of Romanian womanhood,"[40] brought forth arguments echoing the draconian communist anti-abortion policies, whose revival many Romanian women strongly opposed. The ruling Christian Democrats refused to support Moisin's proposal for fear of alienating the female electorate. After lingering in the Senate for two years without real chances of adoption, the proposal was abandoned at the end of the 1996–2000 legislature.

After 2000, the Social Democrat government of Prime Minister Adrian Năstase refused to reintroduce the proposal, contending that no additional law should reconfirm the pro-abortion decree, but he did support a new law that could deny some social categories access to the medical procedure in public hospitals. After legislation introduced in June 2003, women must undergo a psychological check-up before having an abortion. Obstetricians may not perform abortions without notes from psychologists attesting to the mental fitness of the pregnant woman. According to doctors in southeastern Constanța county, the psychological check-up is meant to convince women to carry the pregnancy to term. Women interviewed by local journalists reported that the psychologist could do nothing to change their mind and that the check-up was another method of raising money from a cash-strapped population.[41]

Given the sensitivity of the issue, for a long time, the Orthodox Church avoided formulating an official position toward abortion and contraception.

Unofficial as it was before 2005, the church's position could be gauged from a number of statements in which various clergymen have condemned both practices and from a pamphlet distributed widely by the Orthodox leadership to priests in 1997.[42] Prepared by Father Ilie Moldovan, a moral theology professor at the Sibiu Faculty of Theology and the Orthodox Church's leading authority on the subject, the pamphlet virulently condemned abortion. For Moldovan, the main goal of both marriage and sexual intercourse is procreation. A marriage whose main goal is eluded is "nothing but a legal form of prostitution," and all family planning methods dissociating sexuality from procreation are to be highly condemned. The future child is a person immediately after the egg and the sperm come together; thus any attempt to destroy the impregnated egg imperils "a total human, body and soul," and runs counter to the biblical commandment not to kill. Moldovan also contended that abortion remains unjustified and morally sinful even when the pregnancy endangers the mother's life or health. He went as far as to reject the Ogino calendar-based planning, the only contraception method accepted by the Roman Catholic Church, and that church's arguments that "for just reasons, spouses may wish to space the births of their children" and "the use of infertile periods is in conformity with the objective criteria of morality."[43]

Moldovan's stance relied as much on ethnonational as on religious considerations. For him, abortion was a threat to the very survival of the Romanian nation, amounting to genocide. The author advised his fellow Orthodox priests to refuse communion for seven years to women who had abortions. If a woman died in abortion, he encouraged priests to refuse to bury her. Moldovan's recommendation of a seven-year communion ban appeared to be a lenient version of the punishment prescribed by Orthodox canon law. Following Canon 91 of the Council in Trullo (Quinisext, 692 CE), "those who give drugs for procuring abortion and those who receive poisons to kill the fetus are subject to the penalty of murder." Canon 21 of the Council in Ancyra (314 CE) states that "concerning women who commit fornication, and destroyed that which they have conceived, or who are employed in making drugs for abortion, a former decree excluded them [from receiving communion] until the hour of death, and to this some have assented. Nevertheless, being desirous to use somewhat greater lenity, we have ordained that they fulfill ten years [of penance], according to the prescribed degrees."[44] While few of the married Orthodox priests observe the traditional canons, the charismatic, highly popular, and celibate monks of monasteries generally hand down harsher punishments for abortion.

Social Democrat senator and Orthodox priest Ioan Aurel Rus pointed out that not only the woman but also her partner was guilty for the abortion, since "women could not conceive with trees."[45] Not all the Orthodox leaders agree with such radical views. Father Justin Marchiş, one of the church's pro-reformist voices who favors the Ogino contraceptive method, attacked the pamphlet on theological grounds, criticized Moldovan for arguing that abortion was the gravest sin, a contention not sustained by Orthodox doctrine, and deplored the widespread distribution that only Moldovan's text received.[46] Other priests have maintained that the Orthodox Church's traditional noninterference in spouses' intimate relations means that the calendar is tacitly accepted as a contraceptive method, while all other methods are strongly rejected.[47]

Metropolitan Corneanu was among the few leaders who made clear their opposition to any criminalization of homosexuality and abortion and publicly stated that women, not some institution, had the right to decide whether to stall a pregnancy. In 1998, Corneanu stated that he could not understand the "terrible anti-abortion campaign. Of course, I cannot accept murder, but this is such an intimate problem of the woman that to support condemnation or even punishment is not normal," and added that "it is the right of the prospective mother to decide, together with her husband, if she is married."[48] Romania did not know Western-type anti-abortion protests and picketing at abortion clinics until very recently. Between 19 and 21 December 2005, days before the feast of the Nativity, the increasingly vocal group we mentioned in connection with the Gay Parade, the Noua Dreaptă, organized peaceful anti-abortion protests in Bucharest and Timişoara. Group members dressed in the green colors of the Legionary Movement and picketed abortion clinics in a campaign entitled "Abortion: A Crime against the Romanian Nation." On the third day of the campaign, they also marched in downtown Bucharest and distributed pro-life flyers.[49]

On 25 September 2001, the Orthodox and Roman Catholic Churches joined forces to organize a congress on "Family and Life at the Beginning of a New Christian Millennium" meant to find ways to protect the family, "the nucleus of society." The congress provided the two denominations with a platform for denouncing abortion and homosexuality. In his speech, special guest and head of the Pontifical Council for the Family, Alfonso Lopez Cardinal Trujillo, called for a ban on abortions and for upholding traditional family values in marriages between a man and a woman. He requested the eradication of "recently adopted alternative forms of family" available elsewhere in the world for homosexuals, and he condemned child adoption by homosexual couples as a social danger. Speaking on abortion, Cardinal Trujillo contended that current views on the issue overemphasize the woman's right to dispose of her body and overlook the right to life of the unborn child, a person since conception. Patriarch Teoctist echoed these views, condemned "moral deviations weakening the creation," and declared that the huge number of abortions represents a "real national tragedy" with disastrous consequences for the Romanian nation.[50]

After the congress, the Orthodox Church realized the need to draft a response informed by recent scientific advances, and they established a National Committee on Bioethics to study issues such as abortion, contraceptives, eugenics, euthanasia, in vitro fertilization, surrogate motherhood, the transplantation of human and animal organs, and genetic engineering. While some procedures were unavailable in Romania at the time, the Orthodox Church felt it best to consider them early. The committee has chapters in the university cities of Bucharest, Cluj, and Iaşi, each including five theologians, five scientists, one sociologist, and one law graduate. Drawn from different disciplines, chapter members can bridge the gap between the views of church, science, and law. In November 2001, when the commission first met in Bucharest, Archbishop Anania commented that "several scientific areas, including genetic engineering, raise important moral questions. We are often asked about the position of the church, but for now we cannot answer, because the church is unfamiliar with the issues." Following Gheorghe Scripcaru of the Iaşi Faculty of Medicine, the committee "seeks to connect science and religion so that new [scientific] discoveries do not contradict life and spirituality."[51]

The first draft the committee submitted for the synod's approval came late and dealt with a topic accepted by the Orthodox Church: organ transplant. In spite of this, the draft was the church's first initiative to formulate official statements representing its views while also taking into account the latest scientific discoveries. It is known that Orthodox Churches have neglected to issue public pronouncements comparable to those regularly drafted by the Roman Catholic Church. Rather, they refer to the canon law to respond to social issues. Therefore, the Committee on Bioethics is to be commended for its pioneering work and its effort to increase the transparency and accessibility of Orthodox teaching.

The synod adopted the Committee on Bioethics' pronouncement on abortion and euthanasia on 6 July 2005. Drawing on biblical texts and contemporary scientific knowledge, and taking into account social, psychological, and moral issues, the document offers the following main points with respect to abortion:

a. If a pregnancy endangers the mother's life, the woman's life should be given priority over the child's. This is not because her life is more valuable in itself. Rather, it is due to her relations with and responsibilities for other persons.

b. If genetic investigation reveals an unborn child with abnormalities, we recommend carrying the pregnancy to term thereby observing his right to life. However, this decision belongs to the family after they have been informed by their physician and their father confessor of the crucial moral and physical issues involved. This decision must be made with an eye to the redeeming presence of a disabled [human] being in the life of every person and community.

c. The risk of abortion due to rape or incest must be avoided first of all through education, by teaching citizens not to commit such sins. When pregnancy occurs as a result of rape or incest, the child must be born and given up for adoption, if necessary.

d. Neither a family's economic situation, nor conflict between prospective parents, nor the career of the future mother, nor her physical appearance are moral justifications for abortion.[52]

Thus, the pronouncement is not a blind condemnation of abortion. While not endorsing abortion, the document recognizes instances when abortion may be acceptable.

While titled *Abortion*, the pronouncement also deals with contraception. Contraceptive pills, devices, and surgical procedures to induce temporary or permanent infertility are all condemned because their use is allegedly no less sinful than abortion itself: "The Orthodox Church has always considered the ingestion of medication to cause abortion as a grave sin, whose gravity is equal to the sin of abortion." Following the pronouncement, the use of contraception is condemnable also because of the risks it poses to the life and dignity of the woman. No mention is made of risk-free contraceptive methods like the use of condoms, or the Ogino method accepted by the Roman Catholic Church. Since practical considerations like the health of the woman figure prominently in the document's recommendations, it would seem that risk-free contraceptive methods are acceptable and less sinful than other methods. Like the Roman Catholic documents of its kind, *Abortion* does not distinguish between degrees of sinfulness and therefore fails to differentiate between the prevention of conception through the use of contraceptives and the abortion of an already conceived fetus.

Legalization of Prostitution

Democracy has brought Romania not only freedom but also a booming sex industry involving male and female prostitutes from various age groups. They

cater to a diverse local and foreign clientele. The local mass media have repeatedly commented on the growing number of Bucharest apartments rented
by the hour or the day to high-end prostitutes and their pimps, and the scores
of young women offering their services during the night along the country's
poorly lit roads. According to local journalists, there is a steady clientele of
foreign citizens visiting the Bucharest sex market on a yearly basis. They often
lure unsuspecting Romanian teenagers and young women in search of good
jobs in Western countries into rings of illegal prostitution active throughout
Europe, from Zagreb and Tirana to Paris and Rome. The most desperate cases
involve large families from the poor rural areas of Moldova who sell their sons
and daughters into sexual bondage for as little as a television set or the
equivalent of a monthly wage.

Scholars studying the daily life of Romanians in the interwar period have
noticed that pre-communist Romania had legal prostitution. According to
Scurtu,

> In [interwar] Romania, prostitution was practiced legally, with ap-
> proval from the city hall and under medical and police supervision.
> The "girls" carried a report booklet where personal and health data
> were entered. There were some famous brothels like the one in the
> Crucea de Piatră [Stone Cross] quarter in Bucharest. . . . Female
> prostitutes were recruited from the countryside and city sub-
> urbs. . . . Most were between twenty and thirty years old. In 1930, 91
> percent of the prostitutes were under thirty years old. . . . Besides le-
> gal prostitution, there was widespread underground prostitution, es-
> pecially in ports and big cities. . . . An individualistic opinion trend
> emphasizing individual freedom opposed the mandatory require-
> ment for prostitutes to practice their profession [only] in brothels. The
> Sanitary Law of 1930 based on that trend forbade prostitution
> houses or any businesses where prostitution could be practiced.
> The law allowed women to engage in prostitution privately though, as
> long as they were healthy and had a "health certificate." In practice,
> the authorities lost control of prostitution and venereal diseases
> became widespread.[53]

This historical precedent and the social and medical problems associated with
the expansion of the sex industry convinced some post-communist politicians
and a segment of the Romanian electorate that the country would be better off
legalizing prostitution. Proponents of this view argued that legalization would
control the industry's supply, limit the spread of sexually transmitted diseases
by monitoring sex workers' health, protect sex workers from abuse by their

employers and clients, reduce the number of sex workers denied the right to opt out of the industry, and bring revenue to the national budget through tax collection.

This position was championed in parliament by a woman, Democrat Party deputy Mariana Stoica, head of the Chamber of Deputies European Integration Commission. She announced in January 1998 that the chamber was studying the possibility of legalizing prostitution for the protection of male and female prostitutes and of recognizing prostitution as a profession. There were similarities between Stoica's post-communist law and its pre-communist predecessor. In an effort to address the problem of prostitutes reduced to penniless "human wrecks" after years of harsh treatment by their clients and pimps, both laws gave sex workers a social status and access to a guaranteed pension plan.[54]

Public reaction to Stoica's declaration was mixed. Respected journalist Cornel Nistorescu lamented the fact that Romania's

> national bashfulness is a curtain behind which the sex industry flourishes, our periphery becomes a shambles, and our health decays. For fear of the church and public scandal, Romania avoids discussing sex. [The political elite] uses euphemisms to tackle the issue covertly, for fear of blushing or losing electoral votes. Sexual education made no progress since the shameful silence the socialists kept on the subject.... Until now, only its legalization brought prostitution under a sort of legal, financial, and medical control.

He warned readers that Romanians

> might avoid the question [of legalizing prostitution] for years, while Romanian towns become illegal markets for East European sex. Bucharest's downtown and tourist districts are places of seedy deals, paying no taxes, attracting minors and tacitly contaminating them. Who benefits? Only the pimps and the police officers protecting them. This is a national farce, a cheap operetta masking a dangerous misery.

He added that in the 1996–2000 legislature, Stoica's attempts to launch debates in parliament on such delicate subject "were met by a wall of silence, discreet smiles, and the protests of her elderly [colleagues]."[55]

Indeed, Stoica's hope for a draft law on prostitution to reach the house before the end of her mandate remained unfulfilled. It was only in mid 2003 that eight senators, representing the Social Democrat Party, Greater Romania Party, Humanist Party, and Democratic Union of Magyars in Romania, including two women, introduced a draft bill on prostitution (PL 259).[56] Aimed at eliminating sexually transmitted diseases, the bill defined prostitution as paid sexual activity and gave sexual workers access to pension and health care plans (Articles 2–3). Prostitutes are independent adult workers in good health, offering services either at their residence or in specially designated places, and registered with the mayor's and the revenue offices (Articles 4–5). Set up by persons at least thirty-five years old, of honorable standing, and without a criminal record, sex establishments must be officially registered on the basis of an identity card, an ownership deed or rental agreement for the building where sex services are to be offered, criminal record, local health department permit, and an "honorability" certificate issued by the local police (Articles 9–10). Sex establishments may not be set up near schools and universities, places of worship, public institutions, stadiums, military units, and charitable foundations.

Sex workers have the right to security, dignity, pension and health care plans, as well as the right to choose clients, refuse to render specific services, receive the promised payment, opt out of prostitution, and unilaterally end contracts with sex establishments. They have the obligation to observe prearranged schedules, undergo periodic medical check-ups, present their medical file to clients upon request, notify sex establishment managers of health changes, and not divulge clients' identities (Article 16). Establishment managers set prices and collect fees, dismiss sex workers medically prohibited from working, and reject clients. They must keep the establishment clean, offer clients anonymity and security, not ask sexual workers to perform unwanted sexual acts or unprotected sex, refuse underage clients, post prices visibly, submit to financial audits, respect the security and rights of sex workers, and offer free condoms to clients and free medical check-ups to their workers (Article 17). Prostitution of unauthorized persons or medically unfit individuals, and the filming of persons entering sex establishments are punishable with jail sentence of up to two years. Recruitment of minors, foreigners, and poor people is punishable with jail for up to seven years. Offering sex services in homes with minor children or unauthorized places is punishable with jail for up to a year. Allowing minors access to sex establishments, not submitting to medical check-ups, obliging workers to have unprotected sex, and failing to maintain a clean establishment constitute misdemeanors punishable with fees between 10 million and 100 million lei (Article 23).

After being introduced in the Senate, the bill reached the standing committees. Out of respect for the beginning of Advent, "a period of spiritual purification," members of the committee on gender equality postponed debates. The draft was opposed by the Social Democrat Năstase government on the grounds that it ran counter to the new Criminal and Labor Codes and did not accord with the international convention on the prevention of human trafficking. In its response to parliament, the administration rejected the proposal to set up sex establishments (brothels) but remarked that freelance prostitution would conform to European Union standards.[57]

During debates, Greater Romania Party representative Radu Ciuceanu made the case against legalizing prostitution, dismissing the initiators' claim that legalization would control sexually transmitted diseases. He argued that Western countries where prostitution has been legal for some time registered disease rates higher than Romania's, and he rejected the claim that regular medical check-ups limit the spread of AIDS since prostitutes continue to infect their clients during the incubation period. According to Ciuceanu, the legalization of prostitution would undermine family life and fuel the sex trade, and yet it would not prevent aggression against prostitutes.[58]

Days before the Committee on Gender Equality was to discuss the bill, the Senate prayer group and Committee on Human Rights organized a debate on the legalization of prostitution presided over by Social Democrat senator and Orthodox priest Ioan Aurel Rus and special guest Alexandru Plescan, a Bucharest Orthodox priest. Most senators supported the bill, and Rus stated that "as a senator, I am for the bill, but as a priest, I am against it." By contrast, Plescan denounced prostitution as a "calamity that must be eradicated," condemned women who sold their bodies for money, and urged church and state to curb prostitution. He even argued that the introduction of sexual education in schools led to an increase in prostitution, but the senators dismissed this view.[59] Plescan simply presented the position of the Orthodox Church, which mounted considerable opposition to legalizing prostitution. The church's view on the subject was presented in a roundtable moderated by the respected religious painter Sorin Dumitrescu, known for his close ties to the Group for Social Dialogue, including Romania's preeminent intellectuals. Dumitrescu is head of Anastasia Press, which publishes Orthodox theology works.

The roundtable included Father Ilie Moldovan alongside Orthodox clergy affiliated with the Center for Applied Theological Studies of Craiova. Moldovan summarized the theological arguments against legalizing prostitution, maintaining that prostitution ran counter to the divine order to procreate, two of Moses' divine commandments ("Thou shall not commit adultery" and "Thou shall not covet thy neighbor's wife"), and Paul's warning that "neither fornicators, nor idolaters, nor adulterers, nor the effeminate, nor abusers of themselves with men, nor thieves, nor the covetous, nor drunkards, nor revilers, nor extortionists, shall inherit the kingdom of God."[60] For Moldovan, legalizing prostitution—like abortion and homosexuality—endangered not only the individual but also the community and the nation's "vital energies." Doru

Costache added that prostitution was a form of "spiritual suicide" annulling the difference between human beings and animals. Physician Pavel Chirilă, coauthor of the pamphlet *Faţa nevăzută a prostituţiei legalizate* (The Unseen Face of Legal Prostitution), dismissed the argument that the legalization of prostitution would help control sexually transmitted diseases. The roundtable concluded with Dumitrescu announcing that the ad hoc Initiative Group for the Protection of the Family had sent parliament a comprehensive anti-prostitution document.[61]

As Nistorescu wrote, "there is only one obstacle to legalizing prostitution: the church," whose resistance to change should be dismissed by legislators, since the benefits of legalizing prostitution far exceeded the drawbacks. "The Orthodox Church does not make the laws of a country," Nistorescu wrote, "but guides it spiritually. The legalization of prostitution is the job of parliament. . . . This issue might forever divide parliament and the Orthodox Church, but would not mean the end of the world."[62]

The political elite ultimately did not heed pro-legalization arguments. In November 2003, Patriarch Teoctist condemned the bill in a letter to parliament that rebuked legislators for considering the possibility of legalizing prostitution. His letter denounced the bill's anti-Christian and inhumane character, arguing that it supported "transforming persons into objects of pleasure." The patriarch insisted that crime increased in countries that legalized prostitution and contended that women "caught in the drama of the brothels [were] irremediably affected psychologically and physically." The church leader called on parliament members to remember that they were representatives of an electorate that overwhelmingly opposed the legalization of prostitution.[63] On 17 February 2004, Social Democrat deputy Minodora Cliveti proposed the legalization of prostitution, but the judicial committee rejected her call. The committee agreed on jail sentences of up to one year for prostitution, which it defined as the activity of those persons who derive most of their income from selling sexual services.[64]

Besides mounting pressure on legislators to stall the bill's adoption, the Orthodox Church initiated a number of active and proactive programs against prostitution. In 2000, for example, it launched anti-prostitution campaigns in Bucharest high schools at the prompting of Lucreţia Vasilescu, a Bucharest Faculty of Orthodox Theology professor of social work. The campaign, a joint program developed by the Police General Inspectorate and the Social Assistance Bureau of the patriarchate, explained to high school students the danger of advertisements promising high-paying jobs in other countries; these ads, in fact, concealed the activities of international prostitution rings. The campaign also announced the invitation of the ambassadors of the countries where the majority of Romanian women prostitutes lived to student seminars, alongside priests, sociologists, police officers, and victims of prostitution rings.[65] Far more publicity was gained by the synod decision of April 2003 to suspend ten priests who were filmed blessing illegal brothels, sex shops, and a weapons store. The private Prima TV station filmed the priests undercover performing the blessing in exchange for money and goods. It is traditional for Orthodox priests to bless homes, offices, businesses, cars, gardens, and even animals to ward off the devil, but priests are forbidden to bless places deemed unholy, such as brothels and abortion clinics.[66]

Artificial Insemination

On 16 January 2005, academic Adriana Iliescu gave birth to a healthy baby girl in Bucharest. The news would have been unremarkable if the pregnancy were not the result of nine long years of artificial insemination, the mother were not unmarried and sixty-seven years of age, and both the egg and the sperm were not coming from unknown donors. Because of the mother's age, a world record at the time, the Romanian College of Physicians, the religious denominations, and even the European Union condemned the birth and asked for a thorough investigation of the private Timişoara clinic conducting the treatment. Among religious groups, the Orthodox Church was again the most vocal proponent of a ban on artificial insemination. Since at the time the church had not yet formulated its own position on the subject, it largely echoed the earlier statements of the Roman Catholic Church, which rejected all forms of artificial insemination.

Deputy Bishop Ciprian Campineanu, member of the Orthodox Church's Committee on Bioethics, said his religious group opposed artificial insemination regardless of the mother's age, qualified Iliescu's birth as a "selfish" act that ran counter to Christian moral law, and encouraged Romanians who wished to have children to consider adoption seriously.[67] Father Iustin Marchis announced that the Orthodox Church cannot bless an old mother like Iliescu, as "she did not ask her father confessor's approval" of the insemination, and conceived a child who was not the result of the love between a man and a woman.[68] Metropolitan Nicolae Corneanu of Banat was the only cleric to praise Iliescu's physician, the first doctor to offer in vitro fertilization to Romanian women. According to Corneanu, the doctor "is God's close collaborator, and in a way His competitor because he helps to create new life."[69]

The majority of the local press was merciless, declaring the newborn baby "the fruit of sin. Not a biblical sin, but of the doctors' sin of arrogance and the mother's perverted sin of love, a love colder and more barren than hatred."[70] Minister of Health Care Mircea Cinteza deemed the birth "a great adventure," while the College of Physicians pointed out that in 2001 Romania ratified the Orviedo Protocol calling for ethical principles be observed in medical procedures and the Council of Europe recommended that artificial insemination should not extend beyond a woman's fertile years. France and the Netherlands do not allow women older than forty-five years to undergo artificial insemination. Italy allows married women of up to fifty years to undergo treatment if the couple's infertility is documented. In August 2000, Australia adopted a contested law denying unmarried women and lesbian couples the right to use in vitro fertilization to have children. Romania had no such legal restrictions.

A question mark hangs over the future of Iliescu's daughter. The mother could die or fall ill when she's still a little girl, and some Romanians still question whether an old, single woman with no immediate living relatives could possibly raise a child by herself. By the time Iliescu reaches seventy-two, the average life expectancy for women in Romania, her daughter will barely be five. There are also worries that the child's natural parents—the egg and sperm donors—might seek custody. The birth focused the attention on issues that are bound to become more important as medicine progresses and Romania becomes more prosperous. The College of Physicians adopted specific guidelines banning women at menopause from seeking artificial insemination, and reprimanded the physician who oversaw Iliescu's infertility treatment. The opposition Social Democrats introduced in the Senate a draft law on reproductive health and artificially assisted human reproduction (PL 334/2004) to regulate future cases. The bill banned trade in human sperm, eggs, and embryos and prevented women from selecting their baby's sex. After receiving support from five parliamentary committees and the vote of the legislature, the draft was declared unconstitutional by the Constitutional Court and subsequently returned to parliament. In February 2006, the Chamber of Deputies rejected it. As a result, Romania still lacks a law regulating artificial insemination.

Sexuality within the Orthodox Church

The previous discussion referred to the denominations' involvement in defining acceptable sexual behavior and reproductive practices for Romanian society at large, through new legislation and social programs. While the clergy, together with the rest of society, falls under the jurisdiction of this legislative framework, the debate on sexuality included additional pronouncements and positions affecting bishops, priests, and monks. Sexuality within the Orthodox Church, involving celibate or married clergy, brought additional issues to the fore.

To date, religious denominations in Romania have been spared the allegations of sexual harassment leveled against priests in Western Europe and North America by altar boys who spent some time in the company of their spiritual mentors, celibate Roman Catholic priests. As a minority church closely monitored by both the state and the majority Orthodox Church, the Roman Catholic Church in Romania has paid special attention to its clergy, who so far have never been publicly accused of sexual impropriety. The Orthodox and Greek Catholic Churches accept married priests, whose main temptation seems to be adulterous liaisons, not homosexual relationships or pedophilia.[71] The only case to receive media attention involved the stareț (superior) of the Cernica monastery, situated on the outskirts of Bucharest, who stood accused by two male seminary students of sexual harassment.[72] The monastery runs a pre-university theological school enrolling dozens of teenage students. The accusations apparently had enough validity for the Orthodox Monastic Consistory, a high prosecutorial church body, to investigate the case, temporarily forbid the stareț from celebrating mass, and seek further punishment according to church law.

In so doing, the church leadership asked the police to stop investigating the stareț, on the grounds that the case fell under the jurisdiction of the church rather than secular law. Jurisdiction over criminal cases involving clergy and their close relatives has been a contested issue ever since the Romanian modern state was formed in 1918, with both the Orthodox Church and the state claiming jurisdiction over as many cases as possible. Since 1989 the state has tacitly agreed to allow the church to hear and rule on misdemeanors committed by the clergy. Only special cases have reached the secular courts after the approval of Orthodox Church leadership. Even when the police and the secular courts have begun investigating clergy and monks, the Orthodox Church concerned with its public image has successfully intervened to stop trials. Indeed, the number of cases the church forwarded to the state during the past fifteen years has been negligible, prompting civil society representatives to denounce the Orthodox Church's position of "a state within a state" and other religious denominations to ask for the same privilege or demand that Orthodox criminal jurisdiction be curtailed to levels similar to theirs. Since the agreement between the Orthodox Church and the state is tacit and not formal, it is hard to discern which cases ought to be settled by the church alone and which are to be heard by secular courts. For now, it appears that the church delegates full authority to the state in criminal cases involving members of the clergy (monks, nuns, and priests), while preferring to exert its influence in most civil cases and traffic violations.

The scarcity of reported cases of sexual harassment and homosexual behavior among Orthodox clergy does not mean that these problems are non-existent. For a long time, the church has struggled to hide the homosexual behavior of its monks; this behavior is rumored to be widespread, but the frequency of it cannot be estimated owing to a veil of secrecy. It is also true that accusations of sexual harassment were sometimes used against priests who dared to criticize church leaders. In 2003, Vasile Danion published *Mângâiere și mustrare* (Comforting and Admonishing), a volume of personal interviews with Father Calistrat Chifan, priest at Bârnova, a monastery set up in northern Moldova in 1991. The book's most controversial section was the ten-page chapter on "The Sins of the Priests," in which Chifan commented on "the Orthodox Church's spiritual and intellectual collapse," along with its insensitive bureaucracy, corrupt and ineffective leadership, and venal priesthood. Summarizing current church problems, Chifan said that it was easy to find "drunkard priests, priests owning private shops, priests practicing black magic, priests who did not tell believers about the role of regular confession, communion, mass participation and abandoning sin, or Sunday mass." He criticized the hierarchy's leniency toward priests who too frequently and easily broke canon law and involved themselves in problematic and spiritually harmful activities. The reaction of church leaders to the book and its reception in Orthodox circles speaks for itself. The book was promptly withdrawn from the market on Metropolitan Daniel Ciobotea's order, and Chifan was banned from hearing confession. The official reason for his punishment was related not to his views on the church but to an incident in which four seminary students accused him of sexual harassment, a charge contested by the local press. To date, no religious or secular court has heard Chifan's case.[73]

The Orthodox Church has faced an unprecedented rise in priest divorce and separation rates. Church law bans Orthodox priests from seeking divorce but cannot do anything about divorce initiated by the wife, in which case the husband may not remarry. A number of recent cases involved priests who married previously divorced women or priests who remarried, defying canon law and Orthodox tradition. This old problem escalated after 1989 owing to increased acceptance of divorce and the clergy's loss in prestige and material and social standing. At first the church turned a blind eye, hoping that divorce, separation, remarrying, and marrying unsuitable partners was nothing more than a short-term phenomenon, but recently hierarchs have singled out cases to set examples in the hope of curbing and even reversing the trend. In 2001, a Transylvanian village priest who married a divorced woman lost his parish, while in 2003, a Constanța priest who married for the third time was defrocked.[74]

This latter case provoked much anguish in the local community, which seemed ready to forgive the priest; he argued that his first wife, to whom he was married before being ordained, had died, the second had left him to emigrate to Germany, and for the third marriage he had obtained the verbal approval of the late Archbishop of Tomis Lucian. Archbishop Teodosie, Lucian's successor, opined that "for a priest remarrying is equal to polygamy. The priest cannot celebrate mass again unless he gives up his wife and retires to a monastery as a celibate priest."[75] When Teodosie arrived in the village to remove the accused priest, the parishioners locked him in the church, and only police intervention saved the day. Though some 150 parishioners held a silent procession in his support, the priest was unable to retain his post. Many observers wondered why it took Teodosie four years after the priest's third marriage to defrock him and claimed that the decision to remove him was essentially political.

The Romanian post-communist state has respected the right of religious denominations to regulate the sexuality and marital status of their members. For scholars interested in the interplay between religion and politics, the important issue here is not so much whether the rules on sexual behavior imposed by the Orthodox Church and other religious groups are stricter than those the larger society adopts, but, rather, where the line dividing cases settled by the ecclesiastical courts and cases settled by secular courts falls for each officially registered denomination. For now, the line is determined by informal agreements clearly favoring the majority Orthodox Church. It is hoped that, as Romanian democracy consolidates, the state will find it necessary to be more evenhanded toward different religious groups and to equalize the privileges it grants them in the area of sexual behavior.

Conclusion

In post-communist Romania sexuality has been a contested territory claimed as a private space by civil society representatives and as a largely public space by the state and religious groups. In the early stages of post-communism, the state rolled back its encroachment on sexual life, mostly in an effort to demonstrate a definite break with communist policies. It did this by legalizing abortion, importing contraceptives, and turning a blind eye to prostitution and the booming sex industry. Soon afterward, however, religious groups—especially the dominant Orthodox Church—claimed the territory surrendered by the state as their own and launched an active campaign to regulate sexuality. To do this, the denominations used the religious classes introduced at the pre-university and university levels in an effort to shape public behavior and attitudes. They also exerted direct and indirect pressure on the political elite in an effort to delay and even block permissive legislation.

Our analysis covers primarily the position of the Orthodox Church, the most vocal of Romania's religious groups in the defense of traditional views on sexuality. It is also the most vocal opponent of newer and scientifically informed understandings of sexuality. The Orthodox Church's prominent position in these debates resulted from a combination of factors. Whether a conscious decision or not, religious groups concluded that the Orthodox Church, by sheer numbers, had the best chances of influencing the legislative decision-making process to maintain the ban on homosexuality and prostitution, reverse the legalization of abortion, and restrict the availability of contraception. As the Orthodox position on these matters has often been very conservative, churches with more moderate views on the subject felt no need to intervene in the debate in any forceful way, since by satisfying the Orthodox demands the state would have implicitly fulfilled their demands as well. On the issue of contraception, for example, the Roman Catholic Church in Romania remained silent, although in other countries it made its position very clear. The silence seemingly stemmed from the earlier radical Orthodox position, which rejected even the Catholic-accepted Ogino method of controlling a woman's reproduction. If the Romanian state was to embrace the Orthodox position and ban contraception altogether, the Catholic Church was unlikely to object.

In the fight between religious groups and the post-communist state to regulate sexual practices much depends on society's popular opinion, for whose benefit both church and state have handed down numerous proscriptions. In areas such as the acceptance of homosexual behavior, Romanian society is not as conservative as the Orthodox Church, although it is apprehensive of direct contact with gays and lesbians. However, the society is also not permissive enough to readily embrace new legislation adopted at the insistence of either the European Union or progressive local politicians. With respect to abortion and prostitution, however, Romanian society is far more permissive than either the church or the state. As local civil society acquires more strength and importance in Romania's political life, both church and state will have to consult it more often and listen to it more carefully when searching for long-term social change.

9

Religion, Democratization, and European Union Enlargement

While investigating the relationship between religion and democratic politics in post-communist Romania, we have assumed that the country is committed to Western-style liberal democracy. Explicitly spelled out in the constitution, that commitment has often been voiced by Romanian religious and political actors, and seemingly is attested by the country's recent admission into NATO and its continuous effort to join the European Union. After 1989, Romanian citizens twice had the opportunity to vote on constitutions proclaiming post-communist Romania a secular state, where no religion is "state religion," while church and state retain a respectful distance from each other.

The Romanian state authorities have gradually understood their responsibility to protect the freedom to practice religion for all officially recognized religious denominations. A number of steps have been taken in that direction. The state has upheld a managed quasi-pluralistic model of church-state relations recognizing as many as eighteen religious denominations while regarding religion as complementary to the spheres of education, the arts, and the family. The government financially supported some of their activities, including religious instruction in public schools, taught along denominational lines, and the salaries of the ministers of religious groups requesting such support. The state abolished communist legislation that banned the Greek Catholic Church, thus bringing a degree of moral reparation to that religious group. As a result of foreign and domestic pressure, the state has further abolished legislation punishing homosexual behavior with jail terms, and it has legalized abortion as a fundamental right of women.

As our discussion suggests, additional steps ought to be taken for the country to consolidate its democracy.

First, having just emerged from a dictatorship, individual citizens and even entire organizations (religious denominations included) need to clarify their relationship with the *ancien regime,* not only because those who forget their past risk reenacting it but also because no social reconciliation can be achieved when the victims and their victimizers remain suspicious of each other. True, countries like Spain have opted to "forgive and forget" their dictatorial past, but for various reasons such an option was unpalatable to East European countries. Time and again, the communist past has haunted ordinary Romanians who unexpectedly discovered that the political police made them a target, their politicians and church leaders acted as former spies, and their priests contributed information obtained through confession to the Securitate.

Over the years, ever larger segments of the local electorate have grown displeased with the identified spies' stubborn denial of any wrongdoing, wondering why former spies and high-ranking communist officials insist on denying their past if their actions were innocent and benign. Parliament has already debated several proposals calling for lustration, a process allowing the ban of former communist officials and spies from post-communist politics and positions of responsibility in the economic, academic, and cultural spheres. The adoption of such a law might help make a clean slate for new politicians and religious leaders wishing to enter the public life. As seen, the Orthodox Church has been one of the most vocal opponents of the lustration of its ministers and hierarchs. That denomination has a lot to fear if the opening of the secret archives reveals the extent and depth of its collaboration with Nicolae Ceauşescu's Securitate. The Orthodox Church is not the only one to fear such disclosures. Today, the mass media suspects that some high-ranking leaders of other religious groups were active secret police agents or collaborators.

Second, nationalism remains a powerful sentiment shared by large segments of the population, still educated in a value system that extolls the virtues of Romanianism while paying little heed to ethnic tolerance, cooperation, and inclusiveness. Initially used by the Greek Catholics to foster Romanian national consciousness in Transylvania and then appropriated by the Orthodox Church, nationalism has retained the power to mobilize popular support and restrict the politicians' maneuvering space. Even the communists could not afford to ignore the Orthodox Church, commanding the nationalist ideology.

During the early stages of post-communist transformation, Romanian politics have also been driven by nationalist sentiments. As Tom Gallagher explained, in March 1990 the Transylvanian town of Targu Mures faced the first post-communist interethnic conflict in Eastern Europe, months before tensions flared in Yugoslavia.[1]

Nationalism, and to a lesser extent irredentism related to the return of independent Republic of Moldova to Romania, has figured prominently on the agenda of most important political parties. Nationalism helped the Romanian Orthodox Church to restore the prestige it lost under communism by claiming the unique position of repository of true Romanian traditional values. Opinion polls still list the Orthodox Church as the most trustworthy institution in the eyes of Romanians at the expense of democratically elected bodies like parliament. Romanian nationalism will retain its chauvinist dimensions as long as traditional, backward-looking, and intolerant Orthodox Church leaders set the tone of discussions centered on the nation and the nation-state. Only openness to the world and to other faiths, together with genuine ecumenical spirit, can turn the church into a more tolerant organization and convince it to foster inclusive patriotism instead of exclusive nationalism.

Third, relations between the Orthodox and the Greek Catholic Churches need serious mending. The Orthodox world was very upset by the resurrection of the Greek Catholic Church in Ukraine and Romania in the early 1990s, so much so that Orthodox Churches stalled the ecumenical dialogue with Catholics because of the unsolved issues related to Greek Catholicism. At the national level, the Romanian Orthodox Church has exerted tremendous pressure on politicians in an effort to block, or at least delay, the return of Greek Catholic churches transferred to Orthodox hands in 1948. The joint church commission on property restitution set up in 1990 should only have a consulting role. The final decision should rest with the courts of law, whose orders should be implemented regardless of which denomination is declared the winner. This is perhaps the best solution to the restitution problem, since Orthodox and Catholic canon laws and readings of history understand property differently. By allowing civil courts to exert their powers, the Romanian government would show respect for the separation of the judiciary from the executive and the legislative, which is an essential feature of a democratic state.

As the Greek Catholic Memorandum of 2002 pointed out, the post-communist state—successor to the communist state that confiscated Greek Catholic property in 1948—should assume its responsibility and reassign the property, as ordered by the courts. The view, recently underscored by Metropolitan Bartolomeu Anania of Cluj, that the Orthodox Church leadership has no say in returning Greek Catholic churches because those places of worship have always remained the property of the local community is not reflective of Transylvanian reality. It fails to explain why in some cases property rights were transferred from the Greek Catholic to the Orthodox Church, why the Orthodox have adamantly refused to allow Greek Catholic local congregations to use the village church, why some Romanian courts ordered the property return, and why the European Court of Human Rights recently recognized Greek Catholic petitions for justice as warranted. Perhaps, as more and more Greek Catholic congregations approach the European Court, the Romanian state will have a change of heart and convince the Orthodox Church to relinquish the old churches in order to avoid unfavorable court decisions. Whatever the final outcome, the ongoing conflict over property is likely to scar relations between the Orthodox and the Catholics in Romania for years to come.

Fourth, religion has assumed center place in electoral campaigns, and turned the voters' attention away from the candidate's concrete policy proposals to their readiness to perform religious ritual. In the weeks preceding elections, growing numbers of politicians make almost limitless use of religious symbols and call on support from priests and bishops in order to win seats in government, parliament, and county or local councils. Although repeatedly declaring its neutrality, the dominant Orthodox Church is happy to oblige and give support to various politicians, if certain that its demands will be met. Is association with the political elite repeatedly reflected negatively on the church when it supported corrupt, anti-Semitic, xenophobic, or anti-democratic politicians. Commenting on the Orthodox Church's collaboration with populist politicians like Gigi Becali, who claimed to be "Jesus' athlete" and "God's trumpet" in his bid for the Romanian presidency in 2004, former Ambassador to the Holy See Teodor Baconsky remarked:

> We face the danger of instrumentalizing popular religiosity in demagogical campaigns. This disfigures the fabric of the community and the hierarchy of values. What disturbs me is the fact that the Orthodox Church watches passively the rise of a "carnival Christianity," ignorant and superstitious, meant to deceive the poor and the unemployed. These fragile people risk confounding the pretense to be assisted with the hope to be saved.[2]

While the Orthodox Church has apparently decided to cease its direct involvement in electoral politics, the Reform Church has not. As recently as 2004, Reform clergy warned parishioners that those who did not vote for the Democratic Union of Magyars in Romania would be temporarily excluded from the congregation. Since 1990, the union has constantly polled the ethnic vote of Transylvanian Hungarians, receiving around 7 percent of parliamentary seats.

Fifth, religious education in public schools has perhaps been the most notable achievement of religious denominations in post-communist Romania. All denominations mobilized to convince the state not only to introduce the discipline in the most remote village school but also to fund it entirely from the public purse. Delivered in a denominational fashion, the teaching of religion in schools has occasionally promoted sectarian views about religion and hatred of other religious groups. It has been hoped that exposure to religious instruction will strengthen the Romanian moral fiber, but it remains to be seen whether that hope will become reality. Mindful of international laws protecting the freedom of consciousness and religion, the Romanian law allows students to opt out of religion classes, with the parents' approval. However, since this has to be done formally in writing, few parents take the option. Some denominations, including the Orthodox Church, maintain that religion is compulsory in public schools, denying nonreligious students the right to study alternate subject matters and squarely contradicting the Romanian constitutional guarantee of freedom of religion.

Sixth and finally, sexuality has represented an area that both church and state tried to regulate. While established democracies have removed the ban on homosexual behavior decades ago, they have failed to outline a common policy on the sensitive issues of abortion and prostitution. Having had a draconian anti-abortion communist law, Romania swiftly legalized abortion in 1989, but it took legislators a whole decade and a lot of pressure from the European Union to abolish legislation punishing homosexuality with a jail term. They did so despite bitter opposition coming from all religious denominations in the country. The Romanian Orthodox Church's opposition to homosexuality echoed the Catholic stance and reflected a position shared by other Eastern European Orthodox Churches.

Responding to the European Parliament's nonbinding resolutions to promote the equal rights of same-sex couples, in spring 2000 the Orthodox Church of Greece came out against homosexuality. Its head, Archbishop Christodoulos, stated that granting homosexual couples the same rights as heterosexual couples amounted to "legalizing a sin."[3] Around the same time, the Russian Orthodox Church issued a formal condemnation of homosexuality, artificial insemination, euthanasia, and abortion. When the World Council of Churches authorized a study on sexual diversity, the Russian Church threatened to resign its membership in the ecumenical body. In June 2001, Serbian skinheads led by a retired Orthodox priest attacked the participants in the first Gay Pride march in Belgrade.[4] It will take time for the gay and lesbian community in Romania to be accepted by the general population, and for Romanian women to accept the fact that abortion is not recommended as a family planning strategy.

A Conservative Revival?

As we have seen, the nature of the relationship between religion and politics in Romania depends on the position of the Orthodox Church on key issues such as democratization, European Union membership, the good citizen, and the just society. Recent events demonstrated that the Orthodox Church has gradually steered toward a more conservative stance that could pose problems for the country's political future. These events prove that the church remains an autocratic structure where the leadership enforces decisions made in secrecy without consultations with the clergy and the faithful, that as an organization the church is deeply divided between conservative and reformist factions with opposite agendas, and that the power struggles within the leadership have escalated to the point that short-term struggles between various hierarchs have prevailed over long-term objectives to preserve the unity of the church and strengthen its appeal with the Romanian people.

Faced with the challenge of European Union enlargement and globalization, the Romanian Orthodox Church might be increasingly tempted to succumb to the "tribalization" that Michel Maffesoli has talked about.[5] Paradoxically, Romania's political and economic integration into the larger European family might lead the Orthodox Church to more strongly emphasize its ties to the other Orthodox Churches and take up virulent nationalism. Integration will test the Romanian Orthodox Church's commitment to an understanding of the nation that is in tune with democratic requirements. Since policy pronouncements and discipline derive from the leadership more than the grassroots, the Orthodox Church's future largely depends on who Patriarch Teoctist's successor will be.

In 2005, Archbishop Bartolomeu Anania emerged as leader of the Orthodox Church's large conservative faction, despite his highly controversial past. Born in 1921 as Valeriu Anania, in 1935 he joined the Cluster of Friends, an offshoot for teenagers of the fascist Iron Guard.[6] Briefly arrested for attending the funeral of a prominent Iron Guard leader, he was released in September 1940 when the Iron Guard served as a junior partner in Marshal Ion Antonescu's government. Anania became a monk at the Antim monastery in Bucharest in 1942 and obtained a Bachelor in Theology from the Faculty of Theology in Sibiu in 1948, three years after Romania became a communist country.

After a short ecclesiastical career that brought him close to Patriarch Justinian Marina from 1948 to 1958, Anania was arrested again in 1958 and imprisoned in Aiud together with other Iron Guard members. As an inmate, he was entrusted by prison guards to head an infamous reeducation experiment meant to crush inmates physically and psychologically and brainwash them so they would confess to imaginary abominable crimes and convert to Marxist ideology. Less than a year after his release in August 1964 Anania was sent by the Orthodox Church and the communist authorities as an official envoy to the United States. The appointment raised suspicions that before his departure he convincingly indicated conversion to Marxist ideology and pledged full cooperation with the Romanian communist authorities and their notorious secret police. The opening of the Securitate files will likely illuminate the real reasons for his appointment. According to Ion Mihai Pacepa, the head of the Romanian communist foreign intelligence service until 1977, Anania was to infiltrate the Romanian émigrés communities in the United States, assert control over *Credința* (Faith) magazine and use it to influence foreign opinion about his country, and discredit Bishop Valerian Trifa, who refused to collaborate with the communists, by disclosing his past as a former Iron Guard member. In short, Pacepa claimed that Anania was a Securitate undercover agent, a claim not yet disproved by archival documents.

The death of Metropolitan Antonie Plămădeală of Transylvania in 2005 raised the issue of succession. In such cases, the Holy Synod elects the successor from among its members with a simple majority. Candidates must formally enter the race. Despite media speculation placing him as the frontrunner, Anania did not run for the post, perhaps because of his advanced age (he was eighty-four at the time). He chose to support a rather obscure figure, Archbishop Andrei Andreicuț of Alba Iulia who, in the poll, lost to Bishop Laurențiu Streza of Caransebeș, another little-known figure, elected as Plămădeală's successor on 3 November 2005. Upset that his protégé did not win the important see, the following day Anania proposed the split of the Metropolitanate of Transylvania into two units, dividing the territory and the faithful. The smaller unit continued to be called the Metropolitanate of Transylvania, while the larger unit was named the Metropolitanate of Cluj, Alba, Crisana, and Maramures.[7]

Days later, the synod accepted the proposal in a secret ballot. Further negotiations allowed the new Metropolitanate of Cluj, headed by Anania, to take away several important dioceses from the Metropolitanate of Transylvania and reduce the latter to a fraction of its former size. Anania's proposal for the split of the historical Metropolitanate of Transylvania and subsequent appointment as metropolitan were interpreted as the victory of the conservative hierarchs over their reformist, moderate, and pro-ecumenical colleagues led by Metropolitan Daniel Ciobotea of Moldova. Ciobotea was rumored to have voted, together with Streza, against the split. That Anania could rally to his cause the vast majority of the members of the synod denoted his formidable sway over the Orthodox Church's collective leadership body. Despite protests from civil society representatives and professors of the Faculty of Orthodox Theology in Sibiu, in February 2006 the National Church Assembly endorsed the division, making it official and permanent.

The events were important for a number of reasons. First, a traditional church administrative unit had never before been split because of strictly political divisions within the church leadership. The Orthodox Church has always maintained that tradition takes center stage in all its decisions, but the incident showed that hierarchs were ready to disregard such commitments, without qualms, whenever the move suited their agenda. Second, the split resulted from Anania's refusal to accept the outcome of a seemingly free and fair vote in the synod. The very fact that one single person, even a venerable figure like Anania, could render the result of the vote meaningless by drastically reducing the jurisdiction of the winner (Streza) reflected his enormous power base and the strength of the conservative faction he represented. Third and more important, the events had repercussions on the nomination of the new patriarch. Traditionally, the Metropolitan of Moldova was automatically elevated to the rank of Romanian patriarch after the death of the incumbent, but new rules adopted recently made the appointment contingent on a secret vote taken in the newly formed Church Electoral College consisting of religious leaders and lay persons. The rule could be interpreted as a move toward increased democracy within the Orthodox Church, if it is meant to select the best candidate more than to block Ciobotea's nomination in order to make way for a conservative candidate. A conservative candidate will likely share many of Anania's positions on homosexuality, abortion, and priestly involvement in politics, as though to remove any trace of that much-touted "tradition" recognizing the metropolitan of Moldova precedence relative to other synod members.[8]

European Enlargement and Romanian Religious Actors

Romania's adherence to the European Union on 1 January 2007 represents a highly important factor that will redefine church-state relations in the country. The overwhelming majority of the population and most of the main political groups have showed unconditional support for their country's integration into European structures, mainly as long-overdue reparation for Romania's separation from Europe by the Iron Curtain and because of the expected massive influx of European funds destined to improve the country's infrastructure. Nevertheless, a serious debate on the pros and cons of integration never took place in the country, allowing religious denominations to take center stage with regard to that issue. Geographically, Romania is situated in Europe, so Bucharest has assumed that the European Union could hardly refuse for too long its plea for political and economic integration, regardless of the many conditions imposed by the union and the even more numerous mistakes on the part of Romanian politicians.

The Romanian Orthodox Church was identified as the most formidable opponent to the country's bid to join the European Union, but one should remember that denomination has led only a small flock of Euro-skeptics in the country. Western Europe as a home to secularization, privatization of religion, liberalization, and the loosening of family values and national traditions was perceived by clergy and their hierarchs as a threat to Orthodox values and accepted traditions in Romania. These apprehensions were coupled with a genuine concern that the predominantly Orthodox Romanians could remain second-class citizens in the predominantly Protestant and Catholic enlarged European Union.

In December 2003, for example, Anania criticized European values, while admitting that Romanians overwhelmingly opted for European Union integration. He said, "We find that the New Europe has only two dimensions, political and economic. [They are] very important, but insufficient. Both politics and economics can divide the people. The new Europe lacks two vital dimensions: religious and cultural." He concluded by stating, "We want a Europe belonging to Earth and Heaven."[9] Respected monk Ioanichie Balan echoed these worries: "We don't trust the West! The West is Protestant, it is Catholic, or it is nothing, that is, nihilistic!"[10] These views informed the Orthodox Church's willingness to take up the Roman Catholic project of amending the European Union constitution to recognize the "predominantly Christian" character of European civilization.[11] Together with other conservative intellectuals, historian Gheorghe Ceaușescu defended the proposal: "Mentioning Christianity in the constitution is not a gesture directed against other faiths or the atheists, but reflects a tradition and an important factor that shaped the European spirit."[12]

Other religious denominations in Romania have had less trouble with the country's effort to join the European family, mostly because their own roots were Western European. Roman and Greek Catholics have readily supported the eastward enlargement process, stressing the many benefits the country will enjoy once it is accepted as a full member. The Orthodox Church, too, can play a positive role in the European Union debate if it can help to educate and calm the suspicions of the country's Euro-skeptics, conservative intellectuals, and rural population about the costs and benefits of EU membership. It remains to be seen how well the church will stand up to this challenging opportunity.

Recent proposals include the country's positioning as an Orthodox oasis in the larger European family, without the initiators spelling out the implications of a possible direct competition with the Greek Catholic Church.

For now, Romanian Orthodox theologians ponder over the accession's effect on nationalism. For Răduţ Selişte, "the preaching of Orthodox Christianity to European people represents Romanians' mission in the twenty-first century." He continued: "Romanians have the fortune to be a Latin people, a fact that ties us by blood with most people of the New Europe. At the same time, we are blessed to be Christian Orthodox. God purposely arranged for only one Latin people in Europe to retain the just faith and to avoid heresy. As Latin, we are not foreign to European mentalities. As Orthodox, we love God and other people, and have patience." After joining the European Union, Romania will need greater cooperation with other member countries because "Romanians will have to learn that 'I am Romanian' matters only if one can say 'I am European.'"[13]

Acceptance into the European Union in 2007 of the predominantly Orthodox Romania and Bulgaria is an accomplishment few citizens in that part of the world envisioned in the early 1990s. The two countries' European integration process will likely face a number of difficulties, some of them brought about by their religious majority. Although Romanians in general remain supportive of the process, integration will be successful only to the extent that Orthodox Church leadership is won over to the Euro-supporters' camp. Indeed, Romania presents a paradoxical situation: on the one hand, the majority of its population, which nominally is Orthodox, exhibits unwavering commitment to "entering Europe"; on the other hand, the leadership of the majority Orthodox Church remains the country's most vocal Euro-skeptic. This apparent contradiction stems from ordinary Romanians' attitude toward their church. While proud to be Orthodox and keen to attend church services (such as baptisms, marriages, and funerals), most ordinary Romanians and even some of the priests do not always follow their church leaders' positions in private and public life. The country ranks first in Europe in terms of abortion rates, although the practice is strongly condemned by the Orthodox Church. Similarly, church leaders have repeatedly proved their Euro-skepticism, but Romanians have preferred to follow their own hearts and have embraced accession. Much also depends on the final result of the power struggles being waged within the synod. The Orthodox Church's leadership is divided along generational lines between older, more conservative hierarchs and younger, more reform-minded prelates. Once power reverts to the younger generation, the Orthodox Church leadership will likely be more ecumenically oriented and more ready to support European integration.

Appendix

Romanian Orthodox Church
Serbian Orthodox Episcopate of Timişoara
Roman Catholic Church
Romanian Church United with Rome, Greek Catholic
Archbishopric of the Armenian Church
Russian Church of Ancient Rite in Romania
Reformed Church in Romania
Evangelical Church, Confessio Augustana, in Romania
Evangelical Lutheran Church in Romania
Unitarian Church in Transylvania
Union of the Christian Baptist Churches in Romania
Christian Church according to the Gospel in Romania – Union of
    Christian Churches according to the Gospel in Romania
Romanian Evangelical Church
Pentecostal Union – Apostolic Church of God in Romania
Christian Seventh-day Adventist Church in Romania
Federation of Jewish Communities in Romania
Islam
Jehovah's Witnesses

ORTHODOX CHURCH LEADERS MENTIONED IN THE BOOK

Teoctist Arăpaşu, Patriarch of the Romanian Orthodox Church, Metropolitan of Muntenia and Dobrogea, and Archbishop of Bucharest (Patriarch Teoctist)
Archbishop Bartolomeu Anania of Cluj, Vad, and Feleac (since 2006 also Metropolitan of Cluj, Alba, Crişana, and Maramureş)
Metropolitan Antonie Plămădeală of Transylvania (died in 2005)
Metropolitan Nicolae Corneanu of Banat (also Archbishop of Timişoara)
Bishop Laurenţiu Streza of Caransebeş (since 2006 Archbishop of Sibiu and Metropolitan of Transylvania, replacing Antonie Plămădeală)
Metropolitan Daniel Ciobotea of Moldova and Bukovina (also Archbishop of Iaşi)
Bishop Ioachim Mareş of Huşi
Metropolitan Petru Păduraru of Bessarabia (also archbishop)
Metropolitan Nestor Vornicescu of Oltenia (also Archbishop of Craiova) (died in 2000)
Bishop Casian Crăciun of Dunărea de Jos
Archbishop Pimen Zainea of Suceava
Archbishop Andrei Andreicuţ of Alba Iulia
Archbishop Lucian Florea of Tomis (died in 2001)
Archbishop Teodosie Petrescu of Tomis
Bishop Epifanie Norocel of Buzau

OTHER CHURCHES LEADERS MENTIONED IN THE BOOK

Metropolitan Vlasie Mogîrzan (Old Calendar Orthodox Church)
Bishop Ioan Ploscaru of Lugoj (Greek Catholic)
Archbishop Lucian Mureşan (major archbishop since December 2005) (Greek Catholic)
Bishop Inochentie Micu (Greek Catholic)
Metropolitan Cyril Gundyaev of Smolensk (Russian Orthodox Church)

Notes

All translations in the text are ours unless otherwise noted.

CHAPTER I

1. For example, Adam Przeworski, *Democracy and the Market: Political and Economic Reforms in Eastern Europe and Latin America* (Cambridge: Cambridge University Press, 1991); Karen Dawisha and Bruce Parrot, eds., *The Consolidation of Democracy in East-Central Europe* (Cambridge: Cambridge University Press, 1997); and Terry Cox and Bob Mason, *Social and Economic Transformation in East Central Europe: Institutions, Property Relations and Social Interests* (London: Edward Elgar, 1999). For literature on post-communist Romania, see Lavinia Stan, ed., *Romania in Transition* (Aldershot: Dartmouth, 1997); Steve D. Roper, *Romania: The Unfinished Revolution* (Amsterdam: Gordon and Breach, 2000); Duncan Light and David Phinnemore, eds., *Post-Communist Romania: Coming to Terms with Transition* (New York: Palgrave, 2001); Henry F. Carey, ed., *Romania since 1989: Politics, Economics and Society* (Lanham, Md.: Lexington Books, 2004); and Tom Gallagher, *Modern Romania: The End of Communism, the Failure of Democratic Reform, and the Theft of a Nation* (New York: New York University Press, 2005).

2. Donald Eugene Smith observed that "political development includes, as one of its basic processes, the secularization of politics, the progressive exclusion of religion from the political system" (Donald Eugene Smith, ed., *Religion and Modernization* [New Haven, Conn.: Yale University Press, 1974], 4). Don Swenson's discussion of religion and politics takes for granted the secularization trend in non-Muslim parts of the world (Don Swenson, *Society,*

Spirituality and the Sacred: A Social Scientific Introduction [Peterborough, Ont.: Broadview, 1999], especially chap. 10).

3. Juan J. Linz and Alfred Stepan, *Problems of Democratic Transition and Consolidation: Southern Europe, South America and Post-Communist Europe* (Baltimore: Johns Hopkins University Press, 1996). For levels of religiosity, see Pippa Norris and Ronald Inglehart, *Sacred and Secular: Religion and Politics Worldwide* (Cambridge: Cambridge University Press, 2004).

4. Sabrina P. Ramet, *Balkan Babel: The Disintegration of Yugoslavia from the Death of Tito to the War for Kosovo* (Boulder, Colo.: Westview, 1999), and Vjekoslav Perica, *Balkan Idols: Religion and Nationalism in Yugoslav States* (New York: Oxford University Press, 2004). A noteworthy contribution is Mirella Eberts, "The Roman Catholic Church and Democracy in Poland," *Europe-Asia Studies* 50, no. 5 (1998): 817–842.

5. "Christianity," *Encyclopedia Britannica*, 2006, available at: http://0-search.eb .com.mercury.concordia.ca:80/eb/article-67584 (retrieved 15 February 2006).

6. John Meyendorff, *The Byzantine Legacy in the Orthodox Church* (New York: St. Vladimir's Seminary Press, 1982), 49.

7. "Christianity," *Encyclopedia Britannica*.

8. Deno J. Geanakoplos, "Church and State in the Byzantine Empire: A Reconsideration of the Problem of Caesaropapism," *Church History* 34, no. 4 (1965): 387.

9. Ibid., 388–392.

10. The church's collaboration with the communist authorities included attempts by some of its prominent members to reconcile Orthodox theology with the country's dominant ideology. In his *Apostolat Social*, a collection of essays and sermons spanning his mandate, Patriarch Justinian promoted the concept of "social apostolate," which blended together Marxist-Leninist social analysis and Christian Orthodox theology (Justinian Marina, *Apostolat Social*, 12 vols. [Bucharest: Institutul Biblic și de Misiune al Bisericii Ortodoxe Române, 1948–1971]). The doctrine, whose intrinsic contradictions were never fully resolved, had a major influence on contemporary Romanian theologians who determined the curricula of the theological seminaries and university-level institutes training the priests, especially on the late Metropolitan Antonie Plămădeală of Transylvania.

11. Speaking with the authors in October 2005, a number of prominent Romanian Orthodox hierarchs and theologians insisted that *symphonia* had been abandoned in favor of a new understanding of church-state relations. While not labeling it the established church model, that understanding comes close to the new model proposed in this chapter.

12. Leo A. Kelly and Benedetto Ojetti, *Concordat*, 2003, available at: http:// www.newadvent.org/cathen/04196a.htm (retrieved 16 June 2006).

13. Giovanni Lajolo, *Address of Archbishop Giovanni Lajolo, Secretary for the Holy See's Relations with States at the Pontifical Gregorian University of Rome*, 3 December 2004, available at: http://www.vatican.va/roman_curia/secretariat_state/2004/documents/ rc_seg-st_20041203_lajolo-gregorian-univ_en.html (retrieved 16 June 2006).

14. Ioan Scurtu and Ioan Dordea, eds., *Minoritățile naționale din România 1925– 1931: Documente* (Bucharest: Arhivele Nationale ale României, 1996), 371–379.

15. Rossella Bottoni and Giovanna Giovetti, *I concordati di Giovanni Paolo II*, November 2004, available at: http://www.olir.it/areetematiche/63/index.php (retrieved 16 June 2006).

16. Stephen Monsma and Christopher Soper, *The Challenge of Pluralism: Church and State in Five Democracies* (Lanham, Md.: Rowman and Littlefield, 1997), 10–12. For an examination of the Romanian state's bilateral relations with each religious group, see Sabrina P. Ramet, "Church and State in Romania before and after 1989," in *Romania since 1989: Politics, Economics and Society*, ed. Henry F. Carey (Lanham, Md.: Lexington Books, 2003), 275–296.

17. Monsma and Soper, *Challenge of Pluralism*, 10.

18. According to some researchers, Germany also fits the bill for the model because its Roman Catholic and Lutheran churches enjoy an informal established status, and the government collects public taxes on their behalf.

19. Monsma and Soper, *Challenge of Pluralism*, 10–11.

20. The third model is inspired by Carl H. Esbeck, "A Typology of Church-State Relations in Current American Thought," in *Religion, Public Life, and the American Polity*, ed. Luis Lugo (Knoxville: University of Tennessee Press, 1994), 15–18; and John G. Francis, "The Evolving Regulatory Structure of European Church-State Relationships," *Journal of Church and State* 34, no. 4 (1992): 782.

21. Alfred Stepan, "Religion, Democracy and the 'Twin Tolerations,'" *Journal of Democracy* 11, no. 4 (2000): 37–57; and Alfred Stepan, *Arguing Comparative Politics* (Oxford: Oxford University Press, 2001), 213–254.

22. Max Weber, *The Protestant Ethic and the Spirit of Capitalism* (New York: Routledge, 1992); and Axel Hadenius, *Democracy and Development* (New York: Cambridge University Press, 1992).

23. Serif Mardin, "Civil Society and Islam," in *Civil Society: Theory, History, Comparison*, ed. John A. Hall (Cambridge: Polity Press, 1995), 278–300; and Chris Hann, "Introduction: Political Society and Civil Anthropology," in *Civil Society: Challenging Western Models*, ed. Chris Hann and Elizabeth Dunn (London: Routledge, 1996), 1–26.

24. Samuel P. Huntington, *The Clash of Civilizations and the Remaking of the Modern World* (New York: Simon and Schuster, 1996), 70.

25. Stepan, "Religion, Democracy," 39–40.

26. David Markand and Ronald L. Nettler, eds., *Religion and Democracy* (Oxford: Blackwell, 2000), 2–3.

27. Kenneth D. Wald, "Social Change and Political Response: The Silent Religious Cleavage in North America," in *Politics and Religion in the Modern World*, ed. George Moyser (New York: Routledge and Kegan Paul, 1991), 240.

28. Hans-Gert Poettering, *Mankind, Religion, Europe: The European Union—A Community of Values* (Brussels: Group of the European People's Party [Christian Democrats] and European Democrats in the European Parliament, 2002).

29. The figure is disputed by the Greek Catholic Church, which in 2003 estimated its membership at around 790,000. Available at http://www.greek-catholic.ro (retrieved 10 August 2004).

30. *International Religious Freedom Report: Romania (2003)*, 2003, available at: http://atheism.about.com/library/irf/irf03/blirf_romania.htm (retrieved 10 June 2006).

CHAPTER 2

1. Mihai Barbulescu, Dennis Deletant, Keith Hitchins, Serban Papacostea and Pompiliu Teodor, *Istoria României* (Bucharest: Corint, 2004), 310–311; and Paul E. Michelson, *Romanian Politics 1859–1871: From Prince Cuza to Prince Carol* (Iaşi: Center for Romanian Studies, 1998).

2. *Romanian Constitution of 1866*, available at: http://www.constitutia.ro/consti1866.htm (retrieved 15 December 2005).

3. George Ursul, "From Political Freedom to Religious Independence: The Romanian Orthodox Church, 1877–1925," in *Romania between East and West: Historical Essays in Memory of Constantin C. Giurescu*, ed. Stephen Fischer-Galati, Radu Florescu, and George Ursul (Boulder: East European Monographs, 1982), 217–244. During the sixteenth and seventeenth centuries half of the Moldovan and Wallachian metropolitans were removed from office by the country's political rulers or the Constantinople patriarch, a pattern continued after the principalities came under Russian influence in 1812 (Mircea Păcurariu, *Istoria Bisericii Ortodoxe Române*, 3 vols. [Bucharest: Editura Institutului Biblic şi de Misiune Ortodoxă, 1981], 3:516–526).

4. Aristotle Papanikolaou, "Byzantium, Orthodoxy, and Democracy," *Journal of the American Academy of Religion* 71, no. 1 (2003): 84.

5. *Romanian Constitution of 1923*, available at: http://www.constitutia.ro/consti1923.htm (retrieved 15 December 2005).

6. A list of all government officials responsible for religious affairs is available in State Secretariat for Religious Denominations, *Viaţa religioasă din România* (Bucharest: Paideia, 1999), 86–98.

7. Barbulescu et al., *Istoria României*, 411–412.

8. "Romania," *Encyclopedia Britannica*, 2006, available at: http://0-search.eb.com.mercury.concordia.ca:80/eb/article-42844 (retrieved 25 February 2006).

9. Alexander Webster, *The Price of Prophecy: Orthodox Churches on Peace, Freedom and Security*, 2nd ed. (Washington, D.C.: Ethics and Public Policy Center, 1995); Ronald G. Roberson, "The Church in Romania," *New Catholic Encyclopedia*, Supplement 1989–1995 (Washington, D.C.: McGraw-Hill, 1996), 19:331–337; and Lucian N. Leustean, "Ethno-Symbolic Nationalism, Orthodoxy and the Installation of Communism in Romania: 23 August 1944 to 30 December 1947," *Nationalities Papers* 33, no. 4 (2005): 440.

10. Robert Tobias, *Communist-Christian Encounter in East Europe* (Indianapolis, Ind.: School of Religious Press, 1956), 349.

11. Trevor Beeson, *Discretion and Valour: Religious Conditions in Russia and Eastern Europe*, 2nd ed. (Philadelphia: Collins, 1982), 368; and Tobias, *Communist-Christian Encounter*, 325.

12. For figures on monastic life in the 1950s Romania, see Constantin Aioanei and Frusinica Moraru, "Biserica Ortodoxă în lupta cu diavolul roşu," *Altarul Banatului* 12, nos. 1–3 (2001): 89–90.

13. Tobias, *Communist-Christian Encounter*, 349–350.

14. Webster, *Price of Prophecy*, 111.

15. Lavinia Stan and Lucian Turcescu, "The Devil's Confessors: Priests, Communists, Spies and Informers," *East European Politics and Societies* 19, no. 4 (2005): 655–685.

16. Lavinia Stan and Lucian Turcescu, "Politics, National Symbols and the Romanian National Cathedral," *Europe-Asia Studies* 58, no. 3 (2006): 1119—1139, 1127.

17. For a similar example on Russia, see Perry L. Glanzer and Konstantin Petrenko, "Religion and Education in Post-Communist Russia: Making Sense of Russia's New Church-State Paradigm," paper presented at the Church-State Relations in Post-Communist Eastern Europe symposium, Iaşi, Romania, 5–8 October 2005.

18. The 1991 constitution was amended in 2003 through referendum by the Social Democrat government of Adrian Năstase, but stipulations regarding religious life remained unchanged.

19. Governmental Decision no. 831 of 13 December 1991, *Monitorul Oficial al României* (20 December 1991); and the Law on Legal Off-Work Celebration Days no. 75 of 12 July 1996, *Monitorul Oficial al României* no. 150 (17 July 1996). Law on Preparing the Population for Defense no. 46 of 5 June 1996, *Monitorul Oficial al României* no. 20 (11 June 1996); Decree Law no. 9 of 31 December 1989, *Monitorul Oficial al României* no. 9 (31 December 1989); Decree Law no. 126 of 24 April 1990, *Monitorul Oficial al României* no. 54 (25 April 1990), and the unpublished Decision no. 810 of 1949 (annulled in December 1991).

20. Ronald G. Roberson, ed. *Secretariat for Ecumenical and Interreligious Affairs (SEIA) Newsletter on the Eastern Churches and Ecumenism* 40 (1999): 7.

21. Radio Romania (10 October 1996).

22. Governmental Ordinance no. 225 of 19 August 1994, *Monitorul Oficial al României* (25 May 1994).

23. Decree on the General Regime of Religious Denominations no. 177 of 4 August 1948 in *Monitorul Oficial* 178 (4 August 1948) and also available at: http://legislatie.resurse-pentru-democratie.org/177_1948.php (retrieved on 2 March 2007).

24. Secretary of State for Religious Denominations Laurenţiu Tănase, personal interview by Lucian Turcescu, Bucharest, 9 June 2004.

25. "Biserica Ortodoxă vrea recunoaştere," *Ziua* (23 September 1999).

26. Daniel Barbu, *Şapte teme de politică românească* (Bucharest: Antet, 1997), 119. As Archbishop Anania explained, "we did not ask the state for permission to call ourselves the national church. We are the national church regardless of what this or that [politician] believes. If there is a national state, there must be a national church" (Marius Tudor and Adrian Gavrilescu, *Democraţia la pachet: Elita politică în România postcomunistă* [Bucharest: Compania, 2002], 222).

27. *Biserica Ortodoxă Română* 7–10 (1990): 26.

28. *Biserica Ortodoxă Română* 10–12 (1991): 235.

29. Alina Mungiu-Pippidi, "The Ruler and the Patriarch: The Romanian Eastern Orthodox Church in Transition," *East European Constitutional Review* 7, no. 2 (1998), available at: http://www.law.nyu.edu/eecr/vo17num2/feature/rulerpatriarch.html (retrieved 20 August 1998).

30. "Din nou despre Biserică," *Evenimentul Zilei* (4 April 1999).

31. In 1990, twenty-seven Orthodox bishops qualified for such positions. By 2004, there were thirty (Organizarea BOR, available at: http://www.patriarhia.ro/ BOR/organizareabor.php [retrieved 23 January 2006]). In 2006, the Metropolitanate of Transylvania was divided after Bishop Laurențiu Streza of Caransebeș was elected to replace the late Antonie Plămădeală. The Senate includes 140 members.

32. We thank Fr. Marga for making his unpublished paper available to us (Irimie Marga, "Biserica și politica din perspectivă canonică" [unpublished manuscript, 2005], 5–6). Cf. Article 76 of the 1866 Constitution, Article 72 of the 1932 Constitution, and Article 64 of the 1938 Constitution (Ovidiu Tinca, *Constituții și alte texte de drept public* [Oradea: n.p., 1997], 18, 33, 52–53).

33. The German model was proposed by Metropolitan Daniel Ciobotea of Moldova because of the presence of state support and religious education in public schools, as he indicated in an interview with the authors on 6 October 2005.

34. The church hopes that levels of tax collection would reflect formal church membership more than levels of religiosity, which are much lower and similar to Western European levels. But it is possible that some Orthodox faithful would default on the church tax. For levels of religiosity, see Pippa Norris and Ronald Inglehart, *Sacred and Secular: Religion and Politics Worldwide* (Cambridge: Cambridge University Press, 2004).

35. Lavinia Stan and Lucian Turcescu, "Religious Education in Romania," *Communist and Post-Communist Studies* 38, no. 3 (2005): 381–401; Lavinia Stan and Lucian Turcescu, "Religion, Politics and Sexuality in Romania," *Europe-Asia Studies* 57, no. 2 (2005): 291–310; and Lavinia Stan and Lucian Turcescu, "The Romanian Orthodox Church and Post-Communist Democratization," *Europe-Asia Studies* 52, no. 8 (2000): 1467–1488.

36. "Biserica Ortodoxă vrea reprezentare," *Evenimentul Zilei* (17 April 1998).

37. Vasile Alexandru Talos, "Religious Pluralism in the Romanian Context," available at: http://www.georgefox.edu/academics/undergrad/departments/soc-swk/ rel/reefu1184.html (retrieved 10 December 2005).

38. Dan Bordea, the Roman Catholic advisor to the State Secretary of Religious Denominations, quoted in Tudor and Gavrilescu, *Democrația la pachet*, 221.

39. Tudor and Gavrilescu, *Democrația la pachet*, 217, 223.

40. "Teoctist urechește guvernul," *Monitorul* (13 September 1999).

41. *The Religious Freedom Page*, available at: http://religiousfreedom.lib .virginia.edu (retrieved 1 March 1999).

42. *Forum 18 News Reports*, available at: http://www.forum18.org (retrieved 15 May 2006).

43. Tudor and Gavrilescu, *Democrația la pachet*, 217.

44. *Religious Freedom Page*.

45. Katherine Verdery, *National Ideology under Socialism: Identity and Cultural Politics in Ceaușescu's Romania* (Berkeley: University of California Press, 1991).

46. Peter Siani-Davies, *The Romanian Revolution of December 1989* (Ithaca, N.Y.: Cornell University Press, 2005). The magazine *22* is available online at: http://www.revista22.ro.

47. The week after the 20 May 1990 elections, *22* carried a series of articles under the general heading "The Sunday of the Blind," suggesting that the Romanian electorate must have suffered from blindness when they voted for Iliescu and the former communist officials organized as the National Salvation Front.

48. Many group members remain committed Orthodox, and many more preferred to remain silent on religion and politics.

49. Mihai Chiper, "Biserica Ortodoxă bagă zâzania în lumea politică," *Monitorul* (14 September 1999).

50. Francois Thual, "Stereofonia religie-natiune," *Dilema* (6–12 March 1996).

51. Solidarity for Freedom of Conscience, *The Construction of Churches in Post-Communist Romania and Its Impact on Freedom of Conscience and the Secular State,* prepared by Liviu Andreescu (March 2005): 17, available at: http://www.humanism.ro (retrieved 10 May 2005).

52. Ibid., 29.

53. Alfred Stepan, *Arguing Comparative Politics* (Oxford: Oxford University Press, 2001), 217.

54. Lorne Dawson, *Comprehending Cults: The Sociology of New Religious Movements,* 2nd ed. (Toronto: Oxford University Press, 2006).

55. The Romanian language does not have a word for "privacy."

CHAPTER 3

1. "Nationalism," *Encyclopedia Britannica,* 2006, available at: http://search.eb .com/eb/article-9117287 (retrieved 10 January 2006).

2. Sabrina Ramet, *Whose Democracy? Nationalism, Religion, and the Doctrine of Collective Rights in Post-1989 Eastern Europe* (Lanham, Md.: Rowman and Littlefield, 1997), 15.

3. Ernest Gellner, *Nationalism* (London: Weidenfeld and Nicholson, 1997), 5–13.

4. Paul Latawski, "The Problem of Definition: Nationalism, Nation and Nation-State in East Central Europe," in *Contemporary Nationalism in East Central Europe,* ed. Paul Latawski (New York: St. Martin's, 1995), 1–11.

5. Martyn Rady, "Nationalism and Nationality in Romania," in *Contemporary Nationalism in East Central Europe,* ed. Paul Latawski (New York: St. Martin's, 1995), 131.

6. Ina Merdjanova, "In Search of Identity: Nationalism and Religion in Eastern Europe," *Religion, State and Society* 28, no. 3 (2000): 246–252.

7. Hans Kohn, *The Idea of Nationalism* (New York: Macmillan, 1967); Peter F. Sugar, ed., *Eastern European Nationalism in the Twentieth Century* (Washington, D.C.: American University Press, 1995); Sabrina P. Ramet and Donald Treadgold, eds., *Render unto Caesar: The Religious Sphere in World Politics* (Washington, D.C.:

American University Press, 1995); Sabrina Ramet, *Nihil Obstat: Religion, Politics, and Social Change in East-Central Europe and Russia* (Durham, N.C.: Duke University Press, 1998); Steve Bruce, *Politics and Religion* (Cambridge, Mass.: Polity, 2003); Ina Merdjanova, *Religion, Nationalism, and Civil Society in Eastern Europe: The Post-Communist Palimpsest* (Lewiston, N.Y.: Edwin Mellen, 2002); and Vjekoslav Perica, *Balkan Idols: Religion and Nationalism in Yugoslav States* (New York: Oxford University Press, 2004).

8. See the fine analysis of the Serbian case in Sabrina P. Ramet, "The Serbian Church and the Serbian Nation," in *Render unto Caesar: The Religious Sphere in World Politics,* ed. Sabrina P. Ramet and Donald Treadgold (Washington, D.C.: American University Press, 1995), 301–323. See also Perica, *Balkan Idols.*

9. Olivier Gillet, *Religion et nationalisme: L'Idéologie de l'Eglise orthodoxe roumaine sous le régime communiste* (Brussels: Editions de l'Université du Bruxelles, 1997), 81.

10. In 1945, reconciliation took place with the full recognition of Bulgarian autocephaly within the limits of the Bulgarian state.

11. Katherine Verdery, *National Ideology under Socialism: Identity and Cultural Politics in Ceaușescu's Romania* (Berkeley: University of California Press, 1991), 32–33, quoting Lucian Blaga, *Gîndirea românească din Transilvania în secolul al XVII-lea* (Bucharest: Editura Stiintifica, 1966), 55.

12. Verdery, *National Ideology under Socialism,* 61–63.

13. *Romanian Constitution of 1923,* available at: http://www.constitutia.ro/consti1923.htm (retrieved 15 December 2006).

14. Zigu Ornea, *Anii treizeci: Extrema dreaptă românească* (Bucharest: Editura Fundației Culturale Române, 1995), 113–115. For his anticommunist stance, the communists arrested Crainic in 1947.

15. Nae Ionescu, *Indreptar ortodox* (Wiesbaden: n.p., 1957), as quoted in Gillet, *Religion et nationalisme,* 91–92.

16. Dumitru Stăniloae, "Naționalismul sub aspect moral," *Telegraful Român* 85, no. 4 (1937): 1. Cf. also Dumitru Stăniloae, *Reflecții despre spiritualitatea poporului român* (Bucharest: Editura Elion, 1992).

17. Dumitru Stăniloae, "Idealul național permanent," *Telegraful Român* 88, no. 4 (1940): 1–2; 88, no. 5 (1940): 1. The article was a two-part editorial.

18. Augustine of Hippo, "Eighty-Three Different Questions," in *The Essential Augustine,* ed. Vernon J. Bourke (Indianapolis: Hackett, 1974), 62–63 (questions 1–2, 46); and Lucian Turcescu, "Dumitru Stăniloae (1903–1993)," in *The Teachings of Modern Christianity on Law, Society, and Human Nature,* ed. John Witte Jr. and Frank Alexander (New York: Columbia University Press, 2005), 1:705.

19. Because of his association with Crainic and the Iron Guard, Stăniloae was persecuted by the communist authorities, spending five years in jail and being denied the right to publish (Turcescu, "Dumitru Stăniloae," 687–689).

20. Trond Gilberg, "Religion and Nationalism in Romania," in *Religion and Nationalism in Soviet and East European Politics,* ed. Pedro Ramet (Durham, N.C.: Duke University Press, 1989), 336; and Robert Levy, *Ana Pauker: The Rise and Fall of a Jewish Communist* (Berkeley: University of California Press, 2001), 66. Cf. also Vla-

dimir Tismaneanu, *Stalinism for All Seasons: A Political History of Romanian Communism* (Berkeley, Cal.: University of California Press, 2003).

21. Ramet, "Serbian Church," 301–323. On the importance of collective memory of myths, heroes, and villains as part of ethnicity, see Trond Gilberg, *Nationalism and Communism in Romania* (Boulder, Colo.: Westview, 1990), 4–5.

22. Gillet, *Religion et nationalisme*, 27.

23. Stephen Fischer-Galati, *Twentieth Century Rumania*, 2nd ed. (New York: Columbia University Press, 1991), 112–113.

24. Gheorghe I. Moisescu, "Problema naţională şi rezolvarea ei democratică în Republica Populară Română: Rolul Bisericii în lupta contra şovinismului, anti-semitismului şi antisovietismului," *Studii Teologice*, 2nd series, 1 (1949): 669–690; P. Rezus, "Creştinismul şi dragostea de patrie," *Studii Teologice*, 2nd series, 4 (1952): 109; and E. Vasilescu, "Biserica ortodoxă şi patriotismul," *Studii Teologice*, 2nd series, 7 (1955): 382. All references are quoted in Gillet, *Religion et nationalisme*, 47–71.

25. Gilberg, "Religion and Nationalism in Romania," 338–340.

26. Verdery, *National Ideology under Socialism*, 167–214.

27. Gillet, *Religion et nationalisme*, 78–79; and Anastasia N. Karakasidou, *Fields of Wheat, Hills of Blood: Passages to Nationhood in Greek Macedonia, 1870–1920* (Chicago: University of Chicago Press, 1997).

28. Gillet, *Religion et nationalisme*, 80.

29. Nestor Vornicescu, *Desăvîrşirea unităţii noastre naţionale, fundament al bisericii străbune* (Craiova: Editura Mitropoliei Olteniei, 1988), 10, quoted in Gillet, *Religion et nationalisme*, 83.

30. Gilberg, "Religion and Nationalism in Romania," 342.

31. Sabrina P. Ramet, "Church and State in Romania," in *Romania since 1989: Politics, Economics and Society*, ed. Henry F. Carey (Lanham, Md.: Lexington Books, 2004), 278–279.

32. Henry Percival, ed. and trans., *The Seven Ecumenical Councils of the Undivided Church: Their Canons and Dogmatic Decrees, Nicene and Post-Nicene Fathers*, 2nd series, 14 vols. (New York: Scribner's, 1900), 14:596.

33. Gillet, *Religion et nationalisme*, 93; Maximus of Sardis, *Le patriarcat oecuménique dans l'Eglise orthodoxe: Etude historique et canonique* (Paris: n.p., 1975), 377–387. See also *BibleWorks for Windows*, version 6 (Norfolk, Va.: BibleWorks, 2003).

34. Feliks Gross refers to it as "tribal state" (Feliks Gross, *The Civic and the Tribal State: The State, Ethnicity, and the Multiethnic State* [Westport, Conn.: Greenwood, 1998]).

35. Ioan N. Floca, *Canoanele Bisericii Ortodoxe* (Sibiu, Romania: Polsib, 1992), 27.

36. Nestor Vornicescu, "L'Eglise et la nation dans la théologie roumaine," *Nouvelles de l'Eglise Orthodoxe Roumaine* 20, nos. 3–4 (1988): 7, as quoted in Gillet, *Religion et nationalisme*, 83.

37. Gabriel Andreescu, "Relaţii internaţionale şi ortodoxie în estul şi sud-estul Europei," *Studii internaţionale* 4 (1998): 16, available at: http://studint.org.ro/archive.htm (retrieved 2 July 2000).

38. Ibid., 17.

39. This was the second wave of canonizations carried out by the Orthodox Church. In October 1955, the church canonized nine Romanian saints, five of whom fought against the Greek Catholic Church in Transylvania (Mircea Păcurariu, *Istoria Bisericii Ortodoxe Române*, 3 vols. [Bucharest: Institutul Biblic şi de Misiune al Bisericii Ortodoxe Române, 1981], 3:478–479).

40. Ramet, *Nihil Obstat*, 195–196.

41. Lavinia Stan and Lucian Turcescu, "The Romanian Orthodox Church and Post-communist Democratization," *Europe-Asia Studies* 52, no. 8 (2000): 1480–1481.

42. Ilie Moldovan, *Darul sfînt al vieţii şi combaterea păcatelor împotriva acestuia— Aspecte ale naşterii de prunci în lumina moralei creştine ortodoxe* (Bucharest: n.p., 1997). Before the Orthodox Church's official formulation of its position on abortion in 2005, the pamphlet by Moldovan was the only viewpoint on abortion and contraception to meet the approval of the Orthodox Church and to be distributed to priests.

43. In 1989, Romanians formed 65 percent of Moldova's total population, Ukrainians 14 percent, and Russians 13 percent. The Gagauz, a Christian Orthodox Turkish-speaking minority concentrated in southern Moldova, made up 4 percent. In Transnistria, ethnic Romanians accounted for only 40 percent of the population, followed by Ukrainians (28 percent) and Russians (25 percent). Transnistria accommodated 17 percent of Moldova's total population. Some 98.5 percent of Moldovan citizens were nominal Orthodox Christians, and the Old Russian Orthodox Church believers made up some 3.6 percent of the population. Other registered religions were Roman Catholics, Baptists, Pentecostals, Seventh-Day Adventists, Baha'i, Hare Krishna, Jehovah's Witnesses, and the Church of Jesus Christ of Latter-day Saints. The Jewish community has some 60,000 members (*International Religious Freedom Report: Moldova [2002]*, 7 October 2002, available at: http://www.state.gov/g/drl/rls/irf/2002/13951.htm [retrieved 10 June 2006]). Historical Moldova was split into two parts: the territory on the right bank of the Prut River remained a province of the Romanian state, and the land on the left bank constituted Soviet Moldova.

44. In 1858, Romanians accounted for 66.4 percent of Bessarabia's population, Ukrainians and Russians around 15 percent, Jews 8.6 percent, and Bulgarians 5.2 percent. In 1897, Romanians represented only 47.6 percent, Ukrainians and Russians 27.6 percent, Jews 11.8 percent, and Bulgarians 5.3 percent. By 1930, the Jewish population accounted for 26.6 percent of Moldovan city dwellers (Charles King, *The Moldovans: Romania, Russia and the Politics of Culture* [Stanford, Calif.: Hoover Institution Press, 1999], 43).

45. Ibid., 44.

46. Transnistria, where Ukrainians and Russians made up a majority of the population and Romanian-speakers constituted only one-third, remained in the Soviet Union.

47. Whereas one was titled the Patriarchate of Moscow and All Russia, the other was named the Metropolitanate of Chişinău and All Moldova.

48. *Curierul Ortodox Info: Buletin Informational*, 15 August 2002, available at: http://www.geocities.com/cortodox/notati/05.htm (retrieved 15 November 2002).

49. European Court of Human Rights, *Case of Metropolitan Church of Bessarabia and Others v. Moldova*, 27 March 2002, available at: http://www.echr.coe.int (retrieved 4 January 2004).

50. Bassapress, 23 July 2002.

51. *Pravda*, 19 August 2002, available at: http://english.pravda.ru/society/2002/08/19/34805.html (retrieved 10 June 2006).

52. George Coman, "Mitropolia Moldovei vrea dizolvarea Mitropoliei Basarabiei," *Ziua* (27 May 2002).

53. Writer Horia Roman Patapievici, quoted in Lucian Postu, "Politichia de mărgăritar," *Ziarul de Iaşi* (30 November 1998).

54. Ministerul Apararii Nationale, *Ziua Eroilor*, available at: http://www.mapn.ro/traditii/ziuaeroilor.htm (retrieved 3 August 2005).

55. Bartolomeu Anania, "Totul este să începem construcţia," *Dilema* (24–30 October 1997).

56. Dan Popa, "Deşi trebuia sfinţit astăzi, locul Catedralei Neamului încă n-a fost stabilit," *Ziarul de Iaşi* (5 February 1999).

57. Alexandru Paleologu, "O catedrală a neamului ar fi un kitsch mortal," *22* (30 September–6 October 1997): 10–11.

58. "Bucureştiul şi reperele sacre: Extrase din dezbaterea pe tema proiectului Catedralei Mântuirii Neamului," *22* (7–13 October 1997): 10–11.

59. "Catedrala Mântuirii Neamului se mută în Parcul Carol," *Ziua* (30 April 2003).

60. "Catedrala Mântuirii în Parcul Carol," *Ziua* (7 May 2003).

61. Luminita Vâlcea, "Salvaţi Parcul Carol!," *Evenimentul Zilei* (22 March 2004).

62. "Catedrala Neamului contestată de trecători," *Ziua* (22 March 2004).

63. "Televoting pentru Catedrala Mântuirii Neamului," *Curierul Naţional* (24 March 2004).

64. "Comunicat-protest al Ligii Naţionale a Primarilor şi Consilierilor din România," *Informaţia* (22 March 2004).

65. Lelia Munteanu, "Iisus din tomberon," *Adevărul* (23 March 2004).

66. Cristian Tudor Popescu, "Catedrala Mântuirii în Ţara Mântuielii," *Adevărul* (23 March 2004).

67. "Primarul Capitalei acceptă Catedrala Mântuirii Neamului în Parcul Carol," *Ziua* (22 October 2004).

68. Ciprian Siulea, "O catedrală greşită," *Evenimentul Zilei* (31 October 2004).

69. Gabriel Andreescu, "Umbra teocraţiei asupra Parcului Carol," *Ziua* (4 November 2004).

70. "Catedrala Neamului a intrat în linie dreaptă," *Cotidianul* (9 February 2005).

71. Televiziunea Română, *Mari români*, available at: http://www.tvr.ro (retrieved 17 July 2006). The results were also presented by the major Romanian newspapers.

CHAPTER 4

1. Lavinia Stan, "Access to Securitate Files: The Trials and Tribulations of a Romanian Law," *East European Politics and Societies* 16, no. 1 (2002): 55–90; and Lavinia

Stan, "Moral Cleansing Romanian Style," *Problems of Post-Communism* 49, no. 4 (2002): 52–62. The most important English-language study on the Romanian Securitate remains that of Dennis Deletant, *Ceauşescu and the Securitate: Coercion and Dissent in Romania 1965–1989* (Armonk, N.Y.: M. E. Sharpe, 1996).

2. Kieran Williams and Dennis Deletant, *Security Intelligence Services in New Democracies: The Czech Republic, Slovakia and Romania* (London: Palgrave, 2001); and Lavinia Stan, "Spies, Files and Lies: Explaining the Failure of Access to Securitate Files," *Communist and Post-Communist Studies* 37, no. 3 (2004): 341–359.

3. Law on File Access no. 187 of December 1999 in *Monitorul Oficial* no. 603 (9 December 1999).

4. Stan, "Spies, Files and Lies"; Gabriel Andreescu, "Legea 187/1999 şi primul an de activitate a CNSAS," *Revista Română de Drepturile Omului* 20 (2001): 37–53; and Mircea Stănescu, "Le Conseil National pour L'Etude des Archives de la Securitate et le problème de la gestion de l'héritage communiste," *Asymetria* (10 April 2002): 5–22.

5. Dan Ionescu, "Crisis in the Romanian Orthodox Church," *Report on Eastern Europe* (9 March 1990): 48–51.

6. "Revoluţie în biserică," *România liberă* (31 December 1989).

7. In 1998, Corneanu said he insisted that Teoctist address the Romanians in the first hours of the December 1989 revolution, on grounds that "an era when people were alone ended, the church which was supposed to bring people together failed to do so. Though we could come up with examples to demonstrate the positive role of the church during communist times, at the time we failed to help the people" (22 [3–9 March 1998]).

8. Radio România Actualităţi (4 January 1990).

9. Reported in Ionescu, "Crisis," 50.

10. Agerpress (30 December 1989).

11. BBC Romanian Service (5 February 2000).

12. Decree Law no. 314 of 15 February 1941 as quoted by Dorin Dobrincu, "Patriarhul Teoctist a participat la rebeliunea legionară din 1941," *Ziarul de Iaşi* (13 January 2001). The document incriminating Teoctist, dated 30 January 1950, was found in the Romanian Information Service archive, fond D, file 909, ibid., page 510.

13. "Miscellaneous," *Evenimentul Zilei* (15 January 2001).

14. Ibid.

15. Cornel Nistorescu, "Editorial," *Evenimentul Zilei* (19 January 2001).

16. "Trecutul lui Teoctist, din nou răscolit," *Ziarul de Iaşi* (23 March 2001).

17. Teodora Georgescu, "CNSAS dezgroapă trecutul Patriarhului," *Evenimentul Zilei* (24 March 2001).

18. "CNSAS îi nemulţumeşte şi pe democraţi," *Ziarul de Iaşi* (28 March 2001).

19. Dumitru Stăniloae, *Teologia dogmatică ortodoxă*, 3 vols. (Bucharest: Editura Institutului Biblic şi de Misiune al Bisericii Ortodoxe Române, 1977), 3:234.

20. "Biserica nu se împotriveşte Legii dosarelor," *Cotidianul* (11 July 2001).

21. Ioan N. Floca, *Canoanele Bisericii Ortodoxe* (Sibiu, Romania: Polsib, 1992), 458–459.

22. Marian Alexandru, "Securiști în sutană," *Monitorul* (29 July 1998); "Iliescu pune umărul la îngroparea dosarelor preoților," *Ziarul de Iași* (7 July 2001).

23. Andrei Andreicuț, *S-au risipit făcătorii de basme: Amintiri care dor* (Alba Iulia, Romania: Editura Reîntregirii, 2001), 69.

24. In summer 2005, representatives of the Council for the Study of Securitate Archive told Lavinia Stan that the council had summoned Andreicuț for an interview because some secret documents revealed the archbishop as an informer. Andreicuț's file remains unavailable to the general public, and the council has not yet listed the archbishop among Securitate collaborators. The case shows that, as long as the secret archive is not completely opened to researchers, all individual evaluations remain preliminary.

25. According to Patriarchate data, the total number of Orthodox priests and deacons currently stands at around 13,925. Many priests serve churches built after 1989. There are thus strong reasons to believe that the current number of priests is higher than the number corresponding for the late 1940s, when arrests started (Romanian Orthodox Patriarchate, official website, available at: http://www.patriarhia.ro [retrieved 23 June 2006]).

26. "Stenograma ședinței Biroului Politic al Partidului Comunist Roman" (10 March 1945).

27. Cristian Vasile, *Biserica Ortodoxă Română în primul deceniu communist* (Bucharest: Curtea Veche, 2005), 236.

28. Onisifor Ghibu, *Ziar de lagăr: Caracal, 1945* (Bucharest: Albatros, 1991), 14.

29. Ioan Bardaș, *Calvarul Aiudului: Din suferințele unui preot ortodox* (Bucharest: Anastasia, 1999), 13.

30. Constantin C. Giurescu, *Five Years and Two Months in the Sighet Penitentiary (May 7, 1950–July 5, 1955)* (Boulder, Colo.: East European Monographs, 1994), especially the appendix.

31. Alexandru, "Securiști în sutană."

32. Gheorghe Calciu-Dumitreasa, *Șapte cuvinte pentru tineri* (Munich: Ion Dumitru, 1979).

33. Philip Schaff and Henry Wace, eds., *The Seven Ecumenical Councils* (Peabody, Mass.: Hendrickson, 1994), 599.

34. Andreicuț, *S-au risipit făcătorii*, 66–67.

35. Ibid., 67–68.

36. Gabriela Adameșteanu and Rodica Palade, "Limita între toleranță și intransigență," *22* (3–9 March 1998): 10–12. See also "Msgr. Nicolae Corneanu, metropolite du Banat, reconnait avoir cede aux pressions du pouvoir pendant la periode communiste," *Istina* 42, no. 2 (1997): 203–209.

37. "Am fost turnător din frică, lașite, ignoranța și disperare," *Evenimentul Zilei* (26 March 2001); and "Blestemul Sfintei Vineri," *Evenimentul Zilei* (28 March 2001).

38. Alexandru, "Securiști în sutană."

39. Florian Bichir, "Popii vor să fie reactivați," *Evenimentul Zilei* (10 June 1999).

40. Tudor Flueraș, "Preoții-informatori erau un organ de sondare a opiniei publice," *Evenimentul Zilei* (14 June 1999).

41. Ibid.

42. Among recent contributions, see Lavinia Stan and Lucian Turcescu, "The Romanian Orthodox Church and Post-Communist Democratization," *Europe-Asia Studies* 52, no. 8 (2000): 1467–1488; Olivier Gillet, *Religion et nationalisme: L'Idéologie de L'Eglise orthodoxe roumaine sous le régime communiste* (Brussels: Editions de l'Université de Bruxelles, 1997); and Olivier Gillet, *Les Balkans: Religions et nationalisme* (Brussels: Editions Ousia, 2001).

43. Ionescu, "Crisis," 49.

44. Rompress (12 January 1990).

45. George Enache, *Ortodoxie și putere politică în România contemporană* (Bucharest: Nemira, 2005); and Cristina Păiușan and Radu Ciuceanu, *Biserica Ortodoxă Română sub regimul communist, 1945–1958*, 2 vols. (Bucharest: Institutul Național pentru Studierea Totalitarismului, 2001). There are efforts to rehabilitate Marina, but not Moisescu, probably because Marina was Teoctist's protector.

46. Cristian Vasile, *Intre Vatican și Kremlin: Biserica Greco-Catolică în timpul regimului communist* (Bucharest: Curtea Veche, 2003); and Cristian Vasile, ed., *Istoria Bisericii Greco-Catolice sub regimul communist 1945–1989: Documente și mărturii* (Bucharest: Polirom, 2003).

47. Close to a hundred priests from the Alba Iulia diocese asked for Birdas's resignation in response to his collaboration with local communist authorities. The synod accepted the resignation at its 18 January 1990 extraordinary meeting. For details on the removal, see Andreicuț, *S-au risipit făcătorii*, especially the last chapters.

48. Moisin quoted Bălan's statements from *Biserica Română Unită* (Madrid: n.p., 1952), 278–279.

49. Ioan Ploscaru, *Lanțuri și teroare* (Bucharest: Signata, 1993), 420–422.

50. Radu Ciuceanu, *Intrarea în tunel* (Bucharest: Meridiane, 1991), 319; and Sergiu Grossu, *Calvarul României creștine* (Deva, Romania: Convorbiri Literare, 1992), 262–263.

51. Nicolae Dura, "Pe când canonizarea clericilor și mirenilor martirizați în temnițele comuniste?" *Dreptatea* (8–16 December 1993).

52. Nicolae Dura, "Învățământul teologic universitar ortodox din România de astăzi," *Dreptatea* (15–22 December 1993).

53. Cornel Nistorescu, "Editorial," *Evenimentul Zilei* (19 January 2001).

54. Neculai Constantin Munteanu, "Mînăstirea Secu," *22* (9–15 December 1997).

55. "Publicistul Gabriel Andreescu se leagă de Consiliul pentru Studierea Arhivelor Securității," *Ziarul de Iași* (9 September 2000).

56. "Dosarele înalților prelați religioși vor fi făcute publice," *Ziarul de Iași* (8 March 2001).

57. "Sefii cultelor religioase vor fi audiați la CNSAS," *Ziarul de Iași* (21 August 2001).

58. "Biserica și modernizarea României," *Ziarul de Iași* (16 March 2001).

59. "Invectiva în slujba adevărului," *Ziarul de Iași* (28 March 2001).

60. "Iliescu pune umărul la îngroparea dosarelor preoților."

61. "Accesul la dosarele Secutității provoacă numeroase controverse," *Cotidianul* (3 July 2001).

62. "Preoţii cu pete la dosar bagă dihonia în lumea bisericească," *Ziarul de Iaşi* (4 July 2001).

63. Florian Bichir, "CNSAS scoate la iveală dosarele capilor Bisericii," *Evenimentul Zilei* (10 July 2001).

64. "Petele din dosarele preoţilor le va vedea doar Dumnezeu," *Ziarul de Iaşi* (3 July 2001). Cf. also "Securiştii în sutană, deconspiraţi," *Ziarul de Iaşi* (5 July 2001); and "Dezincriminarea preoţilor turnători are adepţi pe faţă doar în PRM," *Ziarul de Iaşi* (5 July 2001).

65. Cristina Sofronie, "BOR ameninţă," *Evenimentul Zilei* (4 July 2001).

66. "Biserica Ortodoxă precizează că obiecţiile sale la Legea Ticu au fost greşit înţelese," *Cotidianul* (4 July 2001).

67. Ploieşteanu alleged that in 1997 he was threatened with the file's public disclosure after criticizing Premier Victor Ciorbea. Following Ploieşteanu, the blackmailer suggested that the file would conveniently disappear from the archive if his attitude toward the government improved ("In scandalul exceptării preoţilor de la Legea Ticu, Iliescu susţine independenţa Bisericii în raport cu legile statului," *Cotidianul* [9 July 2001]; and Lucian Gheorgiu and Bogdan Marnita, "Biserica nu se împotriveşte Legii dosarelor," *Cotidianul* [11 July 2001]).

68. "Iliescu pune umărul la îngroparea dosarelor preoţilor."

69. Cristian Galeriu, "Sacrificiul Bisericii Ortodoxe Române," *Sfera politicii* 93–94 (2001): 38.

70. "Compromisuri între Onişoru şi Stan," *Cotidianul* (10 July 2001).

71. Lucian Gheorghiu, "CNSAS va verifica preoţii doar cu acceptul Sinodului," *Cotidianul* (2 April 2004).

72. E-mail from Iosif Ţon titled "Deconspirare Iosif Ţon," sent on 17 January 2007 to http://groups.yahoo.com/group/masa_rotunda/message/3182 (retrieved 18 January 2007). A recent report summarizing the position of religious groups toward the Romanian communist regime mentioned Ţon's opposition but euphemistically referred to his secret collaboration as an "anfractuous past." Comisia prezidenţială pentru analiza dictaturii comuniste din Romania, *Raport final* (Bucharest: n.p., 2006): 199, available at: http://www.presicency.ro (retrieved 7 March 2007).

73. Marius David Cruceru, "Despre Dumnezeu, numai de bine: exerciţiu de trăire în adevăr," *Creştinul azi: Revista Bisericilor Creştine Baptiste din România* nos. 4–5 (2006): 6–11.

CHAPTER 5

1. The Greek Catholic Church is known officially as the Romanian Church United with Rome. Some authors refer to it as the Uniate Church, but Greek Catholics consider the term derogatory. For historical details, see Vlad Georgescu, *The Romanians: A History* (Columbus: Ohio State University Press, 1991).

2. Denis Hupchick, *Conflict and Chaos in Eastern Europe* (New York: St. Martin's, 1995), 74.

3. Justinian is quoted by Catherine Durandin, *Histoire des Roumains* (Paris: Fayard, 1995), 375.

4. Nicolae Bălan's 1944 letter to Patriarch Aleksy of Russia is quoted by Cristian Vasile, "Propuneri pentru unificarea celor două biserici românești (1944–1945)," *22* (6–12 April 1999): 10–11.

5. For a recent book of secret police documents on the Romanian Greek Catholic Church under communism, see Cristian Vasile, ed., *Istoria Bisericii Greco-Catolice sub regimul comunist, 1945–1989: Documente și Mărturii* (Iași: Polirom, 2003). Vasile had access to the Securitate archives and published many annotated documents.

6. *Romanian Constitution of 1948*, available at: http://legislatie.resurse-pentru-democratie.org/const_1948.php (retrieved 10 January 2005).

7. Council of Ministers Decision no. 1719 of 27 December 1948, *Monitorul Oficial* (29 December 1948); Decree Law no. 358 of 1 December 1948, *Monitorul Oficial al Republicii Socialiste România* (2 December 1948).

8. *Monitorul Oficial al României, partea a II-a* (12 January 1998).

9. Stephanie Mahieu, *Legal Recognition and Recovery of Property: Contested Restitution of the Romanian Greek Catholic Church Patrimony*, Working Paper no. 69 (Halle, Germany: Max Planck Institute for Social Anthropology, 2004), 4.

10. Censuses carried out by the Romanian National Institute for Statistics, available at: http://www.recensamant.ro (retrieved 2 February 2005 and 26 March 2006).

11. Stéphanie Mahieu, "(Non-)retours à l'Église gréco-catholique roumaine, entre adhésion et transmission religieuse," *Social Compass* 53, no. 4 (2006) 523.

12. Decree Law no. 9 of 31 December 1989, *Monitorul Oficial al României* (31 December 1989); Decree Law no. 126 of 24 April 1990, *Monitorul Oficial* 54 (25 April 1990).

13. According to Stefan Ioniță of the State Secretariat for Religious Denominations (*Monitorul Oficial al României, partea a II-a* [4 November 1997]). By 2002, the number reached 136, according to a memorandum that a group of Greek Catholic laypeople addressed to the Romanian authorities. The memorandum is presented in detail later in this chapter.

14. *Monitorul Oficial al României, partea a II-a* (25 November 1994).

15. "La future collaboration entre greco-catholiques et orthodoxes en Roumanie," *Courrier Oecumenique du Moyen-Orient* 18, no. 3 (1992): 24.

16. The resolution is included in the United Nations database (Vienna Convention on Succession of States in respect of State Property, Archives and Debts of 8 April 1983, available at: http://www.un.org [retrieved 24 May 2005]).

17. From 1992 to 1996, the Social Democrats occupied 117 deputy seats; the Greater Romania Party, 16; and the Democratic Convention, 82 (Richard Rose, Neil Munro, and Tom Mackie, *Elections in Central and Eastern Europe since 1990*, Studies in Public Policy Series 300 [Glasgow: Centre for the Study of Public Policy, University of Strathclyde, 1998]).

18. *Monitorul Oficial al României, partea a II-a* (25 November 1994).

19. Senator Pavel Tănase Tavală read the letter on 29 December 1994 (*Monitorul Oficial al României, partea a II-a* [7 January 1994]).

20. *Monitorul Oficial al României, partea a II-a* (27 June 1997).

21. BBC Romanian Service (27 October 1997).

22. *Monitorul Oficial al României, partea a II-a* (24 December 1997).

23. *Monitorul Oficial al României, partea a II-a* (3 July 1997).

24. Supreme Court of Justice Decision no. 901 of 1996; Constitutional Court Decision no. 23 of 27 April 1993 as quoted in "Protestul Asociaţiei Juriştilor Greco-Catolici din România" (18 March 2002), available at http://www.catholica.ro (retrieved 5 March 2007); Joint International Commission for the Theological Dialogue between the Roman Catholic Church and the Orthodox Church, "The Balamand Statement," *Eastern Churches Journal* 1, no. 1 (1993): 23.

25. Mihai Stoica, "Printr-o scrisoare adresată ministrului Rodica Stănoiu, Teoctist porunceşte justiţiei," *Evenimentul Zilei* (20 March 2002); and Mihai Boeru, "Pentru că scrisoarea Patriarhului Teoctist a ajuns la Curtea de Apel Cluj, Stănoiu şi-a scos subalternul ţap ispăşitor," *Evenimentul Zilei* (23 March 2002).

26. "Ministerul Culturii şi Cultelor cere revocarea Comisiei Mixte de Dialog," *Ziua* (21 March 2002).

27. Laura Dobre, "Greco-catolicii transilvăneni cer sprijinul premierului," *Ziua* (20 April 2002).

28. *Monitorul Oficial* (17 June 2002).

29. Mahieu, "(Non-)retours à l'Église gréco-catholique," 530.

30. *Cotidianul* (19 October 2002); Dan Sarbu, "Irlanda de Nord, varianta ardeleană," *Ziua de Ardeal* (12 March 2002); Victor Toma and Tiberiu Morariu, "Juriştii greco-catolici invocă supremaţia accesului liber la justiţie în faţa procedurii Comisiei Mixte de Dialog," *Ziua* (21 March 2002); and Adolf Crivăţ, "Ierarhii greco-catolici apelează la Ministerul Culturii şi Cultelor pentru restituirea lăcaşelor de cult," *Ziua* (11 April 2002).

31. *Monitorul Oficial al României, partea a II-a* (24 April 1997).

32. *Monitorul Oficial al României, partea a II-a* (26 June 1997).

33. *Monitorul Oficial al României, partea a II-a* (12 February 1998).

34. *Monitorul Oficial al României, partea a II-a* (12 June 1997).

35. Ibid.

36. *Monitorul Oficial al României, partea a II-a* (13 May 1998).

37. *Monitorul Oficial al României, partea a II-a* (17 May 1999).

38. Ibid.

39. *Greek Catholic Memorandum*, September 2002, available at: http://www.greek-catholic.ro/memorandum (retrieved 14 July 2006).

40. "Mitropolitul Corneanu îl contrazice categoric pe preşedintele Ion Iliescu," *România liberă* (11 June 2002). Corneanu did not give the full reference to Ivan.

41. Alexandru Stan to Lucian Turcescu, e-mail dated 17 January 2004.

42. Ion Neagu, "Regimul juridic al lăcaşelor de cult," *Vestitorul ortodoxiei* (15 June 2002): 3, 5.

43. Nicolae Dura, "Este posibilă o reconciliere între ortodocşii şi greco-catolicii din România? Cu ce preţ?" *Renaşterea* 14 (April–June 2003), available at: http://www.episcopia-ramnicului.ro/publicatii/renasterea-2-2003.pdf (retrieved 13 August 2004).

44. Metropolitan Nicolae Corneanu of Banat, personal interview by Lucian Turcescu, Timişoara, 12 June 2004.

45. Ronald Roberson, ed., *Secretariat for Ecumenical and Interreligious Affairs (SEIA) Newsletter on the Eastern Churches and Ecumenism* 123 (31 December 2005).

46. Vasile Gaftone, "Dura lex: Biserica din Suciu de Jos la CEDO Strasbourg," *Graiul Maramureşului* (3 September 2003).

47. The reports can be found on the website of the U.S. Embassy in Bucharest, available at: http://bucharest.usembassy.gov/US_Policy/Reports.html (retrieved 14 July 2006).

CHAPTER 6

1. For example, among others, Michael Shafir, "Romania's Road to 'Normalcy,'" *Journal of Democracy* 8, no. 2 (1997): 144; Liliana Popescu, "A Change of Power in Romania: The Results and Significance of the November 1996 Elections," *Government and Opposition* 32, no. 2 (1997): 172–190; Grigore Pop-Eleches, "Romania's Politics of Dejection," *Journal of Democracy* 12, no. 3 (2001): 156–169; Dorothee de Neve, "Elections in Romania: A Totally Normal Catastrophe?" *Osteuropa* 51, no. 3 (2001): 281–298; Alina Mungiu-Pippidi, "The Return of Populism: The 2000 Romanian Elections," *Government and Opposition* 36, no. 2 (2001): 230–252; Marina Popescu, "The Parliamentary and Presidential Elections in Romania, November 2000," *Electoral Studies* 22, no. 2 (2003): 325–335; Steve D. Roper, "Is There an Economic Basis for Post-Communist Voting? Evidence from Romanian Elections, 1992–2000," *East European Quarterly* 37, no. 1 (2003): 85–100; and Lavinia Stan, "The Opposition Takes Charge: The Romanian General Elections of 2004," *Problems of Post-Communism* 52, no. 3 (2005): 3–15.

2. A related area refers to the 1990 and 1999 calls of the Romanian Orthodox Church to have its leaders, the Holy Synod members, appointed as de jure life senators. Politicians turned down the proposal, wary that the twenty-seven synod members would be a strong parliamentary caucus with great influence on the electorate for decades to come (Orthodox leaders never retire). In 2002, the tiny Humanist Party unsuccessfully sought support for constitutional changes that would appoint only the patriarch a life senator ("PUR cu ochii pe articolul 59 din Constituţie," *Curierul Zilei* [10 June 2002]).

3. Dumitru Sandru, "Biserica din România, 1944–1948," *Arhivele Totalitarismului* 18 (1998): 210–228.

4. Available at http://www.patriarhia.ro (retrieved 14 July 2006).

5. Lavinia Stan and Lucian Turcescu, "Pulpits, Ballots, and Party Cards: Religion and Elections in Romania," *Religion, State and Society* 33, no. 4 (December 2005): 350.

6. Narcis Iordache, "Pentru a ajunge parlamentari, oamenii Bisericii trec cu vederea canoanele acesteia," *Cotidianul* (15 April 2003); Alin Cordos, "Cu Dumnezeu şi PSD inainte!," *Evenimentul Zilei* (3 June 2004); "Primarii argeşeni în sutană nu se consideră incompatibili," *Ziarul de Azi* (15 May 2003); Nicu Amuraritei, "Culoarea politică, mai presus de Cele Sfinte," *Jurnalul Naţional* (30 December 2002).

7. "Biserica declanşează campania electorală," *Ziarul de Iaşi* (17 April 1998).

8. "Ierarhii catolici sunt decişi să nu intre în politică," *Ziarul de Iaşi* (29 April 1998).

9. Cornel Nistorescu, "Slujbaşi la două puteri," *Evenimentul Zilei* (28 April 2000).

10. Eduard Tomaziu, "Ce politică face Biserica?" *Ziarul de Azi* (16 November 2002).

11. "Feţele bisericeşti calcă strâmb," *Ziua* (28 January 2004).

12. Iordache, "Pentru a ajunge parlamentari."

13. Madalina Prundea and Ciprian Iancu, "Puterea în sutană," *Evenimentul Zilei* (2 February 2004). Journalists further claimed that the anticorruption bill (Law no. 161 of 19 April 2003) deemed the positions of priest and mayor incompatible and obliged individuals to choose between them, but the law does not specify the compatibility or incompatibility of public officials who are also priests, and politician priests declared that they would wait for the synod to ask them to renounce their political posts.

14. Francisc Madarasan, "Deputatul Brudaşca cere întoarcerea preoţilor demisionari în PRM," *Informaţia* (1 February 2004); Carmen Radulescu, "Un preot primar din judeţul Argeş renunţă la preoţie în favoarea primăriei," *Informaţia* (13 February 2004); Lia Valendorfean, "Preoţii politicieni, în discuţia Arhiepiscopiei Ortodoxe din Cluj," *România liberă* (29 January 2004); "Preoţii-parlamentari scoşi din Biserică," *Ziarul de Iaşi* (29 January 2004); "PNL vrea preoţi în politică," *Ziarul de Iaşi* (31 January 2004); and Ion Muresan, "Chestiunea transilvană: Popii şi politica," *Evenimentul Zilei* (2 February 2004).

15. "Protopopiatul Botoşani le-a interzis preoţilor să facă politică la predică," *România liberă* (4 February 2004); and Alina Voaides and Florian Bichir, "Preoţii-politicieni, afară din Biserică," *Evenimentul Zilei* (13 February 2004).

16. Synod Decision no. 410 of 12 February 2004, available at http://www .patriarhia.ro (retrieved 10 January 2005).; and "BOR decide azi dacă preoţii pot face politică," *Evenimentul Zilei* (10 February 2004).

17. Sabina Fati, "Politica Bisericii Ortodoxe," *Evenimentul Zilei* (13 February 2004).

18. Ibid.; and Monica Szlavik Dragomir, "Sfântul Sinod respinge ideea politicienilor în sutană," *Curierul Naţional* (13 February 2004).

19. Benone Simionescu, "Preoţii maghiari pot face politică," *Informaţia* (13 February 2004); Cristina Strugari, "Preoţii suceveni se supun Sfântului Sinod," *Informaţia* (15 February 2004); Iulian Uta, "Voi face încă o revoluţie! Declară un popă-primar din Argeş," *Informaţia* (15 February 2004); and "Ierarhii şi preoţii ortodocşi au de ales: Ori Dumnezeu, ori partidul!," *România liberă* (14 February 2004).

20. Catalin Dumitrescu, "Un preot înfruntă Mitropolia Moldovei şi Bucovinei şi candidează la primărie," *România liberă* (2 June 2004).

21. Laura Dobre, "Preot judecat," *Ziua* (19 June 2004).

22. "Ierarhii şi preoţii ortodocşi au de ales: Ori Dumnezeu, ori partidul!" *România libera* (14 February 2004).

23. Francisc Madarasan, "PSD Cluj cere ca preoţii să fie lăsaţi să facă politică," *Informaţia* (18 February 2004); "Ducerea la îndeplinire a hotărîrii Sfîntului Sinod va

contribui la renaşterea morală" and "Retragerea din politică a preoţilor a bulversat listele de candidaţi ale partidului de guvernămînt," *România liberă* (16 February 2004); and Cristian Sutu and Claudia Tipluica, "Cosmânca şi Mischie în război cu Biserica," *Evenimentul Zilei* (14 February 2004).

24. Laura Dobre and Ovidiu Banches, "Preoţii lăsaţi în politică până la alegeri," *Ziua* (24 February 2004); and "PS Calinic al Argeşului nu vrea preoţi membri de partid," *Informaţia* (26 February 2004).

25. Alin Cordos, "Intre Biserică şi PRM," *Evenimentul Zilei* (5 March 2004); "Scurt pe doi," *Evenimentul Zilei* (26 April 2004); and Elena Toporcea, "Mesaj pascal cu îngrijorări laice," *Curierul Naţional* (7 April 2004).

26. Liviu Ioan Stoiciu, "De ce BOR şi-a exclus brusc şi radical clerul din politică," *Cotidianul* (4 March 2004).

27. Ion Zubascu, "Bisericile Catolice din Romania au decis: fără politică!," *România liberă* (19 February 2004).

28. M. S. Avram, "Preoţii ortodocşi şi catolici sălăjeni renunţă la politică," *Evenimentul Zilei* (20 February 2004); "Preoţii PD din Bistriţa au renunţat la politică," *Ziua* (23 February 2004); and "PSD Constanţa a rămas fără şapte preoţi-consilieri," *Cuget Liber* (23 February 2004).

29. Radio Romania (10 October 1996); and Lucian Purcăreanu, "Ion Iliescu: Nu este suficient să transformi în pamflete speranţele oamenilor," *Evenimentul Zilei* (7 December 2000).

30. "Preşedinte cu patrafir," *Evenimentul Zilei* (25 February 2000).

31. "Explicaţie pentru o campanie neruşinată: Legătura dintre stat şi biserică," *România liberă* (19 August 2003); "Maica Domnului, agent electoral PSD," *Adevărul* (16 August 2002); and "Pe spatele icoanelor împărţite la mănăstirea Nicula scria 'Donaţie PSD Cluj,'" *Telegraful de Constanţa* (16 August 2002).

32. Adrian Sorodoc, "Pelerinaj PSD la Talpa lui Cosmâncă," *Evenimentul Zilei* (16 June 2003); Mihnea-Petru Pârvu, "Pentru cine bat clopotele la Talpa lui Cosmâncă?" *Romania liberă* (30 June 2003); "Arhiepiscopul Tomisului, luat prizonier în biserică," *Ziarul de Iaşi* (20 August 2003); and Renata Constanda, "Gheorghe Frigioi pune bazele unei mănăstiri în Crucea," *Replica de Constanţa* (26 October 2004).

33. Neculai Amihulesei, "Preoţii din Tulcea distribuie enoriaşilor în biserici, în timpul slujbei, posterele electorale ale primarului PSD," *România liberă* (14 January 2004); Lucian Ursuletu, "Candidatură interzisă de Biserică," *Evenimentul Zilei* (25 May 2004); and Marius Mitrache, "Roagă-te şi lucrează," *Evenimentul Zilei* (25 May 2004).

34. Mihai Stoica, "Campanie electorală la uşa bisericii," *Evenimentul Zilei* (2 June 2004); Georgeta Petrovici, "Campanie electorală în amvon," *Evenimentul Zilei* (3 June 2004); Octavian Paler, "De ce parte e Biserica?" *Cotidianul* (24 October 2003); and "Năstase: Mesajul meu reflectă relaţia stat-biserică," *Curentul* (11 August 2003).

35. Toporcea, "Mesaj pascal cu îngrijorări laice."

36. "Pregătiri fanariotice la Suceava: PSD l-a confiscat pe Stefan cel Mare," *România liberă* (1 July 2004).

37. "IPS Pimen acuză conducerea ţării," *România liberă* (12 July 2004).

38. "Cei ce trebuiau să-şi ceară scuze sunt autorităţile şi nu arhiepiscopul Pimen" and "Mitropolitul Moldovei se leapădă de Pimen pentru hatârul lui Iliescu," *România liberă* (17 July 2004); and Roxana Andronic, "Puterea în război cu Pimen," *Ziua* (14 July 2004).

39. Gelu Trandafir, "Revoluţia lui Pimen," *Evenimentul Zilei* (15 July 2004).

40. "Cultura şi Cultele, laude, laude şi lozinci," *Ziua* (13 November 2004).

41. "IPS Pimen mulţumeşte Guvernului," *Ziua* (30 October 2004); "Năstase: Pimen ne-a dojenit în anumite cazuri poate pe dreptate," *Curierul Naţional* (1 November 2004); "Marele ctitor şi ocrotitor Adrian Năstase a împădurit Biserica," *România liberă* (30 October 2004); and "Cuprins de fiori înainte de alegeri: Năstase se face frate cu biserica," *Replica de Constanţa* (1 November 2004).

42. Catalin Dumitrescu, "Cuvioasa Paraschiva: Candidatul PSD în cursa pentru Cotroceni," *România liberă* (14 October 2004).

43. Ada Mesesan, "Cosmânca: Băsescu este Satana pe pământ!," *România liberă* (2 November 2004).

44. "Traian Băsescu, susţinător al caselor de toleranţă şi de acord cu căsătoriile între homosexuali," *Adevărul* (27 October 2004). See also "Scandal politic în Biserica Ortodoxă," *Ziua* (2 November 2004).

45. Alina Mihai, "Traian Băsescu a bătut mătănii la biserică," *Evenimentul Zilei* (27 November 2004).

46. Bogdana Păun, "Patriarhia faţă cu impostura lui Vadim," *Ziua* (23 November 2004).

CHAPTER 7

1. Scores of studies propose reforms that would align the Romanian education system to European Union standards. For example, Klaus Hufner, ed., *Higher Education Reform Process in Central and Eastern Europe* (Frankfurt: Peter Lang, 1995); Jan Sadlack, *Education Reform and Policy in East-Central Europe* (New York: Garland, 1995); Cezar Barzea, *Education for Democratic Citizenship* (Strasbourg: Council of Europe, 1996); and Victor Bârsan, ed., *Educaţie pentru Europa* (Bucharest: Pythagora, 1997). Attention was given to history curricula changes and the opening of university-level programs in previously unrecognized domains like political science—for example, Max Kaase and Vera Sparschuh, eds., *Three Social Science Disciplines in Central and Eastern Europe: Handbook on Economics, Political Science and Sociology (1989–2001)* (Berlin: Social Science Information Center, 2000). No study was dedicated specifically to religious education in that country.

2. Mirela-Luminiţa Murgescu, *Intre 'bunul creştin' şi 'bravul roman': Rolul şcolii primare în construirea identităţii naţionale româneşti (1831–1878)* (Iaşi: Editura A'92, 1999), 31–34.

3. Ibid., 32.

4. V. A. Urechia, *Istoria şcoalelor de la 1800–1864*, 2 vols. (Bucharest: n.p., 1892), 1:260.

5. Ibid., 1:202.

6. Gaston Mialaret and Jean Vial, eds., *Histoire mondiale de l'education* (Paris: Presses Universitaires de France, 1981), 6.

7. Aaron Florian, *Catihismul omului creștin, moral și soțial: Pentru trebuința tinerilor din școalele începătoare* (Bucharest: n.p., 1834), 134. The textbook was reedited every two to five years until 1889.

8. Ibid., 88.

9. Ion Heliade-Rădulescu, *Lectura pentru classa I primară: Lecțiuni preparatorie* (Bucharest: n.p., 1861), 62.

10. Writer Ion Creangă encouraged priests to use sermons as education tools (Ion Creangă, *Opere* [Bucharest: Compania, 1993], 235–236).

11. V. A. Urechia, *Opere complete: Didactica*, 2 vols. (Bucharest: n.p., 1883), 1:3.

12. Anton Velini, *Manual de metodică și pedagogie pentru profesorii școlilor primare* (Iași: n.p., 1860), 170.

13. George Radu Melidon, *Manualul învățătorului sau elemente de pedagogie practică pentru usul școalelor populare* (Bucharest: n.p., 1874), 110.

14. Ibid., 119.

15. Ibid.

16. Ibid., 12.

17. Noda Mozes, "The Roman Catholic Denominational Education between the World Wars," *Journal for the Study of Religions and Ideologies* 3 (2002): 123.

18. Cristina Păiușan, " 'Problema cultelor' în România în rapoartele Securității statului, 1949," *Arhivele Totalitarismului* 24–25 (1999): 90.

19. Cristian Vasile, ed., "Rețeaua informativă a Securității din învățământul teologic la sfârșitul anilor '70 și începutul anilor '80," *Arhivele totalitarismului* 11, nos. 3–4 (2003): 47.

20. Cristian Vasile, *Biserica Ortodoxă Română în primul deceniu comunist* (Bucharest: Curtea Veche, 2005), 35.

21. Direcția I a Departamentului Securității Statului, "Raport privind stadiul muncii informativ-operative în mediul elementelor din învățământul teologic" (12 December 1980), ANCSAS, Fond D, file no. 69, vol. 2: 65–66, reprinted in Vasile, "Rețeaua informativă," 49–50.

22. Radio Romania (24 January 1990).

23. Emil Moise, "Interpretarea Bibliei, sursa a discriminărilor de gen în practica religioasă creștină din România," *Revista Română de Drepturile Omului* 23 (2002): 86–96; and Emil Moise, "Relația Stat-Biserică în privința educației religioase în școlile de stat din România" *Journal for the Study of Religions and Ideologies* 7 (2004): 76–100. This chapter greatly benefits from two high-quality materials their author was kind enough to share with us in 2005: Gabriel Andreescu, "Biserica Ortodoxă Română ca actor al integrarii europene," and Gabriel Andreescu, "Relația Stat-Biserică în privința educației religioase în școlile de stat din România." We thank Gabriel for making available his unpublished texts.

24. Memo no. 3808 of 10 September 1990, quoted in Moise, "Relația Stat-Biserică."

25. Declaration no. 510 of 13 February 1991 and Petition no. 1593 of 1 May 1991, quoted in Moise, "Relația Stat-Biserică."

26. Report no. 244 of 25 January 1991, quoted in Moise, "Relaţia Stat-Biserică."

27. *Monitorul Oficial* no. 606 (10 December 1999).

28. *Monitorul Oficial al României, partea a II-a* (23 June 1995), 18, 24–25.

29. Constitutional Court Decision no. 72 of 18 July 1995, *Monitorul Oficial al României* (31 July 1995).

30. Ibid.; *Universal Declaration of Human Rights,* 10 December 1948, available at: www.un.org/Overview/rights.html (retrieved 10 December 2005); *International Covenant on Civil and Political Rights,* 23 March 1976, available at: http://www1.umn.edu/humanrts/instree/b3ccpr.htm (retrieved 10 June 2006); *International Covenant on Economic, Social and Cultural Rights,* 16 December 1966 available at: http://www1.umn.edu/humanrts/instree/b2esc.htm (retrieved 10 June 2006); and *European Convention for the Protection of Human Rights and Fundamental Freedoms,* 4 November 1950, available at: http://www1.umn.edu/humanrts/instree/z17euroco.html (retrieved 10 December 2005).

31. Renate Weber, "Legea învăţământului: între contestare şi supra-apreciere," *Revista Română de Drepturile Omului* 9 (1995): 20.

32. Emergency Ordinance no. 36 of 10 July 1997, *Monitorul Oficial al României* (10 December 1999).

33. Andreescu asked, "How many children and parents know or understand they can take advantage of the possibilities introduced by the [Constitutional Court] Decision no. 72 of 1995, even if they wanted to?" (Andreescu, "Biserica Ortodoxă," 59).

34. Alina Mungiu-Pippidi, "The Ruler and the Patriarch: The Romanian Eastern Orthodox Church in Transition," *East European Constitutional Review* 7, no. 2 (1998), available at: http://www.law.nyu.edu/eecr/vo17num2/feature/rulerpatriarch.html (retrieved 20 August 1998).

35. *Monitorul Oficial al României, partea a II-a* (14 November 1998), 15–17.

36. *Predarea religiei în învăţământul public,* available at: http://www.patriarhia.ro (retrieved 1 September 2005).

37. Oţelariu told us that his is not an official Romanian Orthodox Church website; see Sorin Otelariu, personal website, available at: http://www.invatamantul-religios .go.ro (retrieved 14 May 2005).

38. Elisabeta Stănciulescu, "Sociologia şi reforma sistemului educativ," *Biserica Ortodoxă Română* 62 (2002): 15–28.

39. Moise, "Relaţia Stat-Biserică."

40. Andreescu, "Biserica Ortodoxă," 62; and *Monitorul Oficial al României, partea a II-a* (23 June 1995), 20.

41. Adrian Schiop, "Cruciada ortodoxă în şcoli," *Evenimentul zilei* (4 October 2004).

42. Mădălin Popa, "Biserica din clasă," *Evenimentul Zilei* (6 September 2003).

43. Andreescu, "Biserica Ortodoxă," 62.

44. Schiop, "Cruciada ortodoxă în şcoli."

45. Felix Corley, "Romania: Concerns about Draft Religion Law," *Forum 18 News Service,* 31 January 2006, available at: http://www.forum18.org /(retrieved June 10, 2006).

46. *Propunerea legislativă PL 353/1999: Lege privind regimul general al cultelor religioase* and *Expunere de motive pentru PL 353/1999*, available at: http://www.cdep.ro (retrieved 14 June 2005). See also Ministerul Culturii şi Cultelor, *Proiect de lege: Forma textului Legii privind libertatea religioasă şi regimul cultelor în România stabilită în cadrul întâlnirii finale a Ministerului Culturii şi Cultelor cu cultele recunoscute*, 31 May 2005, available at: http://www.culte.ro/Clintide/proiect_lege_libertate_rel.aspx (retrieved 14 June 2005).

47. Law on Religious Freedom and the General Regime of Religious Denominations no. 489 of 28 December 2006, available at http://www.cdep.ro (retrieved on 2 March 2007).

48. Mihaela Neacşu and Cornel Dragoş, *Religie, Clasa a II-a* (Pitesti, Romania: Carminis, n.d.); and Tudor Demian and Ioan Sauca, *Manual de religie: Clasa a II-a* (Bucharest: Editura Didactică şi Pedagogică, 2002).

49. Related issues were raised during debates on the law on education. Maior told senators that religious proselytism was widespread in Romania, with newcomers recruiting members from among pre-university students and organizing recruitment drives on school premises. The minister worried that religion classes could be misused by new religions for proselytizing purposes. The concern seems unwarranted, since only the eighteen recognized religious groups can offer religious education in public schools (*Monitorul Oficial al României, partea a II-a* [8 June 1995], 18).

50. Ioan Sauca, *Abecedarul micuţului creştin* (Bucharest: Editura Didactică şi Pedagogică, 2002).

51. During debates, Senator Mihail Jurcu made the same observation (*Monitorul Oficial al României, partea a II-a* [23 June 1995], 26).

52. *Monitorul Oficial al României, partea a II-a* (31 May 2001), 24.

53. Nicolae Dascălu and Maria Orzetic, *Religie: Manual pentru clasa a V-a* (Bucharest: Aramis, 1998).

54. Andreescu, "Biserica Ortodoxă," 40.

55. Ioan Sauca, *Manual de Religie, Clasa a IV-a* (Bucharest: Editura Didactică şi Pedagogică, 2002); and Dorin Opriş, Monica Opriş, Irina Horga, and Antoaneta-Firuţă Tacea., *Religie: Manual pentru clasa a IX-a* (Cluj Napoca: Dacia, 2002).

56. Dorin Opriş, Monica Opriş, Irina Horga, Antoaneta-Firuţă Tacea., *Religie: Manual pentru clasa a X-a* (Cluj Napoca: Dacia, 2002).

57. Florin Marcu and Constant Mâneca, *Dicţionar de Neologisme* (Bucharest: Editura Academiei Republicii Socialiste Româna, 1973), 883.

58. Claudiu Dumea, *Manual de religie: Clasa I* (Bucharest: Arhiepiscopia Romano-Catolică, 1991); and Ioan Lucaci, Gelu Miclăuş, and Cristinel Fodor, *Manual de religie: Clasa a II-a* (Iaşi: Editura Presa Bună, 1994).

59. Rompress (15 August 1990).

60. "Senatorul PNTCD Ioan Moisin cere ca Biserica să cenzureze manualele şcolare," *Evenimentul zilei* (18 March 1998).

61. The letter, addressed to Minister of Education Andrei Marga, was eventually published in *22* (24–30 March 1998).

62. Andreescu, "Biserica Ortodoxă," 65.

63. Alice Tudor, "Religia în Universitate, extrase," *22* (23–29 April 1998).

64. *România liberă* (29 March 2004).

CHAPTER 8

1. Paul Goma, *Culoarea curcubeului '77* (Chisinau, Moldova: Flux, 2003), 172, 185.

2. BBC Romanian Service (20 December 2001).

3. Metro Media Transilvania, *Barometru de opinie privind discriminarea în România, 2004,* 2005, available at: http://www.mmt.ro (retrieved 27 January 2006).

4. *Monitorul Oficial,* no. 236 (10 September 1997).

5. Constitutional Court Decision no. 81 of 15 July 1995, available at: http://www.ccr.ro (retrieved 7 May 2005).

6. *Monitorul Oficial,* no. 289 (14 November 1996).

7. Christian Democrat deputy Emil Popescu, quoted in Human Rights Watch and International Gay and Lesbian Human Rights Commission, *Public Scandals: Sexual Orientation and Criminal Law in Romania* (New York: HRW and IGLHRC, 1998).

8. "Biserica ia atitudine față de homosexualitate," *Monitorul* (14 May 1998).

9. Reuters (13 September 2000).

10. Catherine Lovatt, "Legalizing Sex," *Central Europe Review* 2, no. 31 (2000), available at: http://www.tol.cz (retrieved 17 July 2006).

11. Lavinia Stan and Lucian Turcescu, "Religion, Politics and Sexuality in Romania," *Europe-Asia Studies* 57, no. 2 (March 2005): 294.

12. Council of Europe Resolution 1123 on the honoring of obligations and commitments by Romania (24 April 1997). Available at http://assembly.coe.int (retrieved on 4 March 2007).

13. Canons 7 and 62 of Basil of Caesarea, quoted in Philip Schaff and Henry Wace, eds., *The Seven Ecumenical Councils* (Peabody, Mass.: Hendrickson, 1994), 604, 608.

14. Nicolae Steinhardt, *Jurnalul fericirii* (Cluj-Napoca: Dacia, 1991), 56.

15. Alina Mungiu-Pippidi, "The Ruler and the Patriarch: The Romanian Eastern Orthodox Church in Transition," *East European Constitutional Review* 7, no. 2 (1998), available at: http://www.law.nyu.edu/eecr/vo17num2 (retrieved 20 August 1998). Session of the Chamber of Deputies of 14 September 1999 available at http://www.cdep.ro (retrieved 2 March 2007).

16. Ibid.

17. "Biserica ia atitudine față de homosexualitate."

18. BBC Romanian Service (20 December 2001).

19. Nicoleta Vera, "Romania va fi homosexuală sau nu va fi în Europa?" *Evenimentul Zilei* (15 May 1998).

20. Bogdan Stanciu, "AUR va susține reprezentarea bisericilor ortodoxă și greco-catolică în parlament," *Evenimentul Zilei* (16 April 1998).

21. Teodora Georgescu, "Referendum pentru homosexuali," *Evenimentul Zilei* (4 September 2000).

22. Laura Lica, "Biserica Ortodoxă, acuzată că se opune intereselor României," *Evenimentul Zilei* (9 September 2000).

23. *22* (3–9 March 1998).

24. "Homosexualii, la un pas de ieşirea din ilegalitate," *Monitorul* (29 June 2000).

25. HRW and IGLHRC, *Public Scandals*, chapter 4.1.

26. Vera, "Romania va fi homosexuală sau nu va fi în Europa?"

27. *Cotidianul* (26 September 2001).

28. Florian Bichir, "Mitropolitul Vlasie Mogîrzan condamnă legiferarea homosexualităţii," *Evenimentul Zilei* (29 August 2000). For membership figures, see *2002 Romanian Census*, available at: http://www.insse.ro/rp12002rezgen/16.pdf (retrieved 22 May 2004).

29. BBC Romanian Service (20 December 2001).

30. Ben Townley, "Romanian President Makes Way for Pride," 27 May 2005, available at: http://www.gay.com (retrieved 15 June 2005). See also Florin Bichir, "Parada homosexualilor," *Lumea creştină* (July 2005): 48–51. *Lumea creştină* is an illustrated Christian weekly supplement published by the Bucharest-based *Romania liberă* newspaper.

31. *Alternative Media Report*, 4 June 2004, available at: http://romania.indymedia.org/en/2005/06/851.shtml (retrieved 1 June 2006).

32. Bichir, "Parada homosexualilor."

33. Decree 770 of 1 October 1966 regulating the interruption of pregnancy, Buletin oficial no. 60 (1 October 1966).

34. Gail Kligman, *The Politics of Duplicity: Controlling Reproduction in Ceauşescu's Romania* (Berkeley: University of California Press, 1998).

35. John Luxmoore, "Eastern Europe 1995: A Review of Religious Life in Bulgaria, Romania, Hungary, Slovakia, the Czech Republic and Poland," *Religion, State and Society* 24, no. 4 (1996): 363; and "Soaring Abortion Rate Sounds Stalinist Alarm," *Sunday Herald* (9 February 2003).

36. Mihaela Jitea, "Un născut, un avort," *Ziua* (9 February 2004).

37. "Soaring Abortion Rate Sounds Stalinist Alarm." Another study showed that the total induced abortion rate doubled from 1.7 lifetime abortions per woman in 1987–1990 to 3.4 in 1990–1993. The largest increase in abortion occurred among fifteen- to nineteen-year-olds, women with only primary school, Bucharest residents, and women with low socioeconomic status. Some 67 percent of abortions were performed to limit or space births, 20 percent for socioeconomic reasons, 4 percent related to the woman's relationship with her partner, and another 4 percent for health reasons (Lisa Remez, "Romanian Maternal Death Rate Fell by Two-Thirds after the 1989 Revolution," *Family Planning Perspectives* 27, no. 6 [1995]: 263, available at: http://www.findarticles.com/p/articles/mi_qa3634/is_199511/ai_n8722997 [retrieved 17 July 2006]).

38. *Monitorul Oficial al României, partea a II-a* (27 January 1994).

39. *National Catholic Reporter* 30, no. 13 (1994): 4.

40. "Soaring Abortion Rate Sounds Stalinist Alarm."

41. M. Stroie, "Gravidele vor avorta cu aviz de la psiholog," *Telegraful de Constanța* (9 June 2003).

42. Ilie Moldovan, *Darul sfânt al vieții și combaterea păcatelor împotriva acestuia— Aspecte ale nașterii de prunci în lumina moralei creștine ortodoxe* (Bucharest: n.p, 1997). For a long time, this pamphlet was the only viewpoint on abortion and contraception to meet the tacit approval of the Orthodox Church and to be distributed to priests.

43. *The Catechism of the Catholic Church* (Ottawa: Canadian Council of Catholic Bishops, 1999), entries 2368 and 2370. See also Pope Paul VI, *Humanae Vitae* 16, 25 July 1968, available at: http://www.papalencyclicals.net (retrieved 28 August 2005).

44. Schaff and Wace, *Seven Ecumenical Councils,* 73 and 404.

45. "Senatul față în față cu ispitele: Grupul de rugăciune despre 'Păcatul prostituției,'" *Monitorul* (9 October 2003).

46. *22* (3–9 March 1998).

47. *Dilema* (5–11 March 1999).

48. *22* (3–9 March 1998).

49. The Noua Dreaptă (New Right) movement's official website, available at: http://www.nouadreapta.org (retrieved 2 June 2006).

50. Narcis Iordache, "Creștinismul revine la ideile conservatorare," *Cotidianul* (26 September 2001).

51. Narcis Iordache, "B[iserica] O[rtodoxă] R[omână] ia în discuție avorturile și clonarea," *Cotidianul* (14 November 2001).

52. National Committee on Bioethics, *Abortion,* July 2005, available at: http://www.patriarhia.ro (retrieved 10 September 2005).

53. Ioan Scurtu, *Viața cotidiană a românilor în perioada interbelică* (Bucharest: Editura Rao, 2001), 255–257.

54. "1997 a fost un an greu și pentru prostituate," *Monitorul* (1 January 1998).

55. Cornel Nistorescu, "Legalizarea prostituției," *Evenimentul Zilei* (4 May 2001).

56. Chamber of Deputies, official website, available at: http://www.cdep.ro (retrieved 16 July 2005).

57. "Proiectul privind prostituția, amânat pe motiv de post," *Curentul* (27 November 2003); and "Guvernul preferă liber-profesionistele în locul bordelurilor," *Adevărul* (27 November 2003).

58. *Monitorul Oficial al României, partea a II-a* (12 February 2002).

59. "Senatul față în față cu ispitele."

60. *Exodus* 20:14 and 20:17, and I *Corinthians* 6:9–10.

61. Transcript of the roundtable, "Fața ascunsă a prostituției legalizate" (February 2002) available at: http://www.antiprostitutie.ro/conferinta-video (retrieved 5 March 2007).

62. Nistorescu, "Legalizarea prostituției."

63. BBC Romanian Service (13 November 2003); and "Biserica nu vrea legalizarea prostituției," *Monitorul* (13 November 2003).

64. "Deputații au decis: Prostituatele rămân penale," *Adevărul* (18 February 2004).

65. Laura Lica, "Campanie antiprostituţie în licee," *Evenimentul Zilei* (14 October 2000).

66. Associated Press (17 April 2003).

67. Carmen Popescu, "Biserica este împotriva fertilităţii in vitro," *Ziua* (18 January 2005).

68. Georgeta Petrovici, " 'Biserica nu o poate binecuvânta' pe Adriana," *Evenimentul Zilei* (19 January 2005).

69. "Doctorul Munteanu este colaboratorul lui Dumnezeu," *Evenimentul Zilei* (29 January 2005).

70. Cristian Tudor Popescu and Valentin Popescu, "O iubire mai rece şi stearpă decât ura," *Adevărul* (19 January 2005).

71. The canon rule reads that the marital status at the time of ordination must be preserved afterward. This prompts many Orthodox and Greek Catholic seminary and university students to seek marriage before graduation and ordination as priests. Priests who are celibate at the time of ordination are never allowed to marry. Divorced priests also cannot remarry.

72. "Stareţul Mănăstirii Cernica acuzat de hărţuire sexuală," *Evenimentul Zilei* (5 November 2001); and Mariana Bechir, Mihaela Ion, and Andrei Filipache, "Stareţul de la Cernica, destituit pentru abuzuri sexuale," *Evenimentul Zilei* (7 November 2001).

73. Vasile Danion, *Mângâiere şi mustrare* (Bucharest: Editura Sophia, 2003), 888–90; "Reglare de conturi în BOR?" *Ziua* (13 March 2003).

74. Miruna Ionescu, "Un preot face greva foamei," *Evenimentul Zilei* (27 June 2001); and Dana Antohe, "IPS se împotriveşte poligamiei," *Replica de Constanţa* (20 August 2003).

75. Dan Antohe, "IPS se împotriveşte poligamiei," *Replica de Constanţa* (20 August 2003).

CHAPTER 9

1. Tom Gallagher, *Romania after Ceauşescu* (Edinburgh: Edinburgh University Press, 1995).

2. Bogdan Brătescu and Oana Stănciulescu, "Teodor Baconsky: Dezbaterea publică, sufocată de promovarea mediatică a unor figuri interlope," *Prezent* (27 April 2006).

3. Daniel P. Payne, "The Clash of Civilizations: The Church of Greece, the European Union and the Question of Human Rights," *Religion, State and Society* 31, no. 3 (2003): 268.

4. Sabrina P. Ramet, "The Way We Were—And Should Be Again? European Orthodox Churches and the 'Idyllic Past,' " in *Religion in an Expanding Europe*, ed. Timothy A. Byrnes and Peter J. Katzenstein (New York: Cambridge University Press, 2006), 171.

5. Michel Maffesoli, *The Time of the Tribes: The Decline of Individualism in Mass Society* (London: Sage, 1996).

6. The biographical information on Anania is taken from Ion Zubaşcu, "Adevărata biografie," *România liberă* (4 February 2006), and corroborated with information provided by Anania himself in an interview originally given to Rompres: "IPS Bartolomeu Anania: Am fost şi am rămas de dreapta," *Rost* (April 2006), available at: http://www.romfest.org/rost/apr2006/anania.shtml (retrieved 17 July 2006). See also Nistor Chioreanu, *Morminte vii* (Iaşi, 1992), 341–342; Ion Mihai Pacepa, *Red Horizons: Chronicles of a Communist Chief Spy* (Washington, D.C.: Regnery Gateway, 1987), 284–285.

7. Anania admitted in an interview that "if Andreicuţ would have been elected the metropolitan of Transylvania, the metropolitanate would not have been broken in two: there would have been a single metropolitanate with its see in Cluj [rather than Sibiu]" ("In postul Craciunului, ierarhii au dezlegare la lupta pentru putere," *Adevărul* [26 November 2005]).

8. "Noul Patriarh va fi ales prin vot secret," *Evenimentul Zilei* (27 March 2006).

9. "IPS Bartolomeu: Îngrijorat de noua configuraţie a Europei," *Adevărul* (18 December 2003).

10. "Să dea Dumnezeu să nu intrăm în NATO," *România liberă* (5 July 1997).

11. "Teoctist vrea creştinismul în Constituţia UE," *Monitorul* (18 October 2003).

12. Gheorghe Ceauşescu, "Cele trei coline," *România literară* (5–11 November 2003).

13. Marcel Răduţ Selişte, "Biserica Ortodoxă Română şi Noua Europă," *Rost* 35 (2006), available at: http://www.romfest.org/rost/apr_mai2004/oltenia.shtml (retrieved 18 July 2006).

Bibliography

"Accesul la dosarele Securității provoacă numeroase controverse," *Cotidianul* (3 July 2001).

Adameșteanu, Gabriela, and Rodica Palade. "Limita dintre toleranță și intransigență," *22* (3–9 March 1998): 10–12.

Aioanei, Constantin, and Frusinica Moraru. "Biserica Ortodoxă în lupta cu diavolul roșu," *Altarul Banatului* 12, nos. 1–3 (2001): 89–90.

Alexandru, Marian. "Securiști în sutană," *Monitorul* (29 July 1998).

Alternative Media Report. Available at: http://romania.indymedia.org/en/2005/06/851.shtml (retrieved 5 March 2007).

"Am fost turnător din frică, lașitate, ignoranță și disperare," *Evenimentul Zilei* (26 March 2001).

Amihulesei, Neculai. "Preoții din Tulcea distribuie enoriașilor în biserici, în timpul slujbei, posterele electorale ale primarului PSD," *România liberă* (14 January 2004).

Amurăriței, Nicu. "Culoarea politică, mai presus de Cele Sfinte," *Jurnalul Național* (30 December 2002).

Anania, Bartolomeu. "Totul este să începem construcția," *Dilema* (24–30 October 1997).

Andreescu, Gabriel. "Biserica Ortodoxă Română ca actor al integrării europene," unpublished manuscript, 2002.

———. "Legea 187/1999 și primul an de activitate a CNSAS," *Revista Română de Drepturile Omului* 20 (2001): 37–53.

———. "Relația Stat-Biserica în privința educației religioase în școlile de stat din România," unpublished manuscript, 2002.

———. "Relații internaționale și ortodoxie în estul și sud-estul Europei," *Studii internaționale* 4 (1998). Available at: http://studint.org.ro/archive.htm (retrieved 2 July 2000).

————. "Umbra teocrației asupra Parcului Carol," *Ziua* (4 November 2004).

Andreicuț, Andrei. *S-au risipit făcătorii de basme: Amintiri care dor.* Alba-Iulia, Romania: Editura Reîntregirii, 2001.

Andronic, Roxana. "Puterea în război cu Pimen," *Ziua* (14 July 2004).

Antohe, Dana. "IPS se împotrivește poligamiei," *Replica de Constanța* (20 August 2003).

"Arhiepiscopul Tomisului, luat prizonier în biserică," *Ziarul de Iași* (20 August 2003).

Augustine of Hippo. "Eighty-Three Different Questions," in *The Essential Augustine,* ed. Vernon J. Bourke, 62–63. Indianapolis: Hackett, 1974.

Avram, M. S. "Preoții ortodocși și catolici sălăjeni renunță la politică," *Evenimentul Zilei* (20 February 2004).

Barbu, Daniel. *Șapte teme de politică românească.* Bucharest: Antet, 1997.

Bărbulescu, Mihai, Dennis Deletant, Keith Hitchins, Serban Papacostea, and Pompiliu Teodor. *Istoria României.* Bucharest: Corint, 2004.

Bardas, Ioan. *Calvarul Aiudului: Din suferințele unui preot ortodox.* Bucharest: Anastasia, 1999.

Bârsan, Victor, ed. *Educație pentru Europa.* Bucharest: Pythagora, 1997.

Barzea, Cezar. *Education for Democratic Citizenship.* Strasbourg: Council of Europe, 1996.

Bechir, Mariana, Mihaela Ion, and Andrei Filipache. "Starețul de la Cernica, destituit pentru abuzuri sexuale," *Evenimentul Zilei* (7 November 2001).

Beeson, Trevor. *Discretion and Valour: Religious Conditions in Russia and Eastern Europe,* 2nd ed. Philadelphia: Collins, 1982.

BibleWorks for Windows, version 6. Norfolk, Va.: BibleWorks, 2003.

Bichir, Florin. "CNSAS scoate la iveală dosarele capilor Bisericii," *Evenimentul Zilei* (10 July 2001).

————. "Mitropolitul Vlasie Mogîrzan condamnă legiferarea homosexualității," *Evenimentul Zilei* (29 August 2000).

————. "Parada homosexualilor," *Lumea creștină* (July 2005): 48–51.

————. "Popii cer dezlegarea la dosare," *Evenimentul Zilei* (2 July 2001).

————. "Popii vor să fie reactivați," *Evenimentul Zilei* (10 June 1999).

"Biserica declanșează campania electorală," *Ziarul de Iași* (17 April 1998).

"Biserica ia atitudine față de homosexualitate," *Monitorul* (14 May 1998).

"Biserica nu se împotrivește Legii dosarelor," *Cotidianul* (11 July 2001).

"Biserica nu vrea legalizarea prostituției," *Monitorul* (13 November 2003).

"Biserica Ortodoxă precizează că obiecțiile sale la Legea Ticu au fost greșit înțelese," *Cotidianul* (4 July 2001).

"Biserica Ortodoxă vrea reprezentare," *Evenimentul Zilei* (17 April 1998).

Biserica Ortodoxă Română 7–10 (1990): 23–40.

Biserica Ortodoxă Română 10–12 (1991): 57–62.

"Biserica Ortodoxă vrea recunoaștere," *Ziua* (23 September 1999).

Biserica Română Unită. Madrid: n.p., 1952.

"Biserica și modernizarea României," *Ziarul de Iași* (16 March 2001).

"Blestemul Sfintei Vineri," *Evenimentul Zilei* (28 March 2001).

Boeru, Mihai. "Pentru că scrisoarea Patriarhului Teoctist a ajuns la Curtea de Apel Cluj, Stănoiu şi-a scos subalternul ţap ispăşitor," *Evenimentul Zilei* (23 March 2002).

"BOR decide azi dacă preoţii pot face politică," *Evenimentul Zilei* (10 February 2004).

Bottoni, Rossella, and Giovanna Giovetti. *I concordati di Giovanni Paolo II*. November 2004. Available at: http://www.olir.it/areetematiche/63/index.php (retrieved 16 June 2006).

Brătescu, Bogdan, and Oana Stanciulescu. "Teodor Baconsky: Dezbaterea publică, sufocată de promovarea mediatică a unor figuri interlope," *Prezent* (27 April 2006).

Bruce, Steve. *Politics and Religion*. Cambridge, Mass.: Polity, 2003.

"Bucureştiul şi reperele sacre: Extrase din dezbaterea pe tema proiectului Catedralei Mântuirii Neamului," *22* (7–13 October 1997): 10–11.

Calciu-Dumitreasa, Gheorghe. *Şapte cuvinte pentru tineri*. Munich: Ion Dumitru, 1979.

Carey, Henry F., ed. *Romania since 1989: Politics, Economics and Society*. Lanham, Md.: Lexington Books, 2004.

The Catechism of the Catholic Church. Ottawa: Canadian Council of Catholic Bishops, 1999.

"Catedrala Mântuirii în Parcul Carol," *Ziua* (7 May 2003).

"Catedrala Mântuirii Neamului se mută în Parcul Carol," *Ziua* (30 April 2003).

"Catedrala Neamului a intrat în linie dreaptă," *Cotidianul* (9 February 2005).

"Catedrala Neamului contestată de trecători," *Ziua* (22 March 2004).

Ceauşescu, Gheorghe. "Cele trei coline," *România literară* (5–11 November 2003).

"Cei ce trebuiau să-şi ceară scuze sunt autorităţile şi nu arhiepiscopul Pimen," *România liberă* (17 July 2004).

Chamber of Deputies, official website, available at: http://www.cdep.ro (retrieved 20 September 2006).

Chioreanu, Nistor. *Morminte vii*. Iaşi: n.p., 1992.

Chiper, Mihai. "Biserica Ortodoxă bagă zâzania în lumea politică," *Monitorul* (14 September 1999).

"Christianity," *Encyclopedia Britannica*. 2006. Available at: http://o-search.eb.com .mercury.concordia.ca:80/eb/article-67584 (retrieved 15 February 2006).

Ciuceanu, Radu. *Intrarea în tunel*. Bucharest: Meridiane, 1991.

"CNSAS îi nemulţumeşte şi pe democraţi," *Ziarul de Iaşi* (28 March 2001).

Coman, George. "Mitropolia Moldovei vrea dizolvarea Mitropoliei Basarabiei," *Ziua* (27 May 2002).

Comisia prezidenţială pentru analiza dictaturii comuniste din Romania. *Raport final* (Bucharest: n.p., 2006), available at: http://www.presicency.ro (retrieved 7 March 2007)

"Compromisuri între Onişoru şi Stan," *Cotidianul* (10 July 2001).

"Comunicat-protest al Ligii Naţionale a Primarilor şi Consilierilor din România," *Informaţia* (22 March 2004).

Constanda, Renata. "Gheorghe Frigioi pune bazele unei mănăstiri la Crucea," *Replica de Constanţa* (26 October 2004).

Cordos, Alin. "Cu Dumnezeu şi PSD înainte," *Evenimentul Zilei* (3 June 2004).

————. "Intre Biserică şi PRM," *Evenimentul Zilei* (5 March 2004).

Corley, Felix. "Romania: Concerns about Draft Religion Law." *Forum 18 News Service.* 31 January 2006. Available at: http://www.forum18.org (retrieved 10 June 2006).

Country Reports on Human Rights Practices, U.S. Embassy in Bucharest. Available at: http://bucharest.usembassy.gov/US_Policy/Reports.html (retrieved 14 July 2006).

Cox, Terry, and Bob Mason. *Social and Economic Transformation in East Central Europe: Institutions, Property Relations and Social Interests.* London: Edward Elgar, 1999.

Creangă, Ion. *Opere.* Bucharest: Compania, 1993.

Crivăţ, Adolf. "Ierarhii greco-catolici apelează la Ministerul Culturii şi Cultelor pentru restituirea lăcaşelor de cult," *Ziua* (11 April 2002).

Cruceru, Marius David "Despre Dumnezeu, numai de bine: exerciţiu de trăire în adevăr," *Creştinul azi: Revista Bisericilor Creştine Baptiste din România* nos. 4–5 (2006): 6–11

"Cultura şi Cultele, laude, laude şi lozinci," *Ziua* (13 November 2004).

"Cuprins de fiori înainte de alegeri: Năstase se face frate cu biserica," *Replica de Constanţa* (1 November 2004).

Curierul Ortodox Info: Buletin Informaţional. 15 August 2002. Available at: http://www .geocities.com/cortodox.notati/05.htm (retrieved 15 November 2002).

Dascălu, Nicolae, and Maria Orzetic. *Religie: Manual pentru clasa a V-a.* Bucharest: Aramis, 1998.

Dawisha, Karen, and Bruce Parrot, eds. *The Consolidation of Democracy in East-Central Europe.* Cambridge: Cambridge University Press, 1997.

Dawson, Lorne. *Comprehending Cults: The Sociology of New Religious Movements,* 2nd ed. Toronto: Oxford University Press, 2006.

Deletant, Dennis. *Ceauşescu and the Securitate: Coercion and Dissent in Romania 1965– 1989.* Armonk, N.Y.: M. E. Sharpe, 1996.

Demian, Tudor, and Ioan Sauca. *Manual de religie: Clasa a II-a.* Bucharest: Editura Didactică şi Pedagogică, 2002.

De Neve, Dorothee. "Elections in Romania: A Totally Normal Catastrophe?" *Osteuropa* 51, no. 3 (2001): 281–298.

"Deputaţii au decis: Prostituatele rămân penale," *Adevărul* (18 February 2004).

"Dezincriminarea preoţilor turnători are adepţi pe faţă doar în PRM," *Ziarul de Iaşi* (5 July 2001).

"Din nou despre Biserică," *Evenimentul Zilei* (4 April 1999).

Dobre, Laura. "Greco-catolicii transilvăneni cer sprijinul premierului," *Ziua* (20 April 2002).

————. "Preot judecat," *Ziua* (19 June 2004).

Dobre, Laura, and Ovidiu Banches. "Preoţii lăsaţi în politică până în alegeri," *Ziua* (24 February 2004).

Dobrincu, Dorin "Patriarhul Teoctist a participat la rebeliunea legionară din 1941," *Ziarul de Iaşi* (13 January 2001).

"Doctorul Munteanu este colaboratorul lui Dumnezeu," *Evenimentul Zilei* (29 January 2005).

"Dosarele înalţilor prelaţi religioşi vor fi făcute publice," *Ziarul de Iaşi* (8 March 2001).

"Ducerea la îndeplinire a hotărîrii Sfîntului Sinod va contribui la renaşterea morală," *România liberă* (16 February 2004).

Dumea, Claudiu. *Manual de religie: Clasa I.* Bucharest: Arhiepiscopia Romano-Catolică, 1991.

Dumitrescu, Cătălin. "Cuvioasa Paraschiva: Candidatul PSD în cursa pentru Cotroceni," *România liberă* (14 October 2004).

————. "Un preot înfruntă Mitropolia Moldovei şi Bucovinei şi candidează la primărie," *România liberă* (2 June 2004).

Dura, Nicolae. "Este posibilă o reconciliere între ortodocşii şi greco-catolicii din România? Cu ce preţ?" *Renasterea* 14 (April–June 2003). Available at: http://www.episcopia-ramnicului.ro/publicatii/renasterea-2-2003.pdf (retrieved 13 August 2004).

————. "Învăţământul teologic universitar ortodox din România de astăzi," *Dreptatea* (15–22 December 1993).

————. "Pe când canonizarea clericilor şi mirenilor martirizaţi în temniţele comuniste?" *Dreptatea* (8–16 December 1993).

Durandin, Catherine. *Histoire des Roumains.* Paris: Fayard, 1995.

Eberts, Mirella. "The Roman Catholic Church and Democracy in Poland," *Europe-Asia Studies* 50, no. 5 (1998): 817–842.

Enache, George. *Ortodoxie şi putere politică în România contemporană.* Bucharest: Nemira, 2005.

Esbeck, Carl H. "A Typology of Church-State Relations in Current American Thought," in *Religion, Public Life, and the American Polity*, ed. Luis Lugo, 3–34. Knoxville: University of Tennessee Press, 1994.

European Convention for the Protection of Human Rights and Fundamental Freedoms. 4 November 1950. Available at: www1.umn.edu/humanrts/instree/z17euroco.html (retrieved 10 December 2005).

European Court of Human Rights. *Case of Metropolitan Church of Bessarabia and Others vs. Moldova.* 27 March 2002. Available at: http://www.echr.coe.int (retrieved 4 January 2004).

"Explicaţie pentru o campanie neruşinată: Legătura dintre stat şi biserică," *România liberă* (19 August 2003).

Fati, Sabina. "Politica Bisericii Ortodoxe," *Evenimentul Zilei* (13 February 2004).

"Feţele bisericeşti calcă strâmb," *Ziua* (28 January 2004).

Fischer-Galati, Stephen. *Twentieth Century Rumania*, 2nd ed. New York: Columbia University Press, 1991.

Floca, Ioan N. *Canoanele Bisericii Ortodoxe.* Sibiu, Romania: Polsib, 1992.

Florian, Aaron. *Catihismul omului creştin, moral şi soţial: Pentru trebuinţa tinerilor din şcoalele începătoare.* Bucharest: n.p., 1834.

Flueraş, Tudor. "Preoţii-informatori erau un organ de sondare a opiniei publice," *Evenimentul Zilei* (14 June 1999).

Forum 18 News Reports website. Available at: http://www.forum18.org (retrieved 15 May 2006).

Francis, John G. "The Evolving Regulatory Structure of European Church-State Relationships," *Journal of Church and State* 34, no. 4 (1992): 775–804.

Gafton, Vasile. "Dura lex: Biserica din Suciu de Jos la CEDO Strasburg," *Graiul Maramureșului* (3 September 2003).

Galeriu, Cristian. "Sacrificiul Bisericii Ortodoxe Române," *Sfera politicii* 93–94 (2001): 36–40.

Gallagher, Tom. *Modern Romania: The End of Communism, the Failure of Democratic Reform, and the Theft of a Nation.* New York: New York University Press, 2005.

———. *Romania after Ceaușescu.* Edinburgh: Edinburgh University Press, 1995.

Geanakoplos, Deno. J. "Church and State in the Byzantine Empire: A Reconsideration of the Problem of Caesaropapism," *Church History* 34, no. 4 (1965): 381–403.

Gellner, Ernest. *Nationalism.* London: Weidenfeld and Nicholson, 1997.

Georgescu, Teodora. "CNSAS dezgroapă trecutul Patriarhului," *Evenimentul Zilei* (24 March 2001).

———. "Referendum pentru homosexuali," *Evenimentul Zilei* (4 September 2000).

Georgescu, Vlad. *The Romanians: A History.* Columbus: Ohio State University Press, 1991.

Gheorghiu, Lucian, and Bogdan Marnita. "Biserica nu se împotrivește Legii dosarelor," *Cotidianul* (11 July 2001).

———. "CNSAS va verifica preoții doar cu acceptul Sinodului," *Cotidianul* (2 April 2004).

Ghibu, Onisifor. *Ziar de lagăr: Caracal, 1945.* Bucharest: Albatros, 1991.

Gilberg, Trond. *Nationalism and Communism in Romania.* Boulder, Colo.: Westview, 1990.

———. "Religion and Nationalism in Romania," in *Religion and Nationalism in Soviet and East European Politics,* ed. Pedro Ramet, 328–351. Durham, N.C.: Duke University Press, 1989.

Gillet, Olivier. *Les Balkans: Religions et nationalisme.* Brussels: Editions Ousia, 2001.

———. *Religion et nationalisme: L'Idéologie de l'Eglise orthodoxe roumaine sous le régime communiste.* Brussels: Editions de l'Université de Bruxelles, 1997.

Giurescu, Constantin C. *Five Years and Two Months in the Sighet Penitenciary (May 7, 1950–July 5, 1955).* Boulder, Colo.: East European Monographs, 1994.

Glanzer, Perry, and Konstantin Petrenko. "Religion and Education in Post-Communist Russia: Making Sense of Russia's New Church-State Paradigm," paper presented at the Church-State Relations in Post-Communist Eastern Europe symposium, Iași, Romania, 5–8 October 2005.

Goma, Paul. *Culoarea curcubeului '77.* Chisinau, Moldova: Flux, 2003.

Greek Catholic Memorandum. September 2002. Available at: http://www.greek-catholic.ro/memorandum (retrieved 14 July 2006).

Gross, Feliks. *The Civic and the Tribal State: The State, Ethnicity, and the Multiethnic State.* Westport, Conn.: Greenwood, 1998.

Grossu, Sergiu. *Calvarul României creștine.* Deva, Romania: Convorbiri Literare, 1992.

"Guvernul preferă liber-profesionistele în locul bordelurilor," *Adevărul* (27 November 2003).

Hadenius, Axel. *Democracy and Development.* New York: Cambridge University Press, 1992.

Hann, Chris. "Introduction: Political Society and Civil Anthropology," in *Civil Society: Challenging Western Models*, ed. Chris Hann and Elizabeth Dunn, 1–26. London: Routledge, 1996.

Heliade-Radulescu, Ion. *Lectura pentru classa I primară: Lecţiuni preparatorie.* Bucharest: n.p., 1861.

"Homosexualii, la un pas de ieşirea din ilegalitate," *Monitorul* (29 June 2000).

Hufner, Klaus, ed. *Higher Education Reform Process in Central and Eastern Europe.* Frankfurt: Peter Lang, 1995.

Human Rights Watch and International Gay and Lesbian Human Rights Commission. *Public Scandals: Sexual Orientation and Criminal Law in Romania.* New York: HRW and IGLHRC, 1998.

Huntington, Samuel P. *The Clash of Civilizations and the Remaking of World Order.* New York: Simon and Schuster, 1996.

Hupchick, Denis. *Conflict and Chaos in Eastern Europe.* New York: St. Martin's, 1995.

"Ierarhii catolici sunt decişi să nu intre în politică," *Ziarul de Iaşi* (29 April 1998).

"Ierarhii şi preoţii ortodocşi au de ales: Ori Dumnezeu, ori partidul!" *România liberă* (14 February 2004).

"Iliescu pune umărul la îngroparea dosarelor preoţilor," *Ziarul de Iaşi* (7 July 2001).

"In postul Craciunului, ierarhii au dezlegare la lupta pentru putere," *Adevărul* (26 November 2005).

"In scandalul exceptării preoţilor de la Legea Ticu, Iliescu susţine independenţa Bisericii în raport cu legile statului," *Cotidianul* (9 July 2001).

International Covenant on Civil and Political Rights. 23 March 1976. Available at: http://www1.umn.edu/humanrts/instree/b3ccpr.htm (retrieved 10 June 2006).

International Covenant on Economic, Social and Cultural Rights. 16 December 1966. Available at: http://www1.umn.edu/humanrts/instree/b2esc.htm (retrieved 10 June 2006).

International Religious Freedom Report: Moldova (2002). 2002. Available at: http://www.state.gov/rls/irf/2002/13951.htm (retrieved 10 June 2006).

International Religious Freedom Report: Romania (2003). 2003. Available at: http://atheism.about.com/library/irf/irf03/blirf_romania.htm (retrieved 10 June 2006).

"Invectiva în slujba adevărului," *Ziarul de Iaşi* (28 March 2001).

Ionescu, Dan. "Crisis in the Romanian Orthodox Church." *Report on Eastern Europe* (9 March 1990): 48–51.

Ionescu, Miruna. "Un preot face greva foamei," *Evenimentul Zilei* (27 June 2001).

Iordache, Narcis. "B[iserica] O[rtodoxă] R[omână] ia in discuţie avorturile şi clonarea," *Cotidianul* (14 November 2001).

———. "Creştinismul revine la ideile conservatoare," *Cotidianul* (26 September 2001).

———. "Pentru a ajunge parlamentari, oamenii Bisericii trec cu vederea canoanele acesteia," *Cotidianul* (15 April 2003).

"IPS Bartolomeu: Îngrijorat de noua configuraţie a Europei," *Adevărul* (18 December 2003).

"IPS Bartolomeu Anania: Am fost şi am rămas de dreapta," *Rost* (April 2006). Available at: http://www.romfest.org/rost/apr2006/anania.shtml (retrieved 17 July 2006).

"IPS Pimen acuză conducerea ţării," *România liberă* (12 July 2004).

"IPS Pimen mulţumeşte Guvernului," *Ziua* (30 October 2004).

Jitea, Mihaela. "Un născut, un avort," *Ziua* (9 February 2004).

Joint International Commission for the Theological Dialogue between the Roman Catholic Church and the Orthodox Church. "The Balamand Statement," *Eastern Churches Journal* 1, no. 1 (1993): 17–27.

Kaase, Max, and Vera Sparschuh, eds. *Three Social Science Disciplines in Central and Eastern Europe: Handbook on Economics, Political Science and Sociology (1989–2001)*. Berlin: Social Science Information Center, 2000.

Karakasidou, Anastasia. *Fields of Wheat, Hills of Blood: Passages to Nationhood in Greek Macedonia, 1870–1920*. Chicago: University of Chicago Press, 1997.

Kelly, Leo A., and Benedetto Ojetti. *Concordat*. 2003. Available at: http://www.newadvent.org/cathen/04196a.htm (retrieved 16 June 2006).

King, Charles. *The Moldovans: Romania, Russia and the Politics of Culture*. Stanford, Calif.: Hoover Institution Press, 1999.

Kligman, Gail. *The Politics of Duplicity: Controlling Reproduction in Ceauşescu's Romania*. Berkeley: University of California Press, 1998.

Kohn, Hans. *The Idea of Nationalism*. New York: Macmillan, 1967.

"La future collaboration entre greco-catholiques et orthodoxes en Roumanie," *Courrier Oecumenique du Moyen-Orient* 18, no. 3 (1992): 23–26.

Lajolo, Giovanni. *Address of Archbishop Giovanni Lajolo, Secretary for the Holy See's Relations with States at the Pontifical Gregorian University of Rome*. 3 December 2004. Available at: http://www.vatican.va/roman_curia/secretariat_state/2004/documents/rc_seg-st_20041203_lajolo-gregorian-univ_en.html (retrieved 16 June 2006).

Latawski, Paul. "The Problem of Definition: Nationalism, Nation and Nation-State in East Central Europe," in *Contemporary Nationalism in East Central Europe*, ed. Paul Latawski, 1–11. New York: St. Martin's, 1995.

Leustean, Lucian. "Ethno-Symbolic Nationalism, Orthodoxy and the Installation of Communism in Romania: 23 August 1944 to 30 December 1947." *Nationalities Papers* 33, no. 4 (2005): 439–458.

Levy, Robert. *Ana Pauker: The Rise and Fall of a Jewish Communist*. Berkeley: University of California Press, 2001.

Lica, Laura. "Biserica Ortodoxă, acuzată că se opune intereselor României," *Evenimentul Zilei* (9 September 2000).

———. "Campanie antiprostituţie în licee," *Evenimentul Zilei* (14 October 2000).

Light, Duncan, and David Phinnemore, eds. *Post-Communist Romania: Coming to Terms with Transition*. New York: Palgrave, 2001.

Linz, Juan J., and Alfred Stepan. *Problems of Democratic Transition and Consolidation: Southern Europe, South America and Post-Communist Europe*. Baltimore: Johns Hopkins University Press, 1996.

Lovatt, Catherine. "Legalizing Sex," *Central Europe Review* 2, no. 31 (2000). Available at: http://www.tol.cz (retrieved 17 July 2006).

Lucaci, Ioan, Gelu Miclăuş, and Cristinel Fodor. *Manual de religie: Clasa a II-a.* Iaşi: Editura Presa Bună, 1994.

Luxmoore, John. "Eastern Europe 1995: A Review of Religious Life in Bulgaria, Romania, Hungary, Slovakia, the Czeck Republic and Poland," *Religion, State and Society* 24, no. 4 (1996): 357–366.

Madarasan, Francisc. "Deputatul Brudaşcă cere întoarcerea preoţilor demisionari în PRM," *Informaţia* (1 February 2004).

———. "PSD Cluj cere ca preoţii să fie lăsaţi să facă politică," *Informaţia* (18 February 2004).

Maffesoli, Michel. *The Time of the Tribes: The Decline of Individualism in Mass Society.* London: Sage, 1996.

Mahieu, Stephanie. *Legal Recognition and Recovery of Property: Contested Restitution of the Romanian Greek Catholic Church Patrimony.* Working Paper no. 69. Halle, Germany: Max Plank Institute for Social Anthropology, 2004.

———. "(Non-)retours à l'Eglise greco-catholique roumaine, entre adhesion et transmission religieuse," *Social Compass* 53, no. 4 (2006): 515–534.

"Maica Domnului, agent electoral PSD," *Adevărul* (16 August 2002).

Marcu, Florin, and Constant Maneca. *Dicţionar de Neologisme.* Bucharest: Editura Academiei Republicii Socialiste România, 1973.

Mardin, Serif. "Civil Society and Islam," in *Civil Society: Theory, History, Comparison,* ed. John A. Hall, 278–300. Cambridge: Polity Press, 1995.

"Marele ctitor şi ocrotitor Adrian Năstase a împădurit Biserica," *România liberă* (30 October 2004).

Marga, Irimie. "Biserică şi politică din perspectivă canonică," unpublished manuscript, 2005.

Marina, Justinian. *Apostolat Social,* 12 vols. Bucharest: Institutul Biblic şi de Misiune al Bisericii Ortodoxe Române, 1948–1971.

Markand, David, and Ronald L. Nettler, eds. *Religion and Democracy.* Oxford: Blackwell, 2000.

Maximus of Sardis. *Le patriarchat oecumenique dans l'Eglise orthodoxe: Etude historique et canonique.* Paris: n.p., 1975.

Melidon, George Radu. *Manualul învăţătorului sau elemente de pedagogie practică pentru usul şcoalelor populare.* Bucharest: n.p., 1874.

Merdjanova, Ina. "In Search of Identity: Nationalism and Religion in Eastern Europe," *Religion, State and Society* 28, no. 3 (2000): 246–252.

———. *Religion, Nationalism, and Civil Society in Eastern Europe: The Post-Communist Palimpsest.* Lewinston, N.Y.: Edwin Mellen, 2002.

Mesesan, Ada. "Cosmâncă: Băsescu este Satana pe pământ!" *România liberă* (2 November 2004).

Metro Media Transilvania. *Barometru de opinie privind discriminarea în România, 2004.* 2005. Available at: http://www.mmt.ro (retrieved 27 January 2006).

Metzger, Bruce, and Roland Murphy, eds. *The New Oxford Annotated Bible with Apocryphal/Deuterocanonical Books.* New York: Oxford University Press, 1991.

Meyendorff, John. *The Byzantine Legacy in the Orthodox Church.* New York: St. Vladimir's Seminary Press, 1982.

Mialaret, Gaston, and Jean Vial, eds. *Histoire mondiale de l'education.* Paris: Presses Universitaires de France, 1981.

Michelson, Paul E. *Romanian Politics 1859–1871: From Prince Cuza to Prince Carol.* Iaşi: Center for Romanian Studies, 1998.

Mihai, Alina. "Traian Băsescu a bătut mătănii la biserică," *Evenimentul Zilei* (27 November 2004).

Ministerul Apararii Nationale. *Ziua Eroilor.* Available at: http://www.mapn.ro/traditii/ziuaeroilor.htm (retrieved 3 August 2005).

Ministerul Culturii şi Cultelor. *Proiect de lege: Forma textului Legii privind libertatea religioasă şi regimul cultelor în România stabilită în cadrul întâlnirii finale a Ministerului Culturii şi Cultelor cu cultele recunoscute.* 31 May 2005. Available at: http://www.culte.ro/Clintide/proiect_lege_libertate_rel.aspx (retrieved 14 June 2005).

"Ministerul Culturii şi Cultelor cere revocarea Comisiei Mixte de Dialog," *Ziua* (21 March 2002).

"Miscellaneous," *Evenimentul Zilei* (15 January 2001).

Mitrache, Marius. "Roagă-te şi lucrează," *Evenimentul Zilei* (25 May 2004).

"Mitropolitul Corneanu îl contrazice categoric pe preşedintele Ion Iliescu," *România liberă* (11 June 2002).

"Mitropolitul Moldovei se leapădă de Pimen pentru hatârul lui Iliescu," *România liberă* (17 July 2004).

Moise, Emil. "Interpretarea Bibliei, sursă a discriminărilor de gen în practica religioasă creştină din România," *Revista Română de Drepturile Omului* 23 (2002): 86–96.

———. "Relaţia Stat-Biserică în privinţa educaţiei religioase în şcolile de stat din România," *Journal for the Study of Religions and Ideologies* 7 (2004): 76–100.

Moldovan, Ilie. *Darul sfânt al vieţii şi combaterea păcatelor împotriva acestuia: Aspecte ale naşterii de prunci în lumina moralei creştine ortodoxe.* Bucharest: n.p., 1997.

Monsma, Stephen, and Christopher Soper. *The Challenge of Pluralism: Church and State in Five Democracies.* Lanham, Md.: Rowman and Littlefield, 1997.

Mozes, Noda. "The Romanian Catholic Denominational Education between the World Wars," *Journal for the Study of Religion and Ideologies* 3 (2002): 115–130.

"Msgr. Nicolae Corneanu, métropolite de Banat, reconnait avoir cede aux pressions du pouvoir pendant la période communiste," *Istina* 42, no. 2 (1997): 203–209.

Mungiu-Pippidi, Alina. "The Return of Populism: The 2000 Romanian Elections," *Government and Opposition* 36, no. 2 (2001): 230–252.

———. "The Ruler and the Patriarch: The Romanian Eastern Orthodox Church in Transition," *East European Constitutional Review* 7, no. 2 (1998). Available at: http://www.law.nyu.edu/eecr/vo17num2/ (retrieved 20 August 1998).

Munteanu, Lelia. "Iisus din tomberon," *Adevărul* (23 March 2004).

Munteanu, Neculai Constantin. "Mînăstirea Secu," *22* (9–15 December 1997).

Mureşan, Ion. "Chestiunea transilvană: Popii şi politica," *Evenimentul Zilei* (2 February 2004).

Murgescu, Mirela-Luminiţa. *Intre 'bunul creştin' şi 'bravul român': Rolul şcolii primare în construirea identităţii naţionale româneşti (1831–1878)*. Iaşi: Editura A'92, 1999.

"Năstase: Mesajul meu reflectă relaţia stat-biserică," *Curentul* (11 August 2003).

"Năstase: Pimen ne-a dojenit în anumite cazuri poate pe dreptate," *Curierul Naţional* (1 November 2004).

National Catholic Reporter 30, no. 13 (28 January 1994).

National Committee on Bioethics. *Abortion*. July 2005. Available at: http://www .patriarhia.ro (retrieved 10 September 2005).

"Nationalism," *Encyclopedia Britannica*. 2006. Available at: http://search.eb.com/ article-9117287 (retrieved 10 January 2006).

Neacşu, Mihaela, and Cornel Dragoş. *Religie, Clasa a II-a*. Pitesti, Romania: Carminis, n.d.

Neagu, Ion. "Regimul juridic al lăcaşelor de cult," *Vestitorul ortodoxiei* (15 June 2002): 2–7.

"1997 a fost un an greu şi pentru prostituate," *Monitorul* (1 January 1998).

Nistorescu, Cornel. "Editorial," *Evenimentul Zilei* (19 January 2001).

———. "Legalizarea prostituţiei," *Evenimentul Zilei* (4 May 2001).

———. "Slujbaşi la două puteri," *Evenimentul Zilei* (28 April 2000).

Norris, Pippa, and Ronald Inglehart. *Sacred and Secular: Religion and Politics Worldwide*. Cambridge: Cambridge University Press, 2004.

The Noua Dreaptă (New Right) movement's official website available at: http://www .nouadreapta.org (retrieved 2 June 2006).

"Noul Patriarh va fi ales prin vot secret," *Evenimentul Zilei* (27 March 2006).

Opriş, Dorin, Monica Opriş, Irina Horga, Antoaneta-Firuţă Tacea. *Religie: Manual pentru clasa a IX-a*. Cluj Napoca: Dacia, 2002.

———. *Religie: Manual pentru clasa a X-a*. Cluj Napoca: Dacia, 2002.

Organizarea BOR. Available at: http://www.patriarhia.ro/BOR/organizareabor.php (retrieved 23 January 2006).

Ornea, Zigu. *Anii treizeci: Extrema dreaptă românească*. Bucharest: Editura Fundaţiei Culturale Române, 1995.

Oţelariu, Sorin. Personal website. Available at: http://www.invatamantul-religios.go.ro (retrieved 14 May 2005).

Pacepa, Ion Mihai. *Red Horizons: Chronicles of a Communist Chief Spy*. Washington, D.C.: Regnery Gateway, 1987.

Păcurariu, Mircea. *Istoria Bisericii Ortodoxe Române*, 3 vols. Bucharest: Editura Institutului Biblic şi de Misiune Ortodoxă, 1981.

Paiuşan, Cristina. " 'Problema cultelor' în România în rapoartele Securităţii statului, 1949." *Arhivele Totalitarismului* 24–25 (1999): 90–98.

Paiuşan, Cristina, and Radu Ciuceanu. *Biserica Ortodoxă Română sub regimul communist, 1945–1958*, 2 vols. Bucharest: Institutul Naţional pentru Studierea Totalitarismului, 2001.

Paleologu, Alexandru. "O catedrală a neamului ar fi un kitsch mortal," *22* (30 September–6 October 1997): 10–11.

Paler, Octavian. "De ce parte e Biserica?" *Cotidianul* (24 October 2003).

Papanikolaou, Aristotle. "Byzantium, Orthodoxy, and Democracy," *Journal of the American Academy of Religion* 71, no. 1 (2003): 75–98.

Pârvu, Mihnea-Petru. "Pentru cine bat clopotele la Talpa lui Cosmânca?" *România liberă* (30 June 2003).

"Patriarhul Teoctist a participat la rebeliunea legionară din 1941," *Ziarul de Iași* (13 January 2001).

Paun, Bogdana. "Patriarhia față cu impostura lui Vadim," *Ziua* (23 November 2004).

Payne, Daniel P. "The Clash of Civilizations: The Church of Greece, the European Union and the Question of Human Rights," *Religion, State and Society* 31, no. 3 (2003): 261–271.

Percival, Henry, ed. and trans. *The Seven Ecumenical Councils of the Undivided Church: Their Canons and Dogmatic Decrees, Nicene and Post-Nicene Fathers*, 2nd series, 14 vols. New York: Scribner's, 1900.

Perica, Vjekoslav. *Balkan Idols: Religion and Nationalism in Yugoslav States.* New York: Oxford University Press, 2002.

"Pe spatele icoanelor împărțite la mănăstirea Nicula scria 'Donație PSD Cluj,'" *Telegraful de Constanța* (16 August 2002).

"Petele din dosarele preoților le va vedea doar Dumnezeu," *Ziarul de Iași* (3 July 2001).

Petrovici, Georgeta. "'Biserica nu o poate binecuvânta' pe Adriana," *Evenimentul Zilei* (19 January 2005).

———. "Campanie electorală în amvon," *Evenimentul Zilei* (3 June 2004).

Ploscaru, Ioan. *Lanțuri și teroare.* Bucharest: Signata, 1993.

"PNL nu vrea preoți în politică," *Ziarul de Iași* (31 January 2004).

Poettering, Hans-Gert. *Mankind, Religion, Europe: The European Union—A Community of Values.* Brussels: Group of the European People's Party (Christian Democrats) and European Democrats in the European Parliament, 2002.

Popa, Dan. "Deși trebuia sfințit astăzi, locul Catedralei Neamului încă n-a fost stabilit," *Ziarul de Iași* (5 February 1999).

Popa, Mădălin. "Biserica din clasă," *Evenimentul Zilei* (6 September 2003).

Pop-Elecheș, Grigore. "Romania's Politics of Dejection," *Journal of Democracy* 12, no. 3 (2001): 156–169.

Pope Paul VI. *Humanae Vitae* 16. 1968. Available at: http://www.papalencyclicals.net (retrieved 28 August 2005).

Popescu, Carmen. "Biserica este împotriva fertilității in vitro," *Ziua* (18 January 2005).

Popescu, Cristian Tudor. "Catedrala Mântuirii în Țara Mântuielii," *Adevărul* (23 March 2004).

Popescu, Cristian Tudor, and Valentin Popescu, "O iubire mai rece și stearpă decât ura," *Adevărul* (19 January 2005).

Popescu, Liliana. "A Change of Power in Romania: The Results and Significance of the November 1996 Elections," *Government and Opposition* 32, no. 2 (1997): 172–190.

Popescu, Marina. "The Parliamentary and Presidential Elections in Romania, November 2000," *Electoral Studies* 22, no. 2 (2003): 325–335.

Postu, Lucian. "Politichia de mărgăritar," *Ziarul de Iaşi* (30 November 1998).

Pravda. 19 August 2002. Available at: http://english.pravda.ru/ (retrieved 10 June 2006).

Predarea religiei în învăţământul public. Available at: http//www.patriarhia.ro (retrieved 1 September 2005).

"Pregătiri fanariotice la Suceava: PSD i-a confiscat pe Stefan cel Mare," *România liberă* (1 July 2004).

"Preoţii cu pete la dosar bagă dihonia în lumea bisericească," *Ziarul de Iaşi* (4 July 2001).

"Preoţii-parlamentari scoşi din Biserică," *Ziarul de Iaşi* (29 January 2004).

"Preoţii PD din Bistriţa au renunţat la politică," *Ziua* (23 February 2004).

"Preşedinte cu patrafir," *Evenimentul Zilei* (25 February 2000).

"Primarii argeşeni în sutană nu se consideră incompatibili," *Ziarul de Azi* (15 May 2003).

"Primarul Capitalei acceptă Catedrala Mântuirii Neamului în Parcul Carol," *Ziua* (22 October 2004).

"Proiectul privind prostituţia, amânat pe motiv de post," *Curentul* (27 November 2003).

Propunere legislativă PL 353/1999: Lege privind regimul general al cultelor religioase. 1999. Available at: http://www.cdep.ro (retrieved 14 June 2005).

"Protopopiatul Botoşani le-a interzis preoţilor să facă politică la predică," *România liberă* (4 February 2004).

Prundea, Madalina, and Ciprian Iancu. "Puterea în sutană," *Evenimentul Zilei* (2 February 2004).

Przeworski, Adam. *Democracy and the Market: Political and Economic Reforms in Eastern Europe and Latin America.* Cambridge: Cambridge University Press, 1991.

"PS Calinic al Argeşului nu vrea preoţi membri de partid," *Informaţia* (26 February 2004).

"PSD Constanţa a rămas fără şapte preoţi consilieri," *Cuget Liber* (23 February 2004).

"Publicistul Gabriel Andreescu se leagă de Consiliul pentru Studierea Arhivelor Securităţii," *Ziarul de Iaşi* (9 September 2000).

"PUR cu ochii pe articolul 59 din Constituţie," *Curierul Zilei* (10 June 2002).

Purcăreanu, Lucian. "Ion Iliescu: Nu este suficient să transformi în pamflete speranţele oamenilor," *Evenimentul Zilei* (7 December 2000).

Rădulescu, Carmen. "Un preot primar din judeţul Argeş renunţă la preoţie în favoarea primăriei," *Informaţia* (13 February 2004).

Rady, Martin. "Nationalism and Nationality in Romania," in *Contemporary Nationalism in East Central Europe,* ed. Paul Latawski, 127–142. New York: St. Martin's, 1995.

Ramet, Sabrina P. *Balkan Babel: The Disintegration of Yugoslavia from the Death of Tito to the War for Kosovo.* Boulder, Colo.: Westview, 1999.

———. "Church and State in Romania before and after 1989," in *Romania since 1989: Politics, Economics and Society,* ed. Henry F. Carey, 275–296. Lanham, Md.: Lexington Books, 2003.

———. *Nihil Obstat: Religion, Politics, and Social Change in East-Central Europe and Russia*. Durham, N.C.: Duke University Press, 1998.

———. "The Serbian Church and the Serbian Nation," in *Render unto Caesar: The Religious Sphere in World Politics*, ed. Sabrina P. Ramet and Donald Treadgold, 301–323. Washington, D.C.: American University Press, 1995.

———. "The Way We Were—And Should Be Again? European Orthodox Churches and the 'Idyllic Past,' '" in *Religion in an Expanding Europe*, ed. Timothy A. Byrnes and Peter J. Katzenstein, 148–175. New York: Cambridge University Press, 2006.

———. *Whose Democracy? Nationalism, Religion, and the Doctrine of Collective Rights in Post-1989 Eastern Europe*. Lanham, Md.: Rowman and Littlefield, 1997.

Ramet, Sabrina P., and Donald Treadgold, eds. *Render unto Caesar: The Religious Sphere in World Politics*. Washington, D.C.: American University Press, 1995.

"Reglare de conturi în BOR?" *Ziua* (13 March 2003).

The Religious Freedom Page. Available at: http://religiousfreedom.lib.virginia.edu (retrieved 1 March 1999).

Remez, Lisa. "Romanian Maternal Death Rate Fell by Two-Thirds after the 1989 Revolution." *Family Planning Perspectives* 27, no. 6 (1995). Available at: http://www.findarticles.com/p/articles/mi_qa3634/is_199511/ai_n8722997 (retrieved 17 July 2006). "Retragerea din politică a preoților a bulversat listele de candidați ale partidului de guvernământ," *România liberă* (16 February 2004).

"Revoluție în biserică," *România liberă* (31 December 1989).

Roberson, Ronald G. "The Church in Romania," in *New Catholic Encyclopedia*, Supplement 1989–1995, 19:331–337. Washington, D.C.: McGraw-Hill, 1996.

"Romania," *Encyclopedia Britannica*. 2006. Available at: http://o-search.eb.com .mercury.concordia.ca:80/eb/article-42844 (retrieved 25 February 2006).

Romanian Constitution of 1866. Available at: http://www.constitutia.ro/const1866.htm (retrieved 15 December 2005).

Romanian Constitution of 1923. Available at: http://www.constitutia.ro/const1923.htm (retrieved 15 December 2005).

Romanian Constitution of 1948. Available at: http://legislatie.resurse-pentru-democratie .org/const_1948.php (retrieved 10 January 2005).

Romanian Information Service archive, Bucharest, fond D, file 909, page 510.

Romanian National Institute of Statistics website. Available at: http://www .recensamant.ro (retrieved 2 February 2005).

Romanian Orthodox Patriarchate. Official website. Available at: http://www.patriarhia .ro (retrieved 15 July 2006).

Roper, Steve D. "Is There an Economic Basis for Post-Communist Voting? Evidence from Romanian Elections, 1992–2000," *East European Quarterly* 37, no. 1 (2003): 85–100.

———. *Romania: The Unfinished Revolution*. Amsterdam: Gordon and Breach, 2000.

Rose, Richard, Neil Munro, and Tom Mackie. *Elections in Central and Eastern Europe since 1990*. Studies in Public Policy Series 300. Glasgow: Centre for the Study of Public Policy, University of Strathclyde, 1998.

"Să dea Dumnezeu să nu intrăm în NATO," *România liberă* (5 July 1997).

Sadlack, Jan. *Education Reform and Policy in East-Central Europe*. New York: Garland, 1995.

Sandru, Dumitru. "Biserica din România, 1944–1948," *Arhivele Totalitarismului* 18 (1998): 210–228.

Sârbu, Dan. "Irlanda de Nord, varianta ardeleană," *Ziua de Ardeal* (12 March 2002).

Sauca, Ioan. *Abecedarul micuţului creştin*. Bucharest: Editura Didactică şi Pedagogică, 2002.

———. *Manual de Religie: Clasa a IV-a*. Bucharest: Editura Didactică şi Pedagogică, 2002.

"Scandal politic în Biserica Ortodoxă," *Ziua* (2 November 2004).

Schaff, Philip, and Henry Wace, eds. *The Seven Ecumenical Councils*. Peabody, Mass.: Hendrickson, 1994.

Schiop, Adrian. "Cruciada ortodoxă în şcoli," *Evenimentul zilei* (4 October 2004).

"Scurt pe doi," *Evenimentul Zilei* (26 April 2004).

Scurtu, Ioan. *Viaţa cotidiană a românilor în perioada interbelică*. Bucharest: Editura Rao, 2001.

Scurtu, Ioan, and Ioan Dordea, eds. *Minorităţile naţionale din România 1925–1931: Documente*. Bucharest: Arhivele Nationale ale României, 1996.

"Securiştii în sutană, deconspiraţi," *Ziarul de Iaşi* (5 July 2001).

"Sefii cultelor religioase vor fi audiaţi la CNSAS," *Ziarul de Iaşi* (21 August 2001).

Selişte, Marcel Răduţ. "Biserica Ortodoxă Română şi Noua Europă," *Rost* 35 (2006). Available at: http://www.romfest.org/rost/apr_mai2004/oltenia.shtml (retrieved 18 July 2006).

"Senatorul PNTCD Ioan Moisin cere ca Biserica să cenzureze manualele şcolare," *Evenimentul Zilei* (18 March 1998).

"Senatul faţă în faţă cu ispitele: Grupul de rugăciune despre 'Păcatul prostituţiei,' " *Monitorul* (9 October 2003).

Shafir, Michael. "Romania's Road to 'Normalcy,' " *Journal of Democracy* 8, no. 2 (1997): 144–158.

Siani-Davies, Peter. *The Romanian Revolution of December 1989*. Ithaca, N.Y.: Cornell University Press, 2005.

Simionescu, Benone. "Preoţii maghiari pot face politică," *Informaţia* (13 February 2004).

Siulea, Ciprian. "O catedrală greşită," *Evenimentul Zilei* (31 October 2004).

Smith, Donald Eugene. *Religion and Modernization*. New Haven, Conn.: Yale University Press, 1974.

"Soaring Abortion Rate Sounds Stalinist Alarm," *Sunday Herald* (9 February 2003). Available at: www.sundayherald.com.

Sofronie, Cristina. "BOR ameninţă," *Evenimentul Zilei* (4 July 2001).

Solidarity for Freedom of Conscience. *The Construction of Churches in Post-Communist Romania and Its Impact on Freedom of Conscience and the Secular State*. Prepared by Liviu Andreescu. March 2005. Available at: http://www.humanism.ro (retrieved 10 May 2005).

Sorodoc, Adrian. "Pelerinaj PSD la Talpa lui Cosmânca," *Evenimentul Zilei* (16 June 2003).

Stan, Lavinia, "Access to Securitate Files: The Trials and Tribulations of a Romanian Law," *East European Politics and Societies* 16, no. 1 (2002): 55–90.

———. "Moral Cleansing Romanian Style," *Problems of Post-Communism* 49, no. 4 (2002): 52–62.

———. "The Opposition Takes Charge: The Romanian General Elections of 2004," *Problems of Post-Communism* 52, no. 3 (2005): 3–15.

———. "Spies, Files and Lies: Explaining the Failure of Access to Securitate Files," *Communist and Post-Communist Studies* 37, no. 3 (2004): 341–359.

———, ed. *Romania in Transition*. Aldershot: Dartmouth, 1997.

Stan, Lavinia, and Lucian Turcescu. "Church-State Conflict in Moldova: The Bessarabian Metropolitanate," *Communist and Post-Communist Studies* 36, no. 4 (2003): 443–465.

———. "The Devil's Confessors: Priests, Communists, Spies and Informers," *East European Politics and Societies* 19, no. 4 (2005): 655–685.

———. "Politics, National Symbols and the Romanian National Cathedral," *Europe-Asia Studies* 58, no. 3 (2006): 1119–1139.

———. "Pulpits, Ballots and Party Cards: Religion and Elections in Romania," *Religion, State and Society* 33, no. 4 (2005): 347–366.

———. "Religion, Politics and Sexuality in Romania," *Europe-Asia Studies* 57, no. 2 (2005): 291–310.

———. "Religious Education in Romania," *Communist and Post-Communist Studies* 38, no. 3 (2005): 381–401.

———. "The Romanian Orthodox Church and Post-Communist Democratization," *Europe-Asia Studies* 52, no. 8 (2000): 1467–1488.

Stanciu, Bogdan. "AUR va susţine reprezentarea bisericilor ortodoxă şi greco-catolică în parlament," *Evenimentul Zilei* (16 April 1998).

Stănciulescu, Elisabeta. "Sociologia şi reforma sistemului educativ," *Biserica Ortodoxă Română* 62 (2002): 15–28.

Stănescu, Mircea. "Le Conseil National pour l'Etude des Archives de la Securitate et le problème de la gestion de l'héritage communiste," *Asymetria* (10 April 2002): 5–22.

Stăniloae, Dumitru. "Idealul naţional permanent," *Telegraful Român* 88, no. 4 (1940): 1–2, and no. 5 (1940): 1.

———. "Naţionalismul sub aspect moral," *Telegraful Român* 85, no. 4 (1937): 1.

———. *Reflecţii despre spiritualitatea poporului român*. Bucharest: Editura Elion, 1992.

———. *Teologia dogmatică ortodoxă*, 3 vols. Bucharest: Editura Institutului Biblic şi de Misiune al Bisericii Ortodoxe Române, 1978.

"Stareţul Mănăstirii Cernica acuzat de hărţuire sexuală," *Evenimentul Zilei* (5 November 2001).

State Secretariat for Religious Denominations. *Viaţa religioasă din România*. Bucharest: Paideia, 1999.

Steinhardt, Nicolae. *Jurnalul fericirii*. Cluj-Napoca: Dacia, 1991.

"Stenograma şedinţei Biroului Politic al Partidului Comunist Român" (10 March 1945).

Stepan, Alfred. *Arguing Comparative Politics*. Oxford: Oxford University Press, 2001.

———. "Religion, Democracy and the 'Twin Tolerations,'" *Journal of Democracy* 11, no. 4 (2000): 37–57.

Stoica, Mihai. "Campanie electorală la uşa bisericii," *Evenimentul Zilei* (2 June 2004).

———. "Printr-o scrisoare adresată ministrului Rodica Stănoiu, Teoctist porunceşte justiţiei," *Evenimentul Zilei* (20 March 2002).

Stoiciu, Liviu Ioan. "De ce BOR şi-a exclus brusc şi radical clerul din politică?" *Cotidianul* (4 March 2004).

Stroe, Mircea. "Preotul-deputat Pavel Cherescu ia atitudine împotriva Bisericii Ortodoxe," *Informaţia* (25 February 2004).

Stroie, M. "Gravidele vor avorta cu aviz de la psiholog," *Telegraful de Constanţa* (9 June 2003).

Strugari, Cristina. "Preoţii suceveni se supun Sfântului Sinod," *Informaţia* (15 February 2004).

Sugar, Peter F., ed. *Eastern European Nationalism in the Twentieth Century*. Washington, D.C.: American University Press, 1995.

Sutu, Cristian, and Claudia Tipluica. "Cosmânca şi Mischie în război cu Biserica," *Evenimentul Zilei* (14 February 2004).

Swenson, Don. *Society, Spirituality and the Sacred: A Social Scientific Introduction*. Peterborough, Ont.: Broadview, 1999.

Szlavik Dragomir, Monica. "Sfântul Sinod respinge ideea politicienilor în sutană," *Curierul Naţional* (13 February 2004).

Talos, Vasile Alexandru. *Religious Pluralism in the Romanian Context*. Available at: http://www.georgefox.edu/academics/undergrad/departmentrs/soc-swk/rel/reefu1184.html (retrieved 10 December 2005).

Televiziunea Română. *Mari români*. 2006. Available at: http://www.tvr.ro (retrieved 17 July 2006).

"Televoting pentru Catedrala Mântuirii Neamului," *Curierul Naţional* (24 March 2004).

"Teoctist urecheşte guvernul," *Monitorul* (13 September 1999).

"Teoctist vrea creştinismul în Constituţia UE," *Monitorul* (18 October 2003).

Thual, Francois. "Stereofonia religie-natiune," *Dilema* (6–12 March 1996).

Tinca, Ovidiu. *Constituţii şi alte texte de drept public*. Oradea: n.p., 1997.

Tismaneanu, Vladimir. *Stalinism for All Seasons: A Political History of Romanian Communism*. Berkeley, Cal.: University of California Press, 2003.

Tobias, Robert. *Communist-Christian Encounter in East Europe*. Indianapolis, Ind.: School of Religious Press, 1956.

Toma, Victor, and Tiberiu Morariu. "Juriştii greco-catolici invocă supremaţia accesului liber la justiţie în faţa procedurii Comisiei Mixte de Dialog," *Ziua* (21 March 2002).

Tomaziu, Eduard. "Ce politică face Biserica?" *Ziarul de Azi* (16 November 2002).

Țon, Iosif. E-mail titled "Deconspirare Iosif Țon," sent on 17 January 2007 to http://
groups.yahoo.com/group/masa_rotunda/message/3182 (retrieved 18 January
2007).

Toporcea, Elena. "Mesaj pascal cu îngrijorări laice," *Curierul Național* (7 April 2004).

Townley, Ben. *Romanian President Makes Way for Pride.* 27 May 2005. Available at:
http://www.gay.com (retrieved 15 June 2005).

"Traian Băsescu, susținător al caselor de toleranță și de acord cu căsătoriile între
homosexuali," *Adevărul* (27 October 2004).

Trandafir, Gelu. "Revoluția lui Pimen," *Evenimentul Zilei* (15 July 2004).

"Trecutul lui Teoctist, din nou răscolit," *Ziarul de Iași* (23 March 2001).

Tudor, Alice. "Religia în Universitate, extrase," *22* (23–29 April 1998).

Tudor, Marius, and Adrian Gavrilescu. *Democrația la pachet: Elita politică în România
postcomunistă.* Bucharest: Compania, 2002.

Turcescu, Lucian. "Dumitru Staniloae (1903–1993)," in *The Teachings of Modern
Christianity on Law, Society, and Human Nature,* ed. John White Jr. and Frank
Alexander, 1:685–711. New York: Columbia University Press, 2005.

2002 Romanian Census. Available at: http://www.insse.ro/rp12002rezgen/16.pdf
(retrieved 22 May 2004). *United Nations Database.* Available at: http://www.un.org
(retrieved 24 May 2005).

Universal Declaration of Human Rights. 10 December 1948. Available at: http://www
.un.org/Overview/rights.html (retrieved 10 December 2005).

Urechia, V. A. *Istoria școalelor de la 1800–1864,* 2 vols. Bucharest: n.p., 1892.

———. *Opere complete: Didactica,* 2 vols. Bucharest: n.p., 1883.

Ursul, George. "From Political Freedom to Religious Independence: The Romanian
Orthodox Church, 1877–1925," in *Romania between East and West: Historical Essays
in Memory of Constantin C. Giurescu,* ed. Stephen Fischer-Galati, Radu Florescu,
and George Ursul, 217–244. Boulder, Colo.: East European Monographs, 1982.

Ursulețu, Lucian. "Candidatură interzisă de Biserică," *Evenimentul Zilei* (25 May 2004).

Uta, Iulian. "Voi face încă o revoluție! Declara un popă-primar din Argeș," *Informația*
(15 February 2004).

Vâlcea, Luminita. "Salvați Parcul Carol!" *Evenimentul Zilei* (22 March 2004).

Valendorfean, Lia. "Preoții politicieni, în discuția Arhiepiscopiei Ortodoxe din Cluj,"
România liberă (29 January 2004).

Vasile, Cristian. *Biserica Ortodoxă Română în primul deceniu comunist.* Bucharest:
Curtea Veche, 2005.

———. *Intre Vatican și Kremlin: Biserica Greco-Catolică în timpul regimului communist.*
Bucharest: Curtea Veche 2003.

———. "Propuneri pentru unificarea celor două biserici românești (1944–1945)," *22*
(6–12 April 1999): 10–11.

———, ed. *Istoria Bisericii Greco-Catolice sub regimul communist, 1945–1989: Documente
și mărturii.* Bucharest: Polirom, 2003.

———, ed. "Rețeaua informativă a Securității din învățământul teologic la sfârșitul
anilor '70 și începutul anilor '80," *Arhivele Totalitarismului* 11, nos. 3–4 (2003):
47–50.

Velini, Anton. *Manual de metodică și pedagogie pentru profesorii școlilor primare*. Iași: n.p., 1860.

Vera, Nicoleta. "Romania va fi homosexuală sau nu va fi în Europa?" *Evenimentul Zilei* (15 May 1998).

Verdery, Katherine. *National Ideology under Socialism: Identity and Cultural Politics in Ceaușescu's Romania*. Berkeley: University of California Press, 1991. Voaides, Alina, and Florian Bichir. "Preoții-politicieni, afară din Biserică," *Evenimentul Zilei* (13 February 2004).

Wald, Kenneth D. "Social Change and Political Response: The Silent Religious Cleavage in North America," in *Politics and Religion in the Modern World*, ed. George Moyser, 239–284. New York: Routledge and Kegan Paul, 1991.

Weber, Max. *The Protestant Ethic and the Spirit of Capitalism*. New York: Routledge, 1992.

Weber, Renate. "Legea învățământului: între contestare și supra-apreciere," *Revista Română de Drepturile Omului* 9 (1995): 15–25.

Webster, Alexander. *The Price of Prophecy: Orthodox Churches on Peace, Freedom and Security*, 2nd ed. Washington, D.C.: Ethics and Public Policy Center, 1995.

Williams, Kieran, and Dennis Deletant. *Security Intelligence Services in New Democracies: The Czech Republic, Slovakia and Romania*. London: Palgrave, 2001.

Zubașcu, Ion. "Adevărata biografie," *România liberă* (4 February 2006).

———. "Bisericile Catolice din România au decis: fără politică!" *România liberă* (19 February 2004).

LAWS AND DECREES

Constitutional Court Decision no. 72 of 18 July 1995. *Monitorul Oficial al României* (31 July 1995).

Council of Europe Resolution no. 1123 on the honoring of obligations and commitments by Romania (24 April 1997) available at http://assembly.coe.int (retrieved on 4 March 2007).

Council of Ministers Decision no. 1719 of 27 December 1948. *Monitorul Oficial* (29 December 1948).

Decree Law no. 9 of 31 December 1989, *Monitorul Oficial al României* (31 December 1989).

Decree Law no. 126 of 24 April 1990, *Monitorul Oficial* 54 (25 April 1990).

Decree on the General Regime of Religious Denominations no. 177 of 1948. *Monitorul Oficial* 178 (4 August 1948) and also available at: http://legislatie.resurse-pentru-democratie.org/177_1948.php (retrieved on 2 March 2007).

Decree Law no. 358 of 1 December 1948, *Monitorul Oficial al Republicii Socialiste România* (2 December 1948).

Decree on the General Regime of Religious Groups no. 177 of 1948. *Monitorul Oficial* 178 (4 August 1948) and also available at: http://legislatie.resurse-pentru-democratie.org/177_1948.php (retrieved on 2 March 2007).

Decree 770 of 1 October 1966 regulating the interruption of pregnancy, *Buletin Oficial* no. 60 (1 October 1966).

Decision no. 81 of 15 July 1995. Available at: http://www.ccr.ro (retrieved 7 May 2005).

Decision no. 810 of 1949 (annulled in December 1991).

Emergency Ordinance no. 36 of 10 July 1997, *Monitorul Oficial al României* (10 December 1999).

Governmental Decision no. 831 of 13 December 1991, *Monitorul Oficial al României* (20 December 1991).

Governmental Ordinance no. 225 of 19 August 1994, *Monitorul Oficial al României* (25 May 1994).

Law no. 140 of 14 November 1996. *Monitorul Oficial* no. 289 (14 November 1996).

Law Sanctioning Corruption no. 161 of 19 April 2003. *Monitorul Oficial* no. 279 (21 April 2003).

Law on Education no. 84 of 31 July 1995. *Monitorul Oficial* no. 606 (10 decembrie 1999).

Law on File Access no. 187 of December 1999, *Monitorul Oficial* no. 603 (9 December 1999).

Law on Legal Off-Work Celebration Days no. 75 of 12 July 1996, *Monitorul Oficial* (17 July 1996).

Law on Preparing the Population for Defense no. 46 of 5 June 1996. *Monitorul Oficial* no. 120 (11 June 1996).

Law on Religious Freedom and the General Regime of Religious Denominations no. 489 of 28 December 2006, available at http://www.cdep.ro (retrieved 2 March 2007).

Session of the Chamber of Deputies of 14 September 1999 available at http://www.cdep.ro (retrieved 2 March 2007).

Supreme Court of Justice Decision no. 901 of 1996.

Synod Decision no. 1066 of 1996. Available at http://www.patriarhia.ro (retrieved 5 July 2006).

Synod Decision no. 410 of 12 February 2004. Available at http://www.patriarhia.ro (retrieved 5 July 2006).

Vienna Convention on Succession of States in Respect of State Property, Archives and Debts of 8 April 1983, available at: http://www.un.org (retrieved 24 May 2005).

PRESS RELEASES AND RADIO REPORTS

Agerpress, 30 December 1989.

Associated Press, 17 April 2003.

Bassapress, 23 July 2002.

BBC Romanian Service, 27 October 1997, 5 February 2000, 20 December 2001, 13 November 2003.

Cotidianul, 19 October 2002.

Dilema, 5–11 March 1999.

Monitorul Oficial al României, 31 December 1989, 14 November 1996, 10 September 1997.

Monitorul Oficial al României, partea a II-a, 7 January 1994, 27 January 1994, 25 November 2004, 8 June 1995, 23 June 1995, 24 April 1997, 12 June 1997, 26 and

27 June 1997, 3 July 1997, 4 November 1997, 24 December 1997, 12 January 1998, 12 February 1998, 13 May 1998, 14 November 1998, 17 May 1999, 10 December 1999, 31 May 2001, 12 February 2002.

Radio Romania, 24 January 1990 and 10 October 1996.

Radio Romania Actualitati, 4 January 1990.

Religion News Service, 1999.

Reuters, 13 September 2000.

Roberson, Ronald G., ed. *Secretariat for Ecumenical and Interreligious Affairs (SEIA) Newsletter on the Eastern Churches and Ecumenism* 40 (1999).

Roberson, Ronald G., ed. *Secretariat for Ecumenical and Interreligious Affairs (SEIA), Newsletter on the Eastern Churches and Ecumenism* 123 (31 December 2005).

Rompress, 12 January 1990 and 15 August 1990.

22, 30 September–6 October 1997, 7–13 October 1997, 9–15 December 1997, 3–9 March 1998, 24–30 March 1998, and 23–29 April 1998.

Index